P9-DEU-466

# Accounting For Dummies, 2nd Edition

Cheat Sheet

## A Few Quick Accounting Tips for Business Managers and Investors

1. **Business managers and investors need financial information.** Accounting's main function is to supply information about *profit performance*, *financial condition*, and *cash flows.* Managers and investors should meet accountants partway by having a basic familiarity with the financial statements that report this information.

2. **One very important thing accountants do is measure profit — sales revenue less expenses.** The measure of profit for a period depends a great deal on which accounting methods are selected for recording sales and expenses.

3. **Authoritative rules and standards have been established for measuring profit and presenting financial condition and cash flows** — which are called generally accepted accounting principles, or GAAP for short. Business managers should ensure that their financial reports are prepared according to GAAP.

4. **GAAP leave wiggle room for recording profit and financial condition.** A business can adopt stingy or more generous accounting methods to measure profit and to put values on its assets, liabilities, and owners' equity accounts. Managers should understand the effects of their accounting choices — and investors should be aware of them.

5. **The income statement reports bottom-line profit (called net income) and the revenue and expenses leading down to this key figure.** The balance sheet reports assets and liabilities at the stroke of midnight on the last day of the profit period. Even financial reporters, who ought to know better, confuse these two financial statements — but you shouldn't!

6. **The cash flow statement reports the amount of cash flow from the sales and expense operations of the business.** It lists the factors that cause cash flow to be higher or lower than profit for the period. Note that earning profit does not increase cash the same amount during the year.

7. **Business managers need a basic profit model** — to focus on the key variables that determine profit performance, and for making intelligent decisions about how best to protect and improve profit.

8. **Profit margin, sales volume, and variable expenses (separated from fixed expenses) are key features of the accounting profit model for managers.** Profit margin equals sales price less product cost and less the variable expenses of making the sale. Even a small slippage in profit margin can have a devastating impact on profit; even a small gain in the profit margin can have a tremendous positive impact on profit.

9. **A little more sales volume results in a lot more profit.** Fixed expenses for the year are locked in place and cannot be changed over the short-run. A business has to sell enough volume to earn total margin equal to its fixed expenses before breaking into the profit zone. This cross-over volume is called the breakeven point. After the business clears its fixed expenses hurdle, the margin on each additional unit sold goes entirely to profit (before income tax). The business starts making profit hand over fist above its breakeven point.

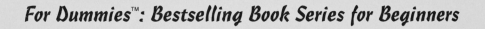

# Accounting For Dummies, 2nd Edition

Cheat Sheet

10. **The profit-making activities of a business propel its balance sheet.** To fathom a balance sheet, you must understand how sales revenue and expenses drive most of the assets and liabilities on the balance sheet. These vital connections between the income statement and the balance sheet are extraordinarily important for managers to understand in planning the capital needs of the business and in controlling the business's financial condition and cash flows.

11. **Business managers should closely scrutinize all costs.** Virtually every cost number that managers see in accounting reports and use in decision-making are based on choices between alternative accounting methods or on arbitrary methods of allocating costs. Managers should have a clear understanding of which choices were made and the logic behind the allocation method.

12. **Some businesses pay income tax, and some don't** — depending on how they are legally organized. Corporations with more than 75 stockholders pay income tax, but corporations with fewer stockholders, and partnerships and limited liability companies, don't pay income tax. They are *pass-through* tax entities; the owners of these entities include their respective shares of the business's taxable income in their individual income tax returns. Cash dividends distributed to stockholders by corporations that pay income tax are also taxable to the individual stockholders (which is called double taxation).

13. **Book values of certain assets may be less than their current replacement cost values.** Inventory is recorded at cost of acquisition and is not written up to recognize increases in replacement cost. Likewise, fixed (long-term) operating assets are recorded at cost and then depreciated over their useful lives. Increases in replacement cost values are not recorded. A business does not benefit from replacement cost increases — unless it can raise the sales prices charged to its customers based on the higher replacement costs of inventory and fixed assets.

14. **Goodwill refers to the capability of a business to make and sustain above-average profit performance.** Unless it has actually been bought and paid for, goodwill is not recorded. Only when another business or group of investors pays cash for the momentum already established by another business does goodwill show up as an asset in a balance sheet. Purchased goodwill is written off to expense over its useful life.

15. **Audits by CPAs of annual financial reports are required of public businesses.** Private businesses may have their annual financial reports audited to satisfy lenders or their outside investors. CPA auditors don't necessarily catch everything, but a clean opinion in an auditor's report provides assurance that the financial statements are presented fairly and have been prepared according to GAAP. Investors should always read the auditor's report to make sure that a clean opinion is being expressed, and if not, then to find out what problems the auditor found with the financial statements.

16. **Business managers should not be intimidated by accountants.** Ask for clear, jargon-free explanations of terms and accounting methods. However, be prepared for the worst. Learning the basic language of accounting has many advantages (see Appendix A, the glossary).

Hungry Minds™

*For Dummies™: Bestselling Book Series for Beginners*

# Praise for *Accounting For Dummies*

"As one of the thousands of people taking graduate-level accounting management courses for the first time, I wanted a step-by-step guide that would quickly bring me up to speed on accounting concepts, approaches, and practices. *Accounting For Dummies* is essential reading for all of us who want to manage our business finances effectively and understand the financial health of companies we may deal with or invest in. I highly recommend it for managers and students of management."

> — Mary Metcalfe, Partner, Envirocomm Communications

"With a keen sense of wit and intelligence, John provides a wealth of practical information on understanding how to manage budgets and financial statements."

> — Jack Rudolph, Former President, Colorado Community First National Bank

"John has an uncanny knack for explaining complicated accounting and financial material to beginners as well as experts in the accounting field. I will definitely use *Accounting For Dummies* in my curriculum."

> — Dale Meyer, Professor, College of Business and Administration, University of Colorado at Boulder

# Praise for John A. Tracy's *How to Read a Financial Report*

"[If] you would like to have a minimal understanding of the numbers that make up a balance sheet, income, and cash flow statement . . . then *How to Read a Financial Report* might be just what you are looking for. Mr. Tracy's book explains in plain English the meaning of the major terms used in financial statements. . . ."

> — *The Wall Street Journal*

"What distinguishes Tracy's efforts from other manuals is an innovative structure that visually ties together elements of the balance sheet and income statement by tracing where and how a line item in one affects an entry in the other."

— *Inc.* Magazine

"An excellent job of showing how to separate the wheat from the chaff without choking in the process."

— *The Miami Herald*

". . . the best book this reviewer has seen in over 20 years of accounting education that is targeted to financial statement users who have little or no knowledge of accounting."

— *The Ohio CPA Journal*

"Tracy has overcome the traditional inability of accountants to talk or write about their subject in a way the layman can understand. . . ."

— *The Chicago Tribune*

". . . gives an easy-to-follow description of the purpose of each type of statement . . . A fine basic handbook for those beginning to perform due diligence on stocks and other investment offerings."

— *Financial Planning*

". . . precise and pragmatic . . . reads with clarity and conciseness, focusing on all business transactions. . . ."

— *Broward Review and Business Record*

". . . written for those non-financial people who would like to pass up all the complicated jargon to get to the real meat and potatoes."

— *Atlanta Business Chronicle*

"A major strength of this book is that it highlights relationships among financial reporting elements that often remain obscure to the non-accountant. It is clearly written and provides detailed guidelines for adjusting accounting numbers to determine cash flow."

— *Journal of Accountancy*

 ™

# *References for the Rest of Us!*®

## BESTSELLING BOOK SERIES

Do you find that traditional reference books are overloaded with technical details and advice you'll never use? Do you postpone important life decisions because you just don't want to deal with them? Then our *For Dummies*® business and general reference book series is for you.

For Dummies business and general reference books are written for those frustrated and hard-working souls who know they aren't dumb, but find that the myriad of personal and business issues and the accompanying horror stories make them feel helpless. *For Dummies* books use a lighthearted approach, a down-to-earth style, and even cartoons and humorous icons to dispel fears and build confidence. Lighthearted but not lightweight, these books are perfect survival guides to solve your everyday personal and business problems.

> *"More than a publishing phenomenon, 'Dummies' is a sign of the times."*
>
> — *The New York Times*

> *"A world of detailed and authoritative information is packed into them..."*
>
> — *U.S. News and World Report*

> *"...you won't go wrong buying them."*
>
> — *Walter Mossberg, Wall Street Journal, on For Dummies books*

**Already, millions of satisfied readers agree. They have made For Dummies the #1 introductory level computer book series and a best-selling business book series. They have written asking for more. So, if you're looking for the best and easiest way to learn about business and other general reference topics, look to *For Dummies* to give you a helping hand.**

Hungry Minds™

# Accounting

## FOR

# DUMMIES®

### 2ND EDITION

## by John A. Tracy, CPA

Hungry Minds™

HUNGRY MINDS, INC.

New York, NY ◆ Cleveland, OH ◆ Indianapolis, IN

# Accounting For Dummies® 2nd Edition

Published by
**Hungry Minds, Inc.**
909 Third Avenue
New York, NY 10022
www.hungryminds.com
www.dummies.com

Library of Congress Control Number: 00-110870

ISBN: 0-7645-5314-3

Printed in the United States of America

10 9 8 7 6 5 4

2O/QY/QT/QR/IN

Distributed in the United States by Hungry Minds, Inc.

Distributed by CDG Books Canada Inc. for Canada; by Transworld Publishers Limited in the United Kingdom; by IDG Norge Books for Norway; by IDG Sweden Books for Sweden; by IDG Books Australia Publishing Corporation Pty. Ltd. for Australia and New Zealand; by TransQuest Publishers Pte Ltd. for Singapore, Malaysia, Thailand, Indonesia, and Hong Kong; by Gotop Information Inc. for Taiwan; by ICG Muse, Inc. for Japan; by Intersoft for South Africa; by Eyrolles for France; by International Thomson Publishing for Germany, Austria and Switzerland; by Distribuidora Cuspide for Argentina; by LR International for Brazil; by Galileo Libros for Chile; by Ediciones ZETA S.C.R. Ltda. for Peru; by WS Computer Publishing Corporation, Inc., for the Philippines; by Contemporanea de Ediciones for Venezuela; by Express Computer Distributors for the Caribbean and West Indies; by Micronesia Media Distributor, Inc. for Micronesia; by Chips Computadoras S.A. de C.V. for Mexico; by Editorial Norma de Panama S.A. for Panama; by American Bookshops for Finland.

For general information on Hungry Minds' products and services please contact our Customer Care Department within the U.S. at 800-762-2974, outside the U.S. at 317-572-3993 or fax 317-572-4002.

For sales inquiries and reseller information, including discounts, premium and bulk quantity sales, and foreign-language translations, please contact our Customer Care Department at 800-434-3422, fax 317-572-4002, or write to Hungry Minds, Inc., Attn: Customer Care Department, 10475 Crosspoint Boulevard, Indianapolis, IN 46256.

For information on licensing foreign or domestic rights, please contact our Sub-Rights Customer Care Department at 650-653-7098.

For information on using Hungry Minds' products and services in the classroom or for ordering examination copies, please contact our Educational Sales Department at 800-434-2086 or fax 317-572-4005.

Please contact our Public Relations Department at 212-884-5163 for press review copies or 212-884-5000 for author interviews and other publicity information or fax 212-884-5400.

For authorization to photocopy items for corporate, personal, or educational use, please contact Copyright Clearance Center, 222 Rosewood Drive, Danvers, MA 01923, or fax 978-750-4470.

Hungry Minds™   is a trademark of Hungry Minds, Inc.

# About the Author

**John A. Tracy** (Boulder, Colorado) is Professor of Accounting, Emeritus, in the College of Business and Administration at the University of Colorado in Boulder. Before his 35-year tenure at Boulder he was on the business faculty for 4 years at the University of California in Berkeley. He has served as staff accountant at Ernst & Young and is the author of several books on accounting, including *The Fast Forward MBA in Finance* and *How To Read a Financial Report*. Dr. Tracy received his MBA and Ph.D. degrees from the University of Wisconsin and is a CPA in Colorado.

# Dedication

For all my grandchildren.

# Author's Acknowledgments

I'm deeply grateful to everyone at Hungry Minds, Inc., who helped produce this book. Their professionalism and their unfailing sense of humor and courtesy were much appreciated. I supplied some raw materials (words), and then the outstanding editors at Hungry Minds molded them into the finished product.

Out of the blue, I got a call one day from Kathy Welton, Vice President and Publisher for the Hungry Minds Consumer Publishing Group. Kathy asked if I'd be interested in doing this book. It didn't take me very long to say yes. She can be very persuasive, and she certainly knows her stuff. Thank you, Kathy!

I can't say enough nice things about Pam Mourouzis, who worked with me as project editor on the first edition of the book. The book is immensely better for her insights and advice. Pam started out as an accounting dummy, and she's now an accounting "smartie." The two copy editors on the book — Diane Giangrossi and Joe Jansen — made innumerable corrections and suggestions which were extraordinarily helpful. You two should also take a bow. I sincerely thank you.

Also, Mark Butler gave me the right nudge back then when I needed it. Mary Metcalfe provided invaluable comments and suggestions on the manuscript as it worked its way through the development process. I don't know Mary personally, but in my mind's eye she is one tough cookie!

I thank Holly McGuire and Jill Alexander for encouraging me to revise the book. The second edition has benefited greatly from the editing by Norm Crampton and Ben Nussbaum. They were extraordinarily helpful in revising the book. Both these gentlemen know their business, that's for sure! I also appreciate their unfailing good humor in working with me on the revision.

In short, it has been my great privilege and pleasure to work with the Hungry Minds team on this book. I couldn't have done it without them.

Also, I owe a debt of gratitude to a faculty colleague at Boulder, an accomplished author in his own right, Professor Ed Gac. He offered very sage advice. Ed was always ready with a word of encouragement when I needed one, and I'm very appreciative.

I often think about why I like to write books. I believe it goes back to an accounting class in my undergraduate days at Creighton University in Omaha. In a course taught by the Dean of the Business School, Dr. Floyd Walsh, I turned in a term paper and he said that it was very well written. I have never forgotten that compliment. I think he would be proud of this book.

## Publisher's Acknowledgments

We're proud of this book; please send us your comments through our Hungry Minds Online Registration Form located at www.dummies.com.

Some of the people who helped bring this book to market include the following:

### Acquisitions, Editorial, and Media Development

**Project Editor:** Norm Crampton

**Acquisitions Editor:** Jill Alexander

**Copy Editor:** Ben Nussbaum

**Acquisitions Coordinator:** Erica Bernheim

**Technical Editor:** David Bray

**Editorial Manager:** Pamela Mourouzis

**Editorial Assistant:** Carol Strickland

### Production

**Project Coordinator:** Leslie Alvarez

**Layout and Graphics:** Adam Mancilla, Jill Piscitelli, Jacque Schneider, Brian Torwelle, Erin Zeltner, Jeremey Unger

**Proofreaders:** Carl Pierce, Linda Quigley, Dwight Ramsey, Charles Spencer, York Graphic Services, Inc.

**Indexer:** York Graphic Services, Inc.

### General and Administrative

**Hungry Minds, Inc.:** John Kilcullen, CEO; Bill Barry, President and COO; John Ball, Executive VP, Operations & Administration; John Harris, CFO

**Hungry Minds Consumer Reference Group**

**Business:** Kathleen A. Welton, Vice President and Publisher; Kevin Thornton, Acquisitions Manager

**Cooking/Gardening:** Jennifer Feldman, Associate Vice President and Publisher

**Education/Reference:** Diane Graves Steele, Vice President and Publisher; Greg Tubach, Publishing Director

**Lifestyles:** Kathleen Nebenhaus, Vice President and Publisher; Tracy Boggier, Managing Editor

**Pets:** Dominique De Vito, Associate Vice President and Publisher; Tracy Boggier, Managing Editor

**Travel:** Michael Spring, Vice President and Publisher; Suzanne Jannetta, Editorial Director; Brice Gosnell, Managing Editor

**Hungry Minds Consumer Editorial Services:** Kathleen Nebenhaus, Vice President and Publisher; Kristin A. Cocks, Editorial Director; Cindy Kitchel, Editorial Director

**Hungry Minds Consumer Production:** Debbie Stailey, Production Director

◆

The publisher would like to give special thanks to Patrick J. McGovern, without whom this book would not have been possible.

◆

# Contents at a Glance

# Cartoons at a Glance

### By Rich Tennant

**The 5th Wave** — By Rich Tennant

"COOKED BOOKS? LET ME JUST SAY YOU COULD SERVE THIS PROFIT AND LOSS STATEMENT WITH A FRUITY ZINFANDEL AND NOT BE OUT OF PLACE."

page 287

**The 5th Wave** — By Rich Tennant

I'm mathematically dyslexic. But it's not that unusual—100 out of every 15 people are.

page 181

**The 5th Wave** — By Rich Tennant

BEAL & WASP ACCOUNTANTS

"OUR GOAL IS TO MAXIMIZE YOUR UPSIDE AND MINIMIZE YOUR DOWNSIDE WHILE WE PROTECT OUR OWN BACKSIDE."

page 93

**The 5th Wave** — By Rich Tennant

They're moving on to chapter 2. That should daze and confuse them enough for us to finish changing the tire and get the heck out of here.

ACCOUNTING TEXT BOOK PUBLISHERS

page 11

**The 5th Wave** — By Rich Tennant

ORIGINAL VAN-GOGH-OF-THE-MONTH CLUB

"SINCE WE BEGAN ON-LINE SHOPPING, I JUST DON'T KNOW WHERE THE MONEY'S GOING."

page 325

**Fax:** 978-546-7747
**E-mail:** richtennant@the5thwave.com
**World Wide Web:** www.the5thwave.com

# Table of Contents

# Introduction

• • • • • • • • • • • • • • • • • • • • • • • • • • • • • • • • • • • • • • • • • • • • • • •

*W*elcome to *Accounting For Dummies.* Why would anyone in their right mind take the time to learn about accounting, you ask? The brief answer is that accounting is your window to the world of business and finance. Understanding accounting can be an excellent means for getting a handle on the financial aspects of your business, investments, income taxes, and personal financial affairs. Accounting paints financial picture — not in colors, but with numbers.

I've written this book for people who need to understand accounting information and financial reports — *not* for accountants and bookkeepers (although they should find this book very interesting and a good refresher course). This book is for people who need to use and understand accounting information — business managers, for example, who need to make profit, turn profit into cash flow, and control the assets and liabilities of their business. If you're a business manager, I'm preaching to the choir when I say that you need a basic familiarity with accounting and financial statements in order to make good business decisions.

Business investors, lawyers, business consultants — pretty much anyone who reads *The Wall Street Journal* — can also benefit from a solid understanding of how to read financial reports and how accounting works.

## About This Book

*Accounting For Dummies* lifts the veil of obscure terminology and lays bare the methods of accounting. This book takes you behind the scenes and explains the language and methods of accounting in a down-to-earth and lighthearted manner — and *in plain English.*

Each chapter in this book is like a tub standing on its own feet — each is designed to stand on its own. Each chapter is self-contained, and you can jump from chapter to chapter as you please (although I encourage you to take a quick tour through the chapters in the order that I present them). I bet you'll discover some points that you may not have expected to find in a book about accounting.

# Conventions Used in Financial Reports

Much of this book focuses on profit and how a business makes profit. Because profit and other financial aspects of a business are reported in *financial statements,* understanding some basic notations and conventions used in these financial reports is important.

I use the following condensed income statement to illustrate some conventions that you can expect to see when reading financial reports. (The actual format of an income statement includes more information about expenses and profit.) These conventions are the common ways of showing figures in financial reports, like saying hello and shaking hands are common conventions that you can expect when you greet someone.

**Abbreviated Income Statement**

| | | |
|---|---|---|
| Sales revenue | | $25,000,000 |
| Cost of goods sold expense | | 15,000,000 |
| Gross margin | | $10,000,000 |
| Marketing expenses | $4,000,000 | |
| Other expenses | 2,000,000 | 6,000,000 |
| Profit | | $4,000,000 |

- ✔ You read a financial statement from the top down. In the sample income statement, for example, sales revenue is listed first, followed by cost of goods sold expense, because this particular expense is the first expense deducted from sales revenue. The other two expenses are listed below the first profit line, which is called gross margin.

- ✔ The sample income statement includes two columns of numbers. Note that the 6,000,000 total of the two expenses in the left column is entered in the right column. Some financial statements display all figures in a single column.

- ✔ An amount that is deducted from another amount — like cost of goods sold expense in the sample income statement — may have parentheses around the amount to indicate that it is being subtracted from the amount just above it. Or, financial statements may make the assumption that you know that expenses are deducted from sales revenue — so no parentheses are put around the number. You see expenses presented both ways in financial reports. But you hardly ever see a minus or negative sign in front of expenses — it's just not done.

✔ Notice the use of dollar signs in the sample income statement. Not all numbers have a dollar sign in front of the number. Financial reporting practices vary on this matter. I prefer to use dollar signs only for the first number in a column and for a calculated number. In some financial reports, dollar signs are put in front of all numbers, but more often they are not.

✔ To indicate that a calculation is being done, a single underline is drawn under the bottom number, as you see below the 15,000,000 cost of goods sold expense number in the sample income statement.

✔ The final number in a column usually is double underlined, as you can see for the $4,000,000 profit number in the sample income statement. This is about as carried away as accountants get in their work — a double underline. Again, actual financial reporting practices are not completely uniform on this point — instead of a double underline on a bottom-line number, the number may appear in **bold.**

When I present an accounting formula that shows how financial numbers are computed, I show the formula in a different font with a gray screen, like this:

```
Assets = Liabilities + Owners' Equity
```

Terminology in financial reporting is reasonably uniform, thank goodness — although you may see a fair amount of jargon. When I introduce a new term in this book, I show the term in *italics* and flag it with an icon (see the section "Icons Used in This Book," later in this Introduction). You can also turn to Appendix A to look up a term that you're unfamiliar with.

# Some Assumptions

This book is designed for all of you who have that nagging feeling that you really should know more about accounting. You don't want to be an accountant, nor do you have any aspirations of ever sitting for the CPA exam. But you worry that ignorance of accounting may hamper your decision-making, and you know deep down that learning more about accounting would help.

Although I assume that you have a basic familiarity with the business world, I take nothing for granted in this book regarding how much accounting you know. Even if you have some experience with accounting and financial statements, I think you'll find this book useful — especially for improving your communication with accountants.

This book is designed for people who need to *use* accounting information. Many different types of people need to understand accounting basics — not all the technical stuff, just the fundamentals. They include the following:

- **Business managers** depend on accounting reports to know how much profit was earned and how it was earned, to see the financial impacts of profit, to determine whether the business is in good financial shape, and to identify the sources and uses of cash flows in the business. Without this kind of information, managers are at a serious disadvantage.

- **Investors** in securities (stocks and bonds), real estate, and other business ventures depend on financial reports to inform them about how things are going and where things stand with their investments. Investors are generally very interested in whether they are getting a fair shake or perhaps are being led down the primrose path. To know what they're getting into (and what happens if they want to get out of an investment), investors can benefit from knowing financial statement basics.

- **Business professionals** need to know how to read financial statements, how accountants measure profit, and what the difference is between profit and cash flow from profit, which are two different things. For example, lawyers who draw up contracts containing accounting terminology and provisions that depend on accounting numbers should definitely understand what the accounting terms and numbers mean.

- **Government regulators, public administrators, and managers in the nonprofit sector of the economy** need a solid underpinning of accounting knowledge. For example, when the U.S. Justice Department investigates a proposed merger of two competitors, they examine financial statements of the businesses — one business may be in a precarious financial condition or not earning enough profit to remain a viable competitor.

- **Bankers and other lenders** depend heavily on financial statements and other accounting information in deciding whether to loan money to businesses and individuals for business and investment purposes. The character and collateral of the borrower count for a lot, but the accounting numbers also have to be in order.

- **Individuals who are trying to decipher their retirement fund reports,** but who can't get to first base on what it all means and what their future retirement benefits are, can benefit from a better understanding of accounting and of how things like compound interest work (see Chapter 4).

- **People who need to understand their personal investments and financial affairs,** such as CDs (certificates of deposit), real estate investments, 401(k) retirement plans, savings accounts, auto loans, home mortgages, and so on, can benefit from some basic accounting knowledge.

✔ **Individuals and families reading books and articles on personal financial planning** bump into accounting terms, concepts, and examples that they don't understand; frequently they are not certain about how things are being accounted for.

✔ **Politicians, social scientists, economists, journalists, and ordinary citizens** need a good understanding of how business and the investment markets work. Accounting provides the fundamental framework.

I assume that you want to know something about accounting because it's an excellent gateway for understanding how business works, and it gives you an indispensable vocabulary for moving up in the business and investment worlds. Finding out more about accounting helps you understand earnings reports, mergers and takeovers, frauds and Ponzi (pyramid) schemes, and business restructurings.

Let me point out one other very practical assumption that I have regarding why you should know some accounting — I call it the *defensive* reason. A lot of people out there in the cold, cruel financial world may take advantage of you, not necessarily by illegal means, but by withholding key information and by diverting your attention away from unfavorable aspects of certain financial decisions. These unscrupulous characters treat you as a lamb waiting to be fleeced. The best defense against such tactics is to learn some accounting basics, which can help you ask the right questions and understand the financial points that tricksters don't want you to know.

# How This Book Is Organized

This book is divided into parts, and each part is further divided into chapters. The following sections describe what you can find in each part.

## Part 1: Accounting Basics

Part I of *Accounting For Dummies* introduces accounting to non-accountants and discusses the basic features of bookkeeping and accounting record-keeping systems. This part also talks about taxes of all kinds involved in running a business, as well as accounting in the everyday lives of individuals.

# Part II: Getting a Grip on Financial Statements

Part II moves on to the end product of the business accounting process — *financial statements.* Three main financial statements are prepared every period — one for each financial imperative of business: making *profit,* keeping *financial condition* in good shape, and controlling *cash flow.* The nature of profit and the financial effects of profit are explained in Chapter 5. Profit is more involved than you probably think, to say the least. The basic format of the profit report, called the *income statement,* is presented — including the topic of unusual gains and losses in addition to the normal revenue and expenses of a business.

Business managers and investors should understand the financial turbulence caused by profit-making activities, which can cause changes in a variety of assets and liabilities. A business has to invest in many different assets to support its profit-making activities. A business has to raise a substantial amount of capital either by borrowing money or by persuading owners to invest money in the business — not easy tasks to accomplish, especially for business managers who do not understand financial statements. The assets, liabilities, and owners' capital invested in a business are reported in the *balance sheet,* which is discussed in Chapter 6.

Cash flow from profit and the *cash flow statement* are explained carefully in Chapter 7. The cash flow statement, which would seem to be the easiest financial statement to understand, is not so easy to grasp. Most people are irritated that profit doesn't simply generate cash flow of an equal amount. I am, too, but getting mad doesn't do any good. I can't think of a more important topic that business managers and investors need to understand clearly.

The last chapter in this part, Chapter 8, explains what managers have to do to get financial statements ready for the annual financial report of the business to its owners. This chapter explains the kinds of disclosures that are included in the annual financial report, in addition to the three financial statements. Also, I discuss frankly and openly the touchy topic of massaging the accounting numbers in financial statements.

# Part III: Accounting in Managing a Business

Business managers should know their financial statements like the backs of their hands. However, just understanding these reports is not the end of accounting for managers. Chapter 9 kicks off this part with an extraordinarily important topic — building a basic profit model that clearly focuses on the key variables that drive profit. This model is necessary, indeed absolutely critical, for decision-making analysis on topics such as changing sales prices, increasing sales volume, changing product costs, and the other factors for which managers are responsible. The importance of profit margin and sales volume is stressed in this chapter.

Chapter 10 discusses accounting-based planning and control techniques, especially *budgeting*. Business managers and owners have to decide on the best business ownership structure, which I discuss in Chapter 11. Managers in manufacturing businesses should be wary of how product costs are determined — as Chapter 12 explains. The chapter also explains other economic and accounting costs that business managers use in making decisions.

Choosing accounting methods for recording expenses is not a cut-and-dried process; managers have to make tough decisions. Chapter 13 identifies and explains the alternative accounting methods for expenses and how the choice of method has a major impact on profit for the period, and on the cost of inventory and fixed assets reported in the balance sheet. This chapter covers how managers can work closely with accountants in selecting the best accounting methods for their businesses — and how investors should be aware of which accounting methods are being used by the business in which they may want to invest.

## *Part IV: Financial Reports in the Outside World*

Part IV explains financial statement reporting for investors. Chapter 14 explains how to speed-read through a financial report. If you were a professional investment manager of a mutual fund with a large staff of financial analysts, you and your staff would read carefully through the entire financial report of every business you've invested in or are thinking of investing in. You're talking about millions of dollars of investments. However, ordinary individual investors do not have this kind of time to spend. Instead, I present a speed-reading approach that concentrates on the key financial ratios to look for in a financial report.

Also, you should read the CPA auditor's report for assurance that the financial statements are reliable, or whether the auditor has some concerns that you should be aware of. The scope of the annual audit and what to look for in the auditor's report are explained in Chapter 15, which also explains the role of CPA auditors as enforcers of financial accounting and disclosure standards.

## Part V: The Part of Tens

This part of the book presents two chapters — Chapter 16 presents some practical ideas for managers to help them put their accounting knowledge to use. Chapter 17 gives business investors some handy tips on things to look for in a financial report, tips that can make the difference between making a good investment and a not-so-good one.

## Appendixes

At the back of the book, you can find two helpful appendixes that can assist you on your accounting safari. Appendix A, "Glossary: Slashing Through the Accounting Jargon Jungle," provides you with a handy, succinct glossary of accounting terms. Appendix B, "Accounting Software," fills you in on the right questions to ask when deciding on an accounting software program for your business, and offers some suggestions on which software packages are best.

# Icons Used in This Book

This icon calls your attention to particularly important points and offers useful advice on practical financial topics. This icon saves you the cost of buying a yellow highlighter pen.

This icon serves as a friendly reminder that the topic at hand is important enough for you to put a note about it in the front of your wallet. This icon marks material that your college professor might put on the board before class starts, noting the important points that you should remember at the end of class.

Accounting is the language of business, and, like all languages, the vocabulary of accounting contains many specialized terms. This icon identifies key accounting terms and their definitions. You can also check the glossary (Appendix A) to find definitions of unfamiliar terms.

This icon is a caution sign that warns you about speed bumps and potholes on the accounting highway. Taking special note of this material can steer you around a financial road hazard and keep you from blowing a fiscal tire. In short — watch out!

I use this icon sparingly; it refers to very specialized accounting stuff that is heavy going, which only a CPA could get really excited about. However, you may find these topics important enough to return to when you have the time. Feel free to skip over these points the first time through and stay with the main discussion.

This icon alerts you that I'm using a practical example to illustrate and clarify an important accounting point. You can apply the example to your business or to a business in which you invest.

This icon points out especially important ideas and accounting concepts that are particularly deserving of your attention. The material marked by this icon describes concepts that are the undergirding and building blocks of accounting — concepts that you should be very clear about, and that clarify your understanding of accounting principles in general.

# Where to Go from Here

If you're new to the accounting game, by all means, start with Part I. However, if you already have a good background in business and know something about bookkeeping and financial statements, you may want to jump right into Part II of this book, starting with Chapter 5. Part III is on accounting tools and techniques for managers and assumes that you have a handle on the financial statements material in Part II. Part IV stands on its own; if your main interest in accounting is to make sense of and interpret financial statements, you can read through Part II on financial statements and then jump to Part IV on reading financial reports. If you have questions about specific accounting terms, you can go directly to the glossary in Appendix A.

I've had a lot of fun writing this book. I sincerely hope that it helps you become a better business manager and investor, and that it aids you in your personal financial affairs. I also hope that you enjoy the book. I've tried to make accounting as fun as possible, even though it's a fairly serious subject. Just remember that accountants never die; they just lose their balance. (Hey, accountants have a sense of humor, too.)

# Part I

# Accounting Basics

The 5th Wave By Rich Tennant

They're moving on to chapter 2. That should daze and confuse them enough for us to finish changing the tire and get the heck out of here.

ACCOUNTING TEXT BOOK PUBLISHERS

## In this part . . .

Accounting is important in all walks of life, and it's absolutely essential in the world of business. Accountants are the bookkeepers and scorekeepers of business. Without accounting, a business couldn't function; it wouldn't know whether it's making a profit, and it wouldn't know its financial situation. Bookkeeping — the recording-keeping part of accounting — must be managed well to make sure that all the financial information needed to run the business is complete, accurate, and reliable, especially the numbers reported in financial statements and tax returns. Wrong numbers in financial reports and tax returns can cause all sorts of trouble.

Speaking of taxes, you can't take more than three or four steps before bumping into taxes. No one likes to pay taxes, but managers must collect and pay taxes in running a business. In addition to income taxes, accounting plays a bigger role in your personal financial affairs than you might realize. This part of the book explains all this and more.

# Chapter 1

# Introducing Accounting to Non-Accountants

*M*ost medium to large businesses employ one or more accountants. Even a very small business needs at least a part-time accountant. Have you ever wondered why? What do these bean counters with the green eye-shades do, anyway? Probably what you think of first is that accountants keep the books — they keep the records of the financial activities of the business. This is true, of course. But accountants perform other very critical, but less well-known, functions in a business:

✔ Accountants carry out vital back-office operating functions that keep the business running smoothly and effectively — including payroll, cash inflows and cash payments, purchases and inventory, and property records.

✔ Accountants prepare tax returns, including the federal income tax return for the business, as well as payroll and property tax returns.

✔ Accountants determine how to measure and record the costs of products and how to allocate shared costs among different departments and other organizational units of the business.

✔ Accountants are the *professional profit scorekeepers* of the business world, meaning that they are the ones who determine exactly how much profit was earned, or just how much loss the business suffered, during the period. Accountants prepare reports for the managers of a business which keep managers informed about costs and expenses, how sales are going, whether the cash balance is adequate, what the inventory situation is, and, the most important thing — accountants help managers understand the reasons for changes in the bottom-line performance of a business.

✔ Accountants prepare *financial statements* that help the owners and stockholders of a business understand where the business stands financially. Stockholders wouldn't invest in a business without a clear understanding of the financial health of the business, which regular financial reports (which are sometimes just called *the financials*) provide.

In short, accountants are much more than bookkeepers — they provide the numbers that are so critical in helping business managers make the informed decisions that keep a business on course toward its financial objectives.

Business managers, investors, and others who depend on financial statements should be willing to meet accountants halfway. People who use accounting information, like spectators at a football game, should know the basic rules of play and how the score is kept. The purpose of this book is to make you a knowledgeable spectator of the accounting game.

# Accounting Everywhere You Look

Accounting extends into virtually every walk of life. You're doing accounting when you make entries in your checkbook and fill out your federal income tax return. When you sign a mortgage on your home, you should understand the accounting method the lender uses to calculate the interest amount charged on your loan each period. Individual investors need to understand some accounting in order to figure the return on capital invested. And every organization, profit-motivated or not, needs to know how it stands financially. Accounting supplies all that information.

Many different kinds of accounting are done by many different kinds of persons or entities for many different purposes:

✔ Accounting for organizations and accounting for individuals

✔ Accounting for profit-motivated businesses and accounting for nonprofit organizations (such as hospitals, homeowners' associations, churches, credit unions, and colleges)

✔ Income tax accounting while you're living and estate tax accounting after you die

✔ Accounting for farmers who grow their products, accounting for miners who extract their products from the earth, accounting for producers who manufacture products, and accounting for retailers who sell products that others make

✔ Accounting for businesses and professional firms that sell services rather than products, such as the entertainment, transportation, and healthcare industries

✔ Past-historical-based accounting and future-forecast-oriented accounting (that is, budgeting and financial planning)

✔ Accounting where periodic financial statements are mandatory (businesses are the primary example) and accounting where such formal accounting reports are not required

✔ Accounting that adheres to cost (most businesses) and accounting that records changes in market value (mutual funds, for example)

✔ Accounting in the private sector of the economy and accounting in the public (government) sector

✔ Accounting for going-concern businesses that will be around for some time and accounting for businesses in bankruptcy that may not be around tomorrow

Accounting is necessary in any free-market, capitalist economic system. It's equally necessary in a centrally controlled, socialist economic system. All economic activity requires information. The more developed the economic system, the more the system depends on information. Much of the information comes from the accounting systems used by the businesses, individuals, and other institutions in the economic system.

Some of the earliest records of history are the accounts of wealth and trading activity, and the need for accounting information was a main incentive in the development of the numbering system we use today. Professor William A. Paton, a well-known accounting professor at the University of Michigan for many years (and who lived to be over 100), expressed the purpose of accounting very well in his classic book, *Essentials of Accounting* (Macmillan):

> *In a broad sense accounting has one primary function: facilitating the administration of economic activity. This function has two closely related phases: (1) measuring and arraying economic data; [and] (2) communicating the results of this process to interested parties.*

# The Basic Elements of Accounting

I like Professor Paton's short definition because it articulates the basic purpose of accounting. However, the definition does sidestep one aspect of accounting — *bookkeeping* (which you can find more about in Chapter 2). Accounting involves bookkeeping, which refers to the painstaking and detailed recording of economic activity and business transactions. But *accounting* is a much broader term than *bookkeeping* because *accounting* refers to the design of the bookkeeping system. It addresses the many problems in measuring the financial effects of economic activity. Furthermore, accounting includes the *financial reporting* of these values and performance measures to non-accountants in a clear and concise manner. Business managers and investors, as well as many other people, depend on financial reports for vital information they need to make good economic decisions.

Accountants design the *internal controls* in an accounting system, which serve to minimize errors in recording the large number of activities that a business engages in over the period. The internal controls that accountants design can detect and deter theft, embezzlement, fraud, and dishonest behavior of all kinds. In accounting, internal controls are the ounce of prevention that is worth a pound of cure.

An accountant seldom prepares a complete listing of all the details of the activities that took place during a period. Instead, he or she prepares a *summary financial statement,* which shows totals, not a complete listing of all the individual activities making up the total. Managers may occasionally need to search through a detailed list of all the specific transactions that make up the total, but this is not common. Most managers just want summary financial statements for the period — if they want to drill down into the details making up a total amount for the period, they ask the accountant for this more detailed backup information. Also, outside investors usually only see summary-level financial statements. For example, they see the total amount of sales revenue for the period but not how much was sold to each and every customer.

Financial statements are prepared at the end of each accounting period. A period may be one month, one quarter (three calendar months), or one year. One basic type of accounting report prepared at the end of the period is a "Where do we stand at the end of the period?" type of report. This is called the *Statement of Financial Condition* or, more commonly, the *balance sheet.* The date of preparation is given in the header, or title above this financial statement. A balance sheet shows two sides of the business.

On the one side are listed the *assets* of the business, which are its economic resources being used in the business. On the other side of the balance sheet is a breakdown of where the assets came from, or the sources of the assets. The asset *values* reported in the balance sheet are the amounts recorded when the assets were originally acquired. For many assets these values are recent — only a few weeks or a few months old. For some assets their values as reported in the balance sheet are the costs of the assets when they were acquired many years ago.

Assets are not like manna from the heavens. They come from borrowing money in the form of loans that have to be paid back at a later date and from owners' investment of capital (usually money) in the business. Also, making profit increases the assets of the business; profit retained in the business is the third basic source of assets. If a business has, say, $2.5 million in total assets (without knowing which particular assets the business holds), I know that the total of its liabilities, plus the capital invested by its owners, plus its retained profit, adds up to $2.5 million.

In this example suppose that the total amount of the liabilities of the business is $1.0 million. This means that the total amount of *owners' equity* in the business is $1.5 million, which equals total assets less total liabilities. Without more information we don't know how much of total owners' equity is traceable to capital invested by the owners in the business and how much is the result of profit retained in the business. But we do know that the total of these two sources of owners' equity is $1.5 million.

The financial condition of the business in this example is summarized in the following *accounting equation* (in millions):

    $2.5 Assets = $1.0 Liabilities + $1.5 Owners' Equity

Looking at the accounting equation you can see why the statement of financial condition is also called the balance sheet; the equal sign means the two sides have to balance.

*Double-entry bookkeeping* is based on the accounting equation — or the fact that the total of assets on the one side are counter-balanced by the total of liabilities, invested capital, and retained profit on the other side. Double-entry bookkeeping is discussed in Chapter 2.

Other financial statements are different than the balance sheet in one important respect: they summarize the significant *flows* of activities and operations over the period. Accountants prepare two types of summary flow reports for businesses:

✔ The **income statement** summarizes the inflows of assets from the sale of products and services during the period. The income statement also summarizes the outflow of assets for expenses during the period — leading down to the well-known *bottom line,* or final profit or loss for the period.

✔ The **cash flow statement** summarizes the business's cash inflows and outflows during the period. The first part of this financial statement calculates the net increase or decrease in cash during the period from the profit-making activities reported in the income statement.

The balance sheet, income statement, and cash flow statement constitute the hard core of a financial report to those persons outside a business who need to stay informed about the business's financial affairs. These individuals have invested capital in the business, or the business owes them money; therefore they have a financial interest in how well the business is doing. These three key financial statements are also used by the managers of a business to keep informed about what's going on and the financial position of the business. They are absolutely essential to helping managers control the performance of a business, identify problems as they come up, and plan the future course of a business. Managers also need other information that is not reported in the three basic financial statements. (Part III of this book explains these additional reports.)

## The jargon jungle of accounting

Financial statements include many terms that are reasonably clear and straightforward, like *cash, accounts receivable,* and *accounts payable.* However, financial statements also use words like *retained earnings, accumulated depreciation, accelerated depreciation, accrued expenses, reserve, allowance, accrual basis,* and *current assets.* This type of jargon in accounting is like ugly on an ape: It's everywhere you look.

Although accounting is often called the "language of business," accountants use some of the most baffling terminology you'll ever hear (well, medical terminology and some legal terms may be worse). Accountants know the definitions of their specialized vocabulary and they assume that non-accountants know all these terms as well. The result is that many financial statements seem to many business managers and investors to be written in Greek. Furthermore, financial statements do not come with a glossary — such as the one that you can find at the end of this book. If you have any doubt about a term as I go along in the book, please take a quick look in Appendix A, which defines many accounting terms in plain English.

# Accounting and Financial Reporting Standards

Imagine if every business could invent its own accounting methods and terminology for measuring profit and for presenting financial statements. As an example from the academic world, what if I give a student an A for a course and a professor at another university gives a student a K? Keeping track of academic performance would be pretty tough without some recognized and accepted standards.

Experience and common sense have taught business and financial professionals that uniform financial reporting standards and methods are critical in a free-enterprise, private, capital-based economic system. A common vocabulary, uniform accounting methods, and full disclosure in financial reports are the goals. How well the accounting profession performs in achieving these goals is an open question, but few disagree that they are worthy goals to strive for.

## The supremacy of GAAP (generally accepted accounting principles)

The most important financial statement and financial reporting standards and rules are called *generally accepted accounting principles (GAAP),* which describe the basic methods to measure profit and to value assets and liabilities, as well as what information should be disclosed in those financial statements released outside a business. Suppose you're reading the financial statements of a business. You're entitled to assume that the business has used GAAP in reporting its cash flows and profit and its financial condition at the end of a financial period — *unless* the business makes very clear that it has prepared its financial report on a comprehensive basis of accounting other than GAAP.

The word *comprehensive* here is very important. A financial report should be comprehensive, or all-inclusive — reflecting all the financial activities and aspects of the entity. If not, the burden is on the business to make very clear that it is presenting something less that a complete and comprehensive report on its financial activities and condition. But, even if the financial report of a business is comprehensive, its financial statements may be based on accounting methods other than GAAP.

If GAAP are not the basis for preparing its financial statements, a business should make very clear which other basis of accounting is being used and should avoid using titles for its financial statements that are associated with GAAP. For example, if a business uses a simple cash receipts and cash disbursements basis of accounting — which falls way short of GAAP — it should not use the terms *income statement* and *balance sheet.* These terms are part and parcel of GAAP, and their use as titles for financial statements implies that the business is using GAAP.

# Financial reporting by government and other not-for-profit entities

In the grand scheme of things, the world of financial reporting can be divided into two hemispheres — for-profit entities (businesses) and not-for-profit entities. Although very prominent, business entities are just one of the main types of institutions in our society. Think of all the non-business institutions that you deal with and that affect your life — governmental, educational, religious, political, medical, cultural, and charitable.

A large body of authoritative rules and standards, called *generally accepted accounting principles,* or *GAAP* for short, have been hammered out over the years to govern accounting methods and financial reporting of business entities. To a lesser extent, accounting and financial reporting standards have evolved or been established for government and other not-for-profit entities. This book centers on business accounting methods and financial reporting. Financial reporting by government and other not-for-profit entities is a broad and diverse territory, which is beyond the scope of this book. I can say only a few words here, and that's it.

In dealing with government and other not-for-profit organizations, people generally don't demand financial reports from these entities. State and local government entities issue formal financial reports that are in the public domain — although very few taxpayers are interested in reading them. When you donate money to a charity, school, or church you don't generally get formal financial reports in return. On the other hand, many private, not-for-profit organizations issue formal financial reports to their members — credit unions, homeowner associations, country clubs, mutual insurance companies (owned by their policy holders), pension plans, labor unions, health care providers, and so on. The members or participants may have an equity interest or ownership share in the organization and, thus, they need financial reports to appraise them of their financial status with the entity.

In summary, government and other not-for profit entities should comply with the established accounting and financial reporting standards that apply to their type of entity. Being acquainted with business GAAP is a good starting point for understanding the financial reports of not-for-profit entities. *Caution:* Many not-for-profit entities use one or more accounting methods different than business GAAP, and the terminology in their financial reports is somewhat different than in the financial reports of business entities.

In brief, GAAP constitute the gold standard for preparing financial statements of business entities — although the gold is somewhat tarnished, which later chapters explain. Readers of a business's financial report are entitled to assume that GAAP have been followed in preparing the financial statements, unless the business makes very clear that it has not complied entirely with GAAP. If the deviations and shortfalls from GAAP are not disclosed, the business may have legal exposure to those who relied on the information in its financial report and suffered a loss attributable to the misleading nature of the information.

## A practical example of GAAP: Why the rules are important

Business managers should know the basic features of GAAP — though certainly not all the technical details — so that they understand how profit is measured. Managers get paid to make profit, and they should be very clear on how profit is measured and what profit consists of. The amount of profit a business makes depends on how *profit* is defined and measured.

For example, a business records the purchase of products at cost, which is the amount it paid for the products. *Inventory* is the stockpile of products being held for sale to customers. Examples include clothes in a department store, fuel in the tanks in a gas station, food on the shelves in a supermarket, books in a bookstore, and so on. The cost of products is put in the inventory asset account and kept there until the products are sold to customers. When the products are eventually sold, the cost of the products are recorded as the cost of goods sold expense, at which time a decrease is recorded in the inventory asset account. The cost of products sold is deducted from the sales revenue received from the customers, which gives a first-step measure of profit. (A business has many other expenses that need to be factored in, which you can read about in later chapters.)

Now, assume that before the business sells the products to its customers, the replacement cost of many of the products being held in inventory awaiting sale increases. The replacement cost value of the products is now higher than the original, actual purchase cost of the products. The company's inventory is worth more, is it not? Perhaps the business could raise the sales prices that it charges its customers because of the cost increase, or perhaps not. In any case, should the increase in the replacement cost of the products be recorded as profit? The manager may think that this holding gain should be recorded as profit. But GAAP accounting standards say that no profit is earned until the products are sold to the customers.

What about the opposite movement in replacement costs of products — when replacement costs fall below the original purchase costs? Should this development be recorded as a loss, or should the business wait until the products are sold? As you'll see, the accounting rule that applies here is called *lower of cost or market,* and the loss is recorded. So the rule requires one method on the upside but another method on the downside. See why business managers and investors need to know something about the rules of the game? I should add that GAAP are not all crystal-clear, which leaves a lot of wiggle room in the interpretation and application of these accounting standards. But first a quick word about GAAP and income tax accounting.

## Income tax and accounting rules

Generally speaking (and I'm being very general when I say the following), the federal income tax accounting rules for determining the annual taxable income of a business are in agreement with GAAP. In other words, the accounting methods used for figuring taxable income and for figuring business profit before income tax are in general agreement. Having said this, I should point out that several differences do exist. A business may use one accounting method for filing its annual income tax returns and a different method for measuring its profit both for management reporting purposes and for preparing its external financial statements to outsiders.

## Flexibility in accounting standards

An often-repeated accounting story concerns three CPAs interviewing for an important position. The CPAs are asked one key question: "What's 2 plus 2?" The first candidate answers, "It's 4," and is told, "Don't call us, we'll call you." The second candidate answers, "Well, most of the time the answer is 4, but sometimes it's 3 and sometimes it's 5." The third candidate answers: "What do you want the answer to be?" Guess who got the job?

The point is that GAAP are not entirely airtight or cut-and-dried. Many accounting standards leave a lot of room for interpretation. *Guidelines* would be a better word to describe some accounting rules. Deciding how to account for certain transactions and situations requires flexibility, seasoned judgment, and careful interpretation of the rules. Furthermore, many estimates have to be made.

Sometimes, businesses use what's called *creative accounting* to make profit for the period look better. Like lawyers who know where to find loopholes, accountants sometimes come up with inventive solutions, but still stay within the guidelines of GAAP. I warn you about these creative accounting

## Accounting depends on many estimates

The importance of estimates in financial accounting is illustrated in a footnote from a recent annual financial report of a well-known business:

"The preparation of financial statements in conformity with generally accepted accounting principles requires management to make estimates and assumptions that affect reported amounts. Examples of the more significant estimates include: accruals and reserves for warranty and product liability losses, post-employment benefits, environmental costs, income taxes, and plant closing costs."

Accounting estimates should be based on the best available information, of course, but most estimates are subjective and arbitrary to some extent. The accountant can choose either pessimistic or optimistic estimates, and thereby record either conservative profit numbers or more aggressive profit numbers.

techniques — also called *massaging the numbers* — at various points in this book. Articles in financial newspapers and magazines regularly focus on such accounting abuses.

# Enforcing Accounting Rules

As I mentioned in the preceding sections, when preparing financial statements a business must follow generally accepted accounting principles (GAAP) — the authoritative ground rules for measuring profit and for reporting values of assets and liabilities. Everyone reading a financial report is entitled to assume that GAAP have been followed (unless the business clearly discloses that it is using another so-called comprehensive basis of accounting).

The basic idea behind GAAP is to measure profit and to value assets and liabilities *consistently* from business to business — to establish broad-scale uniformity in accounting methods for all businesses. The idea is to make sure that all accountants are singing the same tune from the same hymnal. The purpose is also to establish realistic and objective methods for measuring profit and putting values on assets and liabilities. The authoritative bodies write the tunes that accountants have to sing.

GAAP also include minimum requirements for *disclosure,* which refers to how information is classified and presented in financial statements and to the types of information that have to be added to the financial statements in the form of footnotes. Chapter 8 explains these disclosures that are required in addition to the three primary financial statements of a business (the income statement, balance sheet, and cash flow statement).

The official GAAP rule book is *big* — more than a thousand pages! Actually there are eight different sources of authoritative accounting rules in the United States. And, accounting rule-making is becoming more international in scope to keep up with the global operations of many businesses. These rules have evolved over many decades — some rules remaining the same for many years, some being superseded and modified from time to time, and new rules being added. Some think the rules have become too complicated and far too technical. If you flip through the GAAP rule book, you'll see why people come to this conclusion. However, if the rules are not specific and detailed enough, different accountants will make different interpretations which will cause inconsistency from one business to the next regarding how profit is measured and how assets and liabilities are reported in the balance sheet. So, the rule-makers are between a rock and a hard place, and they issue rules that are rather detailed and technical.

How do you know if a business actually has followed the rules faithfully? I think it boils down to two factors. First is the competency and ethics of the accountants who prepared the financial reports. No substitute exists for expertise and integrity. But accountants often come under intense pressure to massage the numbers from the higher-level executives they work for.

Which leads to the second factor that allows you to know of a business has obeyed the dictates of GAAP: Businesses have their financial statements audited by independent certified public accountants (CPAs). In fact, public businesses are required to have annual audits by outside CPAs, and many private businesses hire CPAs to do an annual audit, even if not legally required. Chapter 15 explains audits and why investors should carefully read the auditor's report on the financial statements.

# The Accounting Department: What Goes On in the Back Office

As I discussed earlier in this chapter, bookkeeping (also called *record-keeping*) and financial reporting to managers and investors are the core functions of accounting. In this section, I explain another basic function of a business's accounting department: the back-office functions that keep the business running smoothly.

Most people don't realize the importance of the accounting department. That's probably because accountants do many of the back-office, operating functions in a business — as opposed to sales, for example, which is front-line activity, out in the open and in the line of fire. Go into any retail store, and you're in the thick of sales activities. But have you ever seen a company's accounting department in action?

Folks may not think much about these back-office activities, but they would sure notice if those activities didn't get done. On payday, a business had better not tell its employees, "Sorry, but the accounting department is running a little late this month; you'll get your checks later." And when a customer insists on up-to-date information about how much he or she owes to the business, the accounting department can't very well say, "Oh, don't worry, just wait a week or so and we'll get the information to you then."

Typically, the accounting department is responsible for:

- **Payroll:** The total wages and salaries earned by every employee every pay period, which are called *gross wages* or *gross earnings,* have to be determined. Based on detailed private information in personnel files and earnings-to-date information, the correct amounts of income tax, social security tax, and several other deductions from gross wages have to be determined.

  Next, accountants prepare payroll checks, which must also include various information that has to be reported to employees every pay period. The total amounts of withheld income tax and social security taxes, plus the employment taxes imposed on the employer, have to be paid over to federal and state government agencies right away. Retirement, vacation, sick pay, and other benefits earned by the employees also have to be updated every pay period. In short, payroll is a complex and critical function that the accounting department performs.

- **Cash inflows:** All cash received from sales and from all other sources has to be carefully identified and recorded, not only in the cash account but also in the appropriate account for the source of the cash received. The accounting department makes sure that the cash is deposited in the appropriate checking accounts of the business and that an adequate amount of coin and currency is kept on hand for making change for customers. Accountants balance the checkbook of the business and control who has access to incoming cash receipts. (In larger organizations, the *Treasurer* may be responsible for some of these cash flow and cash-handling functions.)

- **Cash payments:** In addition to payroll checks, a business writes many other checks during the course of a year — to pay for a wide variety of purchases, to pay property taxes, to pay off loans, and to distribute some of its profit to the owners of the business, for example. The accounting department prepares all these checks for the signatures of the officers of the business who are authorized to sign checks. The accounting department keeps all the supporting business documents and files to know when the checks should be paid, makes sure that the amount to be paid is correct, and forwards the checks for signature.

✔ **Purchases and inventory:** Accounting departments usually are responsible for keeping track of all purchase orders that have been placed for inventory (products to be sold by the business) and all other assets and services that the business buys — from postage stamps to forklifts. A typical business makes many purchases during the course of a year, many of them on credit, which means that the items bought are received today but paid for later. So this area of responsibility includes keeping files on all liabilities that arise from purchases on credit so that cash payments can be processed on time. The accounting department also keeps detailed records on all products held for sale by the business and, when the products are sold, records the cost of the goods sold.

✔ **Property accounting:** A typical business holds many different assets called *property* — including office furniture and equipment, retail display cabinets, computers, machinery and tools, vehicles (autos and trucks), buildings, and land. Except for relatively small-cost items, such as screwdrivers and pencil sharpeners, a business has to maintain detailed records of its property, both for controlling the use of the assets and for determining personal property and real estate taxes. The accounting department keeps these property records.

The accounting department may be assigned other functions as well, but I think that this list gives you a pretty clear idea of the back-office functions that the accounting department performs. Quite literally, a business could not operate if the accounting department did not do these functions efficiently and on time.

# Focusing on Business Transactions and Other Financial Events

Understanding that a great deal of accounting focuses on business transactions is very important. *Transactions* are economic exchanges between a business and the persons and other businesses with which the business deals. Transactions are the lifeblood of every business, the heartbeat of activity that keeps the business going. Understanding accounting, to a large extent, means understanding the basic accounting methods and practices used to record the financial effects of transactions.

A business carries on economic exchanges with six basic groups:

- Its **customers,** who buy the products and services that the business sells.

- Its **employees,** who provide services to the business and are paid wages and salaries and provided with a broad range of benefits, such as a retirement plan, health and medical insurance, workers' compensation, and unemployment insurance.

- Its **suppliers** and **vendors,** who sell a wide range of things to the business, such as legal advice, electricity and gas, telephone service, computers, vehicles, tools and equipment, furniture, and even audits.

- Its **debt sources of capital,** who loan money to the business, charge interest on the amount loaned, and have to be repaid at definite dates in the future.

- Its **equity sources of capital,** the individuals and financial institutions who invest money in the business and expect the business to earn profit on the capital they invested.

- The **government,** or the federal, state, and local agencies that collect income taxes, payroll taxes, and property taxes from the business.

Figure 1-1 illustrates the interactions between the business and the other parties in the economic exchange.

Even a relatively small business generates a surprisingly large number of transactions, and all transactions have to be recorded. Certain other events that have a financial impact on the business have to be recorded as well. These are called *events* because they're not based on give-and-take bargaining — unlike the something-given-for-something-received nature of economic exchanges. Events such as the following have an economic impact on a business and have to be recorded:

- A business may lose a lawsuit and be ordered to pay damages. The liability to pay the damages has to be recorded.

- A business may suffer a flood loss that is uninsured. The water-logged assets may have to be written off, meaning that the recorded values of the assets are reduced to a zero if they no longer have any value to the business. For example, products that were being held for sale to customers (until they floated down the river) must be removed from the inventory account.

- A business may decide to abandon a major product line and downsize its workforce, requiring that severance be paid to laid-off employees.

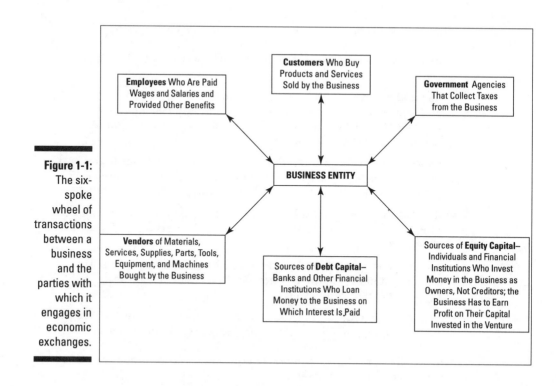

**Figure 1-1:**
The six-
spoke
wheel of
transactions
between a
business
and the
parties with
which it
engages in
economic
exchanges.

**Customers** Who Buy Products and Services Sold by the Business

**Employees** Who Are Paid Wages and Salaries and Provided Other Benefits

**Government** Agencies That Collect Taxes from the Business

**BUSINESS ENTITY**

**Vendors** of Materials, Services, Supplies, Parts, Tools, Equipment, and Machines Bought by the Business

Sources of **Debt Capital**– Banks and Other Financial Institutions Who Loan Money to the Business on Which Interest Is Paid

Sources of **Equity Capital**– Individuals and Financial Institutions Who Invest Money in the Business as Owners, Not Creditors; the Business Has to Earn Profit on Their Capital Invested in the Venture

# *Taking a Closer Look at Financial Statements*

As I mention in the preceding sections, accountants prepare certain basic financial statements for a business. The three basic financial statements are the following:

> ✔ **Statement of financial condition (or balance sheet):** A summary of the financial position of the business at the end of the period.
>
> ✔ **Income statement:** A summary of sales revenue and expenses that determines the profit (or loss) for the period just ended. This is also called the *profit and loss statement,* or simply the *P&L statement.* (Alternative titles also include the *statement of operations* and the *statement of earnings.*)
>
> ✔ **Cash flow statement:** A summary of cash inflows and cash outflows for the period just ended.

This section gives you a description of these statements that constitute a business's financial center of gravity. I show you the general format and content of these three accounting reports. The president and chief executive officer of a business (plus other top-level managers and financial officers) are responsible for seeing that the financial statements are prepared according to financial reporting standards and that proper accounting methods have been used to prepare the financial statements.

If a business's financial statements are later discovered to be seriously in error or misleading, the business and its top executives can be sued for damages suffered by lenders and investors who relied on the financial statements. For this reason, business managers should understand their responsibility for the financial statements and the accounting methods used to prepare the statements. In a court of law, they can't plead ignorance.

I frequently meet managers who don't seem to have a clue about the three primary statements. This situation is a little scary; a manager who doesn't understand financial statements is like an airplane pilot who doesn't understand the instrument readouts in the cockpit. A manager *could* run the business and "land the plane safely," but knowing how to read the vital signs along the way is much more prudent.

In short, business managers at all levels — from the board of directors down to the lower rungs on the management ladder, and especially managers of smaller businesses who have to be a jack-of-all-trades in running the business — need to understand financial statements and the accounting methods used to prepare the statements. Also, lenders to a business, investors in a business, business lawyers, government regulators of business, entrepreneurs, employees who depend on the continued financial success of the business for their jobs, anyone thinking of becoming an entrepreneur and starting a business, and, yes, even economists should know the basics of financial statement accounting. I've noticed that even experienced business journalists, who ought to know better, sometimes refer to the balance sheet when they're talking about profit performance. The bottom line is found in the income statement, not the balance sheet!

## The balance sheet (or statement of financial condition)

The balance sheet is the essential financial statement that reports the main types of assets owned by a business. Assets are only half the picture, however. Almost all businesses borrow money. At the date of preparing the balance sheet, a business owes money to its lenders, who will be paid sometime in the future. Also, most businesses buy many things on credit and at the balance sheet date owe money to their suppliers which will be paid in the future. Amounts owed to lenders and suppliers are called *liabilities*. A balance sheet reports the main types of liabilities of the business, and separates between those due in the short-term and those due in the longer-term.

Could total liabilities be greater than a business's total assets? Well, not likely — unless the business has been losing money hand over fist. In the vast majority of cases a business has more total assets than total liabilities. Why? For two reasons: (1) its owners have invested money in the business, which is not a liability of the business; and, (2) the business has earned profit over the years and some of the profit has been retained in the business. (Profit increases assets.) The sum of invested capital from owners and retained profit is called *owners' equity*. The excess of total assets over total liabilities is traceable to owners' equity. A balance sheet reports the make-up of the owners' equity of a business.

You generally see the balance sheet in the following layout:

### Basic Format of the Balance Sheet

| | |
|---|---|
| **Assets,** or the economic resources the business owns; examples are cash on deposit in bank checking accounts, products held for sale to customers, and buildings. | **Liabilities,** which arise from borrowing money and buying things on credit. |
| | **Owners' Equity,** which arises from two sources: money invested by the owners, and profit earned and retained by the business. |

One reason the balance sheet is called by this name is that the two sides balance, or are equal in total amounts:

```
Total Recorded Amount of Assets = Total Recorded Amount of
        Liabilities + Total Recorded Amount of Owners'
        Equity
```

Owner's equity is sometimes referred to as *net worth*. You compute net worth as follows:

```
Assets - Liabilities = Net Worth
```

*Net worth* is not a particularly good term, because it implies that the business is worth the amount recorded in its owners' equity accounts. Though the term may suggest that the business could be sold for this amount, nothing is further from the truth. (Chapter 6 presents more information about the recorded, or *book,* value of owners' equity reported in the balance sheet, and why current replacement costs of some assets may be higher than the book values of these assets. Chapter 14 discusses the market prices of stock shares, which are units of ownership in a business corporation.)

# The income statement

The income statement is the all-important financial statement that summarizes the profit-making activities (or operations) of a business over a time period. In very broad outline, the statement is reported like this:

---

**Basic Format of the Income Statement**

---

**Sales Revenue** (from the sales of products and services to customers)

**Less Expenses** (which include a wide variety of costs paid by the business, including the cost of products sold to customers, wages and benefits paid to employees, occupancy costs, administrative costs, and income tax)

**Equals Net Income** (which is referred to as the bottom line and means final profit after all expenses are deducted from sales revenue)

The income statement gets the most attention from business managers and investors — not that they ignore the other two financial statements. The very abbreviated versions of income statements that you see in the financial press, such as in *The Wall Street Journal,* report only the top line (sales revenue) and the bottom line (net income). In actual practice, the income statement is more involved than the basic format shown here. Refer to Chapter 5 for more information on income statements.

# The cash flow statement

The cash flow statement presents a summary of the sources and uses of cash in a business during a financial period. Smart business managers hardly get the word *profit* out of their mouths before mentioning *cash flow.* Successful business managers can tell you that they have to manage both profit *and* cash flow; you can't do one and ignore the other. Business is a two-headed dragon in this respect. Ignoring cash flow can pull the rug out from under a successful profit formula. Still, some managers become preoccupied with making profit and overlook cash flow.

For financial reporting, cash flows are divided into three basic categories:

---

**Basic Format of the Cash Flow Statement**

---

(1) Cash flow from the profit-making activities, or **operating activities,** for the period (***Note:*** *Operating means the profit-making transactions of the business.*)

(2) Cash inflows and outflows from **investing activities** for the period

(3) Cash inflows and outflows from the **financing activities** for the period

You determine the bottom-line net increase (or decrease) in cash during the period by adding the three types of cash flows shown in the preceding list.

Part 1 explains why net cash flow from sales revenue and expenses — the business's profit-making operating activities — is more or less than the amount of profit reported in the income statement. The *actual* cash inflows from revenues and outflows for expenses run on a different timetable than when the sales revenue and expenses are recorded for determining profit. It's like two different trains going to the same destination — the second train (the cash flow train) runs on a later schedule than the first train (the recording of sales revenue and expenses in the accounts of the business). Chapter 7 explains the cash flow analysis of profit as well as the other sources of cash and the uses of cash.

Part 2 of the cash flow statement sums up the major long-term investments made by the business during the year, such as constructing a new production plant or replacing machinery and equipment. If the business sold any of its long-term assets, it reports the cash inflows from these divestments in this section of the cash flow statement.

Part 3 sums up the financing activities of the business during the period — borrowing new money from lenders and raising new capital investment in the business from its owners. Cash outflows to pay off debt are reported in this section, as well as cash distributions from profit paid to the owners of the business.

The cash flow statement reports the net increase or net decrease in cash during the year (or other time period), caused by the three types of cash flows. This increase or decrease in cash during the year is never referred to as the *bottom line*. This important term is strictly limited to the last line of the income statement, which reflects net income — the final profit after all expenses are deducted.

Imagine you have a yellow (or pink) highlighter pen in your hand, and the three basic financial statements of a business are in front of you. What are the most important numbers to mark? Financial statements do *not* have any numbers highlighted; they do not come with headlines like newspapers. You have to find your own headlines. *Bottom-line profit* in the income statement is one number you would mark for sure. Another key number is *cash flow from operating activities* in the cash flow statement, or some variation of this number. Cash flow has become very important these days. Chapter 7 explains why this internal source of cash is so important and the various definitions of *cash flow* (did you think there was only one meaning of this term?).

# Accounting as a Career

In our highly developed economy, many people make their living as accountants — and here I'm using the term *accountant* in the broadest possible sense. According to the *1998 Statistical Abstract of the United States* (Table No. 672, page 417), about 1.6 million people in the United States work force are accountants and auditors. A little more than half are women, which is quite an improvement compared to a generation ago. About one-third of these accountants work for independent establishments that offer their accounting and auditing services to the public. Businesses, government agencies, nonprofit organizations, and other organizations and associations employ the other two-thirds.

Because accountants work with numbers and details you hear references to accountants as bean counters, digit heads, number nerds, and other names I don't care to mention here. Accountants take these snide references in stride and with good humor. Actually, accountants come out among the most respected professionals in many polls.

## Certified public accountant (CPA)

In the accounting profession, the mark of distinction is to be a *CPA,* which stands for *certified public accountant.* The term *public* means that the person has had some practical experience working for a CPA firm; it does not necessarily indicate whether that person is presently in *public* practice (as an individual CPA or as an employee or partner in a CPA firm that offers services to the public at large) rather than working exclusively for one organization.

To become a certified public accountant (CPA), you go to college, graduate with an accounting major in a five-year program (in most states), and pass the two-day national CPA exam, which is prepared and graded by the American Institute of Certified Public Accountants. You also must satisfy professional employment experience; this requirement varies from state to state but generally is one or two years. After satisfying the education, exam, and experience requirements, you get a CPA certificate to hang on your wall. More important, you get a permit from your state to practice as a CPA and offer your services to the public. States now require continuing education hours to be satisfied to maintain an active CPA permit.

# The Controller: The chief accountant in an organization

After working for a CPA firm in public practice for a few years, most CPAs leave public accounting and go to work for a business or other organization. Usually, they start at a mid-level accounting position with fairly heavy accounting responsibilities, but some step in as the top accountant in charge of all accounting matters of a business. The top-level accountant in a business organization is usually called the *Controller*.

The Controller designs the entire accounting system of the business and keeps it up-to-date with changes in the tax laws and changes in the accounting rules that govern reporting financial statements to outside lenders and owners. Controllers are responsible for hiring, training, evaluating, promoting, and sometimes firing the persons who hold the various bookkeeping and accounting positions in an organization — which range from payroll functions to the several different types of tax returns that have to be filed on time with different government agencies.

The Controller is the lead person in the financial planning and budgeting process of the business organization. Furthermore, the Controller designs the accounting reports that all the various managers in the organization receive — from the sales and marketing managers to the purchasing and procurement managers. These internal reports should be designed to fit the authority and responsibility of each manager; they should provide information for managers' decision-making analysis needs and the information they need to exercise effective control.

The Controller also designs and monitors the accounting reports that go to the business's top-level vice presidents, the president, the chief executive officer of the business, and the board of directors. All tough accounting questions and problems get referred to the Controller. The Controller needs good people management skills, should know how to communicate with all the non-accounting managers in the organization, and at the same time should be an "accountant's accountant" who has deep expertise in many areas of accounting.

Smaller businesses may have only one or two accountants. The full-time bookkeeper or office manager may carry out many of the duties that would belong to the Controller in a larger organization. Smaller businesses often call in a CPA in public practice to advise their accountants. The CPA may function more or less as a part-time Controller for a small business, preparing the annual income tax returns and helping to prepare the business's external financial reports.

# Chapter 2

# Bookkeeping 101: From Shoeboxes to Computers

*M*ost folks are lousy bookkeepers just because they really don't do much bookkeeping. Admit it: Maybe you balance your checkbook against your bank statement every month and somehow manage to pull together all the records you need for your annual federal income tax return. But you probably stuff your bills in a drawer and just drag them out once a month when you're ready to pay them. (Hey, that's what I do.) And you almost certainly don't prepare a detailed listing of all your assets and liabilities (even though a listing of assets is a good idea for fire insurance purposes). Two or three popular personal computer programs make book-keeping for individuals a lot easier, but you still have to enter a lot of data into the program, and most people decide not to put forth the effort.

I don't prepare a summary statement of my earnings and income for the year or a breakdown of what I spent my money on and how much I saved. Why not? Because I don't need to! Individuals can get along quite well without much bookkeeping — but the exact opposite is true for a business.

One key difference between individuals and businesses is that a business must prepare periodic *financial statements,* the accuracy of which is critical to the business's survival. The business uses the accounts and records generated by its bookkeeping process to prepare these statements; if the accounting records are incomplete or inaccurate, the financial statements are incomplete or inaccurate. And inaccuracy simply won't do.

Obviously, then, business managers have to be sure that the company's bookkeeping and accounting system is adequate and reliable. This chapter shows managers what bookkeepers and accountants do — mainly so that you can make sure that the information coming out of your accounting system is complete, timely, and accurate.

# Bookkeeping versus Accounting

*Bookkeeping* is essentially the process (some would say the drudgery) of recording all the information regarding the transactions and financial activities of a business — the record-keeping aspects of *accounting.* Bookkeeping is an indispensable subset of accounting. The term *accounting* goes much further, into the realm of designing the bookkeeping system in the first place, establishing controls to make sure that the system is working well, and analyzing and verifying the recorded information. Bookkeepers follow orders; accountants give orders.

Accounting can be thought of as what goes on before and after bookkeeping. Accountants prepare reports based on the information accumulated by the bookkeeping process — financial statements, tax returns, and various confidential reports to managers. Measuring profit is a very important task that accountants perform, a task that depends on the accuracy of the information recorded by the bookkeeper. The accountant decides how to measure sales revenue and expenses to determine the profit or loss for the period. The tough questions about profit — where it is and what it consists of — can't be answered through bookkeeping alone.

The rest of this book doesn't discuss bookkeeping in any detail — no talk of debits and credits and all that stuff. All you really need to know about bookkeeping, as a business manager, is contained in this chapter alone.

# Pedaling through the Bookkeeping Cycle

Figure 2-1 presents an overview of the bookkeeping cycle side-by-side with elements of the accounting system. You can follow the basic bookkeeping steps down the left side. The accounting elements are shown in the right column. The basic steps in the bookkeeping sequence, explained briefly, are as follows. (See also "Managing the Bookkeeping and Accounting System," later in this chapter, for more details on some of these steps.)

1. **Record *transactions* — the economic exchanges between a business and the other persons and businesses that the bookkeeper's business deals with.**

   Transactions have financial effects that must be recorded — the business is better off, worse off, or at least "different off" as the result of its transactions. Examples of typical business transactions include paying employees, making sales to customers, borrowing money from the bank, and buying products that will be sold to customers. The bookkeeping process begins by identifying all transactions and capturing the relevant information about each transaction.

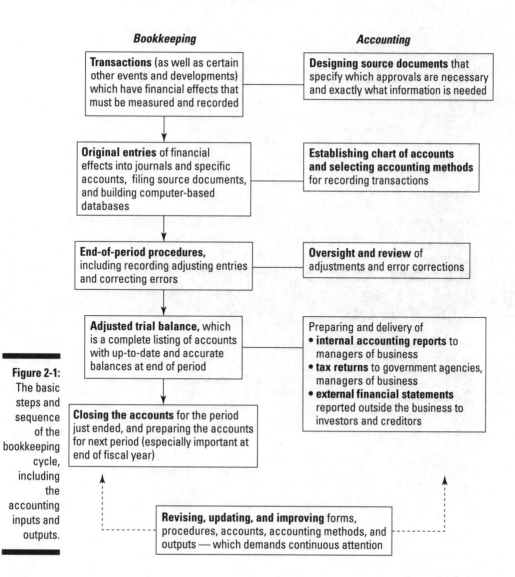

**Figure 2-1:**
The basic
steps and
sequence
of the
bookkeeping
cycle,
including
the
accounting
inputs and
outputs.

*Bookkeeping*                    *Accounting*

**Transactions** (as well as certain other events and developments) which have financial effects that must be measured and recorded

**Designing source documents** that specify which approvals are necessary and exactly what information is needed

**Original entries** of financial effects into journals and specific accounts, filing source documents, and building computer-based databases

**Establishing chart of accounts and selecting accounting methods** for recording transactions

**End-of-period procedures,** including recording adjusting entries and correcting errors

**Oversight and review** of adjustments and error corrections

**Adjusted trial balance,** which is a complete listing of accounts with up-to-date and accurate balances at end of period

Preparing and delivery of
• **internal accounting reports** to managers of business
• **tax returns** to government agencies, managers of business
• **external financial statements** reported outside the business to investors and creditors

**Closing the accounts** for the period just ended, and preparing the accounts for next period (especially important at end of fiscal year)

**Revising, updating, and improving** forms, procedures, accounts, accounting methods, and outputs — which demands continuous attention

2. **Prepare and collect *source documents* — transaction documentation that the bookkeeper uses to record the transactions.**

   When buying products, a business gets a *purchase invoice* from the supplier. When borrowing money from the bank, a business signs a *note payable,* a copy of which the business keeps. When a customer uses a credit card to buy the business's product, the business gets the *credit card slip* as evidence of the transaction. When preparing payroll checks, a business depends on *salary rosters* and *time cards.* All of these key business forms serve as sources of information into the bookkeeping system — in other words, information the bookkeeper uses in recording the financial effects of the transaction.

3. **Record original entries (the financial effects of the transactions) into journals and accounts.**

   Using the source document(s) for every transaction, the bookkeeper makes the first, or original, entry into a journal and then into the business's accounts. Only an official, established chart of accounts should be used in recording transactions. A *journal* is a chronological record of transactions in the order in which they occur — like a very detailed personal diary. In contrast, an *account* is a separate record for each asset, each liability, and so on. One transaction affects two or more accounts. The journal entry records the whole transaction in one place; then each piece is recorded in the two or more accounts changed by the transaction.

   Here's a simple example that illustrates recording of a transaction in a *journal* and then *posting* the changes caused by the transaction in the *accounts.* Expecting a big demand from its customers, a retail bookstore purchases, on credit, 50 copies of *Accounting For Dummies* from the publisher, IDG Books Worldwide, Inc. The books are received and placed on the shelves. (50 copies is a lot to put on the shelves, but my relatives promised to rush down and buy several copies each.) The bookstore now owns the books and also owes IDG $600.00, which is the cost of the 50 copies. You look only at recording the purchase of the books, not recording subsequent sales of the books and paying the bill to IDGB.

   The bookstore has established a specific inventory account called "Inventory-Trade Paperbacks" for books like mine. And the purchase liability to the publisher should be entered in the account "Accounts Payable-Publishers." So the journal entry for this purchase is recorded as follows:

   | | |
   |---|---|
   | Inventory-Trade Paperbacks | + $600.00 |
   | Accounts Payable-Publishers | + $600.00 |

   This pair of changes is first recorded in one journal entry. Then, sometime later, each change is *posted,* or recorded in the separate accounts — one an asset and the other a liability.

In ancient days, bookkeepers had to record these entries by hand, and even today there's nothing wrong with a good hand-entry (manual) bookkeeping system. But bookkeepers now can use computer programs that take over many of the tedious chores of bookkeeping. Computers have come to the rescue — of course, typing has replaced hand cramps with carpal tunnel syndrome, but at least the work gets done more quickly and with fewer errors! (See Appendix B for more about popular accounting software packages for personal computers.)

I can't exaggerate the importance of entering transaction data correctly and in a timely manner. For example, an important reason that most retailers these days use cash registers that read bar-coded information on products is to more accurately capture the necessary information and to speed up the entry of this information.

4. **Perform end-of-period procedures — preliminary steps for preparing the accounting reports and financial statements at the end of every period.**

A *period* can be any stretch of time — from one day to one month to one quarter (three months) to one year — and is determined by the needs of the business. A year is the longest period of time that a business would wait to prepare its financial statements. As a matter of fact, most businesses need accounting reports and financial statements at the end of each quarter, and many need monthly financial statements.

Before the accounting reports can be prepared at the end of the period (see Figure 2-1), the bookkeeper needs to bring the accounts of the business up-to-date and complete the bookkeeping process. One step, for example, is recording the *depreciation expense* for the period (see Chapter 6 for more on depreciation). Another step is getting an actual count of the business's inventory so that the inventory records can be adjusted to account for shoplifting, employee theft, and so on.

The accountant needs to take the final step and check for errors in the business's accounts. Data entry clerks and bookkeepers may not fully understand the unusual nature of some business transactions and may have entered transactions incorrectly. One reason for establishing *internal controls* (discussed in "Protect the family jewels: Internal controls," later in this chapter) is to keep errors to an absolute minimum. Ideally, accounts should contain very few errors at the end of the period, but the accountant can't make any assumptions and should make a final check for any errors that fell through the cracks.

5. **Prepare the adjusted trial balance for the accountants.**

After all the end-of-period procedures have been completed, the bookkeeper prepares a complete listing of all accounts, which is called the *adjusted trial balance*. Modest-sized businesses maintain hundreds of accounts for their various assets, liabilities, owners' equity, revenue, and expenses. Larger businesses keep thousands of accounts, and very large businesses may keep more than 10,000 accounts. In contrast, external financial statements, tax returns, and internal accounting reports to managers contain a relatively small number of accounts. For example, a typical external balance sheet reports only 20 to 25 accounts, and a typical income tax return contains less than 100 accounts.

The accountant takes the adjusted trial balance and telescopes similar accounts into one summary amount that is reported in a financial report or tax return. For example, a business may keep hundreds of separate inventory accounts, every one of which is listed in the adjusted trial balance. The accountant collapses all these accounts into one summary inventory account that is presented in the external balance sheet of the business.

In short, the large number of specific accounts listed in the adjusted trial balance is condensed into a comparatively small number of accounts that are reported in financial statements and tax returns. In grouping the accounts, the accountant should comply with established financial reporting standards and income tax requirements.

6. ***Close the books*** — **bring the bookkeeping for the fiscal year just ended to a close and get things ready to begin the bookkeeping process for the coming fiscal year.**

   *Books* is the common term for *accounts.* A business's transactions are a constant stream of activities that don't end tidily on the last day of the year, which can make preparing financial statements and tax returns challenging. The business has to draw a clear line of demarcation between activities for the year (the 12-month accounting period) ended and the year yet to come by *closing the books* for one year and starting with fresh books for the next year.

The business may have an *accounting manual* that spells out in great detail the specific accounts and procedures for recording transactions. But all businesses change over time, and they occasionally need to review their accounting system and make revisions. Companies do not take this task lightly; discontinuities in the accounting system can be major shocks and have to be carefully thought out. Nevertheless, bookkeeping and accounting systems can't remain static for very long. If these systems were never changed, bookkeepers would still be sitting on high stools making entries with quill pens and ink in leather-bound ledgers.

# Managing the Bookkeeping and Accounting System

In my experience, far too many business managers either ignore their bookkeeping and accounting systems or take them for granted — unless something obvious goes wrong. The managers assume that if the books are in balance, then everything is okay. The section "Recording transactions using debits and credits," later in this chapter, covers just exactly what "the books being in balance" means — it does *not* necessarily mean that everything is okay.

To determine whether your bookkeeping system is up to snuff, check out the following sections, which, taken as a whole, provide a checklist of the most important elements of a good system.

## Categorize your financial information: The chart of accounts

Suppose that you're the accountant for a corporation and you're faced with the daunting task of preparing the annual federal income tax return for the business. This demands that you report the following kinds of expenses (and this list contains just the minimum!):

- Advertising
- Bad debts
- Charitable contributions
- Compensation of officers
- Cost of goods sold
- Depreciation
- Employee benefit programs
- Interest
- Pensions and profit-sharing plans
- Rents
- Repairs and maintenance
- Salaries and wages
- Taxes and licenses

You must provide additional information for some of these expenses. For example, the cost of goods sold expense is determined in a schedule that also requires inventory cost at the beginning of the year, purchases during the year, cost of labor during the year (for manufacturers), other costs, and inventory cost at year-end.

Where do you start? Well, if it's March 1 and the tax return deadline is March 15, you start by panicking — unless you were smart enough to think ahead about the kinds of information your business would need to report. In fact, when your accountant first designs your business's accounting system, he or she should dissect every report to managers, the external financial statements, and the tax returns, breaking down all the information into categories such as those I just listed.

For each category, you need an *account,* a record of the activities in that category. An account is basically a focused history of a particular dimension of a business. Individuals can have accounts, too — for example, your checkbook is an account of the cash inflows and outflows and the balance of your checking account (assuming that you remember to record all activities and balance your checkbook against your bank statement). I doubt that you keep a written account of the coin and currency in your wallet, pockets, glove compartment, and sofa cushions, but a business needs to.

*Note:* The term *account* in the bookkeeping sense means a basic category of information in which the financial effects of transactions are recorded and which serves as the source of information for preparing financial statements, tax returns, and reports to managers. In general usage, the term refers to a personal checking account in a bank, or a charge account you have at a store, or an investment account you have established for saving money for your retirement. In the following discussion, I use the term in its business bookkeeping sense.

The term *general ledger* refers to the complete set of accounts established and maintained by a business. The *chart of accounts* is the formal index of these accounts — the complete listing and classification of the accounts used by the business to record its transactions. *General ledger* usually refers to the actual accounts and often to the balances in these accounts at some particular time.

The chart of accounts, even for a relatively small business, normally contains 100 or more accounts. Larger business organizations need thousands of accounts. The larger the number, the more likely that the accounts are given number codes according to some scheme — all assets may be in the 100 to 300 range, all liabilities in the 400 to 500 range, and so on.

As a business manager, you should make sure that the person in charge of accounting (or perhaps an outside CPA) reviews the chart of accounts periodically to determine whether the accounts are up-to-date and adequate for the business's needs. Over time, income tax rules change, the company goes into new lines of business, the company adopts new employee benefit plans, and so on. Most businesses are in constant flux, and the chart of accounts has to keep up with these changes.

## *Standardize source document forms and procedures*

Businesses move on paperwork. Placing an order to buy products, selling a product to a customer, determining the earnings of an employee for the month — virtually every business transaction needs paperwork, known as *source documents*. Source documents serve as evidence of the terms and conditions agreed upon by the business and the other person or organization that it's dealing with. Both parties receive some kind of source document. For example, for a sale at a cash register, the customer gets a sales receipt, and the business keeps a running tape of all transactions in the register.

Clearly, an accounting system needs to standardize the forms and procedures for processing and recording all normal, repetitive transactions and should control the generation and handling of these source documents.

From the bookkeeping point of view, these business forms and documents are very important because they provide the input information needed for recording transactions in the business's accounts. Sloppy paperwork leads to sloppy accounting records, and sloppy accounting records just won't do when the time comes to prepare tax returns and financial statements.

Check out a business office-supply store to see the kinds of forms that you can buy right off the shelf. You can find many — maybe all — of the basic forms and documents that you need for recording business transactions, although most firms have to design at least some of their own forms. Also, personal computer accounting software packages (see Appendix B for more detail) provide templates for common business forms.

## More than you want to know right now about account classes and types

Accounts fall into two basic *classes,* with three *types* of accounts in one class and two in the other:

- ✔ Balance sheet accounts: (1) assets, (2) liabilities, and (3) owners' equity accounts

- ✔ Income statement accounts: (1) revenue and income accounts and (2) expense and loss accounts

In other words, the accounts are divided between those that constitute the financial condition of the business (assets, liabilities, and owners' equity accounts) and those that summarize the profit-making operations of the business (revenue and expenses, plus income and loss accounts). Business managers and investors are mainly interested in the two financial statements that report the financial position of the business and its profit performance. You should be clear about how accounts shake out between these two key financial statements.

*Note:* Although your business reports a cash flow financial statement in addition to the financial condition and profit statements, the cash flow amounts that are reported in the cash flow statement are prepared from information already included in the balance sheet and income statement accounts (see Chapter 7). So rest assured that the balance sheet and income statement accounts taken together are all the accounts a business needs.

## Don't be penny-wise and pound-foolish: The need for competent, trained personnel

What good is meticulously collecting source documents if the information on those documents isn't entered into your system correctly? You shouldn't try to save a few bucks by hiring the lowest-paid people you can find. Book-keepers and accountants, like all other employees in a business, should have the skills and knowledge needed to perform their functions. No-brainer, right? Well, determining what that level is *can* be difficult. Here are some guidelines for choosing the right people to enter and manipulate your business's data and for making sure that those people *remain* the right people:

- **College degree:** Many accountants in business organizations have a college degree with a major in accounting. However, as you move down the accounting department, you find that more and more employees do not have a college degree and perhaps don't even have any courses in accounting — they learned bookkeeping methods and skills through on-the-job training. Although these employees may have good skills and instincts, my experience has been that they tend to do things by the book; they often lack the broader perspective necessary for improvising and being innovative. So your best bet is to at least look twice at a potential employee who has no college-based accounting background.

- **CPA or CMA:** For the higher-level accountants in a business organization, asking whether they should be certified public accountants (CPAs) is extremely important. Most larger businesses insist on this credential, along with a specific number of years' experience in public accounting. The other main professional accounting credential is the *CMA,* or *certified management accountant,* sponsored by the Institute of Management Accountants (IMA). Unlike the CPA license, the CMA designation of professional achievement is not regulated by the state. The CMA is evidence that the person has passed tough exams and has a good understanding of business accounting and income tax. In my opinion, a business is prudent to require the CPA or CMA credential for its chief accountant (who usually holds the title of Controller), or a business should regularly consult with a CPA in public practice for advice on its accounting system and on accounting problems that come up.

- **Continuing education:** Bookkeepers and accountants need continuing education to keep up with changes in the income tax law and financial reporting requirements as well as changes in how the business operates. Ideally, bookkeepers and accountants should be able to spot needed improvements and implement these changes — to make accounting reports to managers more useful, for example. Fortunately, many short-term courses, home-study programs, and the like are available at very reasonable costs for keeping up on the latest accounting developments.

Many continuing education courses are available on the Internet. States require that CPAs in public practice must take 30 to 40 hours per year of continuing education in approved courses to keep their licenses.

✔ **Integrity:** What's possibly the most important quality to look for is also the hardest to judge. Bookkeepers and accountants need to be honest people because of the control they have over your business's financial records. Do a careful background check when hiring new accounting personnel. After you hire them, periodically (and discreetly) check whether their lifestyles match their salaries. Of course, you can't invade their privacy, and you have to be extremely careful in accusing them of anything. Small-business owners and managers have closer day-in and day-out contact with their accountants and bookkeepers, which can be a real advantage — they get to know their accountants and bookkeepers on a personal level. Even so, you can find many cases where a trusted bookkeeper has embezzled many thousands of dollars over the years.

## *Protect the family jewels: Internal controls*

Every accounting system should establish and vigorously enforce *internal controls* — basically, additional forms and procedures over and above what's needed strictly to move operations along that serve to deter and detect errors (honest mistakes) and all forms of dishonesty by employees, customers, suppliers, and even managers themselves. Internal controls are like highway truck weigh stations, which make sure that a truck's load doesn't exceed the limits and that the truck has a valid plate. You're just checking that your staff is playing by the rules.

For example, to prevent or minimize shoplifting, most retailers now have video surveillance, tags that set off the alarms if the customer leaves the store with the tag still on the product, and so on. Likewise, a business has to implement certain procedures and forms to prevent as much as possible any theft, embezzlement, kickbacks, and fraud (and simple mistakes) by its own employees and managers.

In my experience, smaller businesses tend to think that they're immune to embezzlement and fraud by their loyal and trusted employees. Yet a recent study found that small businesses are hit the hardest by fraud, and usually can least afford the consequences. Even in a friendly game of poker with my buddies, we always cut the deck before dealing the cards around the table. Your business, too, should put checks and balances into place to discourage dishonest practices and to uncover any fraud and theft as soon as possible. For example, virtually every retailer that deals with the general public installs protections against shoplifting. Likewise, every business should guard against "internal shoplifting," or fraud by its employees and managers.

## A new perspective on paperwork: Controlling against mistakes and theft

Accounting is characterized by a lot of paperwork — forms and procedures are plentiful. Most business managers and employees have their enthusiasm under control when it comes to the paperwork and procedures that the accounting department requires. One reason for this attitude, in my experience, is that non-accountants fail to appreciate the need for the accounting controls that are an essential part of many forms and procedures.

These controls are designed to minimize errors in bookkeeping, which has to process a great deal of detailed information and data. Equally important, controls are necessary to deter employee fraud, embezzlement, and theft, as well as fraud and dishonest behavior against the business from the outside. Unfortunately, every business is a target for fraud and theft, such as customers who shoplift; suppliers who deliberately ship less than the quantities invoiced to a business and hope that the business won't notice the difference (called *short-counts*); and even dishonest managers themselves, who might pad expense accounts or take kickbacks from suppliers or customers.

A business has to avoid being an easy target for dishonest behavior by its employees, customers, and suppliers. Every business should institute and enforce certain control measures; many of these controls are designed into the accounting process. Following are five common examples of control measures:

- Requiring a second signature on cash disbursements over a certain dollar amount

- Matching up receiving reports based on actual counts and inspections of incoming shipments with purchase orders before cutting checks for payment to suppliers

- Requiring both a sales manager's and another high-level manager's approval for formal *write-offs* of customers' overdue receivable balances (that is, closing the accounts on the assumption that they won't be collected), including a checklist of collection efforts that were undertaken

- Having auditors or employees who do not work in the warehouse take surprise counts of products stored in the company's warehouse and compare the counts with inventory records

- Requiring mandatory vacations by every employee, including bookkeepers and accountants, during which time someone else does that person's job (a second person may notice irregularities or deviations from company policies)

## *Keep the scale in balance with double-entry accounting*

A business needs to be sure that *both* sides of the economic exchange are recorded for all its transactions. Economic exchanges involve a give and take, or something given for something received. Businesses (and other entities as well) use the *double-entry accounting method* to make sure that both sides of their transactions are recorded and to keep their books in balance. This method, which has been used for hundreds of years, involves recording certain changes as debits and the counterbalancing changes as credits. See "Double-Entry Accounting for Non-Accountants," later in this chapter, for more details.

## Check your figures: End-of-period procedures checklist

Like an airplane pilot before takeoff, an accountant should have a clear checklist to follow at the end of each period and especially at the end of the accounting year. Two main things have to be done at the end of the period:

- ✔ **Normal, routine *adjusting entries* for certain expenses:** For example, depreciation isn't a transaction as such and therefore hasn't been recorded as an expense in the flow of transactions recorded in the day-to-day bookkeeping process. (Chapter 6 explains depreciation expense.) Similarly, certain other expenses and some revenues may not have been associated with a specific transaction and have not been recorded. These kinds of adjustments are necessary for providing complete and accurate reports.

- ✔ *Careful sweep of all matters* **to check for other developments that may affect the accuracy of the accounts:** For example, the company may have discontinued a product line. The remaining inventory of these products may have to be removed from the asset account, with a loss recorded in the period. Or the company may have settled a long-standing lawsuit, and the amount of damages needs to be recorded. Layoffs and severance packages are another example of what the chief accountant needs to look for before preparing reports.

Lest you still think of accounting as dry and dull, let me tell you that end-of-period accounting procedures can stir up controversy of the heated-debate variety. These procedures require that the accountant make decisions and judgment calls that upper management may not agree with. For example, the accountant may suggest recording major losses that would put a big dent in profit for the year or cause the business to report a loss. The outside CPA auditor (assuming that the business has an audit of its financial statements) often gets in the middle of the argument. These kinds of debates are precisely why you business managers need to know some accounting: to hold up your end of the argument and participate in the great sport of yelling and name-calling — strictly on a professional basis, of course.

## *Keep good records: Happy audit trails to you!*

The happy trails that accountants like to walk are called *audit trails*. Good bookkeeping systems leave good audit trails. An audit trail is a clear-cut path of the sequence of events leading up to an entry in the accounts; an accountant starts with the source documents and follows through the bookkeeping steps in recording transactions to reconstruct this path. Even if a business doesn't have an outside CPA do an annual audit, the accountant has frequent occasion to go back to the source documents and either verify certain information in the accounts or reconstruct the information in a different manner. For example, suppose that a salesperson is claiming some suspicious-looking travel expenses; the accountant would probably want to go through all this person's travel and entertainment reimbursements for the past year.

If the IRS (Internal Revenue Service) comes in for a field audit of your business, you'd better have good audit trails to substantiate all your expense deductions and sales revenue for the year. The IRS has rules about saving source documents for a reasonable period of time and having a well-defined process for marking bookkeeping entries and keeping accounts. Think twice before throwing away source documents. Also, ask your accountant to demonstrate and lay out for your inspection the audit trails for key transactions — such as cash collections, sales, cash disbursements, inventory purchases, and so on. Even in computer-based accounting systems, the importance of audit trails is recognized. Well-designed computer programs provide the ability to backtrack through the sequence of steps in the recording of specific transactions.

## *Look out for unusual events and developments*

Business managers should encourage their accountants to be alert to anything out of the ordinary that may require attention. Suppose that the accounts receivable balance for a particular customer is rapidly increasing — that is, the customer is buying more and more from your company on credit but isn't paying for these purchases quickly. Maybe the customer has switched more of his or her company's purchases to your business and is buying more from you only because he or she is buying less from other businesses. But maybe the customer is planning to stiff your business and take off without paying his or her debts. Or maybe the customer is secretly planning to go into bankruptcy soon and is stockpiling products before the company's credit rating heads south.

Don't forget internal time bombs: A bookkeeper's refusal to take a vacation could mean that he or she is reluctant to let anyone else look at the books.

To some extent, accountants have to act as the eyes and ears of the business. Of course, that's one of your main functions as business manager, but your accounting staff can play an important role as well.

## Design truly useful accounting reports for managers

I have to be careful in this section; I have strong opinions on this matter. I have seen too many off-the-mark accounting reports to managers — difficult to decipher and not very useful or relevant to the manager's decision-making needs and control functions.

Part of the problem lies with the managers themselves. As a business manager, have you told your accounting staff what you need to know, when you need it, and how to present it in the most efficient manner? Probably not. When you stepped into your position, you probably didn't hesitate to rearrange your office and maybe even insisted on hiring your own support staff. Yet you most likely lay down like a lapdog regarding your accounting reports. Maybe you've assumed that the reports have to be done a certain way and that arguing for change is no use.

On the other hand, accountants bear a good share of the blame for the poor reports. Accountants should proactively study the manager's decision-making responsibilities and provide the information that is most useful, presented in the most easily digestible manner.

In designing the chart of accounts, the accountant should also keep in mind the type of information needed for management reports. To exercise control, managers need much more detail than what's reported on tax returns and external financial statements. And as Chapter 9 explains, expenses should be regrouped into different categories for management decision-making analysis. A good chart of accounts looks to both the external and the internal (management) needs for information.

So what's the answer for a manager who receives poorly formatted reports? Demand a report format that suits your needs! See Chapter 9 for a useful profit analysis model (and make sure that your accountant reads that chapter as well).

# Double-Entry Accounting for Non-Accountants

A business is a *two-sided* entity. It accumulates assets on one side — by borrowing money, persuading investors to put money in the business as owners, purchasing assets on credit, and making profit. Profit (net income) is essentially an increase in assets, not from increasing liabilities and not from additional capital infusion from owners, but rather as the net result of sales revenue less expenses. As my old accounting professor used to say, "Assets don't fall on a business like manna from heaven." He meant that assets have *sources,* and these sources are *claims* of one sort or another on the assets of a business. He asked the class, "Shouldn't a business keep track of the sources of assets, according to the type of claim each source has against the assets?" We all said "yes," of course. He then told us that this is precisely the reason for and nature of *double-entry accounting.*

## The two-sided nature of a business entity and its activities

In a nutshell, double-entry accounting means *two-sided* accounting. Both the assets of a business and the sources of and claims on its assets are accounted for. Suppose that a business reports $10 million in total assets. That means the total sources of and claims on its assets are also reported at a total of $10 million. Each asset source has a different type of claim. Some liabilities charge interest and some don't; some have to be paid soon, and other loans to the business may not come due for five or ten years. Owners' equity may be mainly from capital invested by the owners and very little from retained earnings ( profit not distributed to the owners). Or the mix of owners' equity sources may be just the reverse.

The sources of and claims on the assets of a business fall into two broad categories: *liabilities* and *owners' equity.* With a few technical exceptions that I don't go into, the dollar amount of liabilities the business reports are the amounts that will be paid to the creditors at the maturity dates of the liabilities. In other words, the dollar amounts of liabilities are definite amounts to be paid at certain future dates.

In contrast, the dollar amounts reported for owners' equity are *historical* amounts, based on how much capital the owners invested in the business in the past and how much profit the business has recorded. Owners' equity, unlike the liabilities of a business, has no maturity date at which time the money has to be returned to the owners. When looking at the amount of owners' equity reported in a balance sheet, don't think that this amount could be taken out of the business. Owners' equity is tied up in the business indefinitely.

So one reason for double-entry accounting is the two-sided nature of a business entity — assets are on one side, and the sources of and claims on assets are on the other side. The second reason for double-entry accounting is the *economic exchange* nature of business activities, referring to the give-and-receive nature of the transactions that a business engages in to pursue its financial objectives. Consider a few typical transactions:

- A business borrows $10 million: It receives money, so the company's cash increases. In exchange, the business promises to return the $10 million to the lender at some future date, so the company's debt increases. Interest on the loan is paid in exchange for the use of the money over time.

- The business buys products that it will later resell to its customers: It gives money for the products (the company's cash decreases) and receives the products (the company's inventory increases).

- The business sells products: It receives cash or promises of cash to come later (the company's accounts receivable increases), and it gives the products to the customer (the company's inventory decreases). Of course, the business should sell the products for more than cost. The excess of the amount received over product cost is called *gross profit,* from which many other expenses have to be deducted. (Chapter 5 explains the profit-making transactions leading to bottom-line profit or loss.)

## Recording transactions using debits and credits

Using *debits and credits* is a marvelous technique for making sure that both sides of exchanges are recorded and for keeping both sides of the accounting equation in balance. The recording of every transaction requires the same value for the debits on one side and the credits on the other side. Just think back to math class in your school days: What you have on one side of the equal sign (in this case, in the accounting equation) must equal what you have on the other side of the equal sign.

See Table 2-1 for how debits and credits work in the balance sheet accounts of a business.

| Table 2-1 | The Rules of Debits and Credits | |
|---|---|---|
| *Changes* | *In Assets* | *In Liabilities and Owners' Equities* |
| Increases | Debit | Credit |
| Decreases | Credit | Debit |

*Note:* Sales revenue and expense accounts, which are not listed in Table 2-1, also follow debit and credit rules. A revenue increases owners' equity (thus is a credit), and an expense decreases owners' equity (thus is a debit).

As a business manager, you don't need to know all the mechanics and technical aspects of using debits and credits. Here's what you do need to know:

✔ **The basic premise of the accounting equation:** Assets equal the sources of the assets and the claims on the assets. That is, the total of assets on the one side should equal the sum of total liabilities and total owners' equity on the other side.

✔ **The important difference between liabilities and owners' equity accounts:** Liabilities need to be paid off at definite due dates in the future. Owners' equity has no such claims for definite payments at definite dates. As such, these two accounts must be kept separate.

✔ **Balanced books don't necessarily mean correct balances:** If debits equal credits, the entry for the transaction is correct as far as recording equal amounts on both sides of the transaction. However, even if the debits equal the credits, other errors are possible. The bookkeeper may have recorded the debits and credits in a wrong account, or may have entered wrong amounts, or may have missed recording an entry altogether. Having balanced books simply means that the total of accounts with debit balances equals the total of accounts with credit balances. The important thing is whether the books (the accounts) have *correct* balances, which depends on whether all transactions and other developments have been recorded and accounted for correctly.

✔ **The use of debits and credits has been around for more than 500 years:** Okay, you don't really need to know this bit of trivia. But to impress your accounting staff with the depth of your accounting knowledge, you may want to casually mention that a book published in 1494 described how business traders and merchants of the day used debits and credits in their bookkeeping. Stops 'em cold every time.

# Juggling the Books to Conceal Embezzlement and Fraud

One of the problems I faced as a business professor was what to say to students about fraud and dishonest practices in the business world. Business textbooks say little about these negative topics — which is kind of like a marriage textbook not mentioning adultery. (*Auditing* textbooks, however, do cover the topic of fraud.) I certainly didn't encourage students to embezzle or to commit fraud, of course, but I had to point out that these things happen in the business world. Even people you know and like may engage in fraud of one kind or another. In my experience, the large majority of business managers and employees don't commit fraud. But I know for sure that a significant minority do.

TIP

---

# Some tricks of the trade in bookkeeping

Bookkeeping for even a relatively small business requires recording a large number of transactions over the course of one year. A few errors and mistakes are normal. Here are some ways in which a bookkeeper can find the errors and correct them:

✔ At the end of the period, the bookkeeper should definitely take a *trial balance.* This listing of all accounts puts debit accounts in one column and credit accounts in a second column, to check whether the total of all debit balance accounts equals the total of all credit balance accounts. If the two totals don't agree, one trick is to divide the difference by 9. If the answer is a whole number (without digits after the decimal point), chances are good that a *transposition error* was made. Suppose that the actual $34,564.60 balance in an account was transposed as $35,464.60. Notice that the $900.00 error is divisible by 9 to give the whole number 100.

If this step doesn't find the answer, the bookkeeper can divide the amount of the imbalance by 2 and then search for any accounts that have a balance of this amount. Perhaps a debit balance was listed wrongly as a credit balance, or vice versa, which would cause the trial balance to have a difference twice the balance of the account.

✔ Sometimes a business receives money without any clear indication of why the money was sent. Some people just like to

part with their money for no reason. My wife, Fay, who did bookkeeping for her employer, calls this money "mystery checks." The bookkeeper increases the cash account when he or she deposits the money, but what account is credited? The answer is to create what's called a *suspense* account (also known as a *clearing* or *wash* account) as a temporary holding place for the credit so that the books stay in balance. Of course, the bookkeeper should find out as soon as possible the reason behind the cash receipt. Then the bookkeeper should credit the appropriate account and reduce the suspense account to a zero balance.

✔ I had fun in my accounting classes teasing students with the following question: What's the WITTB account? They hadn't seen such an account title in their textbooks. *WITTB* stands for "what it takes to balance." You use this account to force the trial balance into balance, meaning that if you have an unaccounted-for credit, you put a balancing debit in the WITTB account, and if you have an unaccounted-for debit, you put a balancing credit in the WITTB account. This account should serve as a temporary means of balancing the accounts until you can find the error at a more convenient time. I don't recommend this technique if the trial balance is out of balance by a large difference, in which case you should immediately do some serious studying of the accounts to get them reconciled.

*Fraud* is a catch-all term; I'm using the term in its broadest sense to include any type of dishonest, unethical, immoral, or illegal practice. My concern here is with the effects of fraud on a business's accounting records, not with the broader social and criminal aspects of fraud — which are very serious, of course, but which are outside the scope of this book.

A business should capture and record faithfully all transactions in its accounting records. Having said this, I have to admit that some business activities are deliberately *not* accounted for or are accounted for in a way that disguises their true nature. For example, *money laundering* involves taking money from illegal sources (such as drug dealing) and passing it through a business to make it look legitimate — to give the money a false identity. This money can hardly be recorded as "revenue from drug sales" in the accounts of the business.

Fraud occurs in large corporations and in one-owner/manager-controlled small businesses — and every size business in between. Some types of fraud are more common in small businesses, including *sales skimming* (not recording all sales revenue, to deflate the taxable income of the business and its owner) and the recording of personal expenses through the business (to make these expenses deductible for income tax). Some kinds of fraud are committed mainly by large businesses, including paying bribes to public officials and entering into illegal conspiracies to fix prices or divide the market. The purchasing managers in any size business can be tempted to accept kickbacks and under-the-table payoffs from vendors and suppliers.

I should mention another problem that puts accountants in the hot seat: In many situations, two or more businesses are controlled by the same person or the same group of investors. Revenue and expenses can be arbitrarily shifted among the different business entities under common control. For one person to have a controlling ownership interest in two or more businesses is perfectly legal, and such an arrangement often makes good business sense. For example, a retail business rents a building from a real estate business, and the same person is the majority owner of both businesses. The problem arises when that person arbitrarily sets the monthly rent to shift profit between the two businesses; a high rent generates more profit for the real estate business and lower profit for the retail business. This kind of maneuver may be perfectly legal, but it raises a fundamental accounting issue.

Readers of financial statements are entitled to assume that all activities between the business and the other parties it deals with are based on what's called *arm's-length bargaining,* meaning that the business and the other parties have a purely business relationship. When that's not the case, the financial report should — but usually doesn't — use the term *related parties* to describe persons and organizations who are not at arm's length with the business. According to financial reporting standards, your accountant should advise you, the business manager, to disclose any substantial related-party transactions in your external financial statements.

In short, fraud occurs in the business world. Most of these schemes require *cooking the books* — which means altering entries in the accounts to cover the fraud or simply not recording certain entries that should be recorded. If you saw an expense account called *bribes,* you would want to be a little suspicious, but unethical bookkeepers and accountants are usually a tad more clever than that.

When the books have been cooked, the financial statements prepared from the accounts are distorted, incorrect, and probably misleading. Lenders, other creditors, and the owners who have capital invested in the business rely on the company's financial statements. Also, a business's managers and board of directors (the group of people who oversee a business corporation) may be misled — assuming that they're not a party to the fraud, of course — and may also have liability to third-party creditors and investors for their failure to catch the fraud. Creditors and investors who end up suffering losses have legal grounds to sue the managers and directors (and perhaps the auditors who did not catch the fraud) for damages suffered.

Persons engaging in fraud generally cheat on their federal income taxes; they don't declare the ill-gotten income. Needless to say, the IRS is on constant alert for fraud in federal income tax returns — both business and personal returns. The IRS has the authority to come in and audit the books of the business and also the personal income tax returns of its managers and investors. Conviction for income tax evasion is a felony, I might point out.

# Chapter 3

# Taxes, Taxes, and More Taxes

● ● ● ● ● ● ● ● ● ● ● ● ● ● ● ● ● ● ● ● ● ● ● ● ● ● ● ● ● ● ● ● ● ● ● ● ● ● ● ● ● ● ● ● ● ● ● ● ● ●

### In This Chapter

▶ Paying taxes as an employer and a property owner

▶ Putting on your tax agent hat and collecting sales tax

▶ Determining how much of business profit goes to the government

▶ Allowing income tax methods to override good accounting methods

▶ Looking at the different ways income tax works for different business structures

● ● ● ● ● ● ● ● ● ● ● ● ● ● ● ● ● ● ● ● ● ● ● ● ● ● ● ● ● ● ● ● ● ● ● ● ● ● ● ● ● ● ● ● ● ● ● ● ● ●

*A*s an employer, a business pays taxes. As a property owner, a business pays taxes. As a retailer, a business collects sales taxes paid by customers and remits the amounts to state and local governments. And, of course, a business or its owners must pay federal income tax. Yikes! Is there no escaping the tax millstone?

Nope, afraid not (short of resorting to illegal activity or a sly move to another country — you'll have to find another book to tell you about those options). But you can take advantage of the many options in tax laws that can minimize how much you pay and delay your payment (a perfectly legal strategy known as *tax avoidance*). This chapter starts you on your way by explaining the various types of taxation that a business faces.

I say that this chapter "*starts* you on your way" because I can't possibly provide you with exhaustive detail in one chapter. And besides, no one can give you good tax advice without first looking at your specific situation — consult a professional tax expert for that.

Some critics say that income tax is a real disincentive to investing in business. But you can also look at how much income tax you pay as a measure of your success. One of my colleagues says that he'd love to pay a million dollars of income tax every year. He's got a good point. To pay this much income tax, he would have to have an annual taxable income of about $3 million. Hey, you can't get away from taxes (you know the old saying about death and taxes), so you may as well try for a positive outlook.

# Taxing Wages and Property

Even if you don't earn a profit in your business, you still have to pay certain taxes. Unlike income tax, which is a *contingent* or *conditional* tax that depends on whether a business earns taxable income for the year, the two major types of non-income taxes — *employer payroll taxes* and *property taxes* — always have to be paid. (See "Taxing Your Bottom Line: Income Taxes," later in this chapter, for more about income tax.)

## Putting Uncle Sam on the payroll: Employer taxes

In addition to deducting federal, state, and local taxes from employees' wages and remitting those amounts to the proper government agencies, businesses need to pay the following employee-related taxes: social security and Medicare taxes, unemployment tax, and workers' compensation insurance. (Actually, that last one isn't really a tax, but I won't get technical.)

### Social security and Medicare tax

Most folks don't realize that they pay only half of their social security tax — the employer picks up the rest of the tab. The social security law stipulates that the tax burden be divided 50-50 between an employee and an employer.

I don't want to get into a debate about the social security system and the financial problems it's facing; I'll just say that the amount you'll pay in social security taxes almost certainly won't diminish in the future. Here's an idea of what a business pays in social security taxes: In 2000, the first $76,200.00 of annual wages were taxed at 6.20 percent on the employee and 6.20 percent on the employer, for a maximum of $4,724.40 paid by each. Wages are also taxed 1.45 percent on both the employee and the employer for the Medicare program. Wages subject to Medicare taxes have no ceiling.

So for employees who earn less than $76,200.00, the total tax rate for social security and Medicare is 7.65 percent. A business pays this 7.65 percent tax in addition to the wages that it pays an employee in this wage range. That is, for every $100.00 paid to an employee, the employer's total cost is $107.65. (Tell *that* to Pat in Marketing the next time he gripes about the tax deductions in his paycheck!)

### Unemployment tax

Another tax that an employer pays is the *unemployment tax,* which provides funds for individuals thrown out of work through no fault of their own. A worker who is laid off because of downsizing is entitled to unemployment benefits, for example, but a worker who is fired *for cause* is not. (The specific rules about who qualifies and for how long vary from state to state.)

The unemployment tax rate (through 2007) is 6.2 percent on a maximum of $7,000 wages paid to each employee, or a maximum of $434 per employee. (Note, however, that unlike with social security, employees don't pay any of this tax.) This program is a joint federal-state venture, so the employer pays part of the unemployment tax to the state in which its employees work and part to the federal government.

Whereas the social security and Medicare taxes are *flat* taxes — the rates are fixed and cannot be reduced — the unemployment tax rate is reduced for employers that have a stable work force and do not lay off employees very often. It's never reduced all the way to zero, though; every business pays *some* unemployment tax.

---

# The way to an employee's heart is through the payroll department

Remember the first time you received a real paycheck? Your jaw dropped when you compared the *gross wages* (the amount before deductions) and the *net,* or *take-home pay* (the amount you actually received), right? A business's accountants need to track how much of the following, by law, to deduct from employees' paychecks:

✔ Social security tax

✔ Medicare tax

✔ Withholdings for federal, state, and local income taxes

✔ Other, non-tax-related withholdings that the employee agrees to (such as union dues, retirement plan contributions, and health insurance costs paid by the employee)

✔ Other non-tax-related withholdings required by a court order (for example, a business may be ordered to withhold part or all of an employee's wages and remit the amount to a legal agency or a creditor to which the employee owes money)

For all these deductions, a business serves as a collection agent and remits the appropriate amount of wages to the appropriate party. As you can imagine, this task requires lots of additional accounting and record-keeping. *Tip:* Don't underestimate the cost and importance of an experienced, well-trained payroll accounting staff to keep all the necessary records, file all the required reports on time, answer employees' questions, and make corrections for the inevitable errors that occur. Employee morale is very important, and one surefire way to screw it up is to have a lousy payroll department that makes many mistakes and is short-tempered with employees.

You can't do anything to answer your employees' gripes about how much tax is deducted, but you can certainly do your best to make the payroll system as painless for them as possible.

### Workers' compensation insurance

Although, strictly speaking, workers' compensation insurance isn't a tax, state laws require that every business purchase this insurance (or self-insure under state rules). The purpose of this insurance coverage is to provide replacement income to employees who suffer work-related injuries and other job-related disabilities that keep them from performing their normal duties for a specified period of time. Employees don't pay for the insurance; the employer bears all the cost.

Unfortunately, collecting workers' compensation benefits has become a cottage industry for some dishonest employees — and their unscrupulous doctors and lawyers, who help them submit bogus claims for faked or exaggerated injuries. These false or exaggerated claims drive up the costs of providing benefits to honest employees who suffer actual injuries on the job and who should be compensated for the weeks they miss a paycheck.

A business owner friend had serious problems with employees filing false claims and driving up the premiums for his workers' compensation insurance. He decided to start screening job applicants more carefully by sending their information to a company that maintains a national database on people who have filed workers' compensation claims (as well as people with driving violations and other criminal convictions). My friend has to ask for permission from the job applicants before submitting their information to the company. He won't hire job applicants with too many workers' compensation claims or other bad marks on their records. He's very careful to conduct this background check on all job applicants — without regard to gender, minority ethnic status, age, and so on.

## Taxing everything you can put your hands on: Property taxes

Businesses have to pay two basic types of property taxes:

- ✔ **Real estate tax:** Owners of land and buildings and other permanent improvements on the land (such as a concrete driveway or a paved parking lot) pay annual taxes to county and other local-level governments. Real estate is taxed in virtually all states, although the tax rates vary from state to state.

- ✔ **Tangible personal property tax:** Many states and localities tax *inventory* (products held for sale) and *portable assets* (office furniture, computers, cars and trucks, and so on). Vehicles are taxed in all states; other types of assets are taxed in some states and not in others.

Property taxes are based on *assessed values* of assets. The main thing you have to do is make sure that the assessed values of your real estate and personal property assets are correct and not higher than they should be. Believe it or not, the government has been known to make mistakes (say it isn't so!); in fact, government assessment methods are always open to question and challenge. A friend of mine routinely challenges his annual real estate tax assessment — and gets it lowered more often than not.

Your assets may qualify for exemption under various state and local laws or may be eligible for special reductions (called *abatements*). Property taxation is a legal thicket — laws, terminology, procedures, and forms differ a great deal from state to state and county to county — so consult your tax advisor.

Generally speaking, only property located within the jurisdiction of the government entity on the assessment date is taxed. If the property happens to be outside the vicinity on the assessment date, it may not be subject to the property tax. Many companies let their inventory levels drop as low as possible on the tax assessment date — by delaying incoming shipments or delaying purchase orders. However, a business should be careful not to illegally move property out of the state on the tax date if the only reason is to avoid paying tax. Talk to a good property tax lawyer first.

Property taxes can take a big chunk out a business's profit. In large organizations, an in-house accountant who deals with property taxes and knows the tax law language and methods is responsible for developing strategies to minimize property taxes. Small-business owners may want to consult with a CPA or an attorney who specializes in property tax law — it may be money well spent.

# 'Cause I'm the Tax Man: Collecting Sales Tax

Most states, counties, and municipal governments levy *retail sales taxes* on certain products and services sold within their jurisdictions. The final consumer of the product or service pays the sales tax — in other words, the sales tax is tacked onto the product's price tag at the very end of the economic chain. The business that is selling the product or service collects the tax and remits it to the appropriate tax agency. Businesses that operate earlier in the economic chain (that is, those that sell products to other businesses that in turn resell the products) generally do not pay sales tax.

For example, when you run to your local bookstore to buy *Taxes For Dummies* because you simply can't get enough of this tax business, you pay the bookstore the cost of the book plus sales tax. But the bookstore didn't pay sales tax when it bought the book from IDG Books Worldwide. Only you, the final consumer, pay sales tax. (Lucky you!)

Businesses that make retail sales must register with a government agency and obtain a *retail sales tax number,* thus becoming a designated sales tax collector. As a designated sales tax collector, the business does not pay sales tax on products that it buys from other businesses for resale to its customers. If you're a small-business owner/manager, be aware that if you overlook this role imposed on your business by the state, you're still responsible for paying over the sales tax to the government. Suppose that you make a sale for $100 but don't add the $6 sales tax into the total amount you collect from the customer. Big Brother says that you did collect the sales tax, whether you think you did or not. So you still have to pay the government $6, which leaves you only $94 in sales revenue.

As anyone who has traveled to various U.S. states knows, sales tax is anything but nationally uniform. In addition to the differences in sales tax rates from state to state, the following issues complicate state sales tax:

✔ Some products, such as clothing and newspapers, are subject to sales tax in some states and not others.

✔ Some products and services are always taxed — namely, the sales of liquor, beer, and cigarettes. These taxes are referred to as *sin taxes.*

✔ Health care products and services, such as prescription drug sales and medical and hospital charges, are specifically exempted from retail sales taxes in many states.

✔ Sales of professional services (legal or accounting advice, for example) generally are not taxed, although some states have considered doing so.

Tracking and recording retail sales tax is a big responsibility for many businesses, especially if the business operates out of more than one state. Having a well-trained accounting staff manage this side of the business is well worth the cost.

# Taxing Your Bottom Line: Income Taxes

You may think that Uncle Sam is a trusting soul; after all, he doesn't send any bills for income tax. Instead, he trusts that individuals and businesses will determine their taxable income honestly and will file the appropriate, accurately filled-out tax returns to the Internal Revenue Service (IRS) yearly. But just like your seemingly trusting spouse who expects that you'll do your chores without being asked, Uncle Sam will raise Cain if you don't do what you're supposed to.

This chapter focuses on the tax dimensions of business entities. Chapter 4 presents a basic income tax model for individuals.

Every business must determine its annual *taxable income,* which is the amount of profit subject to income tax. A business's tax return reports its *gross income,* which is very broadly defined to include sales revenue, investment income, and any other cash inflow or realized increase in wealth. Gross income is either *exempt,* meaning that it's not subject to taxation, or *taxable,* the meaning of which should be painfully obvious. To determine annual *taxable income,* you deduct certain allowed expenses from gross income. Income tax law rests very roughly on the premise that all income is taxable unless expressly exempted, and nothing can be deducted unless expressly allowed.

Broadly speaking, a business uses either the *cash basis* or the *accrual basis* of accounting to determine its annual taxable income. The cash basis of accounting, as the name implies, is limited to recording only cash inflows and outflows. Under the cash basis, taxable income equals cash receipts from sales and other income less cash payments for deductible expenses. The cash basis can be used only by certain kinds of businesses — see the sidebar "A word on cash basis accounting." Businesses that sell products and all businesses having over $5 million in annual sales revenue must use the accrual basis of accounting.

The accrual basis of accounting goes way beyond recording only cash inflow and cash outflow transactions. For example, under the accrual method, assets purchased on credit are recorded as soon as the purchase takes place — by increasing the asset and increasing the liability account to recognize the obligation to pay for the purchase later. The assets and liabilities you see in a balance sheet are the result of using the accrual basis of accounting. Furthermore, the accrual-based profit measure for a period is different from what it would be under the cash basis — an extremely important difference between the two accounting methods. Under the accrual basis of accounting, for example, revenue is recorded as soon as sales are made on credit, even though the cash is not actually received from customers until later. Under the cash basis, no entry is made to record revenue until cash is received from customers.

When you read an income statement that summarizes a business's sales revenue and expenses for a period and ends with bottom-line profit, keep in mind that the accrual basis of accounting has been used to record sales revenue and expenses — unless the business makes very clear that it's using the cash basis instead. The accrual basis gives a more trustworthy and meaningful profit number. But accrual-based sales revenue and expense numbers are not cash inflows and outflows during the period. So the bottom-line profit does not tell you the impact on cash from the profit-making activities of the business. You have to convert the revenue and expense amounts reported in the income statement to a cash basis in order to determine the net cash increase or decrease. Well, actually, you don't have to do this — the cash flow statement does this for you, which Chapter 7 explains.

---

# A word on cash basis accounting

Cash basis accounting (also known as *check-book accounting*) isn't generally acceptable in the world of business, but is permitted by income tax law for some businesses. To use cash basis accounting, a business must

✔ Not deal in inventories (products sold to customers).

✔ Keep accounting records for cash receipts and cash payments only, even though it may buy some things on credit that it doesn't pay for right away, and even if it allows its customers to pay a few weeks after the sale. (As long as the business does not formally record these payables and receivables in its bookkeeping process, the IRS does not insist that it do so for tax purposes.)

✔ Have no more than $5 million in annual sales revenue.

For the great majority of businesses, cash basis accounting is not acceptable, neither for reporting to the IRS nor for preparing financial statements. This method falls short of the information needed for even a relatively small business. Accrual basis accounting, described in Chapters 5 and 6, is the only real option for most businesses. Even small businesses that don't sell products should carefully consider whether cash basis is adequate for

✔ Preparing external financial statements for borrowing money and reporting to owners

✔ Dividing profit among owners

For all practical purposes, only sole proprietorships (one-owner businesses) that sell just services and no products can use cash basis accounting. Other businesses must use the accrual basis — which provides a much better income statement for management control and decision-making, and a much more complete picture of the business's financial condition.

---

Although you determine your business's taxable income as an annual amount (for 12 consecutive months, which can end on March 31 or September 30 instead of December 31), you don't wait until you file your tax return to make that calculation and payment. Instead, the income tax law requires you to estimate your income tax for the year and, based on your estimate, to make four (quarterly) installment payments on your income tax during the year. When you file the final tax return — with the official, rather than the estimated, taxable income amount — after the close of the year, you pay any remaining amount of tax you owe or claim a refund if you have overpaid your income tax during the year. If you grossly underestimate your taxable income for the year and thus end up having to pay a large amount of tax after the end of the year, you probably will owe a late payment penalty.

You must keep adequate accounting records to determine your business's annual taxable income. If you report the wrong taxable income amount, you can't plead that the bookkeeper was incompetent or that your accounting records were inadequate or poorly organized — in fact, good old Uncle Sam may decide that your poor accounting was intentional and is evidence of income tax evasion. If you underreport your taxable income by too much, you may have to pay interest and penalties in addition to the tax that you owe.

## Tax law can be very ... well ... *taxing!*

Did I mention that I can't possibly do justice to tax law in just a single chapter? Federal income tax law is extraordinarily complex and is constantly evolving. Most businesses hire tax professionals to

✔ Keep the business in compliance with tax laws and regulations.

✔ Help the business prepare and file all the necessary returns and schedules completely, correctly, and on time.

✔ Give advice on the many options in the tax law for minimizing taxable income and for general tax planning.

When I talk about adequate accounting records, I'm not talking about the accounting *methods* that you select to determine annual taxable income — Chapter 13 discusses choosing among alternative accounting methods for certain expenses. After you've selected which accounting methods you'll use for these expenses, your bookkeeping procedures must follow these methods faithfully. Choose the accounting methods that minimize your current year's taxable income — but make sure that your bookkeeping is done accurately and on time and that your accounting records are complete. If your business's income tax return is audited, the IRS agents first look at your accounting records and bookkeeping system.

Furthermore, you must stand ready to present evidence for expense deductions. Be sure to hold on to receipts and other relevant documents. In an IRS audit, the burden of proof is on *you.* The IRS doesn't have to disprove a deduction; you have to prove that you were entitled to the deduction. *No evidence, no deduction* is the rule to keep in mind.

The following sections paint a rough sketch of the main topics of business income taxation. (I *don't* go into the many technical details of determining taxable income, however.)

## Different tax rates on different levels of business taxable income

A business's annual taxable income isn't taxed at a flat rate. In writing the income tax law, Congress gave the little guy a break. As of 1999, corporate income tax rates start at only 15 percent on the first $50,000 of taxable income, then quickly move up to a 34 percent rate on taxable income in the range of $335,000 to $10,000,000, and settle into a 35 percent rate on taxable income of $18,333,333 or more. The income tax on the taxable income for the year is calculated using these tax rates. However, the *actual* amount of tax due to the government may be less than this amount, indeed far less — due to special credits that are direct offsets against the normal income tax. (By the way, in a footnote to the financial statements, a business is required by GAAP to reconcile its actual income tax for the year with the amount of income tax that would be due based on the earnings before income tax reported in its income statement for the year.)

In years past, corporate income tax rates were considerably higher, and the rates could go up in the future — although most experts don't predict any increase. Congress looks at the income tax law every year and makes some changes virtually every year. Many changes have to do with the accounting methods allowed to determine annual taxable income. For instance, the methods for computing annual *depreciation expense,* which recognizes the wear and tear on a business's long-lived operating assets, have been changed back and forth by Congress over the years.

## Profit accounting and taxable income accounting

You're probably thinking that this section of the chapter is about how a business's bottom-line profit — its net income — drives its taxable income amount. Actually, I want to show you the exact opposite: how income tax law drives a business's profit accounting. That's right: Tax law plays a large role in how a business determines its profit figure, or more precisely the accounting methods used to record revenue and expenses.

Before you explore that paradox, you need to understand something about the accounting methods for recording profit. For measuring and recording many expenses (and some types of revenue), no single accounting method emerges as the one, only, dominant method. Accountants have a certain amount of legitimate leeway in measuring and reporting the revenue and expenses that drive the profit figure. (See Chapter 13 for further discussion of alternative accounting methods.) Therefore, two different accountants, recording the same profit-making activities for the same period, would most likely come up with two different profit figures — the numbers would be off by at least a little, and perhaps by a lot.

And that inconsistency is fine — as long as the differences are due to legitimate reasons. I'd like to be able to report to you that in measuring profit, accountants always aim right at the bull's-eye, the dead center of the profit target. One commandment in the accountants' bible is that annual profit should be as close to the truth as can be measured; accounting methods should be objective and fair. As the late sportscaster Howard Cosell used to say, "Tell it like it is." But in the real world, profit accounting doesn't quite live up to this ideal.

Be aware that a business may be tempted to deliberately *overstate* or *understate* its profit. When a business overstates its profit in its income statement, some amount of its sales revenue has been recorded too soon and/or some amount of its expenses has not yet been recorded (but will be later). Overstating profit is a dangerous game to play because it deceives investors and other interested parties into thinking that the business is doing better than it really is. Audits of financial reports by CPAs (as discussed in Chapter 15) keep such financial reporting fraud to a minimum but don't necessarily catch every case.

More to the point of this chapter is the fact that most businesses are under some pressure to *understate* the profit reported in their annual income statements. Businesses generally record sales revenue correctly (with some notable exceptions), but they may record some expenses sooner than these costs should be deducted from sales revenue. Why? Businesses are preoccupied with minimizing income tax, which means minimizing *taxable income.* To minimize taxable income, a business chooses accounting methods that record expenses as soon as possible. Keeping two sets of books (accounting records) — one for tax returns and one for internal profit accounting reports to managers — is not very practical, so the business uses the accounting methods kept for tax purposes for other purposes as well. And that's why tax concerns can drive down a business's profit figure.

In short, the income tax law permits fairly conservative expense accounting methods — expense amounts can be *front-loaded,* or deducted sooner rather than later. The reason is to give a business the option to minimize its current taxable income (even though this course has a reverse effect in later years). Many businesses select these conservative expense methods — both for their income tax returns and for their financial statements reported to managers and to outside investors and lenders. Thus financial statements of many businesses tilt to the conservative, or understated, side.

Of course, a business should report an accurate figure as its net income, with no deliberate fudging. If you can't trust that figure, who knows for sure exactly how the company is doing? Not the owners, the value of whose investment in the business depends mostly on profit performance, and not even the business's managers, whose business decisions depend on recorded profit performance. Every business needs a reliable profit compass to navigate its way through the competitive environment of the business world — that's just common sense and doesn't even begin to address ethical issues.

I should say that many businesses do report their annual profit correctly — sales revenue and expenses are recorded properly and without any attempt to manipulate either side of the profit equation.

Refer to Chapter 13 for more about how choosing one expense accounting method over another method impacts profit. (*Note:* The following sections, which discuss expenses and income that are not deductible or are only partially deductible, have nothing to do with choosing accounting methods.)

---

## Other reasons for understating profit

Minimizing taxable income is a strong motive for understating profit, but businesses have other reasons as well. Imagine for the moment that business profit isn't subject to income tax (you wish!). Even in this hypothetical, no-tax world, many businesses probably would select accounting methods that measure their profit on the low side rather than the high side. Two possible reasons are behind this decision:

✔ **Don't count your chickens before they hatch philosophy:** Many business managers and owners tend to be financially conservative; they prefer to err on the low side of profit measurement rather than on the high side.

✔ **Save for a rainy day philosophy:** A business may want to keep some profit in reserve so that during a future downturn, it has a profit cushion to soften the blow.

The people who think this way tend to view *overstating profit* as a form of defrauding investors but view *understating profit* as simply being prudent. Frankly, I think that putting your thumb on either side of the profit scale (revenue being one side and expenses the other) is not a good idea. *Let the chips fall where they may* is my philosophy. Adopt the accounting methods that you think best reflect how you operate the business. The income tax law has put too much downward pressure on profit measurement, in my opinion.

---

## *Nondeductible expenses*

To be deductible, business expenses must be *ordinary and necessary* — that is, regular, routine stuff that you need to do to run your business. You're probably thinking that you can make an argument that *any* of your expenses meet the ordinary and necessary test. And you're mostly right — almost all business expenses meet this twofold test.

However, the IRS considers certain business expenses to be anything but ordinary and necessary; you can argue about them until you're blue in the face, and it won't make any difference. Here's a list of expenses that are *not* deductible or are only partially deductible when determining annual taxable income:

✔ **Customer entertainment expenses:** You can generally deduct only 50 percent of your customer entertainment expenses.

✔ **Bribes, kickbacks, fines, and penalties:** Oh, come on, did you really think that you could get rewarded for doing stuff that's illegal or, at best, undesirable? If you were allowed to deduct these costs, that would be tantamount to the IRS encouraging such behavior — a policy that wouldn't sit too well with the general public.

✔ **Lobbying costs:** You can't deduct payments made to influence legislation. Sorry, but you can't deduct the expenses you ran up to persuade Senator Hardnose to give your bicycle business special tax credits because riding bicycles is good exercise for people.

✔ **Start-up costs:** A new business is not permitted to deduct these costs immediately. You divide these costs over five years or longer and take a fractional deduction in each of those years. This area of the tax law can get a little hairy. If you have just started a new business, you may be wise to consult a tax professional on this question, especially if your start-up costs are rather large.

✔ **Unreasonable compensation:** The IRS generally doesn't question salaries and wages, but a special rule applies to all publicly owned corporations. If one or more of the top five executives (CEO, president, executive president, and so on) are paid more than $1 million in annual wages, the compensation over that amount must be based on objective performance criteria, or else the excess is not deductible. The IRS doesn't question the first $1 million. Likewise, *golden parachute payments* — generous severance packages given to executives who were suddenly dismissed (because of a merger, for example) — may not be fully deductible.

Privately owned companies may put someone from the business owner's family on the payroll (which is a type of nepotism). Hiring your son or daughter (or Uncle Harry, for that matter) is all right, but family members must be paid an amount that's consistent with their actual contribution to the business. An IRS auditor will laugh herself silly while she disallows a huge salary paid to your nephew who just makes coffee and copies. (This rule also applies to publicly owned companies, although privately owned businesses have more of a tendency to overpay family members.) You may have to consult a tax professional to determine exactly who is considered a family member under the income tax law.

✔ **Life insurance premiums:** A business may buy life insurance coverage on key officers and executives, but if the business is the beneficiary, the premiums are not deductible. The proceeds from a life insurance policy are not taxable income to the business if the insured person dies, because the cost of the premiums was not deductible. In short, premiums are not deductible, and proceeds upon death are excluded from taxable income.

✔ **Travel and convention attendance expenses:** Some businesses pay for rather lavish cruise ship conventions for their managers and spend rather freely for special meetings at attractive locations that their customers attend for free. The IRS takes a dim view of such extravagant expenditures and may not allow a full deduction for these types of expenses. The IRS holds that such conventions and meetings could have been just as effective for a much more reasonable cost. In short, a business may not get a 100 percent deduction for its travel and convention expenses if the IRS audits these expenditures.

✔ **Transactions with related parties:** Income tax law takes a special interest in transactions where the two parties are related in some way. For example, a business may rent space in a building owned by the same people who have money invested in the business; the rent may be artificially high or low in an attempt to shift income and expenses between the two tax entities or individuals. In other words, these transactions may not be based on what's known as *arm's-length bargaining*. A business that deals with a related party must be ready to show that the price paid or received is consistent with what the price would be for an unrelated party.

## Nontaxable income

Whereas having some nondeductible or partially deductible expenses is common for a business, having income that's not taxable or only partially taxable isn't all that common. The two sources of nontaxable income are

✔ Interest income from municipal bonds (bonds issued by state and local governments)

✔ Cash dividends received from other corporations in which the business owns stock

Not many businesses invest in municipal bonds, but a fair number own stock in other corporations, either as investors or as members of an affiliated group of corporations. A business can deduct 70, 80, or 100 percent of dividends received from the corporations it has invested in, depending on how many shares it owns. The purpose of this *dividend-received deduction* is to avoid taxing the receiving corporation again on money earned by the paying corporation, which has already paid income tax on its profit. In other words, the dividends received have already been taxed once, and the idea is to avoid double taxation between the two corporations.

In sharp contrast, when a corporation pays dividends to its individual stockholders (real-live persons such as you and I), the dividends are taxed a second time as income to the individuals. This is called the *double taxation* of corporate profit — once in the hands of the corporation and again in the hands of the individual stockholders. Corporations that are owned by a relatively small number of individuals can avoid this double taxation of corporate profit by making the corporation a *pass-through entity* for income tax purposes. The corporate entity pays no tax on its taxable income for the year; that's the good news. The bad news is that the individual stockholders have to include their respective shares of the corporation's taxable income on their individual income tax returns for the year. See the "Who Pays the Income Tax?" section later in this chapter.

## Equity capital disguised as debt

The general term *debt* refers to money borrowed from lenders who require that the money be paid back by a certain date, and who require that interest be paid on the debt until it is repaid. *Equity* is money invested by owners (such as stockholders) in a business in return for hoped-for, but not guaranteed, profit returns. Interest is deductible, but cash dividends paid to stockholders are not — which gives debt capital a big edge over equity capital at tax time.

Not surprisingly, some businesses try to pass off equity capital as debt on their tax returns so that they can deduct the payments to the equity sources as interest expense to determine taxable income. Don't think that the IRS is ignorant of these tactics: Everything that you declare as interest on debt may be examined carefully, and if the IRS determines that what you're calling debt is really equity capital, it disallows the interest deduction. The business can make payments to its sources of capital that it calls and treats as interest — but this does not mean that the IRS will automatically believe that the payments are in fact interest. The IRS follows the general principle of substance over form. If the so-called debt has too many characteristics of equity capital, the IRS treats the payments not as interest but rather as dividend distributions from profit to the equity sources of capital.

In summary, debt must really be debt and must have few or none of the characteristics of equity. Drawing a clear-cut line between debt and equity has been a vexing problem for the IRS, and the rules are complex. You'll probably have to consult a tax professional if you have a question about this issue. Be warned that if you attempt to disguise equity capital as debt, your charade may not work — and the IRS may disallow any "interest" payments you have made.

# Who Pays the Income Tax?

You may not know this, but many businesses do not pay income tax on their taxable income. No, these businesses are not breaking the law and evading income tax. Whether a business actually pays income tax depends on its legal organizational structure. A business may be organized as a corporation and have more than 75 owners (called *stockholders*). This type of business entity does not have a choice — it pays the income tax on its annual taxable income.

Corporations with 75 or fewer owners can choose to be pass-through tax entities. Also, other types of noncorporate businesses do not have to pay income tax. Don't jump to the conclusion that this is a big loophole in the tax law. These non-taxpaying kinds of business entities pass the amount of their annual taxable income through to their owners, who must include their respective shares of the business's taxable income on their individual tax returns. Chapter 11 explains income taxation of different types of business entities.

# Chapter 4

# Accounting and Your Personal Finances

*I*n this chapter, I look at you as an *individual*. I look over your financial shoulder at four different roles in which some accounting smarts can help you — as a taxpayer, as a borrower, as an investor, and as a retirement planner. The federal income tax law requires individuals to do some accounting once a year to determine their taxable income and income tax. You may farm out your income tax return preparation to a tax professional. Even so, you should keep in mind the income tax consequences of earning and spending your income.

# The Accounting Vise You Can't Escape

All of us have to earn income, right? Therefore, we're all subject to the federal income tax law, whether we like it or not. The federal income tax law is written in the complex and frustrating language of accounting. It's sometimes called the "Accountants' Relief and Welfare Act" because it provides employment for a large number of accountants who are hired to prepare the annual tax returns of individuals and businesses. The alternative to using an accountant is to grit your teeth and do your own taxes. Either way, I strongly suggest that you see the forest and not get lost in all the trees. A thumbnail-sized model of how the income tax law works helps you in making many important financial decisions and is very useful for mapping your overall financial strategy.

The basic income tax model is also useful for testing investment opportunities that seem too good to be true. I have seen too many people get suckered into questionable investments because of alleged income tax advantages. I'm sure you've heard the often-repeated saying, "There's a sucker born every minute."

Don't let the extraordinary complexity of the federal income tax law stop you from trying to understand how it works. Here's a basic income tax model for a married couple that's very useful, even though just four factors (numbered 1 through 4) affect the amount of the income tax in this example.

| Basic Income Tax Accounting Model | |
| --- | --- |
| (1)  Annual Income | $62,700 |
| (2)  Less Personal Exemptions | $5,500 |
| (3)  Less Standard Deduction for a Married Couple | 7,200 |
| Equals Taxable Income | $50,000 |
| (4)  Times the Tax Rates (15% on first $43,050 and 28% on excess) | |
| Equals Amount of Income Tax | **$8,404** |

*Note:* Some sources of income are not taxable or are subject to more favorable tax treatment. Some personal expenditures are deductible, and some are not. Persons over 65 or blind get . . . Hold on! Once you start getting into technical details, you're on a slippery slope, and there's no turning back. My purpose here is not to provide a detailed tax guide but to provide a simple, hands-on income model to show the basic income tax effects of your financial decisions. Several good tax guides are available, including *Taxes For Dummies,* which is updated yearly, by Eric Tyson and David Silverman (published by IDG Books Worldwide, Inc.).

Following is a brief — and I do mean *brief* — explanation of each factor in the basic income tax model:

✔ **(1) Income:** Money flowing your direction from working or owning assets is subject to income tax — unless the income tax law specifically makes the inflow not subject to income tax. (Two examples are interest income on municipal bonds and insurance proceeds received upon the death of the insured.) A good general rule is that every dollar of income comes with a potential income tax burden.

✔ **(2) Personal Exemptions:** The income tax law gives every individual a so-called *personal exemption.* The term *exemption* means that a certain amount of income is excused from income tax. For 1999 (the amount changes from year to year), the personal exemption was $2,750 per person, or $5,500 for a married couple filing a joint return (one combined income tax return for both persons, as shown in the preceding basic income tax accounting model).

✔ **(3) Deductions:** In writing the income tax law, Congress decided that you can deduct certain personal expenditures — but not others — to determine taxable income. For example, you can deduct interest paid on home mortgages, charitable contributions, and property taxes. In place of itemizing deductions, the income tax law allows a *standard deduction* of a flat amount. For 1999, a married couple filing a joint return could deduct a $7,200 standard deduction instead of itemizing specific expenditures, whether or not they made deductible-type expenditures.

✔ **Taxable Income:** The first $12,700 of income earned by the married couple in the basic income tax model shown is *not* subject to income tax — equal to the personal exemption of $5,500 plus the standard deduction of $7,200. Income above this amount is taxable. The married couple's taxable income is $50,000 because the $12,700 of income is offset by exemptions and deductions. You multiply the taxable income by the tax rates — one rate for the first layer of taxable income and a higher rate for the next layer — to determine the income tax amount.

✔ **(4) Tax Rates:** The federal income tax law is based on the *progressive taxation* philosophy — as your income progresses, your tax rate progresses. Taxable income is subdivided into *brackets* or *layers;* each higher one is subject to a higher income tax rate. The lowest rate is 15 percent; the top rate is 39.6 percent on taxable income in excess of $283,150. The brackets and rates can change from year to year, but don't worry — Uncle Sam keeps you informed in the booklet that comes with your annual income tax forms. Instead of our progressive tax rate structure, the *flat tax* proposal argues that the taxable income of individuals should be taxed at one rate — see the sidebar "The flat tax: Sounds good, but . . ."

✔ **Income Tax Amount:** In 1999, the tax rate on $50,000 taxable income was 15 percent on the first $43,050. The rate almost doubles to 28 percent on the next bracket of taxable income. As you can see in the example, the income tax on the $50,000 taxable income is $8,404.

In this example, the income tax of $8,404 is 16.8 percent of the $50,000 taxable income and 13.4 percent of the $62,700 gross income. However, the *marginal tax rate* gets the most attention. The marginal tax rate is the rate that applies to the margin, or highest layer of taxable income. The margin in this example is the taxable income in excess of $43,050, or $6,950. By earning $1,000 more income, the married couple's income tax would increase by 28 percent or $280. They are in the 28 percent marginal income tax bracket.

## The flat tax: Sounds good, but . . .

Congress is under constant pressure to simplify the tax law, but the pressure to promote certain expenditures (contributions to churches, for example) is equally great. For example, a *flat tax,* where you pay a standard tax rate on all income without having to make all sorts of mind-numbing calculations, seems like a great idea — until you realize that a flat tax won't let you deduct your home mortgage interest anymore.

Behind the flat tax idea is the concept that all taxpayers should be treated exactly the same,

regardless of whether they earn $10,000, $100,000, or $1 million in annual income. Incomes are not flat, so don't pin your hopes on a flat tax anytime soon. Maybe someday you'll be able to figure your annual income tax in one short, simple calculation, but — and I hate to sound like a sourpuss — I don't think anyone will ever see that day.

The marginal tax rate starts at 15 percent on the first dollar of *taxable* income. Remember that you do not have any taxable income until your annual income exceeds the total of your personal exemption(s) plus the standard deduction. For the married couple in the example, the first $12,700 of their income is not taxable because the total of their personal exemptions and standard deduction equals this amount. Their next $43,050 of income is taxed at 15 percent, and the remaining $6,950 is taxed at 28 percent.

## The $300 TV that cost me $450

When I taught accounting, I often asked my students what the cost of a television set was that I had bought for $300. They would look at me rather strangely, especially when I told them the true economic cost was really $450. That's how much I had to earn, before federal and state income tax, to pay for the TV. In other words, I paid $300 to the retailer and $150 to the government in income taxes.

The cost of a television is a personal expense and is not deductible when determining taxable

income. In contrast, if I had increased my contributions to my church by $300, I would need to earn only $300 to pay for that contribution, because contributions to qualified nonprofit organizations are deductible. (If I use the standard deduction instead of itemizing deductions, however, things are a little more complicated and I would, indeed, have to earn $450 to pay for a $300 charitable contribution.)

I find that using a combined total federal and state *marginal* income tax rate of 33 percent, which is based on a 28 percent federal income tax plus a 5 percent state income tax, is generally accurate and computationally convenient. This number may be too high or too low for a specific individual or married couple, but it's reasonably accurate for a broad range of taxpayers. (If you're a multi-millionaire, you probably should shift up to a 45 percent marginal tax rate.) In other words, most of the readers of this book can assume that if they receive a $1,000 raise, about 33 percent of that will be lost to taxes. Or, if you'd like to buy a new pair of jogging shoes that cost $67 at the sporting goods store, you need $100 of income before taxes to have $67 left over, after taxes, for the shoes.

# The Ins and Outs of Figuring Interest and Return on Investment (ROI)

In addition to understanding the basic model of income tax accounting, you should have a good grip on the calculation of periodic interest and how return on investment is measured. Most people pay interest on loans (credit cards, home mortgages, car loans) and earn interest on savings accounts. When you borrow, you ought to understand the accounting for your interest cost and the paydown of the amount borrowed. Likewise, when you save, you ought to understand the accounting for your interest income and for the accumulation of your savings balance. And when you invest, you ought to understand accounting for return on investment (ROI).

Interest rates and ROI rates are tossed around freely as if everyone were intimately familiar with how these important ratios are calculated. In fact, many people do not understand these key accounting calculations. In my experience, most people get sweaty palms when they have to think about how interest is actually calculated and how investment performance is measured. The following sections should reduce your anxiety about these matters, which have a big impact on your personal financial affairs.

## Individuals as borrowers

Everyone borrows money — for car loans, for home mortgages, on unpaid credit card balances, and so on. In my experience, everyone knows that interest is the extra amount you have to pay the lender in addition to paying back the amount you borrowed. But most people (even some experienced business people) are not entirely clear on how interest is figured. When you borrow money, you agree to a method of interest accounting, whether you understand the method or not. You should be clear on the following points:

  ✔ If you make more than one loan payment per year, divide the annual interest rate by the number of loan payments to determine the interest rate per period, which usually is a month or a quarter. In other words, the quoted annual rate is simply the number to divide into to get the real interest rate per month or per quarter.

✔ When you make two or more loan payments, each payment goes first to the interest amount; the remainder is deducted from the loan balance, called the *principal*. The amount of the principal paydown each period is referred to as the *amortization* of the loan. The total amount borrowed has to be amortized, or paid back to the lender over the life of the loan.

✔ Shortening the term of a very long-term loan, say from 30 years to 15 years, results in a dramatic decrease in the total interest paid over the life of the loan but a relatively small increase in the monthly loan payment amount.

✔ A monthly interest rate should not be multiplied by 12 to determine the *effective annual interest rate;* likewise, a quarterly interest rate should not be multiplied by 4 to determine the effective annual interest rate. Annual effective rates assume the *compounding* of interest during the year. Compounding means paying interest on interest; it is an extremely important building block for understanding financial matters.

A good example to illustrate several of these points is a typical home mortgage loan.

### Home mortgage example

The biggest loan in most individuals' financial lives is a home mortgage. Compared with a short-term auto loan, a home mortgage loan runs up to 30 years, and the amount borrowed is usually much larger than for an automobile (unless you buy a Ferrari).

Suppose that you just bought the home of your dreams and qualified for a $180,000 first mortgage loan for 30 years at a 9 percent annual interest rate. The loan requires equal monthly payments, so you divide the annual interest rate by 12 to determine the monthly rate, which is 0.75 percent (or ¾ of 1 percent) per month. How much would each of your 360 loan payments be? How do you determine this amount? You probably would assume that the lender's quoted amount is correct — and you'd be pretty safe in this assumption. But how can you be sure?

Relatively inexpensive hand-held business/financial calculators are available to quickly determine monthly loan payments. These handy tools have special keys for entering each of the variables of a loan. To determine the monthly payment in this example, I pulled out my hand-held calculator and punched in the following numbers for each variable:

✔ **N** = number of periods — 360 months in this example

✔ **INT** = interest rate per period — 0.75 percent per month in this example (these calculators expect that the interest is given in a percentage, so I typed .75, not .0075)

✔ **PV** = present value, or amount borrowed today (the present time) — $180,000 in this example

✔ **FV** = future value, or principal amount owed after the final monthly loan payment is made — $0 in this example (which means that the loan is fully amortized and paid off after the last monthly loan payment; otherwise, there would be a *balloon* payment due at the end of the loan)

✔ **PMT** = payment per period based on the four numbers just entered — $1,448.32 in this example, which is the amount you solve for (and which appears as a negative number, meaning that you have to pay this amount per month)

The big advantage of a business/financial hand-held calculator is that you can enter the known numbers (the first four) and then simply hit the button for the unknown number, which appears instantly. Another big advantage is that you can keep all these numbers in the calculator and make "what if" changes very, very quickly. For example, what if the annual interest rate was 8.4 percent? Just re-enter the new interest rate (0.7 percent per month) and then call up the new monthly payment amount, which is $1,371.31. The monthly payment difference times 360 payments is $27,725 less interest over the life of the loan. So you might decide to shop around for a lower rate.

If you don't have a business/financial calculator but use the Internet, you can find many Web sites that provide online financial calculators. For instance, I went to a search engine site, selected the search tab, and then entered "mortgage calculations." Many Web sites were found; one was exactly suited to my purpose.

Now, here's a short test to see if you've been paying attention. Suppose the lender did not charge interest — in other words, the interest rate was zero. What would your monthly payments be in the example I just used? The monthly payments would be simply $180,000 divided by 360 months, or only $500 per month. At a 9 percent annual interest rate, you have to pay $1,448.32 per month. This does not mean that the extra $948.32 more per month, or $11,379.85 per year, is for interest. Interest is accounted for differently, and just how interest is accounted for makes a big difference to you.

Each mortgage payment is divided between interest and principal amortization (paydown). For the first month, the interest amount is $1,350 ($180,000 loan balance × 0.75 percent monthly interest rate = $1,350). Therefore, the first month's principal paydown is only $98.32. Right off, you can see that the loan's principal balance will go down very slowly — and that a 30-year mortgage loan involves a lot of interest. Lenders provide you with a loan payoff (amortization) schedule. I encourage you to take a look — although trying to follow down a table of 360 rows of monthly payments is tough going.

Figure 4-1 presents the annual amounts of interest cost and principal reduction for this mortgage loan example. (I generated this data from a Microsoft Excel spreadsheet payoff schedule for the loan). Note that the annual principal amortization doesn't overcome annual interest cost until the *23rd year.* In other words, you pay mostly interest during the first 22 years! The right column in the figure shows how slowly the loan balance goes down.

| Year | Payments | Annual Interest Cost | Annual Amortization, or Reduction of Principal |
|---|---|---|---|
| 1 | $17,379.85 | $16,150.09 | $1,229.75 |
| 2 | $17,379.85 | $16,034.73 | $1,345.11 |
| 3 | $17,379.85 | $15,908.55 | $1,471.30 |
| 4 | $17,379.85 | $15,770.54 | $1,609.31 |
| 5 | $17,379.85 | $15,619.57 | $1,760.28 |
| 6 | $17,379.85 | $15,454.44 | $1,925.40 |
| 7 | $17,379.85 | $15,273.83 | $2,106.02 |
| 8 | $17,379.85 | $15,076.27 | $2,303.58 |
| 9 | $17,379.85 | $14,860.18 | $2,519.67 |
| 10 | $17,379.85 | $14,623.82 | $2,756.03 |
| 11 | $17,379.85 | $14,365.28 | $3,014.57 |
| 12 | $17,379.85 | $14,082.49 | $3,297.36 |
| 13 | $17,379.85 | $13,773.18 | $3,606.67 |
| 14 | $17,379.85 | $13,434.85 | $3,945.00 |
| 15 | $17,379.85 | $13,064.78 | $4,315.07 |
| 16 | $17,379.85 | $12,660.00 | $4,719.85 |
| 17 | $17,379.85 | $12,217.24 | $5,162.61 |
| 18 | $17,379.85 | $11,732.95 | $5,646.89 |
| 19 | $17,379.85 | $11,203.24 | $6,176.61 |
| 20 | $17,379.85 | $10,623.83 | $6,756.02 |
| 21 | $17,379.85 | $9,990.07 | $7,389.78 |
| 22 | $17,379.85 | $9,296.85 | $8,083.00 |
| 23 | $17,379.85 | $8,538.61 | $8,841.24 |
| 24 | $17,379.85 | $7,709.24 | $9,670.61 |
| 25 | $17,379.85 | $6,802.07 | $10,577.77 |
| 26 | $17,379.85 | $5,809.81 | $11,570.04 |
| 27 | $17,379.85 | $4,724.46 | $12,655.39 |
| 28 | $17,379.85 | $3,537.29 | $13,842.56 |
| 29 | $17,379.85 | $2,238.77 | $15,141.08 |
| 30 | $17,379.85 | $818.43 | $16,561.42 |
| Totals | $521,395.46 | $341,395.46 | $180,000.00 |

**Figure 4-1:** Annual summary for a 30-year home mortgage payoff schedule.

One alternative that you should definitely consider when taking out a home mortgage is a 15-year loan instead of a 30-year loan. For this home mortgage example, the monthly payment on a 15-year loan is $1,825.68, which is an additional $377.36 per month. The total interest over the life of the 15-year loan is about $149,000, compared with $341,000 on the 30-year loan. The 15-year loan saves you about $192,000 in total interest over the life of the mortgage, and you own your home free and clear 15 years sooner. Of course, you have to come up with $377.36 more per month, which may not be possible in the short run. But after a few years of paying the 30-year amount, you can step up the amount you pay each month and pay off your mortgage sooner. Figure 4-1A (A is for *alternative*) shows the annual interest and principal payments for the 15-year mortgage.

You may be tempted to focus on the amount of the monthly payment and how this amount fits into your personal budget. But you should also look closely at the pattern of interest versus principal payments over the life of the loan. In my experience, overlooking interest versus principal payments is the biggest mistake borrowers make. You should always know how fast you're paying off principal, and you should keep track of your loan balance.

| Year | Payments | Annual Interest Cost | Annual Amortization, or Reduction of Principal | Loan Balance At End of Year |
|---|---|---|---|---|
| 1 | $21,908.16 | $15,958.55 | $5,949.61 | $174,050.39 |
| 2 | $21,908.16 | $15,400.44 | $6,507.72 | $167,542.67 |
| 3 | $21,908.16 | $14,789.97 | $7,118.19 | $160,424.48 |
| 4 | $21,908.16 | $14,122.23 | $7,785.93 | $152,638.56 |
| 5 | $21,908.16 | $13,391.86 | $8,516.30 | $144,122.26 |
| 6 | $21,908.16 | $12,592.97 | $9,315.19 | $134,807.07 |
| 7 | $21,908.16 | $11,719.14 | $10,189.02 | $124,618.06 |
| 8 | $21,908.16 | $10,763.34 | $11,144.82 | $113,473.24 |
| 9 | $21,908.16 | $9,717.88 | $12,190.28 | $101,282.97 |
| 10 | $21,908.16 | $8,574.35 | $13,333.81 | $87,949.16 |
| 11 | $21,908.16 | $7,323.55 | $14,584.61 | $73,364.55 |
| 12 | $21,908.16 | $5,955.41 | $15,952.75 | $57,411.80 |
| 13 | $21,908.16 | $4,458.93 | $17,449.23 | $39,962.57 |
| 14 | $21,908.16 | $2,822.07 | $19,086.08 | $20,876.49 |
| 15 | $21,908.16 | $1,031.67 | $20,876.49 | $0.00 |
| Totals | $328,622.37 | $148,622 | $180,000 | |

**Figure 4-1A:** Annual summary for a 15-year home mortgage payoff schedule.

## Tools of the trade

I advise everyone to invest the time and effort (plus a relatively small cost) to learn how to use one of two indispensable tools of the trade for analyzing savings and investments: a handheld business/financial calculator and a personal computer spreadsheet program, such as Excel, Quattro Pro, or Lotus 1-2-3.

A powerful business/financial handheld calculator costs under $100. I use a financial calculator every day. You have to take some time and go through a few examples to learn how to operate the thing, but I think the time is well spent. The owner's manuals for the Hewlett Packard business/financial calculators are very well written and have good practical examples. When negotiating my most recent home mortgage, I brought my HP calculator along and caught the loan officer in a major error.

If you already use a computer spreadsheet program, take advantage of its financial functions. For example, you can easily print out loan payoff schedules, savings plans, retirement fund accumulations, estimated retirement income, and many more useful tables and schedules and convert these into charts for easier viewing. The spreadsheet owner's manuals are terrible, I know. I suggest buying the *For Dummies* book for the spreadsheet program you use.

## Individuals as savers

Ben Franklin said, "A penny saved is a penny earned." His point is that one penny not spent today is a penny kept for another day. Until that later day arrives, the penny saved can earn interest income. These days, 100 pennies saved for one year earn about 6 pennies in interest income, or 6 percent per year.

*Saving* is done for income and safety of principal and not for market value appreciation. Suppose you save $10,000 for one year. You expect to earn the going interest rate, *and* you expect to have little or no risk of losing any of your money during the year. You do not expect your savings to appreciate in value other than from interest income. Assuming that the going interest rate is 6 percent, you expect that your savings will grow to $10,600 by the end of the year — the $10,000 you started with plus 6 percent interest (or $6 per $100) earned on that money. The interest income increases your taxable income by the same amount, so keep in mind the marginal income tax rate that takes a bite out of your $600 in interest income.

### The power of compounding (which means not spending your interest income)

Suppose you have some money that you want to save. You can deposit your money in a savings account at a savings and loan association, a bank, or a credit union. Or you can buy a CD — not the music kind or the kind you insert into a computer, but a certificate of deposit issued by a bank or other financial institution. Or you can put your money in a money market fund. You can save money through many different types of vehicles and instruments, which are explained in Eric Tyson's excellent book *Personal Finance For Dummies* (IDG Books Worldwide). My purpose is to demonstrate how your savings grow or do not grow depending on what you do with the interest income each period.

Suppose you have $100,000 in savings. (Larger amounts of money are more interesting than smaller amounts.) You leave the money alone for one year, and at the end of the year your savings balance has grown to $106,000. Therefore, you earned a 6 percent annual interest income:

```
$6,000 increase in savings balance ÷ $100,000 balance at start
        of year = 6%
```

Now you have a critical choice to make: Should you withdraw the $6,000 income and spend the money, or should you leave the $6,000 in savings? Many people depend on income from their savings for living expenses. Others want to build up their money over time. Suppose you're in the second group; you leave the first year's interest income in your savings account for a second year.

Suppose at the end of the second year, your savings amount is $112,360 — $6,360 more than at the start of the year. Therefore, for the second year, you also earned a 6 percent annual interest rate:

```
$6,360 increase in savings balance ÷ $106,000 balance at
        start of year = 6%
```

You earned more interest income in the second year because you had more in savings at the start of the year. Notice that at the end of the second year you have two years of interest income accumulated: $6,000 from year one and $6,360 from year two, for $12,360 total increase in your savings amount.

If you continue to plow back annual earnings for 12 years, how much would you have at the end of the 12 years — starting with $100,000, earning 6 percent per year, and resaving interest income every year? Without touching my calculator, I know that your savings balance after 12 years would about double, or would be about $200,000. This quick-and-dirty method is based on the *rule of 72* (see the sidebar "The rule of 72"). To be more precise, your savings balance at the end of 12 years would be $201,220. I did this computation with my calculator. (If you use Microsoft Excel, you might double-check this amount by using the FV financial function; or you can go to a Web site that has a financial calculator.)

*Note:* I use the terms *plow back* and *resaving* in order to avoid the term *reinvesting.* Reinvesting implies an investment, which, strictly speaking, involves market value fluctuation risk. Saving does not involve this risk. (I should warn you that there is always a small risk that part of the money in a savings account or instrument will be lost or will be delayed in being returned to you — witness the savings and loan association scandals of several years ago.)

Figure 4-2 illustrates how your savings balance would grow year by year, assuming a 6 percent annual interest rate for all 12 years. This growth comes at a price — you can't take out annual earnings. Not withdrawing annual earnings is called *compounding;* the term *compound interest* refers to not withdrawing interest income. Compounding means that you save more and more each year. To emphasize this important point, notice in Figure 4-2 that I include a column for the amount of interest income withdrawn each year (which is zero every year in this example).

Furthermore, the entire interest income each year is subject to individual income tax — unless the money is invested in a tax-deferred retirement fund such as a 401(k) account. For instance, in year 4 your interest income is $7,146 (see Figure 4-2). At the 33 percent marginal tax rate (federal plus state), you would owe $2,358 income tax on your interest income.

Unfortunately, compounding of earnings is often touted as a sort of magical way to build wealth over time or to make your money double. Don't be suckered by this claim. You sacrifice 12 years of earnings to make your money grow; you don't get to spend the interest income on your savings for 12 years. I don't call this magic; I call it *frugal.*

# The rule of 72

A handy trick of the trade is called the rule of 72. In Figure 4-2, at the end of the 12th year, notice that your savings balance is about $200,000 (rounded off) — exactly twice what you started with. This is a good example of the rule of 72. The rule states that if you take the periodic earnings rate as a whole number and divide it into 72, the answer is the number of periods it takes to double what you started with. Sure enough: 72 ÷ 6 = 12. Doubling your money at 6 percent per year takes 12 years.

The rule of 72 assumes compounding of earnings. It's amazingly accurate over a broad range of earnings rates and number of periods. For example, how long does it take to double your money at an 8 percent annual earnings rate? It takes nine years (72 ÷ 8 = 9). If you earn 18 percent per year, you double your money in just four years.

One caution: For very low and very high earnings rates, the rule is not accurate and should not be used.

| Year | Savings Balance at Start of Year | Annual Interest Rate | Interest Income on Savings Balance | Amount of Interest Income Withdrawn | Savings Balance at End of Year |
|---|---|---|---|---|---|
| 1 | $100,000 | x 6% = | $6,000 | $0 | $106,000 |
| 2 | $106,000 | x 6% = | $6,360 | $0 | $112,360 |
| 3 | $112,360 | x 6% = | $6,742 | $0 | $119,102 |
| 4 | $119,102 | x 6% = | $7,146 | $0 | $126,248 |
| 5 | $126,248 | x 6% = | $7,575 | $0 | $133,823 |
| 6 | $133,823 | x 6% = | $8,029 | $0 | $141,852 |
| 7 | $141,852 | x 6% = | $8,511 | $0 | $150,363 |
| 8 | $150,363 | x 6% = | $9,022 | $0 | $159,385 |
| 9 | $159,385 | x 6% = | $9,563 | $0 | $168,948 |
| 10 | $168,948 | x 6% = | $10,137 | $0 | $179,085 |
| 11 | $179,085 | x 6% = | $10,745 | $0 | $189,830 |
| 12 | $189,830 | x 6% = | $11,390 | $0 | $201,220 |

**Figure 4-2:** Growth in savings balance assuming no withdrawals and full compounding of annual interest income.

In your economic life, you constantly make many spend-versus-save decisions. I didn't have to take my wife out to a nice dinner on her birthday. If I had saved the $100 and earned a 6 percent annual interest rate and compounded the income for 12 years, I would have $201. By then, I'd be almost 80 years old. Compounding is not magical — it's a conservative way to build wealth that requires you to forgo a lot of spending along the way.

## Individuals as investors

The last two decades have seen a remarkable explosion in the number of individuals who invest in the stock market — either directly by buying and selling stock shares or indirectly by putting their money in shares of mutual funds (open-end investment companies that act as intermediaries for individuals). Also during this time span, a sea change has occurred in the arena of retirement planning, mainly a fundamental shift away from traditional *defined-benefit* pension plans (which are based on years of service to an employer and salaries during the final years of employment) to *defined-contribution* plans (which are based on how much money has been put into individual retirement investment accounts and the earnings performance of the investments).

Social security is the federal government-sponsored defined-benefit retirement plan. Your monthly retirement benefit depends on how many years you have worked and your salary levels during those years. In the private sector, a large percentage of retired employees still depend on traditional defined-benefit pension plans. However, the growth of defined-contribution plans has been phenomenal — although I think most individuals don't realize that this type of retirement plan puts much more of a burden on them to understand investment performance accounting.

### The twofold nature of return on investment

Putting money into savings, such as a savings account or a certificate of deposit (CD), is low risk. In contrast, putting money into an *investment,* such as corporate stocks and bonds or real estate, means that you are taking on more risk — that you may lose part of the amount of money you invest and that the earnings from your investment may fluctuate from year to year. There's no such thing as a free lunch. If you want the higher earnings, you must take greater risk.

Earnings from *investing* capital are generally not referred to as earnings on investment, but rather as *return on investment* (ROI). ROI consists of two parts: (1) *cash income* (if in fact there is cash income) and (2) *market value appreciation or depreciation.* When you invest, you put your money in stocks and bonds (which are called *securities*), or mutual funds, or real estate, or pork belly futures, or whatever. The range of possible investments is diverse, to say the least. I recommend Eric Tyson's *Investing For Dummies* (IDG Books Worldwide). He explains the wide range of investments open to individuals, from mutual funds to real estate and most things in between. Investors should understand how return on investment is accounted for — no matter which type of investment they choose.

The return on investment, or ROI, for a period is computed as follows, and is usually expressed as a percentage:

```
Return for Period ÷ Amount Invested at Start of Period = Rate
              of Return on Investment (ROI)
```

Suppose, for example, that your $100,000 investment at the start of the year provided $2,500 cash flow income during the year, and the market value of your investment asset increased $7,500 during the year. Your total return is $10,000 for the year, and your ROI is 10 percent for the year: $10,000 return ÷ $100,000 invested = 10 percent ROI.

Often, people use the term *ROI* when they really mean *rate,* or *percentage* of ROI. Like some words that have a silent character, ROI is frequently used without rate or percentage. Anytime you see the % symbol, you know that the *rate* of ROI is meant. In any case, the ROI rate is not a totally satisfactory measure. For instance, suppose you tell me that your investments earned 18 percent ROI last year. I know your wealth, or capital, increased 18 percent — although I don't know how much of this return you received in cash income and how much was an increase in the market value of your investment, and I don't know whether you spent your cash income or reinvested it.

Individuals, financial institutions, and businesses always account for the cash income component of investment return. However, the market value gain or loss during the period may or may not be recorded. Most individuals who invest in real estate, farms, stocks, and bonds do not record the gain or loss in the market value of their investments during the period. So they do not have a full and complete accounting of ROI for the period.

My father-in-law has owned a farm in Iowa since 1940. He keeps very good accounting records for the annual revenue and expenses of the farm so that he can determine net income (or loss) for the year, which he reports in his annual income tax return. But he does not record a gain or loss from changes in the market value of the farm from year to year. He knows the approximate market value of the farm, but he does not account for changes in the market value. Only the original 1940 cost is on his books.

He doesn't plan on selling the farm. For one thing, he would have to pay a 20 percent capital gains tax (at the 2000 rate) if he did. He plans to leave the farm in his estate. In short, accounting for the return on his farm investment is restricted to cash income (or loss) for the year. Only mentally does he compare the cash income against the current market value of the farm — which is as close as he gets to calculating an ROI rate for the year.

The investment accounting that most individuals do is governed largely by what's required for income tax purposes. Unrealized market value gains are not taxed, so most investors do not record market value gains. Nevertheless, they keep an eye on market value ups and downs, in addition to their cash income. For example, real estate investors generally do not measure and record market value changes each year, although they keep an eye on the prices of comparable properties.

In contrast, financial institutions, including banks, mutual funds, insurance companies, and pension funds, are governed by generally accepted accounting principles (GAAP). They invest in marketable securities that are held for sale or trading or that are available for sale. GAAP requires that changes in market value of these investments be recognized. On the other hand, GAAP does not require the recording of market value gains and losses for their investments in fixed-income debt securities (for example, bonds and notes) that are held until maturity.

The main point of this discussion is that you should be very clear about what's included and not included in ROI. As just discussed, many individuals do not capture market value changes during the year in accounting for the return, or earnings on their investments — they account for only the cash income part, which gives an incomplete measure of ROI. On the other hand, when a mutual fund advertises that its annual ROI was 18 percent last year, you can be sure that it *does* include the market value gains in this rate (as well as cash income, of course).

### A real-world example of ROI accounting

Suppose you invest $94,757.86 today in a U.S. Treasury Note that has three years to go until its maturity date. The face, or par, value of this debt security is $100,000, which is its maturity value three years hence and also is the basis on which interest is computed. (U.S. debt securities issued with less than ten years to maturity are called *notes* instead of bonds.) This note pays 6 percent annual interest, which is paid semiannually. The 6 percent rate is sometimes called the *coupon rate* because in the good old days (before direct deposit by electronic funds transfer), investors in debt securities had to clip one of the interest coupons attached to the debt certificate as it came due and mail the coupon for payment of the interest.

Every six months, the U.S. Treasury Department sends you $3,000 (depositing the amount directly in your checking account). Assume that you spend the $3,000 semiannual interest income. So far, so good. But now comes a tough question: What's your ROI rate on this investment?

By paying $94,757.86, you buy the Treasury Note at a *discount* from its $100,000 maturity value. The discount provides part of your return on investment in addition to your cash flow interest income. Most of your ROI consists of cash income every six months. But part consists of *market value appreciation* as the note moves closer to its maturity date. This second component does not provide cash flow until the maturity date is reached. Taking both parts into account, your ROI rate is more than the 6 percent annual interest rate based on the par value of the note.

Tell you what: Guess that the correct ROI rate is 4 percent per period (every six months), and see whether this rate is correct. I'll walk you quickly through the accounting in this example to test out the 4 percent ROI rate. Figure 4-3 demonstrates that in each period, the return on the investment indeed equals 4 percent of the amount invested at the start of the period. The investor receives only $3,000 per period of cash income. The increase in the value of the note each period as it moves toward its maturity value provides the remainder of the return each period. The total increase in value over the three years is not received until the maturity date, at which time the investment is cashed out. At this time, the individual has to find another investment to put his or her $100,000 into.

**Figure 4-3:**
Investing in a debt security at a discount from its maturity value to illustrate a higher ROI rate than the periodic interest rate paid on the debt instrument.

| Period | Investment at Start of Period | Total Return (ROI = 4.0% on Starting Amount) | Two Components of Return — Cash Income | | Increase in Value | Investment at End of Period |
|---|---|---|---|---|---|---|
| 1 | $94,757.86 | $3,790.31 | $3,000.00 | + | $790.31 | $95,548.18 |
| 2 | $95,548.18 | $3,821.93 | $3,000.00 | + | $821.93 | $96,370.10 |
| 3 | $96,370.10 | $3,854.80 | $3,000.00 | + | $854.80 | $97,224.91 |
| 4 | $97,224.91 | $3,889.00 | $3,000.00 | + | $889.00 | $98,113.91 |
| 5 | $98,113.91 | $3,924.56 | $3,000.00 | + | $924.56 | $99,038.46 |
| 6 | $99,038.46 | $3,961.54 | $3,000.00 | + | $961.54 | $100,000.00 |
| Totals = | | $23,242.14 | $18,000.00 | | $5,242.14 | |

*Please Note:* Only the increase in value is compounded, or reinvested each period. The $3,000 cash income each period is not compounded but is, instead, withdrawn from the investment. The amount invested grows period to period only by the increase in value. The total return each period equals 4.0% of the amount invested at the start of the period.

### An important note regarding annualized ROI rates

In the investment example in Figure 4-3, the increase in value each period is not received in cash. Therefore, it is "automatically" reinvested, or compounded. Due to this compounding, the amount invested increases period to period — see the left column. As a result, the increase in the value amount is larger from period to period.

Seems odd, doesn't it? A 4 percent ROI earned each half-year is treated as equivalent to 8.16 percent ROI earned for the whole year. The purpose is to put all investments on the same footing, as it were — so that annual ROI rates can be compared among different investments. The standard practice in the world of finance is to express ROI rates on the basis of a one-year period — even though the investment may be for a shorter period of time. When a less-than-one-year ROI rate (or interest rate) is converted into an equivalent full-year rate, the shorter-term rate is *annualized.* Usually the word *annualized* is not included; it is assumed that you understand that shorter-term rates have been converted into an equivalent annual rate. Any investment income received during the year is assumed to be compounded (reinvested) for the rest of the year to determine the annualized ROI rate, or I should say just the ROI rate.

Suppose you have been in an investment for some time — say, 5, 10, or 20 years. Your ROI rate probably has fluctuated from year to year, high in some years and low in others. Now, suppose I ask how you have done on this investment over the years. You could give me the yearly ROI rates. But the more common practice in the investment world is to calculate the *average* ROI — the equivalent constant, or flat rate that would have resulted in the same ending value of your investment.

*Average ROI* rates are commonly used to summarize the historical investment performance of a mutual fund. You see this measure in several other places as well — for example, in the reporting of investment performance to individuals by their retirement fund managers. Be very careful about using these ROI rates. Keep in mind that the average ROI rate masks the actual year-by-year volatility in investment performance.

For example, suppose that five years ago you put $100,000 in an investment that paid no cash income any year; all the return was in annual changes in the value of the investment. Figure 4-4 summarizes the yearly performance of your investment. Your $100,000 original investment five years ago is now worth $248,832. But the annual returns fluctuated widely; you had some good ROI years and some bad years. (Many investors would not tolerate the annual ROI volatility of this type of investment.) What is the average annual ROI for your investment?

Believe it or not, the average ROI for this investment is 20 percent. You may ask: How can this be correct? Well, 20 percent is indeed correct. The average annual ROI rate is the uniform rate that would make the investment grow from the original amount invested ($100,000 in this example) to the final value at the end of the investment ($248,832 in this example). You may not be convinced that the average annual ROI rate is 20 percent unless you actually walk through what would have happened if your investment had increased 20 percent in value each year.

| | Year | Investment Value at Start of Year | Market Value Change During Year | Investment Value at End of Year | ROI For Year |
|---|---|---|---|---|---|
| **Figure 4-4:** Yearly investment performance over five years. | 1 | $100,000 | $70,000 | $170,000 | 70% |
| | 2 | $170,000 | $70,418 | $240,418 | 41% |
| | 3 | $240,418 | $0 | $240,418 | 0% |
| | 4 | $240,418 | ($24,042) | $216,376 | -10% |
| | 5 | $216,376 | $32,456 | $248,832 | 15% |

Figure 4-5 shows this imaginary year-by-year investment value growth. Note that the investment value at the end of the fifth year is exactly $248,832. Of course, you didn't actually earn 20 percent ROI each year, as a comparison with the actual investment performance in Figure 4-4 reveals. But advertising that the average annual ROI for this investment is 20 percent is legal and even accurate. Let the investor beware!

| | Year | Investment Value at Start of Year | Imputed 20% ROI For Year | Investment Value at End of Year |
|---|---|---|---|---|
| **Figure 4-5:** Proof that the average annual ROI rate for the five-year investment is 20 percent. | 1 | $100,000 | $20,000 | $120,000 |
| | 2 | $120,000 | $24,000 | $144,000 |
| | 3 | $144,000 | $28,800 | $172,800 |
| | 4 | $172,800 | $34,560 | $207,360 |
| | 5 | $207,360 | $41,472 | $248,832 |

# An Accounting Template for Retirement Planning

The transition from being employed to being retired involves psychological, social, and financial aspects. I recently retired from 41 years working as a CPA and a professor of accounting. Of course, the main financial concern of most persons as they approach retirement is whether they will have enough retirement income in addition to what they will receive from social security. How much retirement income do you need? How should you take money out of your retirement account, assuming that you have choices? What are the income tax effects of withdrawals from your tax-deferred retirement funds?

I can't begin to answer these questions here. But I can offer a basic template to get you going and to help you negotiate the first steps in financial retirement planning. Figure 4-6 is illustrates how to calculate your *replacement ratio,* which you compute by dividing retirement income by pre-retirement income. The point is that your retirement income replaces your wage, or salary, or other earned income, and that it's very important to calibrate your retirement income as a percentage of your pre-retirement income. Most financial advisors recommend that your replacement ratio should be at least 70 percent, in order to maintain your standard of living at a reasonably comparable level.

For this example, I used numbers based on reasonable assumptions and typical conditions. Prior to retirement, Pat (as I call the person in this example) was earning $6,000 per month. Upon retirement, this regular paycheck stops coming. Pat has to depend on either the company's pension plan (in a defined-benefit retirement plan) or on the accumulated investment amount (in a defined-contribution plan). Without going into details, assume that Pat's monthly retirement income will be $3,000 per month, which is only half of Pat's pre-retirement income. But hold on; you have to consider several other important factors.

| Monthly Income and Deductions | Before Retirement | After Retirement |
|---|---|---|
| Gross Income, Before Deductions | $6,000 | |
| Retirement Income | | $3,000 |
| Social Security Tax (at 6.2%) | ($372) | |
| Social Security Income | | $1,200 |
| Medicare Tax (at 1.45%) | ($87) | |
| Medicare Part B Cost | | ($46) |
| Employee's Retirement Plan Contribution (at 5%) | ($300) | |
| Medical and Hospital Insurance | ($200) | ($200) |
| Take Home Income Before Income Tax | $5,041 | $3,954 |
| Replacement Ratio | 78% | |

**Figure 4-6:** Accounting template for figuring retirement income replacement ratio.

In 1999, an employee had to pay 6.2 percent social security tax on the first $76,200 of annual earned income. Once retired, Pat doesn't have to pay the tax; instead Pat starts receiving social security income, which is $1,200 in the example (a fairly reasonable estimate given Pat's salary). Pat also stops paying Medicare tax, although Medicare Part B coverage (for physicians and medical care) will cost Pat about $46 per month (in 2000). Also, Pat stops making retirement contributions. Pat, like most people, probably will buy supplemental medical and hospital insurance (called Medigap insurance). This cost is difficult to estimate, so it's kept the same during Pat's retirement.

The bottom line is that Pat's take-home monthly income, before income tax, is $3,954 after retirement and $5,041 before retirement — which is a replacement ratio of 78 percent. Most financial advisors consider this ratio adequate, although it would be better, of course, if Pat's retirement nest egg had been bigger to provide more income during the golden years. The template shown in Figure 4-6 allows you to start with a replacement ratio goal, say 85 percent, and then work back to how much your retirement income would have to be. Good luck on accumulating enough in your retirement fund to provide the income you need.

# Part II

# Getting a Grip on Financial Statements

The 5th Wave      By Rich Tennant

BEAL & WASP
ACCOUNTANTS

"OUR GOAL IS TO MAXIMIZE YOUR UPSIDE AND MINIMIZE YOUR DOWNSIDE WHILE WE PROTECT OUR OWN BACKSIDE."

## *In this part . . .*

Financial statements are like the tip of an iceberg — the only visible part, underneath which are a lot of record-keeping, accounting methods, and reporting decisions. The managers of a business, the investors in a business, and the lenders to a business need a firm grasp on these accounting communications. They need to know which handles to grab hold of and how to find both the good and bad signals in financial statements — and, ugh, this includes the small print footnotes that go with financial statements.

Accountants prepare three primary financial statements. The *income statement* reports the profit-making activities of the business and how much profit or loss the business made. (Sounds odd, doesn't it, to say a business *made a loss?* But to make profit, a business has to take the risk that it may suffer a loss.) The *balance sheet* reports the financial situation and position of the business at a point in time — usually the last day of the profit period. The *cash flow statement* reports how much cash was actually realized from profit and other sources of cash, and what the business did with this money. In short, the financial life of a business is revealed in its financial statements, as this part of the book exposes.

# Chapter 5

# Profit Mechanics

● ● ● ● ● ● ● ● ● ● ● ● ● ● ● ● ● ● ● ● ● ● ● ● ● ● ● ● ● ● ● ● ● ● ● ● ● ● ● ● ● ● ● ● ● ● ● ●

## In This Chapter

▶ Getting the lowdown on profit

▶ Analyzing the different steps in making profit

▶ Locating where the profit ends up

▶ Reporting profitor loss in the income statement

▶ Reporting unusual gains and losses in the income statement

● ● ● ● ● ● ● ● ● ● ● ● ● ● ● ● ● ● ● ● ● ● ● ● ● ● ● ● ● ● ● ● ● ● ● ● ● ● ● ● ● ● ● ● ● ● ● ●

*I*n this chapter, I lift up the hood and investigate how the profit engine runs. Profit is the main financial goal of a business. Accountants are the professional profit-measurers in the business world — measuring profit is their expertise. I find profit accounting a fascinating challenge. You have to understand the way a business operates and its strategies to account for its profit. At first glance, making profit may seem fairly simple — sell stuff and control expenses. Bring in more dollars from sales revenue than the dollars paid out for expenses. The excess of revenue over expenses is profit. What's the big deal?

Well, making a profit and determining its amount isn't nearly as simple as you may think. Managers have the very demanding tasks of making sales and controlling expenses — and accountants have the tough tasks of measuring revenue and expenses and preparing profit reports that summarize the profit-making activities every period. Also, accountants are called on to explain to managers where profit went if the cash account doesn't increase by the same amount as profit — and it usually doesn't.

This chapter starts with a simple case in which the increase in cash is equal to profit — the business collects cash for all of its sales during the period and pays out cash for all of its expenses, and profit equals the cash left over. But alas, the business world is not so simple. So the chapter continues one step at a time to build a realistic profit model. Walking through this example lets you answer one very important question: At the end of the day, where exactly is your profit that you worked so hard to earn?

# Swooping Profit into One Basic Equation

For a business that sells products, its profit equation is simply sales revenue – expenses = profit, which almost always is reported in a vertical format like this:

| Basic Profit Equation | |
|---|---|
| Sales Revenue | $1,000,000 |
| Less Expenses | 940,000 |
| Equals Profit | $ 60,000 |

Profit, in short, equals what's left over from sales revenue after you deduct all expenses. (You never see the term *net sales revenue* instead of *profit.*) This business earned $60,000 on $1,000,000 total sales revenue for the period, which is 6 percent. Expenses used up 94 percent of sales revenue. Although it may seem rather thin, a 6 percent profit margin on sales is typical for many businesses — although some businesses consistently make a bottom-line profit of 10 to 20 percent of sales, and others are satisfied with a 1 or 2 percent profit margin on sales revenue. Normal profit ratios vary widely from industry to industry.

Businesses that sell services instead of products also use the term *sales revenue* for *gross income* (total income before deducting expenses) from sales of their services — but you also see variations on this term. Businesses that don't sell anything as such — financial institutions that earn investment income, for example — use other terms for their gross income.

Notice the following points about the basic profit equation:

✔ Even though you're deducting expenses from sales revenue, you generally don't use a minus sign or parentheses to indicate that the expense amount is a negative number (although some people do).

✔ Using a double underline under the profit number is common practice but not universal. Some people use bold type. You generally don't see anything as garish as a fat arrow pointing to the profit number or a big smiley encircling the profit number — but again, tastes vary.

✔ Profit isn't usually called *profit.* It's called *net income* or the *bottom line* or — particularly on financial reports intended for people outside the business — *net earnings.* (Can't accountants agree on *anything?*) Through-out this book, I use the terms *net income* and *profit* pretty much interchangeably.

✔ *Sales revenue* is the total amount of money or other assets received from sales of the company's products for the entire year. The number used in the profit equation represents all sales — you can't tell how many different sales were made, how many different customers the company sold products to, or how the sales were distributed over the 12 months of the year.

Sales revenue is strictly what belongs to the business and doesn't include money that anyone else can claim (for example, sales tax that the business collects from customers and then remits to the government).

*Note:* A business may have other sources of income in addition to the sales revenue from its products. One common alternative source of income is interest or other return earned on investments the company makes. In the profit report, investment income goes on a separate line and is not included with sales revenue — to make clear that this source of income is secondary to the mainstream sales revenue of the business.

✔ *Expenses* consist of a wide variety of costs of operating the business and making sales, starting with the cost of the goods (products) sold to the customers and including many other costs of operating the business:

- Payroll costs (wages, salaries, and benefits paid to employees)
- Insurance costs
- Property taxes on buildings and land
- Cost of gas and electric utilities
- Telephone and Internet charges
- Depreciation of operating assets that last more than one year (such as buildings, cars and trucks, computers, office furniture, tools and machinery, and shelving)
- Advertising and sales promotion costs
- Office supplies
- Legal and audit costs
- Interest paid on loans
- Income taxes

As is the case with sales revenue, you can't tell from the amount reported as an expense how much was spent on each component making up the total. For example, the total depreciation expense amount doesn't tell you how much was for buildings and how much was for trucks.

## The P word

I'm sure you won't be surprised to hear that the financial objective of every business is to make profit. In the pursuit of profit, a business should behave ethically, stay within the law, care for its employees, and be friendly to the environment. I don't mean to preach here. But the blunt truth of the matter is that *profit* is a dirty word to many people, and the profit motive is a favorite target of many critics, who blame it for unsafe working conditions, exploitation of child labor, wages that are below the poverty line, and other ills of the economic system. The profit motive is blamed for how incomes and wealth are distributed in our economic system as well.

Businesses should find that earning profit by doing things the right way rather than by cutting corners is in their own interest. But even on their best behavior, businesses will continue to come under the fire of criticism for the profit motive. It's an easy target.

You hear a lot about the profit motive of business, but you hardly ever see the *P* word in external financial reports. In the financial press, the most common term you see instead is *earnings*. Both *The Wall Street Journal* and *The New York Times* cover the profit performance of public corporations and use the term *earnings reports*. If you look in financial statements, the term *net income* is used most often for the bottom-line profit that a business earns. Accountants prefer *net income,* although they also use other names, like *net earnings* and *net operating earnings*.

In short, *profit* is more of a street name; in polite company, you generally say *net income*.

By the way, notice that only one total is shown for all the business's expenses — to keep the profit equation as short as possible. However, when preparing a formal profit report — which is called an *income statement* — expenses are broken down into several basic categories. (See "Reporting Profit to Managers and Investors: The Income Statement" at the end of the chapter.)

# Measuring the Financial Effects of Profit-Making Activities

In the basic profit equation example introduced earlier in this chapter, a business earned $60,000 net income for the year. That means it's $60,000 richer now, right? Well, that could happen in a make-believe world, and I start this section with a hypothetical profit example in which the business checking account *does* increase by $60,000 — but this example is extremely oversimplified. In the real world, nothing is that simple.

The financial effects of making profit go far beyond a fatter bank account. To get a clear picture, a balance sheet equation is handy to sort out the various effects. The general format of the balance sheet equation (also called the *accounting equation*) is as follows:

```
Assets = liabilities + owners' equity
```

See Chapter 2 for more information about this equation.

Making a profit increases the assets of a business. Assets also increase when the owners invest money in the business and when the business borrows money. These two types of increases in assets are not profit. Profit is the net increase of assets from sales revenue less expenses, not from borrowing and not from its owners investing capital in the business.

Most businesses do not distribute all of their annual profit to their owners; they could, but they don't. Instead, the increase in assets from making profit is used to expand the resource base of the business. Profit not distributed is called *retained earnings.* The nature of retained earnings is shown the following rearrangement of the balance sheet equation:

```
Assets - liabilities - invested capital = retained earnings
```

# So why is it called retained earnings?

The retained earnings account, like all balance sheet accounts, reports the net balance in the account after recording both the increases and the decreases in the account through the end of the period. The retained earnings account increases when the business makes a profit and then decreases when the business distributes some of the profit to the owners. That is, the total amount of profit paid out to the owners is recorded as a decrease in the retained earnings account. (Exactly how the profit is divided among the owners depends on the ownership structure of the business — see Chapter 11.)

**Bonus question:** Why doesn't a business pay out all its profit to owners? One reason is that the business may not have converted all its profit into cash by the end of the year and may not have enough cash to distribute the profit to the owners. (In fact, the increase in cash seldom equals the amount of profit.) Or the business may have had the cash but needed it for other purposes, such as growing the company by buying new buildings and equipment or spending the money on research and development of new products. Reinvesting the profit in the business in this way is often referred to as *plowing back* earnings. A business should always make good use of its profit cash flow instead of letting the cash pile up in the cash account. See Chapter 7 for more on cash flow from profit.

The key idea here is that if you start with total assets and then take away how much of the assets came from liabilities and how much was invested by the owners, the remainder must have come from retained earnings. For example, if a business has $6 million in assets, $2 million in liabilities, and $3 million in invested capital, the remaining $1 million must be due to retained earnings.

The retained earnings account is *not* — I repeat, *not* — an asset, even though its name may suggest otherwise. It is a *source*-of-assets account, not an asset account. See the "So why is it called retained earnings?" sidebar for more information about the retained earnings account.

The profit-making activities of a business affect several assets and also some liabilities — not the kind recorded when borrowing money (interest-bearing debt), but the kind recorded for expenses that have not been paid immediately. The accounts used to record unpaid expenses are referred to as *operating liabilities.* Interest is paid on debt (borrowed money), but not on operating liabilities. The term *operating* simply refers to the sales and expense operations of a business that are necessary for making profit.

An example: During a period, a business records the full cost of all wages and benefits that its employees earn. The full cost is the correct amount of expense to record in the period to measure profit for the period. But at the end of the period, some part of this total cost has not been paid. The unpaid balance of the total cost is recorded in an operating liability account.

## Preparing the balance sheet equation

Each asset of a business is different from the others, but cash is in a class by itself. Furthermore, the cash flow aspects of profit are receiving a great deal of attention these days — almost to the level of being an equal concern with profit itself. So separating assets into cash and noncash assets is useful. Moreover, separating liabilities into operating liabilities and borrowed money (generally referred to as *debt*) is useful, and separating owners' equity into invested capital and retained earnings is useful. This six-fold subdivision of the balance sheet equation looks like this:

```
Cash + noncash assets = operating liabilities + debt +
            invested capital + retained earnings
```

On the one hand, this expansion of the balance sheet equation helps clarify the different types of assets, liabilities, and owners' equity. On the other hand, for exploring the profit-making process, debt and invested capital are not needed because revenue and expenses do not involve these two types of accounts. Debt and invested capital are excess baggage for the following journey through the profit-making process of a business. So to simplify the equation, assume that the business has no debt and no invested capital (not realistic, but very convenient here). Thus the balance sheet equation that I use in the following sections is as follows:

**Cash + Noncash Assets = Operating Liabilities + Retained Earnings**

A simple, all-cash example to start things off: Suppose your business collected all sales revenue for the year immediately in cash and paid all expenses for the year immediately in cash. Your profit for the year was $60,000. Here's how that profit affects the financial condition of your business (to simplify, dollar signs are not used):

**Cash + Noncash Assets = Operating Liabilities + Retained Earnings**

| | |
|---|---|
| +60,000 | +60,000 |

The cash asset account increases by $60,000, which is the net difference between sales revenue and expenses — your business checking account balance is $60,000 higher at the end of the year than at the beginning of the year. (If you had distributed some of the profit, the balance of the retained earnings account would be the amount you distributed subtracted from $60,000, and your cash would be lower by the same amount.)

# Exploring the Profit-Making Process One Step at a Time

I don't mean to scare you off, but the profit picture gets more complex than the simple all-cash example just discussed. Many businesses sell their products on credit rather than cash, for example, and usually don't collect all their sales revenue by the end of the year. Some of the expenses for the year aren't paid by the end of the year, in other words. Each of the following steps adds a layer of reality, one at a time, to make the profit picture more realistic. The following sections start with the all-cash scenario as the point of departure and then make one change at a time to show you how the additional factor affects the balance sheet equation.

## Making sales on credit

If your business allows customers to buy its products or services on credit, you need to add an asset account called *accounts receivable,* which records the total amount owed to the business by its customers who made purchases "on the cuff" and haven't paid up yet. You probably wouldn't have collected all your receivables by the end of the year, especially for credit sales that occurred in the last weeks of the year. However, you still record the sales revenue and the cost-of-goods-sold expense for these sales in the year in which the sales occurred. The initial scenario in which all sales were collected in cash and all expenses were paid in cash is used as the point of reference in the following steps.

Your business had sales revenue of $1 million and total expenses of $940,000, all of which were paid by year-end, making for a bottom-line profit of $60,000. Now assume that $80,000 of the sales revenue came from credit sales that haven't yet been collected at the end of the year. Here's what the financial effects look like (for convenience, dollar signs in the balance sheet equation are not used):

| Cash | + | Noncash Assets | = | Operating Liabilities | + | Retained Earnings |
|---|---|---|---|---|---|---|
| +60,000 | | | | | | +60,000 |
| | | Accounts receivable | | | | |
| –80,000 | | +80,000 | | | | |

Note that the first line in the balance sheet equation (which is underlined) is from the initial all-cash scenario and serves as the point of reference. Everything in the new scenario is the same as in the all-cash scenario except for the changes shown below the line. Also note that the name of the specific noncash asset — in this case, accounts receivable — is entered in the balance sheet equation column. When a change in a noncash asset is entered in the balance sheet equation, the corresponding effect on cash is shown in the cash column.

The $80,000 of uncollected sales revenue at year-end has the effect of decreasing the cash you have by $80,000. Accounts receivable represents cash waiting in the wings to be collected in the near future (assuming that all your customers will pay their accounts receivable to you on time). But until the money is actually received, your business is without the $80,000 cash inflow. This situation may appear to be pretty serious. But hang on; there are several more steps to go.

Whether collected entirely in cash or not, the entire $1 million in sales revenue for the year is recorded and used to calculate profit. So bottom-line profit is $60,000 — the same as in the all-cash scenario. But the cash effects between the two scenarios are quite different. When making sales on credit, you count the sales in calculating your profit, even though the cash is not collected from customers until sometime later. This is one feature of the *accrual basis of accounting,* which is explained in Chapter 3. The accrual basis of accounting records revenue when sales are made and records expenses when these costs are incurred. When sales are made on credit, the accounts receivable asset account is increased; later, when cash is received from the customer, cash is increased and the accounts receivable account is decreased.

## Depreciation expense

*Depreciation expense accounting* is the method of spreading out the cost of a fixed asset instead of charging the entire cost to the year of purchase. That way, each year of use bears a share of the total cost. *Fixed assets* are long-lived operating assets — buildings, machinery, office equipment, vehicles, computers and data-processing equipment, shelving and cabinets, and so on. Of course, depreciation applies only to fixed assets that you buy, not those you rent or lease. (If you lease or rent fixed assets, which is quite common for some fixed assets, the rent you pay each month is charged to *rent expense.* Rent expense is the substitute for depreciation expense when you rent rather than buy your fixed assets.)

For example, cars and light trucks are depreciated over five years for income tax purposes. (Businesses apply the five-year rule to other kinds of assets as well.) The basic idea of depreciation is to charge a fraction of the total cost to depreciation expense for each of the five years. (The actual fraction each year depends on which method of depreciation you choose, which is explained in Chapter 13.)

---

### Appreciating the positive impact of depreciation on cash flow

Whereas making sales on credit does not generate immediate cash inflow and thus has a temporarily negative impact on your cash flow, depreciation is good news for cash flow. This concept gets a little complex, so stay with me here.

Fundamentally, a business sets its sales prices high enough to recover its expenses plus provide a profit. In a real sense, the business is passing on the cost of its fixed assets to its customers and recovering some of the cost of the fixed assets each year through sales revenue. A good example to illustrate this critical point is a taxicab driver who owns his cab. He sets his fares high enough to pay for his time; to pay for the insurance, license, gas, and oil; and to recover the cost of the cab. Included in each fare is a tiny fraction of the cost of the cab, which over the course of the year adds up to the depreciation expense that he passed on to his passengers and collected in fares. At the end of the year, he has collected a certain amount of money that pays him back for part of the cost of the cab.

In short, fixed assets are gradually *liquidated,* or turned back into cash, each year. Part of sales revenue recovers a fraction of the cost of fixed assets, which is why the decrease in the fixed assets account to record depreciation expense has the effect of increasing cash (assuming your sales revenue was collected in cash during the year). What the company does with this cash recovery is another matter. Sooner or later, you need to replace the fixed assets to continue in business. In this chapter, I do not look beyond the cash recovery of part of the original cost invested in the fixed asset.

Suppose your $940,000 total of expenses for the year includes $25,000 depreciation for fixed assets. (You bought these assets for $125,000 and are charging one-fifth of the cost each year for five years.) But you didn't actually pay anything for the fixed assets this year — you bought the assets in previous years. Depreciation is a real expense, but not a *cash outlay* expense after the fixed assets are already bought and paid for. (See the "Appreciating the positive impact of depreciation on cash flow" sidebar if you're confused about this point.)

Here's what the financial effects of depreciation expense look like:

| Cash | + | Noncash Assets | = | Operating Liabilities | + | Retained Earnings |
|---|---|---|---|---|---|---|
| +60,000 | | | | | | +60,000 |
| | | Fixed assets | | | | |
| +25,000 | | –25,000 | | | | |

Compared with the cash flow effects of accounts receivable, depreciation is good news. Let me put it this way: If all sales revenue had been collected and all expenses except depreciation had been paid during the year, your cash would have increased $85,000. The company would have realized $60,000 from your profit-making activities plus the $25,000 depreciation recovery during the year. The positive impact of depreciation on cash is just the prelude. Next in line are the favorable cash flow effects of unpaid expenses.

## Unpaid expenses

A typical business pays many expenses after the period benefited by the expense. For example, your business hires a law firm that does a lot of legal work for the company during the year, but you don't pay the bill until the following year. Your business may match retirement contributions made by employees, but you may not pay your share until the following year. Or your business may have unpaid bills for telephone, gas, electricity, and water that it has used during the year.

Accountants use three different types of operating liability accounts to record a business's unpaid expenses:

> ✓ **Accounts payable:** For items that the business buys on credit and for which it receives an invoice (a bill). For example, your business receives an invoice from its lawyers for legal work done. As soon as you receive the invoice, you record in the accounts payable liability account the amount that you owe. Later, when you pay the invoice, you subtract that amount from the accounts payable account — and your cash goes down by the same amount, of course.

✔ **Accrued expenses payable:** For unpaid costs that a business generally has to estimate because it doesn't receive an invoice for them. Examples of accrued expenses are unused vacation and sick days that your employees carry over to the following year, which you will have to pay for in the coming year; unpaid bonuses to salespeople; the cost of future repairs and part replacements on products that customers have bought and haven't yet returned for repair; and the daily accumulation of interest on borrowed money that won't be paid until the end of the loan period.

As you can imagine, without invoices to refer to, you have to examine your business operations carefully to determine which liabilities of this sort to record.

✔ **Income tax payable:** For income taxes that a business still owes to the IRS. At the end of the year, your business may not have paid all its income tax expense for the year — it may still owe a fraction to the IRS. You record the unpaid amount in the income tax payable account, and you record the full amount of the income tax on the taxable income earned for the year (including the paid and unpaid portions) as an expense. In other words, the income tax expense for the year is the total amount based on the taxable income for the entire year — the large part of which is paid by year-end, but a small part of which is still unpaid at year-end. This unpaid part is recorded in the income tax payable liability account.

*Note:* A business may be organized legally as a *pass-through tax entity* for income tax purposes, which means that it doesn't pay income tax itself but instead passes its taxable income on to its owners. Chapter 11 explains these types of business entities. This example assumes that your business is an ordinary (or C) corporation that pays income tax.

Your business has each of the three operating liabilities I just listed. Some of your total expenses for the year are unpaid at year-end — part in the accounts payable account, part in the accrued expenses payable account, and part in the income tax payable account. Here's what the financial effects of your unpaid expenses look like in the balance sheet equation:

| Cash | + | Noncash Assets | = | Operating Liabilities | + | Retained Earnings |
|---|---|---|---|---|---|---|
| +60,000 | | | | | | +60,000 |
| +30,000 | | | | Accounts payable +30,000 | | |
| +35,000 | | | | Accrued expenses payable +35,000 | | |
| +5,000 | | | | Income tax payable +5,000 | | |

The total of these three unpaid operating liabilities is $70,000 ($30,000 accounts payable + $35,000 accrued expenses + $5,000 income tax payable). Your balance sheet would report these liabilities because they are claims against the business. You may think that liabilities are bad, but for cash flow, liabilities are good. Your business has not yet paid $70,000 of the expenses for the year, and your cash balance is higher by this amount — you get to hang onto the cash until you pay the liabilities. Of course, you have to pay these liabilities next year, but isn't it nice to have your balance sheet show a big, fat cash increase for this year even though you have to show the liabilities as well?

## Prepaid expenses

*Prepaid expenses* are the opposite of unpaid expenses. For example, a business buys fire insurance and general liability insurance (in case a customer who slips on a wet floor or is insulted by a careless salesperson sues the business). You pay insurance premiums ahead of time, before the period in which you're covered, but you charge that expense to the actual period benefited. At the end of the year, the business may be only halfway through the insurance coverage period, so it charges off only half the premium cost as an expense (for a six-month policy, you charge one-sixth of the premium cost to each of the six months covered). So at the time you pay the premium, you charge the entire amount to the prepaid expenses asset account, and for each month of coverage, you transfer the appropriate fraction of the cost to the insurance expense account.

Another example of when to use a prepaid expenses asset account is when your business pays cash to stock up on office supplies that it may not use for several months. You record the cost in the prepaid expenses asset account at the time of purchase; then, when you finally use the supplies, you subtract the amount from the prepaid expenses asset account and add the expense to the office supplies expense account.

Using the prepaid expenses asset account is not so much for the purpose of reporting all the assets of a business, because the balance in the account compared with other assets and total assets is typically small. Rather, using this account is an example of allocating costs to expenses in the period benefited by the costs and not necessarily in the period in which the business pays for the costs.

Your business has prepaid some expenses, like the examples just discussed. Here's what the financial effects of your prepaid expenses look like in the balance sheet equation:

| Cash | + | Noncash Assets | = | Operating Liabilities | + | Retained Earnings |
|---|---|---|---|---|---|---|
| +60,000 | | | | | | +60,000 |
| | | Prepaid expenses | | | | |
| −15,000 | | +15,000 | | | | |

The buildup of prepaid expenses has a negative impact on the business's cash. In other words, you had to write checks for the prepaid expenses, so your cash balance is smaller. The prepayment of these expenses lays the groundwork for continuing your operations seamlessly into next year. What it comes down to is that certain costs of your profit-making operations must be paid in advance — you don't have a choice. Remember that although your business is $15,000 cash poorer, profit remains the same ($60,000) as it is in all the previous scenarios.

# Inventory and cost of goods sold expense

*Cost of goods sold* is one of the primary expenses of businesses that sell products. It's just what its name implies: the cost that a business paid for the products it sells to customers. A business makes profit by setting its sales prices high enough to cover the actual costs of products sold, the costs of operating the business, interest on borrowed money, and income taxes (assuming that the business pays income tax), with something left over for profit.

When the business acquires a product, the cost of the product goes into an *inventory asset account* (and, of course, the cost is either deducted from the cash account or added to the accounts payable liability account, depending on whether the business paid with cash or bought on credit). When a customer buys that product, the business transfers the cost of the product from the inventory asset account to the cost-of-goods-sold expense account because the product is no longer in the business's inventory; the product has been delivered to the customer.

The first step in determining profit for the period is deducting the cost-of-goods-sold expense from the sales revenue for the goods sold. Most income statements report the cost of goods sold as a separate expense (refer to "Reporting Profit to Managers and Investors: The Income Statement," later in this chapter).

So assume that your business did, in fact, start the year with a sizeable stock of products, whose cost is recorded in the inventory asset account. As your business sold the products early in the year, the cost of the goods sold was removed from the inventory account, and that cost was charged to expense.

Your business sells products, so you need to have a stock of products on hand to sell to your customers. This stockpile of goods on the shelves waiting to be sold (or in storage space in the backroom) is called *inventory*. When you drive by an auto dealer and see all the cars, SUVs, and pickup trucks waiting to be sold, remember that these products are called inventory. The cost of unsold products (goods held in inventory) is not charged to expense until the products are actually sold. In this way, the cost-of-goods-sold expense is correctly matched against the sales revenue from the goods sold.

During the year, you increased the number of products offered for sale. Therefore, your total purchases of products during the year was $55,000 more than your total cost of goods sold. In other words, you increased the size of your inventory by $55,000 cost. The financial effects of your ending inventory increase in the balance sheet equation are as follows:

| Cash | + | Noncash Assets | = | Operating Liabilities | + | Retained Earnings |
|------|---|------|---|------|---|------|
| +60,000 | | | | | | +60,000 |
| | | Inventory | | | | |
| −55,000 | | +55,000 | | | | |

You not only replaced the products sold to customers during the year, but you also bought additional products that cost $55,000. This inventory buildup requires cash — notice the $55,000 drain on cash. Your increase in inventory may be a smart move, but it did use $55,000 in cash.

An increase in the accounts payable liability account may provide part of the inventory increase because businesses that have established good credit histories can buy their inventory on credit. However, I didn't want to add another change in the accounts payable account. And in most situations, a good part of the inventory increase would have to be paid for by the end of the year.

# So Where's Your Hard-Earned Profit?

As a business manager, not only should you make profit, but you should also understand and manage the financial effects of profit. In particular, understand that profit does not simply mean an increase in cash. Sales revenue and expenses, the two factors of profit, affect many assets and operating liabilities — making sales on credit impacts accounts receivable, expenses paid in advance impact prepaid assets, unpaid expenses impact operating liabilities, and so on. You simply can't have expenses without a smorgasbord of changes in assets and operating liabilities.

Knowing how much profit your business made isn't enough. You need to take another step and ask, "Did the profit generate an increase in cash equal to the profit, and because it hardly ever does, where is the rest of the profit?"

So far, I've looked at each step along the reality road separately, as if it were the only change from the simple cash basis example. Now I assemble all the steps together that I've analyzed since starting with the simple all-cash example. In reading the following summary, remember that increases in assets hurt your cash balance, but that increases in operating liabilities help your cash balance:

### Summary of Changes During Year in Noncash Assets and Operating Liabilities

| Changes in Noncash Assets: | | |
|---|---|---|
| Accounts receivable | +$80,000 | |
| Inventory | +$55,000 | |
| Prepaid expenses | +$15,000 | |
| Fixed assets | –$25,000 | |
| Net increase in non-cash assets | | $125,000 |
| **Changes in Operating Liabilities:** | | |
| Accounts payable | +$30,000 | |
| Accrued expenses payable | +$35,000 | |
| Income tax payable | +$5,000 | |
| Increase of operating liabilities | | 70,000 |
| Net decrease in cash balance during year | | $55,000 |

My purpose right now is simply to explain that $55,000 of your profit for the year is not found in an increase in cash, but rather consists of the changes in noncash assets and operating liabilities. Profit is a mixture, or you could say a smorgasbord, of changes in the assets and operating liabilities that are an integral part of the profit-making process.

If it isn't in cash, where is it? The following schedule summarizes the changes in your noncash assets and operating liabilities caused by the profit-making steps I showed you earlier in this chapter:

| Changes in Noncash Assets | | |
|---|---|---|
| Accounts receivable | +80,000 | |
| Inventory | +55,000 | |
| Prepaid expenses | +15,000 | |
| Fixed assets | −25,000 | |
| Net increase of assets | | +125,000 |
| **Changes in Operating Liabilities** | | |
| Accounts payable | +30,000 | |
| Accrued expenses payable | +35,000 | |
| Income tax payable | +5,000 | |
| Less increase of operating liabilities | | −70,000 |
| Noncash components of profit | | +55,000 |

*Note:* The amounts shown in this summary are the *changes* — the increases and decreases — in the accounts caused by the sales revenue and expense transactions of your business during the year.

And there you have the story of the $60,000 profit — equal to the $5,000 increase of cash plus the $125,000 increase of noncash assets minus the $70,000 increase in operating liabilities. Probably your biggest surprise here is that, even though your business earned $60,000 in profit for the year, your cash balance increased only $5,000. In managing your profit-making activities (sales revenue and expenses) during the year, you caused cash and three other assets to increase, one asset to decrease, and three operating liabilities to increase. Notice that I've put the onus on you, the owner or manager of the business. The point is that these increases and decreases don't happen automatically — they are the result of management decisions.

By the by, you may not like referring to expenses as profit-making activity, but they are! The main point is that expenses (unless you're talking about totally wasteful expenditures like throwing money out the window) generate sales revenue. Advertising expense creates the incentive in customers to buy products sold by the business. Buying products at $60 cost per unit and selling them for $100 per unit generates $40 profit before other expenses are considered — even though the business has $60 of expense (cost of goods sold). Much of business profit-making is built on the model of incurring, say, $90 in expenses to generate, say, $100 in sales revenue.

Isn't profit simpler than what I just explained? Well, no, not really. Making profit in a highly sophisticated economic system is somewhat involved, to put it mildly. The earning of profit drives the several changes in assets and operating liabilities that you see in this summary.

---

## The mark-to-market method of accounting

*Financial statement* accounting, what this book is mainly concerned with, records the actual revenue and expense transactions and operations of a business and, generally speaking, does not record market value increases in the assets of a business. The basic alternative to this accounting model is the *mark-to-market* method, which goes like this: You record market values of assets and liabilities at the end of each year and compare the year-end net value with the net value a year ago. The increase (or decrease) in the net value equals profit for the year (not counting any additional capital investment by the owners and adding back any distributions of profit to the owners). The mark-to-market accounting method depends heavily on having readily available, reliable, and accurate market values for assets. This is realistic for a mutual fund that invests only in marketable securities.

One benefit of the mark-to-market method is that the balance sheet is up-to-date and not "contaminated" with historical costs of some assets (such as fixed assets in particular) that may be lower than the assets' current market or replacement values. If a business or investment venture makes profit from the appreciation of assets that are held for sale, then the mark-to-market method makes sense — assuming that current market values can be determined.

*Caution:* This method is not practical or appropriate for businesses that sell products and services, because these businesses do not stand ready to sell their assets (other than inventory); they need their assets for operating the business in the future. At the end of their useful lives, assets are sold for their disposable values (or traded in for new assets).

---

Other transactions also change the assets, debt, and owners' equity accounts of a business — such as borrowing money and buying new fixed assets. The balance sheet, in other words, is changed by all the business's transactions. The profit-making transactions (sales and expenses) are the main transactions changing the balance sheet, but many other transactions are recorded in the asset, liability, and owners' equity accounts. Therefore, a separate summary of the profit-making transactions — limited to sales revenue and expenses — that ends with the profit for the period is a standard part of a complete financial report. This separate profit report is called the *income statement.*

# Reporting Profit to Managers and Investors: The Income Statement

At the end of each period, the accountant prepares a profit report called an *income statement.* You may think that the report would be called the *net income statement* because the bottom-line profit term preferred by accountants is *net income* — but the word *net* is dropped off the title. Other variations of the term are also used, such as *statement of operating results* and *statement of earnings.* Traditionally, the income statement has been called the *profit and loss statement,* or simply the *P&L* — although in external financial reports, very few businesses use this term for the income statement, and accountants generally dislike this term.

The income statement reports the business's sales and expense transactions for the period, with the final profit result on the bottom line. These transactions are *inflows* and *outflows:* Sales revenue is an inflow, and expenses are outflows. Profit, the bottom line, is the *net* inflow. Please note that I didn't say "*cash* flow." Making profit involves the inflows and outflows of many assets other than cash, as demonstrated in the steps in the profit-making process examined earlier in the chapter. In the business example earlier in the chapter, the earning of profit involved cash and four other asset accounts as well as three operating liabilities.

The annual income statement included in an external financial report that circulates outside a business has two basic sections (or *layers*):

- ✔ The first section presents the usual, ordinary, continuing sales and expense operations of the business for the year.

- ✔ The second section presents any unusual, extraordinary, and non-recurring gains and losses that the business recorded in the year.

However, a business that didn't experience any extraordinary gains or losses wouldn't include that second section in its income statement — its income statement would consist simply of the first section.

## *Reporting normal, ongoing profit-making operations*

The top section of an income statement (which is the only section of the income statement if the business doesn't have extraordinary gains or losses to report) typically breaks down total expenses for the year into at least four basic classes. (Refer to the sample income statement at the end of this section for an example.)

- ✔ **Cost-of-goods-sold-expense:** The cost of the products sold to customers for which the company received the sales revenue reported on the first line of the income statement. The profit line following the deduction of this expense from sales revenue is called *gross margin* (or *gross profit*) — that's your profit before you factor in the other expenses.

  *Note:* Companies that sell services rather than products (airlines, movie theaters, CPA firms, and so on) do not have a cost-of-goods-sold expense line in their income statements.

✔ **Sales, administrative, and general expenses:** A broad, catchall category for all expenses except those reported on the other lines in the income statement. This expense combines such things as legal fees, the president's salary, advertising costs, travel and entertainment costs, and much more — probably including some of the company's dirty laundry buried deep within.

The next profit line, which is generally called *earnings before interest and tax* and abbreviated EBIT, is the result after deducting the sales, administrative, and general expenses from gross margin.

✔ **Interest expense:** Interest paid on borrowed money (applies only to businesses that have borrowed money, obviously). This expense is usually reported on a separate line even though it may be relatively small. The profit line after deducting interest expense from earnings before interest and tax is typically called *earnings before income tax* or something similar. (Unfortunately, accounting terminology is not entirely uniform and standardized; you see variations from business to business.)

✔ **Income tax expense:** Income taxes paid by the business, *not* including property and employer payroll taxes, which are included in the sales, administrative, and general expenses line. Income tax expense is always reported on a separate line. The final profit line, the bottom line after you deduct income tax, is called *net income* — the bottom-line profit figure, unless the business has extraordinary gains and losses to report. If so, the nonrecurring gains and losses are included to get down to the bottom line.

*Note:* Chapter 11 explains that a business may be organized as a *pass-through tax entity,* which means that it does not pay income tax itself but instead passes its taxable income through to its owners, who end up paying the income tax.

To close the business example that I've been using throughout this chapter, here is your annual income statement:

**Annual Income Statement for the Example**

| | |
|---|---|
| Sales revenue | +1,000,000 |
| Cost of goods sold expense | –600,000 |
| Gross margin | +400,000 |
| Sales, administrative, and general expenses | –285,000 |
| Earnings before interest and income tax | +115,000 |
| Interest expense | –25,000 |
| Earnings before income tax | +90,000 |
| Income tax expense | –30,000 |
| Net income | +60,000 |

Here are two key points to keep in mind about income statements:

✔ The income statement format that I discuss here is what you find in *external* reports released outside the business that are directed to its absentee owners who do not participate in the day-to-day management of the business. If you owned shares in General Motors, for example, this is the sort of income statement you would receive. The external income statement does not provide the level of detail about sales revenue and expenses needed for management purposes. (Refer to Chapter 9 for more information about what type of information and format managers should request when they want to analyze profit.) Managers must have reports that drill down to the relevant detail they need to make specific decisions and for control purposes. The external income statement is a fairly condensed summary.

✔ The income statement does not report the financial effects of sales revenue and expenses — the increases and decreases in the assets and operating liabilities that revenue and expenses cause. Readers of the profit report have to look at the balance sheet to see the assets and liabilities of the business. Actually, the cash flow statement that Chapter 7 explains is the link between the income statement and the balance sheet. In short, the income statement is not really a standalone financial statement; you have to put it into the financial context of the business's other two primary financial statements: the balance sheet and the cash flow statement.

## Reporting unusual gains and losses

The road to profit is anything but smooth and straight. Every business experiences an occasional *discontinuity* — a serious disruption that comes out of the blue, doesn't happen regularly or often, and can dramatically affect bottom-line profit. In other words, a discontinuity is something that disturbs the basic continuity of business operations — the regular flow of profit-making activities.

Here are some examples of discontinuities:

✔ **Downsizing and restructuring the business:** Layoffs require severance pay or early retirement costs; major segments of the business may be disposed of at large losses.

✔ **Abandoning product lines:** When you decide to discontinue selling a line of products, you lose at least some of the money that you paid for obtaining or manufacturing the products, either because you sell the products for less than you paid or because you just get rid of the products you can't sell.

✔ **Settling lawsuits and other legal actions:** Damages and fines that you pay — as well as damages that you *receive* in a favorable ruling — are obviously nonrecurring extraordinary losses or gains (unless you're in the habit of being taken to court every year).

✔ **Writing down (also called *writing off*) damaged and impaired assets:** If your products become damaged and unsellable, or your fixed assets need to be replaced unexpectedly, you need to remove these items from the assets account. Even if certain assets are in good physical condition, if they lose their ability to generate future sales or other benefits to the business, accounting rules say that the assets have to be taken off the books or at least written down.

✔ **Changing accounting methods:** A business may decide to use different methods for recording revenue and expenses than it did in the past, in some cases because the accounting rules (set by the authoritative accounting governing bodies) have changed. Often, the new method requires a business to record a large expense or loss that had not been recognized in previous years.

✔ **Correcting errors from previous financial reports:** If you or your accountant discover that a past financial report had an accounting error, you can't very well revise and reissue that financial report. So you do a catch-up correction in the current financial report instead, which means that you record a loss or gain that had nothing to do with your performance this year.

With all these extraordinary losses and gains, how can you distinguish the profit that a business earned from its normal revenue and expense activities from profit caused by other forces entirely? This is one case where accounting rules are actually working *for you,* the non-accountant reader of financial reports.

According to financial reporting standards, a business must make these one-time losses and gains very visible in the income statement. So in addition to the normal part of the income statement, which reports normal profit activities, a business with unusual, extraordinary losses or gains must add a second layer to the income statement to report on *these* happenings.

If a business has no unusual gains or losses in the year, its income statement ends with one bottom line, usually called *net income.* When an income statement includes a second layer, that line becomes *net income from continuing operations before unusual gains and losses.* Below this line, those unusual gains and losses appear for each significant, nonrecurring gain or loss.

Say that a business suffered a relatively minor loss from quitting a product line and a very large loss from adopting a new accounting standard. Here's what the second layer of this business's income statement looks like:

| | |
|---|---|
| Net income from continuing operations | +267,000,000 |
| Discontinued operations, net of applicable income taxes | −20,000,000 |
| Earnings before cumulative effect of changes in accounting principles | +247,000,000 |
| Cumulative effect of changes in accounting principles, net of applicable income taxes | −456,000,000 |
| Net earnings (loss) | −209,000,000 |

What new accounting standards could possibly cause a $456 million charge? A very likely scenario could be that this charge is the result of the Financial Accounting Standards Board (FASB) changing the way a business records medical benefits to retired employees. This business probably hadn't been recording those benefits all along, while the employees were still working (see Chapter 13 for more about recording these kinds of future expenses). For a mature business with many retired employees, the accumulated cost for those benefits could quite conceivably reach that high.

The gains and losses reported in the second layer of the external income statement are generally complex and are not always fully explained in the financial report. So where does that leave you? As I advise in Chapter 14, your best bet is to seek the counsel of expert financial report readers — financial reports are, for all practical purposes, designed for an audience of stockbrokers, sophisticated readers of *The Wall Street Journal,* and the like, so don't feel bad that you can't understand a report without a degree in accounting-ese.

Even if you have someone else analyze a two-layer income statement for you, you should be aware of controversial issues that extraordinary losses or gains raise. To really get some respect from your stockbroker or from Joe in Accounting, ask these questions about an unusual loss that a business reports:

- Were the annual profits reported in prior years overstated?
- Why wasn't the loss recorded on a more piecemeal and gradual year-by-year basis instead of as a one-time charge?
- Was the loss really a surprising and sudden event that could not have been anticipated?
- Will such a loss occur again in the future?

Every company that stays in business for more than a couple of years experiences a discontinuity of one sort or another. But beware of a business that takes advantage of discontinuities in either of the following ways:

✔ **Discontinuities become "continuities":** This business makes an extraordinary loss or gain a regular feature on its income statement. Every year or so, the business loses a major lawsuit, abandons product lines, or restructures itself. It reports "nonrecurring" gains or losses from the same source on a recurring basis every year.

✔ **A discontinuity becomes an opportunity to dump all sorts of write-downs and losses:** When recording an unusual loss (such as settling a lawsuit), the business opts to record other losses at the same time — everything but the kitchen sink (and sometimes that, too) gets written off. This *big-bath theory* says that you may as well take a big bath now in order to avoid taking little showers in the future.

Obviously, a business may just have the bad (or good) luck of experiencing certain discontinuities on a regular basis. And if you're facing a major, unavoidable expense this year, cleaning out all your other expenses in the same year so you can start off fresh next year can be a clever, legitimate accounting tactic. But these accounting practices come uncomfortably close to profit manipulation, accounting gimmickry, and fraud. All I can advise you to do is stay alert to these potential problems. And if you have reason to believe that a business is using questionable accounting practices, remember that you have the ultimate power: Use your buy-and-sell decisions as your vote against this kind of behavior.

## Putting the income statement in perspective

The income statement occupies center stage; the bright spotlight is on this financial statement because it reports profit or loss for the period. But think of the three primary financial statements — the other two being the balance sheet and the cash flow statement — as a three-ring circus. The income statement may draw the most attention, but you have to watch what's going on in all three places. As important as profit is to the financial success of a business, the income statement is not an island unto itself. To understand and manage profit, managers have to follow through to the financial effects of revenue and expenses on the assets and liabilities of the business and pay particular attention to cash flow, which Chapter 7 explores.

The term *financial report* is the umbrella term referring to a complete set of financial statements. Financial statements are supplemented with footnotes and other commentary from a business's managers. If the financial statements have been audited, the CPA firm includes a short report stating whether the financial statements follow generally accepted accounting principles. Most financial reports, even by small businesses, are bound between two covers.

A financial report can be anywhere from 5 pages to more than 50 pages to even 100 pages for very large, publicly owned business corporations. More and more public corporations make their annual financial reports available on their Web sites. (You can guess the Web address from the name or nickname of the company.)

The term *financial statement* refers to one of the following three key summaries prepared periodically by every business:

- **Income statement:** Summarizes sales revenue and expenses and ends with the net income (profit) earned for the period, or the loss suffered for the period

- **Balance sheet:** Summarizes the balances in the business's assets, liabilities, and owners' equity accounts at the close of the period

- **Cash flow statement:** Summarizes the sources and uses of cash during the period

The annual financial report of a business must include all three of these financial statements. Some businesses also prepare other schedules and summaries of a more limited focus that may also be called a financial statement — but in this book, the term *financial statement* refers only to the three primary financial statements that I just listed.

In response to contractual or regulatory requirements, some businesses issue special financial reports that do not include a complete set of financial statements with all footnote disclosures, or that adopt other than generally accepted accounting principles for certain matters. The distribution of these special financial reports is limited to specific parties. These special reports should be distinguished from the *general-purpose* financial reports that are distributed to the owners and creditors of the business based on generally accepted accounting principles (GAAP).

# Chapter 6

# The Balance Sheet from the
# Income Statement Viewpoint

. . . . . . . . . . . . . . . . . . . . . . . . . . . . . . . . . . . . . . . .

### In This Chapter

▶ Coupling the income statement with the balance sheet

▶ Seeing how sales revenue and expenses drive assets and liabilities

▶ Sizing up assets and liabilities

▶ Drawing the line between debt and owners' equity

▶ Grouping short-term assets and liabilities to determine solvency

▶ Understanding costs and other balance sheet values

. . . . . . . . . . . . . . . . . . . . . . . . . . . . . . . . . . . . . . . .

*T*his chapter explores one of the three primary financial statements reported by businesses — the *balance sheet,* or, to be more formal, the *statement of financial condition.* This key financial statement may seem to stand alone — like an island to itself — because it's presented on a separate page in a financial report. In fact, the assets and liabilities reported in a balance sheet are driven mainly by the transactions the business engages in to make profit. These sale and expense transactions of a business are summarized for a period in its *income statement,* which is explained in Chapter 5.

You've probably heard the expression that it takes money to make money. For a business it takes *assets* to make profit. This chapter identifies the particular assets needed to make profit. Also, the chapter identifies the particular liabilities involved in the pursuit of profit. Accounting for profit would be a lot simpler if all sales were made for cash and if all expenses were paid in cash in the same period that sales are made. But life in the business world is not so simple. Accounting for profit requires accounting for increases and decreases of several assets and liabilities. Profit accounting, in other words, requires balance sheet accounting. You can't separate the two; they are like Siamese twins.

In brief, a business needs a lot of assets to open its doors and to carry on its profit-making activities — making sales and operating the business day-to-day. For example, companies that sell products need to carry an *inventory* of products that are available for delivery to customers when sales are made.

A business can purchase products for its inventory on credit, and delay payment for the purchase (assuming it has a good credit rating). In most cases, however, the business has to pay for these purchases before all the products have been sold — the inventory holding period is considerably longer than the credit period. The business needs cash to pay for its inventory purchases. Where does the cash come from?

In fact a business needs many more assets than only inventory. Where does the money for these assets come from? Assets are the first act of a two-act play. The second act looks at where the money comes from, or the *sources of capital* for businesses. As Chapter 1 explains, the *balance sheet* of a business is the financial statement that reports its assets on one side and the sources of capital on the other side.

Of course, as I repeat throughout this book, you need to use all three primary financial statements to paint a business's complete financial picture. The *income statement* details sales revenue and expenses, which directly determine the amounts of assets (and two or three of the liabilities) that are summarized in the *balance sheet*. The *cash flow statement* answers the important question of how much of the profit has been converted to cash, and the company's other sources and uses of cash during the period.

This chapter connects sales revenue and expenses, which are reported in the income statement, with their corresponding assets and liabilities in the balance sheet. The chapter also explains the sources of capital that provide the money a business uses to invest in its assets.

# Coupling the Income Statement with the Balance Sheet

Sales revenue generates the inflow of assets and expenses cause the outflow of assets — and these increases and decreases in assets have to be recorded. Also, some expenses spawn short-term liabilities that have to be recorded. In short, accounting for profit involves much more than keeping track of cash inflows and outflows. Which specific assets and liabilities are directly involved in recording the sales revenue and expenses of a business? And how are these assets and liabilities reported in a business's balance sheet at the end of the profit period? These are the two main questions that this chapter answer.

This chapter explains how the profit-making transactions reported in the income statement connect with the assets (and some operating liabilities) reported in the balance sheet. I stress the dovetail fit between these two primary financial statements (the income statement and the balance sheet). And don't forget that business accounting also keeps track of where the money for the assets comes from — to invest in its assets, a business needs to raise money by borrowing and persuading owners to put money in the business. You shouldn't look at assets without also looking at where the money (the capital) for the assets comes from.

The *balance sheet,* or statement of financial condition, summarizes a business's assets, liabilities, and owners' equity at a point in time and, as shown in Chapter 5, can be summarized in the following equation:

| ASSETS | | LIABILITIES | | | OWNERS' EQUITY | |
|---|---|---|---|---|---|---|
| | Non-cash | Operating | | | Invested | Retained |
| Cash | + Assets = | Liabilities | + Debt | + | Capital | + Earnings |

Figure 6-1 shows a balance sheet for a fictitious company — not from left to right as shown in the accounting equation just above, but rather from top to bottom, which is a vertical expression of the accounting equation. This balance sheet is boiled down to the bare-bone essentials — please note that it would need a little tidying up before you'd want to show it off to the world in an external financial report (see Chapter 8).

| Assets | | |
|---|---|---|
| Cash | | $ 2,000,000 |
| Accounts Receivable | | $ 2,500,000 |
| Inventory | | $ 3,575,000 |
| Prepaid Expenses | | $ 480,000 |
| Fixed Assets (at Original cost) | $ 11,305,000 | |
| Accumulated Depreciation | $ (5,780,000) | $ 5,525,000 |
| Total | | $ 14,080,000 |

| Liabilities and Owners' Equity | | |
|---|---|---|
| Accounts Payable | $ 800,000 | |
| Accrued Expenses Payable | $ 1,200,000 | |
| Income Tax Payable | $ 80,000 | |
| Total Operating Liabilities | | $ 2,080,000 |
| Notes Payable (Interest-bearing debt) | | $ 5,000,000 |
| Owners' Invested Capital | | $ 2,000,000 |
| Retained Earnings | | $ 5,000,000 |
| Total | | $ 14,080,000 |

**Figure 6-1:** A balance sheet example showing a business's various assets, liabilities, and owners' equity.

A balance sheet doesn't have a punch line like the income statement does — the income statement's punch line being the net income line (which is rarely humorous to the business itself, but can cause some snickers among analysts). You can't look at just one item on the balance sheet, murmur an appreciative "ah-hah," and rush home to watch the game. You have to read the whole thing (sigh) and make comparisons among the items. See Chapters 8 and 14 for more information on interpreting financial statements.

At the most basic level, the best way to understand a balance sheet (most of it, anyway) is to focus on the assets that are generated by the company's profit-making activities — in other words, the cause-and-effect relationship between an item that's reported in the income statement and an item that's reported in the balance sheet.

Figure 6-2 lays out the vital links between sales revenue and expenses and the assets and liabilities that are driven by these profit-seeking activities. You can refer back to each connection as sales revenue and expenses are discussed below. The format of the income statement is virtually the same as the format introduced in Chapter 5, except that depreciation expense is reported on a separate line (in Chapter 5, depreciation is buried in the sales, administrative, and general expenses account).

| INCOME STATEMENT (in thousands) | | BALANCE SHEET (in thousands) | |
|---|---|---|---|
| Sales Revenue | $ 25,000 | **Assets** | |
| Cost of Goods Sold Expense | 15,000 | Cash | $ 2,000 |
| Gross Margin | $ 10,000 | Accounts Receivalbe | 2,500 |
| Sales, Administrative, and General Expenses | 6,000 | Inventory | 3,575 |
| Depreciation Expense | 1,200 | Prepaid Expenses | 480 |
| Earnings Before Interest and Income Tax | $ 2,800 | Fixed Assets | 11,305 |
| Interest Expense | 400 | Accumulated Depreciation | (5,780) |
| Earnings Before Income Tax | $ 2,400 | Total | $ 14,080 |
| Income Tax Expense | 800 | **Liabilities & Owners' Equity** | |
| Net Income | $ 1,600 | Accounts Payable | $ 800 |
| | | Accrued Expenses Payable | 1,200 |
| | | Income Tax Payable | 80 |
| | | Notes Payable | 5,000 |
| | | Owners' Invested Capital | 2,000 |
| | | Retained Earnings | 5,000 |
| | | Total | $ 14,080 |

**Figure 6-2:** Connections between the assets and operating liabilities of a business and its sales revenue and expenses.

The amounts reported in the income statement are the cumulative totals for the whole year (or other time period). In contrast the amounts reported in the balance sheet are the *balances* at the end of the year — the net amount, starting with the balance at the start of the year, adjusted for increases and decreases that occur during the year. For example the total cash inflows and outflows over the course of the entire year were much more than the $2 million ending balance for cash.

**JARGON ALERT**

## Turning over assets

Assets should be *turned over,* or put to use by making sales. The higher the turnover — the more times the assets are used and then replaced — the better. The more sales, the better, because every sale is a profit-making opportunity. The *asset turnover ratio* compares annual sales revenue with total assets:

Annual sales revenue ÷ total assets = asset turnover ratio

Some industries are very capital-intensive; they have low asset turnover ratios, which means that they need a lot of assets to support their sales. For example, public gas and electric utilities are capital-intensive. Many retailers, on the other hand, do not need a lot of assets to make sales. Their asset turnover ratios are relatively high; their annual sales are three, four, five, or

more times their assets. Putting it another way, they bring in $300, $400, $500, or more in sales from every $100 of their assets.

The asset turnover ratio is interesting as far as it goes, but it unfortunately doesn't go very far. This ratio looks only at total assets as a glob, or aggregate total. And the ratio looks only at sales revenue. The expenses of the business for the year are not considered — even though expenses are responsible for most of the assets of a business.

**Note:** The asset turnover ratio is a quick-and-dirty test of how well a business is using its assets to generate sales. The ratio does not evaluate profitability; profit is not in the calculation. Basically, the ratio indicates how well assets are being used to generate sales — nothing more.

The purpose of Figure 6-2 is to highlight the connections between the particular assets and operating liabilities that are tightly interwoven with sales revenue and expenses. Business managers need a good grip on these connections to control assets and liabilities. And outside investors need to understand these connections to interpret the financial statements of a business (see Chapter 14).

Cash itself — an extremely important asset, of course — increases when sales are made for cash. Many expenses are paid in cash, decreasing the cash amount. But cash doesn't increase when sales are made on credit, and many expenses do not decrease cash at the time of recording them.

Most people intuitively understand that sooner or later sales revenue increases cash and expenses decrease cash. (The exception is depreciation expense, as explained in Chapters 5 and 7). It's the "sooner or later" that gives rise to the assets and liabilities involved in making profit.

The assets and liabilities driven by sales revenue and expenses are as follows:

> ✔ Sales revenue derives from selling products and services to customers. Customers pay *cash* at the time of sale, or they pay sometime later if the business is willing to extend them credit. The total amount of credit sales goes in the *accounts receivable* asset account. A business that doesn't make any sales on credit doesn't have accounts receivable.

✔ The cost of goods sold expense is what the business paid for the products that it sells to its customers. You can't charge the cost of products to this expense account until you actually sell the goods, so that cost goes into the *inventory* asset account until the goods are sold. Inventory acts like a holding account that delays letting the cost go into expense until the goods are actually sold.

✔ The sales, administrative, and general expenses (SA&G) category covers many different operating expenses (such as advertising, travel, and telephone costs). Many of these expenses are paid at the time of recording the expenses and cash is decreased — but many of these expenses are paid either before or after being recorded. SA&G expenses drive the following items on the balance sheet:

  • The *prepaid expenses* asset account holds the total amount of cash payments for future expenses — amounts that aren't recorded as expenses until the next period (according to the accrual basis of accounting, you charge a cost to the period actually benefited by the cost, not to the period when you pay the cost; for example, you pay insurance premiums before the policy goes into effect, so you charge those premiums to the months covered by the policy).

  • The *accounts payable* liability account is the total amount of expenses that haven't been paid yet but that affect the current period. For example, you receive a bill for electricity that you used the month before, so you charge that bill to the month benefited by the electricity — again thanks to the accrual basis of accounting.

  • The *accrued expenses payable* account is the opposite of the prepaid expenses asset account: this liability account holds costs that are paid after the cost is recorded as an expense. An example is the accumulated vacation pay that the company's employees have earned by the end of the year; when the employees take their vacations next year, the company pays this liability. The company has received the benefit of their labor but hasn't yet paid the employees for their vacation pay, and the accumulated amount is recorded in the accrued expenses payable liability account.

✔ The purpose of depreciation is to spread out the original cost of a *fixed asset* over the course of the asset's life. If you buy a truck that's going to serve you for five years, you charge one-fifth of the cost to depreciation expense each of the five years. (Instead of charging this straight line, or level amount to each year, a business can choose an accelerated depreciation method, as explained in Chapter 13.) Rather than decreasing the fixed assets account directly (which would make some sense), accountants put depreciation expense in an offset account called *accumulated depreciation,* the balance of which is deducted from the original cost of fixed assets. Thus, both the original cost and how much of the original cost has been depreciated to date are available in separate accounts — both items of information are reported in the balance sheet.

✔ Interest expense depends on the amount of money that the business borrows and the interest rate that the lender charges. *Debt* is the generic term for borrowed money; and debt bears interest. *Notes payable* is the most common term you see for most debt because the borrower (the business) signs a legal instrument called a *note*. A business that hasn't borrowed any money has no interest expense and no debt. Normally, the total interest expense for a period hasn't been paid by the end of the period. So the unpaid part is recorded in *accrued expenses payable* (or in a more specific account of this type called *accrued interest payable*).

✔ A small part of the total income tax owed on the corporation's taxable income for the year probably would not be paid by the end of the year, and the unpaid part is recorded in the *income tax payable* account.

✔ A final note: The bottom-line profit (net income) for the year increases the *retained earnings* account, which is one of the two owners' equity accounts.

# Sizing Up Assets and Liabilities

Although the business example shown in Figure 6-2 is hypothetical, I didn't make up the numbers at random — not at all. I use a medium-sized business that has $25 million in annual sales revenue as the example. (Your business may be a lot smaller or larger than one with $25 million annual sales revenue, of course). All the other numbers in both the income statement and the balance sheet of the business are realistic relative to each other. I assume the business earns 40 percent gross margin ($10 million gross margin ÷ $25 million sales revenue = 40 percent), which means its cost of goods sold expense is 60 percent of sales revenue. The sizes of particular assets and liabilities compared with their relevant income statement numbers vary from industry to industry, and even from business to business in the same industry.

Based on its history and policies, the managers of a business can estimate what the size of each asset and liability should be — and these estimates provide very useful *control benchmarks*, or yardsticks against which the actual balances of the assets and liabilities are compared with, to spot any serious deviations. In other words, assets (and liabilities, too) can be too high or too low in relation to the sales revenue and expenses that drive them, and these deviations can cause problems that managers should try to correct as soon as possible.

For example, based on the credit terms extended to customers and the company's actual policies regarding how aggressive the business is in collecting past-due receivables, a manager can determine the range for how much a proper, or within-the-boundaries, balance of accounts receivable should be. This figure would be the control benchmark. If the actual balance is reasonably close to this control benchmark, accounts receivable is under control. If not, the manager should investigate why accounts receivable is smaller or larger than what it should be.

The following sections discuss the relative sizes of the assets and liabilities in the balance sheet that result from sales and expenses. The sales and expenses are the *drivers,* or causes of the assets and liabilities. If a business earned profit simply by investing in stocks and bonds, for example, it would not need all the various assets and liabilities explained in this chapter. Such a business — a mutual fund, for example — would have just one income-producing asset: investments in securities. But this chapter focuses on businesses that sell products to make profit.

## Sales revenue and accounts receivable

In Figure 6-2 the annual sales revenue is $25.0 million. Accounts receivable is one-tenth of this, or $2.5 million. In rough terms, the average customer's credit period is about 36 days — 365 days in the year times the 10 percent ratio of ending accounts receivable balance to annual sales revenue. Of course, some customer's balances owed to the business may be past 36 days and some quite new. It's the overall average that you should focus on. The key question is whether or not a customer-credit period averaging 36 days is reasonable or not.

Suppose that the business offers all its customers a 30-day credit period, which is fairly common in business to business selling (although not typical for a retailer selling to individual consumers). The relatively small deviation of about 6 days (36 days average credit period versus 30 days normal credit terms) may not be a significant cause for concern. But suppose that, at the end of the period, the accounts receivable had been $3,750,000, which is 15 percent of annual sales, or about a 55-day average credit period. Such an abnormally high balance should sound an alarm — the responsible manager should look into the reasons for the abnormal accounts receivable balance. Perhaps several customers are seriously late in paying and should not be extended new credit until they pay up.

## Cost of goods sold expense and inventory

In Figure 6-2 the annual cost of goods sold expense is $15.0 million. The inventory is $3,575,000, or about 24 percent. In rough terms, the average product's inventory holding period is 87 days — 365 days in the year times the 24 percent ratio of ending inventory to annual cost of goods sold. Of course, some products may remain in inventory longer than the 87-day average and some products may sell in a much shorter period than 87 days. It's the overall average that you should focus on. Is an 87-day average inventory holding period reasonable?

The "correct" average inventory holding period varies from industry to industry. In some industries, the inventory holding period is very long, three months or longer — especially for manufacturers of heavy equipment and high-tech products. The opposite is true for high-volume retailers, such as retail supermarkets, that depend on getting products off the shelves as quickly as possible. The 87-day average holding period in the example is reasonable for many businesses, but would be far too high for many other businesses. The managers should know what the company's average inventory holding period should be — in other words, they should know what the control benchmark is for the inventory holding period. If inventory is much above this control benchmark, managers should take prompt action to get inventory back in line — which is easier said than done, of course. If inventory is at abnormally low levels this should be looked into as well — the manager should determine the reasons for the lower-than-normal inventory balance. Perhaps some products are out of stock and should be immediately reordered to avoid lost sales. Most customers want immediate delivery of products and are not willing to wait.

## SA&G expenses and the four balance sheet accounts that are connected with the expenses

Note that in Figure 6-2 sales, administrative, and general (SA&G) expenses connect with four balance sheet accounts — cash, prepaid expenses, accounts payable, and accrued expenses payable. The broad SA&G expense category includes many different types of expenses that are involved in making sales and operating the business. (Separate expense accounts are maintained for specific expenses; depending on the size of the business and the needs of its various managers, hundreds or thousands of specific expense accounts are established.)

Cash is paid when recording payroll, mailing, and some other expenses. In contrast, insurance and office supplies costs are prepaid, and then released to expense gradually over time. So, cash is paid before the recording of the expense. Some of these expenses are not paid until weeks after being recorded; to recognize the delayed payment the amounts owed are recorded in an accounts payable or an accrued expenses payable liability account. I won't go through all the details of how I came up with the balances in prepaid expenses, accounts payable, and accrued expenses payable (aren't you lucky). But, if I did I would follow the same logic from the sections on accounts receivable and inventory.

One point I would like to repeat is that the company's managers should adopt benchmarks for each of these accounts that are connected with the operating expenses of the business. For example, the $1.2 million ending balance of accrued expenses payable is 20 percent of the $6.0 million SA&G for the year. Is this ratio within control limits? Is it too high? Managers should ask and answer questions like these for every asset and liability connected with the expenses of the business.

## Fixed assets and depreciation expense

As explained in Chapter 5, depreciation is a truly unique expense. Depreciation is like other expenses in that all expenses are deducted from sales revenue to determine profit. Other than this, however, depreciation is very different. None of the depreciation expense recorded to the period requires cash outlay during the period. Rather, depreciation expense for the period is that portion of the total cost of a business's fixed assets that is allocated to the period to record an amount of expense for using the assets during the period. Depreciation is an imputed cost, based on what fraction of the total cost of fixed assets is assigned to the period.

The higher the total cost of its fixed assets, the higher a business's depreciation expense. However, there is no standard ratio of depreciation expense to the total cost of fixed assets. The amount of depreciation expense depends on the useful lives of the company's fixed assets and which depreciation method the business selects. (How to choose depreciation methods is explained in Chapter 13.) The annual depreciation expense of a business seldom is more than ten or fifteen percent of the total cost of its fixed assets. The depreciation expense for the year is either reported as a separate expense in the income statement (as in Figure 6-2) or the amount is disclosed in a footnote.

Because depreciation is based on the cost of fixed assets, the balance sheet reports not one but two numbers: the original cost of the fixed assets and the *accumulated depreciation* amount (the amount of depreciation that has been charged as an expense from the time of acquiring the fixed asset to the current balance sheet date).

The point isn't to confuse you by giving you even more numbers to deal with. Seeing both numbers gives you an idea of how old the fixed assets are and also tells you how much these fixed assets originally cost.

In the example the business has, over several years, invested $11,305,000 in its fixed assets (that it still owns and uses), and it had already charged off depreciation of $4,580,000 in previous years. In this year, the business records $1,200,000 depreciation expense (you can't tell from the balance sheet how much depreciation was charged this year; you have to look at the income statement in Figure 6-2). The remaining undepreciated cost of this business's fixed assets at the end of the year is $5,525,000. So the fixed assets part of this year's balance sheet looks like this:

| | |
|---|---|
| Fixed assets | $11,305,000 |
| Accumulated depreciation | (5,780,000) |
| Net amount included in total assets | $5,525,000 |

You can tell that the collection of fixed assets includes both old and new assets because the company has recorded $5,780,000 total depreciation since the assets were bought, which is a fairly sizable percent of original cost (more than half). But, many businesses use accelerated depreciation methods which pile up a lot of the depreciation expense in the early years and less in the back years (see Chapter 13 for more details), so it's hard to estimate the average age of the assets.

## Debt and interest expense

The business example whose balance sheet and income statements are presented in Figure 6-2 has borrowed $5 million on notes payable, which at an 8 percent annual interest rate is $400,000 in interest expense for the year. (The business may have had more or less borrowed at certain times during the year, of course, and the actual interest expense depends on the debt levels from month to month.)

For most businesses, a small part of their total annual interest is unpaid at year-end; the unpaid part is recorded to bring the expense up to the correct total amount for the year. In Figure 6-2, the accrued amount of interest is included in the more inclusive accrued expenses payable liability account. You seldom see accrued interest payable reported on a separate line in a balance sheet, unless it happens to be a rather large amount or if the business is seriously behind in paying interest on its debt.

## Income tax expense

In Figure 6-2, earnings before income tax — after deducting interest and all other expenses from sales revenue — is $2,400,000. (The actual taxable income of the business for the year probably would be somewhat more or less than this amount because of the many complexities in the income tax law which are beyond the scope of this book.) In the example I use a tax rate of one-third for convenience, so the income tax expense is $800,000 of the pretax income of $2,400,000. (The precise marginal federal tax rate is 34 percent on corporations' taxable income in this range; and, the business may have to pay state income tax as well.)

## What about cash?

A business's cash account consists of the money it has in its checking accounts plus the money that it keeps on hand to make change for its customers. Cash is the essential lubricant of business activity. Sooner or later, virtually everything passes through the cash account.

Every business needs to maintain a working cash balance as a buffer against fluctuations in day-to-day cash receipts and payments. You can't try to get by with a zero cash balance, hoping that enough customers will come in and pay cash to cover all the cash payments that you need to make that day. Can you imagine starting the day with no money in your business's checking account? (Of course, your bank wouldn't like this either).

How much of a cash balance should a business maintain? This question has no right answer. A business needs to determine how large a cash safety reserve it's comfortable with to meet unexpected demands on cash while keeping the following wisdom in mind:

- Excess cash balances are nonproductive and don't earn any profit for the business.

- Insufficient cash balances can cause the business to miss taking advantage of opportunities that require quick action and large amounts of cash — such as snatching up a prized piece of real estate that just came on the market, which the business has had its eye on for some time, or buying out a competitor when the business comes up for sale.

The cash balance of the business whose balance sheet is presented in Figure 6-2 is $2,000,000 — which would be too large for some other businesses and too small for others. Again, what's right for a particular business is an individual thing.

Most of the federal income tax for the year must be paid over to the IRS before the end of the year. But a small part is usually still owed at the end of the year. The unpaid part is recorded in the *income tax payable* liability account — as you see in Figure 6-2. In the example, the unpaid part is $80,000 of the total $800,000 income tax for the year — but I don't mean to suggest that this ratio is typical. Generally, the unpaid income tax at the end of the year is fairly small, but just how small depends on several technical factors. You may want to check with your tax professional to make sure you have paid over enough of the annual income tax by the end of the year to avoid a penalty for late payment.

## *The bottom line (net income) and cash dividends (if any)*

A business may have other sources of income during the year, such as interest income on investments. In this example, however, the business has only sales revenue, which is gross income from the sale of products and services. All expenses — starting with cost of goods sold down to and including income tax — are deducted from sales revenue to arrive at the last, or bottom-line of the income statement. The preferred term for bottom-line profit is *net income*, as you see in Figure 6-2.

The $1,600,000 net income for the year increases *retained earnings* by the same amount, so see the line of connection from net income and retained earnings in Figure 6-2. The $1,600,00 profit (here I go again using the term profit instead of net income) either stays in the business, or some of it is paid out and divided among the owners of the business. If the business had paid out cash dividends from profit during the year these cash payments to its owners (shareholders) are deducted from retained earnings. You can't tell from the income statement or the balance sheet whether any cash dividends were paid. You have to look in the cash flow statement for this information — which is explained in Chapter 7.

# Financing a Business: Owners' Equity and Debt

You may have noticed in Figure 6-2 that two balance sheet accounts have no lines of connection from the income statement to them — notes payable and owners' invested capital. Revenue and expenses do not affect these two key balance sheet accounts (nor the fixed assets account for that matter, which is explained in Chapter 7). But, both debt and owners' invested capital are extremely important for making profit.

To run a business, you need financial backing, otherwise known as *capital.* Capital is all incoming funds that are not derived from sales revenue (or from selling off assets). A business raises capital by borrowing money, getting owners to invest money in the business, and making profit that is retained in the business. Borrowed money is known as *debt;* invested money and retained profits are the two sources of *owners' equity.* Those two sources need to be kept separate, according to the rules of accounting. See Chapters 5 and 9 for more about profit.

How much capital does the business shown in Figure 6-2 have? Its total assets are $14,080,000, but this is not quite the answer. The company's profit-making activities generated three operating liabilities — accounts payable, accrued expenses payable, and income tax payable — and in total these three liabilities provided $2,080,000 of the total assets of the business. So, deducting this amount from total assets gives the answer: the business has $12 million in capital. Where did this capital come from? Debt provided $5 million and the two sources of owners' equity provided the other $7 million (see Figure 6-1 or 6-2 to check these numbers).

Accounts payable, accrued expenses payable, and income tax payable are short-term, non-interest-bearing liabilities that are sometimes called *spontaneous liabilities* because they arise directly from a business's expense activities — they aren't the result of borrowing money but rather are the result of buying things on credit or delaying payment of certain expenses.

This particular business has decided to finance itself through debt and equity in the following mix:

| | |
|---|---|
| Debt | $5,000,000 |
| Owners' equity | 7,000,000 |
| Total sources of capital | $12,000,000 |

Deciding how to divide your sources of capital can be tricky. In a very real sense, the debt-versus-equity question never has a final answer; it's always under review and reconsideration by most businesses. Some companies, just like some individuals, are strongly anti-debt, but even they may find that they need to take on debt eventually to keep up with changing times.

Debt is both good and bad, and in extreme situations it can get very ugly. The advantages of debt are:

- ✔ Most businesses can't raise all the capital they need from owners' equity, and debt offers another source of capital (though, of course, many lenders may provide only half or less of the capital that a business needs).

- ✔ Interest rates charged by lenders are lower than rates of return expected by owners. Owners expect a higher rate of return because they're taking a greater risk with their money — the business is not required to pay them back the same way that it's required to pay back a lender. For example, a business may pay 8 percent interest on its debt and have to earn a 13 percent rate of return on its owners' equity. (See Chapter 14 for more on earning profit for owners.)

The disadvantages of debt are:

- ✔ A business must pay the fixed rate of interest for the period even if it suffers a loss for the period.

- ✔ A business must be ready to pay back the debt on the specified due date, which can cause some pressure on the business to come up with the money on time. (Of course, a business may be able to *roll over* its debt, meaning that it replaces its old debt with an equivalent amount of new debt, but the lender has the right to demand that the old debt be paid and not rolled over.)

If you default on your debt contract — you don't pay the interest on time, or you don't pay back the debt on the due date — you face some major unpleasantries. In extreme cases, a lender can force you to shut down and liquidate your assets (that is, sell off everything you own for cash) to pay off the debt and unpaid interest. Just as you can lose your home if you don't pay your home mortgage, your business can be forced into involuntary bankruptcy if you don't pay your business debts.

# Trading on the equity: taking a chance on debt

The large majority of businesses borrow money to provide part of the total capital needed for their assets. The main reason for debt, by and large, is to close the gap between how much capital the owners can come up with and the amount the business needs. Lenders are willing to provide the capital because they have a senior claim on the assets of the business. Debt has to be paid back before the owners can get their money out of the business. The owners' equity provides the permanent base of capital and gives the lenders a cushion of protection.

The owners use their capital invested in the business as the basis to borrow. For example, for every two bucks the owners have in the business, lenders may be willing to add another dollar (or even more). Thus, for every two bucks of owners' equity the business can get three dollars total capital to work with. Using owners' equity as the basis for borrowing is called *trading on the equity*. It is also referred to as *financial leverage,* because the equity is the lever for increasing the total capital of the business.

These terms also refer to the potential gain a business can realize from making more EBIT (earnings before interest and income tax) on the amount borrowed than the interest on the debt. For a simple example, assume that debt supplies one-third of the total capital of a business (and owners' equity two-thirds, of course), and the business's EBIT for the year just ended is a nice, round $3,000,000. Fair is fair, so you could argue that the lenders, who put up one-third of the money, should get one-third or $1,000,000 of the

profit. This is not how its works. The lenders (investors) get only the interest amount on their loans (their investments). Suppose this total interest is $750,000. The financial leverage gain, therefore, is $250,000. The owners would get their two-thirds share of EBIT plus the $250,000 pretax financial leverage gain.

Trading on the equity may backfire. Instead of a gain, the business may realize a financial leverage loss — one-third of its EBIT may be *less* than the interest due on its debt. That interest has to be paid no matter what amount of EBIT the business earns. Suppose the business just breaks even, which means its EBIT equals zero for the year. Nevertheless, it must pay the interest on its debt. So, the business would have a bottom-line loss for the year.

I haven't said much about the situation in which a business has a loss for the year, instead of a profit. A loss has the effect of decreasing the assets of a business (whereas a profit increases its assets). To keep it simple, assume cash is the only asset decreased by the loss (other assets could also decrease as a result of the loss). Basically, cash goes down by the amount of the loss; and, on the other side of the balance sheet, the retained earnings account goes down the same amount. The owners do not have to invest additional money in the business to cover the loss. The impact on the owners is that their total equity (the recorded value of their ownership in the business) takes a hit equal to the amount of the loss.

A lender may allow the business to try to work out its financial crisis through bankruptcy procedures, but bankruptcy is a nasty business that invariably causes many problems and can really cripple a business.

# Reporting Financial Condition: The Classified Balance Sheet

The assets, liabilities, and owners' equity of a business are reported in its *balance sheet,* which is prepared at the end of the income statement period.

The balance sheet is not a flows statement but a *position* statement, which reports the financial condition of a company at a precise moment in time. The balance sheet is unlike the income and cash flow statements (which report inflows and outflows). The balance sheet presents a company's assets, liabilities, and owners' equity that exist at the time the report is prepared.

An accountant can prepare a balance sheet at any time that a manager wants to know how things stand financially. However, balance sheets are usually prepared only at the end of each month, quarter, and year. A balance sheet is always prepared at the close of business on the last day of the profit period, so that the financial effects of sales and expenses (reported in the income statement) also appear in the assets, liabilities, and owners' equity sections of the balance sheet.

The balance sheet shown in Figure 6-1 is a bare-bones statement of financial condition. Yes, the basic assets, liabilities, and owners' equity accounts are presented. However, for both internal management reporting and for external reporting to investors and lenders, the balance sheet must be dressed up more than the one shown in Figure 6-1.

For internal reporting to managers, balance sheets include much more detail, either in the body of the financial statement itself, or more likely, in supporting schedules. For example, only one cash account is shown in Figure 6-1, but the chief financial officer of a business needs to see the balances in each of the business's checking accounts.

As another example, the balance sheet shown in Figure 6-1 includes just one total amount for accounts receivable, but managers need details on which customers owe money and whether any major amounts are past due. Therefore, the assets and liabilities of a business are reported to its managers in greater detail, which allows for better control, analysis, and decision-making. Management control is very detail-oriented: Internal balance sheets and their supporting schedules should provide all the detail that managers need to make good business decisions.

In contrast, balance sheets presented in *external* financial reports (which go out to investors and lenders) do not include much more detail than the balance sheet shown in Figure 6-1. However, external balance sheets must classify (or group together) short-term assets and liabilities. For this reason, external balance sheets are referred to as *classified balance sheets*. This classification is not mandatory for internal reporting to managers, although separating short-term assets and liabilities is also useful for managers.

Business balance sheets are not vetted by the CIA to make sure no secrets are being disclosed that would harm national security. The term "classified" applied to a balance sheet does not mean restricted or top secret; rather, the term means that assets and liabilities are sorted into basic classes, or groups for external reporting. Classifying certain assets and liabilities into current categories is done mainly to help readers of the balance sheet more easily compare total current assets with total current liabilities for the purpose of judging the short-term solvency of the business.

Solvency refers to the ability of a business to pay its liabilities on time. Delays in paying liabilities on time can cause very serious problems for a business. In extreme cases, a business could be thrown into *bankruptcy* — even the threat of bankruptcy can cause serious disruptions in the normal operations of a business, and profit performance is bound to suffer. If current liabilities become too high relative to current assets — which are the first line of defense for paying those current liabilities — managers should move quickly to raise additional cash to reduce one or more of the current liabilities. Otherwise, a low current ratio will raise alarms in the minds of the outside readers of the business's financial report.

Figure 6-3 presents the *classified* balance sheet for the same company. What's new? Not the assets, liabilities, and owners' equity accounts and their balances. These numbers are the same ones shown in Figure 6-1. The classified balance sheet shown in Figure 6-3 includes the following new items of information:

✔ The first four asset accounts (cash, accounts receivable, inventory, and prepaid expenses) are added to give the $8,555,000 subtotal for *current assets*.

✔ The $5,000,000 total debt of the business is divided between $2,000,000 short-term notes payable and $3,000,000 long-term notes payable.

✔ The first four liability accounts (accounts payable, accrued expenses payable, income tax payable, and short-term notes payable) are added to give the $4,080,000 subtotal for *current liabilities*.

| Assets | | |
|---|---|---|
| Cash | | $ 2,000,000 |
| Accounts Receivable | | $ 2,500,000 |
| Inventory | | $ 3,575,000 |
| Prepaid Expenses | | $ 480,000 |
| Current Assets | | $ 8,555,000 |
| Fixed Assets (at original cost) | $11,305,000 | |
| Accumulated Depreciation | $ (5,780,000) | $ 5,525,000 |
| Total Assets | | $ 14,080,000 |
| | | |
| **Liabilities and Owners' Equity** | | |
| Accounts Payable | | $ 800,000 |
| Accrued Expenses Payable | | $ 1,200,000 |
| Income Tax Payable | | $ 80,000 |
| Short-term Notes Payable | | $ 2,000,000 |
| Current Liabilities | | $ 4,080,000 |
| Long-term Notes Payable | | $ 3,000,000 |
| Owners' Invested Capital | $ 2,000,000 | |
| Retained Earnings | $ 5,000,000 | $ 7,000,000 |
| Total Liabilities and Owners' Equity | | $ 14,080,000 |

**Figure 6-3:** Example of an external (classified) balance sheet for a business.

## Current (short-term) assets

Short-term, or *current,* assets are

- ✔ Cash
- ✔ Marketable securities that can be immediately converted into cash
- ✔ Operating assets that are converted into cash within one *operating cycle*

*Operating cycle* refers to the process of putting cash into inventory, selling products on credit (which generates accounts receivable), and then collecting the receivables in cash. In other words, the operating cycle is the "from cash — through inventory and accounts receivable — back to cash" sequence. The term *operating* refers to those assets that are directly part of making sales and directly involved in the expenses of the company.

## Current (short-term) liabilities

Short-term, or *current,* liabilities are those non-interest-bearing liabilities that arise from the operating activities of the business, as well as interest-bearing notes payable that have a maturity date one year or less from the balance sheet date. Current liabilities also include any other liabilities that must be paid within the upcoming financial period.

Current liabilities are generally paid out of current assets. That is, current assets are the first source of money to pay the current liabilities when those liabilities come due. Thus, total current assets are compared against total current liabilities in order to compute the *current ratio*. For the balance sheet shown in the preceding section, you can compute the current ratio as follows:

```
$8,555,000 current assets ÷ $4,080,000 current liabilities =
            2.1 current ratio
```

The general rule is that a company's current ratio should be 2.0 or higher. However, business managers know that the current ratio depends a great deal on how the business's short-term operating assets are financed from current liabilities. Some businesses do quite well with a current ratio less than 2.0. Therefore, take the 2.0 current ratio rule with a grain of salt. A lower current ratio does not necessarily mean that the business won't be able to pay its short-term (current) liabilities on time. Chapters 14 and 17 explain current ratios in more detail.

# Costs and Other Balance Sheet Values

The balance sheet summarizes the financial condition for a business at a point in time. Business managers and investors should clearly understand the values reported in this primary financial statement. In my experience, understanding balance sheet values can be a source of confusion for both business managers and investors, who tend to put all dollar amounts on the same value basis. In their minds, a dollar is a dollar, whether it's in the accounts receivable, inventory, fixed assets, or accounts payable. Assigning the same value to every account value tends to gloss over some important differences and can lead to serious misinterpretation of the balance sheet.

A balance sheet mixes together several different types of accounting values:

- ✔ **Cash:** Amounts of money on hand in coin and currency; money on deposit in a bank in checking accounts

- ✔ **Accounts receivable:** Amounts not yet collected from credit sales to customers

- ✔ **Inventory:** Amounts of purchase costs or production costs for products that haven't sold yet

- ✔ **Fixed assets (or, Property, Plant & Equipment):** Amounts of costs invested in long-life, tangible, productive operating assets

✔ **Accounts payable** and **accrued liabilities:** Amounts for the costs of unpaid expenses

✔ **Notes payable:** Amounts borrowed on interest-bearing liabilities

✔ **Capital stock:** Amounts of capital invested in the business by owners (stockholders)

✔ **Retained earnings:** Amounts remaining in the owners' equity account

In short, a balance sheet represents a diversity or a rainbow of values — not just one color. This is the nature of the generally accepted accounting principles (GAAP) — the accounting methods used to prepare financial statements.

*Book values* are the amounts recorded in the accounting process and reported in financial statements. Do not assume that the book values reported in a balance sheet necessarily equal the current *market values.* Book values are based on the accounting methods used by a business. Generally speaking — and I really mean *generally* here because I'm sure that you can find exceptions to this rule — cash, accounts receivable, and liabilities are recorded at close to their market or settlement values. These receivables will be turned into cash (at the same amount recorded on the balance sheet), and liabilities will be paid off at the amounts reported in the balance sheet. It's the book values of inventory and fixed assets that most likely are lower than current market values, as well as any other non-operating assets in which the business invested some time ago.

A business can use alternative accounting methods to determine the cost of inventory and the cost of goods sold, and to determine how much of a fixed asset's cost is allocated to depreciation expense each year. A business is free to use very conservative accounting methods — with the result that its inventory cost value and the undepreciated cost of its fixed assets may be much lower than the current replacement cost values of these assets. Chapter 13 explains more about choosing different accounting methods. (You may also want to check out the sidebar in Chapter 5, "The mark-to-market method of accounting.")

# Chapter 7

# Cash Flows and the Cash Flow Statement

● ● ● ● ● ● ● ● ● ● ● ● ● ● ● ● ● ● ● ● ● ● ● ● ● ● ● ● ● ● ● ● ● ● ● ● ● ● ● ● ●

## In This Chapter

▶ Separating the three types of cash flows

▶ Figuring out how much actual cash increase was generated by profit

▶ Looking at a business's other sources and uses of cash

▶ Being careful about free cash flow

▶ Evaluating managers' decisions by scrutinizing the cash flow statement

● ● ● ● ● ● ● ● ● ● ● ● ● ● ● ● ● ● ● ● ● ● ● ● ● ● ● ● ● ● ● ● ● ● ● ● ● ● ● ● ●

*T*his chapter talks about *cash flows* — which in general refers to cash inflows and outflows over a period of time. Suppose you tell me that last year you had total cash inflows of $145,000 and total cash outflows of $140,000. I know that your cash balance increased $5,000. But I don't know where your $145,000 cash inflows came from: Did you earn this much in salary? Did you borrow money from the bank? Did you receive an inheritance from your rich uncle? Likewise, I don't know what you used your $140,000 cash outflow for: Did you make large payments on your credit cards? Did you lose a lot of money in Las Vegas? Did you invest in a piece of land that you think will appreciate in value? In short, cash flows have to be sorted into different sources and uses to make much sense.

## The Three Types of Cash Flows

Accountants categorize the cash flows of a business into three types:

✔ Cash inflows from making sales and cash outflows for expenses; sales and expense transactions are called the *operating activities* of a business (although they could be called profit activities just as well, because their purpose is to make profit).

✔ Cash outflows for making investments in new assets (buildings, machinery, tools, and so on), and cash inflows from liquidating old investments (assets no longer needed that are sold off); these transactions are called *investment activities.*

✔ Cash inflows from borrowing money and from the additional investment of money in the business by its owners, and cash outflows for paying down debt, returning capital that the business no longer needs to owners, and making cash distributions of profit to its owners; these transactions are called *financing activities.*

The cash flow statement (or *statement of cash flows*) summarizes the cash flows of a business for a period according to this three-way classification. Generally accepted accounting principles (GAAP) require that whenever a business reports its income statement, it must also report its cash flow statement for the same period — a business shouldn't report one without the other. A good reason exists for this dual financial statement requirement.

The income statement is based on the *accrual basis of accounting* that records sales when made whether or not cash is received at that time, and records expenses when incurred whether or not the expenses are paid at that time. (Chapter 3 explains accrual basis accounting.) Because accrual basis accounting is used to record profit, you can't equate bottom-line profit with an increase in cash. Suppose a business's annual income statement reports that it earned net $1.6 million income for the year. This does not mean that its cash balance increased $1.6 million during the period. You have to look in the cash flow statement to find out how much its cash balance increased (or, possibly, decreased!) from its operating activities (sales revenue and expenses) during the period.

In the chapter, I refer to the net increase (or decrease) in the business's cash balance that results from collecting sales revenue and paying expenses as *cash flow from profit,* as the alternative term for *cash flow from operating activities.* Cash flow from profit seems more user-friendly than cash flow from operating activities, and in fact the term is used widely. In any case, do not confuse cash flow from profit with the other two types of cash flow — from the business's investing activities and financing activities during the period.

Before moving on, here's a short problem for you to solve. Using the three-way classification of cash flows explained earlier, a summary of the business's net cash flows for the year just ended, with one amount missing, is presented here (in thousands):

| | |
|---|---|
| (1) From profit (operating activities) | ? |
| (2) From investing activities | – $1,275 |
| (3) From financing activities | + $160 |
| Decrease in cash balance during year | – $15 |

Note that the business's cash balance from all sources and uses decreased $15,000 during the year. The amounts of net cash flows from the company's investing and financing activities are given. So you can determine that the net cash flow from profit was $1,100,000 for the year. Understanding cash flows from investing activities and financing activities is fairly straightforward. Understanding the net cash flow from profit, in contrast, is more challenging — but business managers and investors should have a good grip on this very important number.

# Setting the Stage: Changes in Balance Sheet Accounts

The first step in understanding the amounts reported by a business in its cash flow statement is to focus on the *changes* in the business's assets, liabilities, and owners' equity accounts during the period — the increases or decreases of each account from the start of the period to the end of the period. These changes are found in the comparative, two-year balance sheet reported by a business. Figure 7-1 presents the increases and decreases during the year in the assets, liabilities, and owners' equity accounts for a business example. Figure 7-1 is not a balance sheet but only a summary of *changes* in account balances. I do not want to burden you with an entire balance sheet, which has much more detail than is needed here.

Take a moment to scan Figure 7-1. Note that the business's cash balance decreased $15,000 during the year. (An increase is not necessarily a good thing, and a decrease is not necessarily a bad thing; it depends on the overall financial situation of the business.) One purpose of reporting the cash flow statement is to summarize the main reasons for the change in cash — according to the three-way classification of cash flows explained earlier. One question on everyone's mind is this: How much cash did the profit for the year generate for the business? The cash flow statement begins by answering this question.

| Assets | |
|---|---|
| Cash | (15) |
| Accounts Receivable | 800 |
| Inventory | 975 |
| Prepaid Expenses | 145 |
| Fixed Assets | 1,275 |
| Accumulated Depreciation* | (1,200) |
| Total | 1,980 |
| **Liabilities & Owners' Equity** | |
| Accounts Payable | 80 |
| Accrued Expenses Payable | 1,20 |
| Income Tax Payable | 20 |
| Short-term Notes Payable | 200 |
| Long-term Notes Payable | 300 |
| Owners' Invested Capital | 60 |
| Retained Earnings | 1,200 |
| Total | 1,980 |

**Figure 7-1:** Changes in balance sheet assets and operating liabilities that affect cash flow from profit.

\* Accumulated Depreciation is a negative asset account which is deducted from Fixed Assets. The negative $1,200 change increases the negative balance of the account.

# Getting at the Cash Increase from Profit

Although all amounts reported on the cash flow statement are important, the one that usually gets the most attention is *cash flow from operating activities,* or *cash flow from profit* as I prefer to call it. This is the increase in cash generated by a business's profit-making operations during the year, exclusive of its other sources of cash during the year (such as borrowed money, sold-off fixed assets, and additional owners' investments in the business). *Cash flow from profit* indicates a business's ability to turn profit into available cash — cash in the bank that can be used for the needs of business. Cash flow from profit gets just as much attention as net income (the bottom-line profit number in the income statement).

Before presenting the cash flow statement — which is a rather formidable, three-part accounting report — in all its glory, in the following sections I build on the summary of changes in the business's assets, liabilities, and owners' equities shown in Figure 7-1 to explain the components of the $1,100,000 increase in cash from the business's profit activities during the year. (The $1,100,000 amount of cash flow from profit is determined earlier in the chapter by solving for the unknown factor.)

The business in the example experienced a rather strong growth year. Its accounts receivable and inventory increased by relatively large amounts. In fact, all the relevant accounts increased; their ending balances are larger than their beginning balances (which are the amounts carried forward from the end of the preceding year). At this point, I need to provide some additional information. The $1.2 million increase in retained earnings is the net difference of two quite different things.

The $1.6 million net income earned by the business increased retained earnings by this amount. As you see in Figure 7-1, the account increased only $1.2 million. Thus there must have been a $400,000 decrease in retained earnings during the year. The business paid $400,000 cash dividends from profit to its owners (the shareholders) during the year, which is recorded as a decrease in retained earnings. The amount of cash dividends is reported in the *financing activities* section of the cash flow statement. The entire amount of net income is reported in the *operating activities* section of the cash flow statement.

## Computing cash flow from profit

Here's how to compute cash flow from profit based on the changes in the company's balance sheet accounts presented in Figure 7-1:

### Computation of Cash Flow from Profit (in thousands of dollars)

|  | Negative Cash Flow Effects | Positive Cash Flow Effects |
|---|---|---|
| Net income for the year |  | $1,600 |
| Accounts receivable increase | $800 |  |
| Inventory increase | $975 |  |
| Prepaid expenses increase | $145 |  |
| Depreciation expense |  | $1,200 |
| Accounts payable increase |  | $80 |
| Accrued expenses payable increase |  | $120 |
| Income tax payable increase |  | $20 |
| Totals | $1,920 | $3,020 |
| Cash flow from profit ($3,020 positive increases minus $1,920 negative increases) | $1,100 |  |

Note that net income for the year — which is the correct amount of profit based on the accrual basis of accounting — is listed in the positive cash flow column. This is only the starting point. Think of this the following way: If the business had collected all its sales revenue for the year in cash, and if it had made cash payments for its expenses exactly equal to the amounts recorded for the expenses, then the net income amount would equal the increase in cash. These two conditions are virtually never true, and they are not true in this example. So the net income figure is just the jumping-off point for determining the amount of cash generated by the business's profit activities during the year.

I'll let you in on a little secret here. The analysis of cash flow from profit asks what amount of profit would have been recorded if the business had been on the cash basis of accounting instead of the accrual basis. This can be confusing and exasperating, because it seems that two different profit measures are provided in a business's financial report — the true economic profit number, which is the bottom line in the income statement (usually called *net income*), and a second profit number called *cash flow from operating activities* in the cash flow statement.

When the cash flow statement was made mandatory in 1987, many accountants worried about this problem, but the majority opinion was that the amount of cash increase (or decrease) generated from the profit activities of a business is very important to disclose in financial reports. In reading the income statement, you have to wear your accrual basis accounting lenses, and in the cash flow statement you have to put on your cash basis lenses. Who says accountants can't see two sides of something?

The following sections explain the effects on cash flow that each balance sheet account change causes (refer to Figure 7-1).

## Getting specific about changes in assets and liabilities

As a business manager, you should keep a close watch on each of your assets and liabilities and understand the cash flow effects of increases (or decreases) caused by these changes. Investors should focus on the business's ability to generate a healthy cash flow from profit, so investors should be equally concerned about these changes.

### Accounts receivable increase

Remember that the accounts receivable asset shows how much money customers who bought products on credit still owe the business; this asset is a promise of cash that the business will receive. Basically, accounts receivable is the amount of uncollected sales revenue at the end of the period. Cash does not increase until the business collects money from its customers.

But the amount in accounts receivable _is_ included in the total sales revenue of the period — after all, you did make the sales, even if you haven't been paid yet. Obviously, then, you can't look at sales revenue as being equal to the amount of cash that the business received during the period.

To calculate the actual cash flow from sales, you need to subtract from sales revenue the amount of credit sales that you did not collect in cash over the period — but you add in the amount of cash that you collected during the period just ended for credit sales that you made in the _preceding_ period. Take a look at the following equation for the business example, which is first introduced in Chapter 6 — the income statement figures used here are given in Figure 6-2, and the asset and liability changes are shown in Figure 7-1. (No need to look back to Figure 6-2 unless you want to review the income statement.)

```
$25.0 million sales revenue - $0.8 million increase in
         accounts receivable = $24.2 million cash collected
         from customers during the year
```

The business started the year with $1.7 million in accounts receivable and ended the year with $2.5 million in accounts receivable. The beginning balance was collected during the year, but the ending balance had not been collected at the end of the year. Thus the _net_ effect is a shortfall in cash inflow of $800,000, which is why it's called a negative cash flow factor. The key point is that you need to keep an eye on the increase or decrease in accounts receivable from the beginning of the period to the end of the period.

- ✔ If the amount of credit sales you made during the period is greater than what you collected from customers during the period, your accounts receivable _increased_ over the period, and you need to _subtract_ from sales revenue that difference between start-of-period accounts receivable and end-of-period accounts receivable. In short, an increase in accounts receivable hurts cash flow by the amount of the increase.

- ✔ If the amount you collected from customers during the period is greater than the credit sales you made during the period, your accounts receivable _decreased_ over the period, and you need to _add_ to sales revenue that difference between start-of-period accounts receivable and end-of-period accounts receivable. In short, a decrease in accounts receivable helps cash flow by the amount of the decrease.

In the example I've been using, accounts receivable increased $800,000. Cash collections from sales were $800,000 less than sales revenue. Ouch! The business increased its sales substantially over last period, so you shouldn't be surprised that its accounts receivable increased. The higher sales revenue was good for profit but bad for cash flow from profit.

An occasional hiccup in cash flow is the price of growth — managers and investors need to understand this point. Increasing sales without increasing accounts receivable is a happy situation for cash flow, but in the real world you can't have one increase without the other (except in very unusual circumstances).

### Inventory increase

Inventory is the next asset in Figure 7-1 — and usually the largest short-term, or *current,* asset for businesses that sell products. If the inventory account is greater at the end of the period than at the start of the period — because either unit costs increased or the quantity of products increased — what the business actually paid out in cash for inventory purchases (or manufacturing products) is more than what the business recorded as its cost-of-goods-sold expense in the period. Therefore, you need to deduct the inventory increase from net income when determining cash flow from profit.

In the example, inventory increased $975,000 from start-of-period to end-of-period. In other words, this business replaced the products that it sold during the period *and* increased its inventory by $975,000. The easiest way to understand the effect of this increase on cash flow is to pretend that the business paid for all its inventory purchases in cash immediately upon receiving them. The inventory on hand at the start of the period had already been paid for *last* period, so that cost does not affect this period's cash flow. Those products were sold during the period and involved no further cash payment by the business. But the business did pay cash *this* period for the products that were in inventory at the end of the period.

In other words, if the business had bought just enough new inventory (at the same cost that it paid out last period) to replace the inventory that it sold during the period, the actual cash outlay for its purchases would equal the cost-of-goods-sold expense reported in its income statement. Ending inventory would equal the beginning inventory; the two inventory costs would cancel each other out and thus would have a zero effect on cash flow. But this hypothetical scenario doesn't fit the example, because the company increased its sales substantially over the last period.

To support the higher sales level, the business needed to increase its inventory level. So the business bought $975,000 more in products than it sold during the period — and it had to come up with the cash to pay for this inventory increase. Basically, the business wrote checks amounting to $975,000 more than its cost-of-goods-sold expense for the period. This step-up in its inventory level was necessary to support the higher sales level, which increased profit — even though cash flow took a hit.

It's that accrual basis accounting thing again: The cost that a business pays *this* period for *next* period's inventory is reflected in this period's cash flow but isn't recorded until next period's income statement (when the products are actually sold). So if a business paid more *this* period for *next* period's inventory than it paid *last* period for *this* period's inventory, you can see how the additional expense would adversely affect cash flow but would not be reflected in the bottom-line net income figure. This cash flow analysis stuff gets a little complicated, I know, but hang in there. The cash flow statement, presented later in the chapter, makes a lot more sense after you go through this background briefing.

### Prepaid expenses increase

The next asset, after inventory, is prepaid expenses (refer to Figure 7-1). A change in this account works the same way as a change in inventory and accounts receivable, although changes in prepaid expenses are usually much smaller than changes in those other two asset accounts.

Again, the beginning balance of prepaid expenses is recorded as an expense this period, but the cash was actually paid out last period, not this period. This period, a business pays cash for next period's prepaid expenses — which affects this period's cash flow but doesn't affect net income until next period. So the $145,000 increase in prepaid expenses from start-of-period to end-of-period in this business example has a negative cash flow effect.

As it grows, a business needs to increase its prepaids for such things as fire insurance (premiums have to be paid in advance of the insurance coverage) and its stocks of office and data processing supplies. Increases in accounts receivable, inventory, and prepaid expenses are the price a business has to pay for growth. Rarely do you find a business that can increase its sales revenue without increasing these assets.

### The simple but troublesome depreciation factor

Depreciation expense recorded in the period is both the simplest cash flow effect to understand and, at the same time, one of the misunderstood elements in calculating cash flow from profit. (Refer to Chapters 5 and 6 for more about depreciation.) To start with, depreciation is not a cash outlay during the period. The amount of depreciation expense recorded in the period is simply a fraction of the original cost of the business's fixed assets that were bought and paid for years ago. (Well, if you want to nit-pick here, some of the fixed assets may have been bought during this period, and their cost is reported in the investing activities section of the cash flow statement.) Because the depreciation expense is not a cash outlay this period, the amount is added back to net income in the calculation of cash flow from profit — so far so good.

When measuring profit on the accrual basis of accounting, you count depreciation as an expense. The fixed assets of a business are on an irreversible journey to the junk heap. Fixed assets have a limited, finite life of usefulness to a business (except for land); depreciation is the accounting method that allocates the total cost of fixed assets to each year of their use in helping the business generate sales revenue. Part of the total sales revenue of a business constitutes *recovery of cost invested in its fixed assets*. In a real sense, a business "sells" some of its fixed assets each period to its customers — it factors the cost of fixed assets into the sales prices that it charges its customers. For example, when you go to a supermarket, a very small slice of the price you pay for that box of cereal goes toward the cost of the building, the shelves, the refrigeration equipment, and so on. (No wonder they charge so much for a box of flakes!)

Each period, a business recoups part of the cost invested in its fixed assets. In other words, $1.2 million of sales revenue (in the example) went toward reimbursing the business for the use of its fixed assets during the year. The problem regarding depreciation in cash flow analysis is that many people simply add back depreciation for the year to bottom-line profit and then stop, as if this is the proper number for cash flow from profit. It ain't so. The changes in other assets as well as the changes in liabilities also affect cash flow from profit. You should factor in *all* the changes that determine cash flow from profit, as explained the following section.

Adding net income and depreciation to determine cash flow from profit is mixing apples and oranges. The business did not realize $1,600,000 cash increase from its $1,600,000 net income. The total of the increases of its accounts receivable, inventory, and prepaid expenses is $1,920,000 (refer to Figure 7-1), which wipes out the net income amount and leaves the business in a cash balance hole of $320,000. This cash deficit is offset by the $220,000 increase in liabilities (explained later), leaving a $100,000 net income *deficit* as far as cash flow is concerned. Depreciation recovery increased cash flow $1.2 million. So the final cash flow from profit equals $1.1 million. But you'd never know this if you simply added depreciation expense to net income for the period.

---

# Net income + depreciation expense does not equal cash flow from profit!

The business in my example earned $1.6 million in net income for the year, plus it received $1.2 cash flow because of the depreciation expense built into in its sales revenue for the year. The sum of these is $2.8 million. Is $2.8 million the amount of cash flow from profit for the period? The knee-jerk answer of many investors and managers is "yes." But as they say in Iowa, "Hold 'er down, Newt!" If net income + depreciation truly equals cash flow, then *both* factors in the brackets — both net income and depreciation — must be fully realized in cash. Depreciation is, but the net income amount is not fully realized in cash because the company's accounts receivable, inventory, and prepaid expenses increased during the year, and these increases have negative impacts on cash flow.

The managers did not have to go outside the business for the $1.1 million cash increase generated from its profit for the year. Cash flow from profit is an *internal* source of money generated by the business itself, in contrast to *external* money that the business raises from lenders and owners. A business does not have to "go begging" for external money if its internal cash flow from profit is sufficient to provide for its growth.

In passing, I should mention that a business could have a negative cash flow from profit for a year — meaning that despite posting a net income for the period, the changes in the company's assets and liabilities caused its cash balance to decrease. In reverse, a business could report a bottom-line *loss* in its income statement yet have a *positive* cash flow from its operating activities: The add-back of depreciation expense plus decreases in its accounts receivable and inventory could amount to more than the amount of loss. More realistically, a loss often leads to negative cash flow or very little positive cash flow.

### Operating liabilities increases

The business in the example, like almost all businesses, has three basic liabilities that are inextricably intertwined with its expenses: accounts payable, accrued expenses payable, and income tax payable. When the beginning balance of one of these liability accounts is the same as the ending balance of the same account (not too likely, of course), the business breaks even on cash flow for that account. When the end-of-period balance is higher than the start-of-period balance, the business did not pay out as much money as was actually recorded as an expense on the period's income statement.

In the example I've been using, the business disbursed $720,000 to pay off last period's accounts payable balance. (This $720,000 was reported as the accounts payable balance on last period's ending balance sheet.) Its cash flow this period decreased by $720,000 because of these payments. But this period's ending balance sheet shows the amount of accounts payable that the business will need to pay next period: $800,000. The business actually paid off $720,000 and recorded $800,000 of expenses to the year, so this time, cash flow is *richer* than what's reflected in the businesses net income figure by $80,000 — the increase in accounts payable has a positive cash flow effect, in other words. The increases in accrued expenses payable and income tax payable work the same way.

Therefore, liability increases are favorable to cash flow — in a sense, the business borrowed more than it paid off. Such an increase means that the business delayed paying cash for certain things until next year. So you need to add the increases in the three liabilities to net income to determine cash flow from profit, following the same logic as adding back depreciation to net income. The business did not have cash outlays to the extent of increases in these three liabilities.

The analysis of the changes in assets and liabilities of the business that affect cash flow from profit is complete for the business example. The bottom line (oops, I shouldn't use that term when referring to a cash flow amount) is that the company's cash balance increased $1.1 million from profit. You could argue that cash should have increased $2.8 million — $1.6 million net income plus $1.2 million depreciation that was recovered during the year — so the business is $1.7 million behind in turning its profit into cash flow ($2.8 million less the $1.1 million cash flow from profit). This $1.7 million lag in converting profit into cash flow is caused by the $1,920,000 increase in assets less the $220,000 increase in liabilities, as shown in Figure 7-1.

# Presenting the Cash Flow Statement

The cash flow statement is one of the three primary financial statements that a business must report to the outside world, according to generally accepted accounting principles (GAAP). To be technical, the rule says that whenever a business reports an income statement, it should also report a cash flow statement. The *income statement* summarizes sales revenue and expenses and ends with the bottom-line profit for the period. The *balance sheet* summarizes a business's financial condition by reporting its assets, liabilities, and owners' equity. (Refer to Chapters 5 and 6 for more about these reports.)

You can probably guess what the *cash flow statement* does by its name alone: This statement tells you where a business got its cash and what the business did with its cash during the period. I prefer the name given in the old days to the predecessor of the cash flow statement, the *Where Got, Where Gone* statement. This nickname goes straight to the purpose of the cash flow statement: asking where the business got its money and what it did with the money.

To give you a rough idea of what a cash flow statement reports, I repeat some of the questions I asked at the start of the chapter: How much money did you earn last year? Did you get all your income in cash (did some of your wages go straight into a retirement plan, or did you collect a couple of IOUs)? Where did you get other money (did you take out a loan, win the lottery, or receive a gift from a rich uncle)? What did you do with your money (did you buy a house, support your out-of-control Internet addiction, or lose it in Saturday night poker)?

Getting a little too personal for you? That's exactly why the cash flow statement is so important: It bares a business's financial soul to its lenders and owners. Sometimes the cash flow statement reveals questionable judgment calls that the business's managers made. At the very least, the cash flow statement reveals how well a business handles the cash increase from its profit.

## The history of the cash flow statement

The cash flow statement was not required for external financial reporting until 1987. Until then, the accounting profession had turned a deaf ear to calls from the investment community for cash flow statements in annual financial reports. (Accountants had presented a _funds flow statement_ prior to 1987, but that report proved to be a disaster — the term _funds_ included more assets than just cash and represented a net amount after deducting short-term liabilities from short-term, or current, assets.)

In my opinion, the reluctance to require cash flow statements came from fears that the _cash flow_

_from profit_ figure would usurp net income — people would lose confidence in the net income line.

Those fears have some justification — considering the attention given to cash flow from profit and what is called "free cash flow" (discussed later in the chapter). Although the income statement continues to get most of the fanfare (because it shows the magic bottom-line number of net income), cash flow gets a lot of emphasis these days.

As explained at the start of the chapter, the cash flow statement is divided into three sections according to the three-fold classification of cash flows for a business:

- ✔ Cash flow from **operating activities** (which I also call _cash flow from profit_ in the chapter): The activities by which a business makes profit and turns the profit into cash flow (includes depreciation and changes in operating assets and liabilities)

- ✔ Cash flow from **investing activities:** Investing in long-term assets needed for a business's operations; also includes money taken out of these assets from time to time (such as when a business disposes of some of its long-term assets)

- ✔ Cash flow from **financing activities:** Raising capital from debt and owners' equity, returning capital to these capital sources, and distributing profit to owners

The cash flow statement reports a business's net cash increase or decrease based on these three groupings of the cash flow statement. Figure 7-2 shows what a cash flow statement typically looks like — in this example, for a _growing_ business (which means that its assets, liabilities, and owners' equity increase during the period).

| Cash Flow Statement For Year (in thousands of dollars) | | |
|---|---|---|
| **Cash Flows From Operating Activities** | | |
| Net Income | | $ 1,600 |
| Accounts Receivable Increase | $ (800) | |
| Inventory Increase | $ (975) | |
| Prepaid Expenses Increase | $ (145) | |
| Depreciation Expense | $ 1,200 | |
| Accounts Payable Increase | $ 80 | |
| Accrued Expense Increase | $ 120 | |
| Income Tax Payable Increase | $ 20 | $ (500) |
| Cash Flow From Operating Activities | | $ 1,100 |
| | | |
| **Cash Flows From Investing Activities** | | |
| Purchases of Property, Plant & Equipment | | $ (1,275) |
| | | |
| **Cash Flows From Financing Activities** | | |
| Short-term Debt Borrowing Increase | $ 200 | |
| Long-term Debt Borrowing Increase | $ 300 | |
| Capital Stock Issue | $ 60 | |
| Dividends Paid Stockholders | $ (400) | $ 160 |
| Increase (Decrease) In Cash During Year | | $ (15) |
| Beginning Cash Balance | | $ 2,015 |
| Ending Cash Balance | | $ 2,000 |

**Figure 7-2:** Cash flow statement for the business in the example.

The trick to understanding cash flow from profit is to link the sales revenue and expenses of the business with the changes in the business's assets and liabilities that are directly connected with its profit-making activities. Using this approach earlier in the chapter, I determine that the cash flow from profit is $1.1 million for the year for the sample business. This is the number you see in Figure 7-2 for cash flow from operating activities. In my experience, many business managers, lenders, and investors don't fully understand these links, but the savvy ones know to keep a close eye on the relevant balance sheet changes.

# Where to put depreciation?

Where the depreciation line goes within the first section (operating activities) of the cash flow statement is a matter of personal preference — no standard location is required. Many businesses report it in the middle or toward the bottom of the changes in assets and liabilities — perhaps to avoid giving people the idea that cash flow from profit simply requires adding back depreciation to net income.

What do the figures in the first section of the cash flow statement (refer to Figure 7-2) reveal about this business over the past period? Recall that the business experienced rapid sales growth over the last period. However, the downside of sales growth is that operating assets and liabilities also grow — the business needs more inventory at the higher sales level and also has higher accounts receivable.

The business's prepaid expenses and liabilities also increased, although not nearly as much as accounts receivable and inventory. The rapid growth of the business yielded higher profit but also caused quite a surge in its operating assets and liabilities — the result being that cash flow from profit is only $1.1 million compared with $1.6 million in net income — a $500,000 shortfall. Still, the business had $1.1 million at its disposal after allowing for the increases in assets and liabilities. What did the business do with this $1.1 million of available cash? You have to look to the remainder of the cash flow statement to answer this key question.

A very quick read through the rest of the cash flow statement (refer to Figure 7-2) goes something like this: The company used $1,275,000 to buy new fixed assets, borrowed $500,000, and distributed $400,000 of the profit to its owners. The bottom line (or should I use that term here?) is that cash decreased $15,000 during the year. Shouldn't the business have increased its cash balance, given its fairly rapid growth during the period? That's a good question! Higher levels of sales generally require higher levels of operating cash balances. However, you can see in its balance sheet at the end of the year (refer to Figure 6-2) that the company has $2 million in cash, which, compared with its $25 million annual sales revenue, is probably enough.

## A better alternative for reporting cash flow from profit?

I call your attention, again, to the first section of the cash flow statement in Figure 7-2. You start with net income for the period. Next, changes in assets and liabilities are deducted or added to net income to arrive at cash flow from operating activities (the cash flow from profit) for the year. This format is called the *indirect method*. The alternative format for this section of the cash flow statement is called the *direct method* and is presented like this (using the same business example, with dollar amounts in millions):

| | |
|---|---|
| Cash inflow from sales | $24.2 |
| Less cash outflow for expenses | 23.1 |
| Cash flow from operating activities | $1.1 |

You may remember from the earlier discussion that sales revenue for the year is $25 million, but that the company's accounts receivable increased $800,000 during the year, so cash flow from sales is $24.2 million. Likewise, the expenses for the year can be put on a cash flow basis. But I "cheated" here — I have already determined that cash flow from profit is $1.1 million for the year, so I plugged the figure for cash outflow for expenses. I would take more time to explain the direct approach, except for one main reason.

Although the Financial Accounting Standards Board (FASB) expresses a definite preference for the direct method, this august rule-making body does permit the indirect method to be used in external financial reports — and, in fact, the overwhelming majority of businesses use the indirect method. Unless you're a CPA, I don't think you need to know much more about the direct method.

# Sailing through the Rest of the Cash Flow Statement

After you get past the first section, the rest of the cash flow statement is a breeze. The last two sections of the statement explain what the business did with its cash and where cash that didn't come from profit came from.

## Investing activities

The second section of the cash flow statement reports the investment actions that a business's managers took during the year. Investments are like tea leaves, which serve as indicators regarding what the future may hold for the company. Major new investments are the sure signs of expanding or modernizing the production and distribution facilities and capacity of the business. Major disposals of long-term assets and shedding off a major part of the business could be good news or bad news for the business, depending on many factors. Different investors may interpret this information differently, but all would agree that the information in this section of the cash flow statement is very important.

Certain long-lived operating assets are required for doing business — for example, Federal Express wouldn't be terribly successful if it didn't have airplanes and trucks for delivering packages and computers for tracking deliveries. When those assets wear out, the business needs to replace them. Also, to remain competitive, a business may need to upgrade its equipment to take advantage of the latest technology or provide for growth. These investments in long-lived, tangible, productive assets, which I call *fixed assets* in this book, are critical to the future of the business and are called *capital expenditures* to stress that capital is being invested for the long haul.

One of the first claims on cash flow from profit is capital expenditures. Notice in Figure 7-2 that the business spent $1,275,000 for new fixed assets, which are referred to as *property, plant, and equipment* in the cash flow statement (to keep the terminology consistent with account titles used in the balance sheet, because the term *fixed assets* is rather informal).

Cash flow statements generally don't go into much detail regarding exactly what specific types of fixed assets a business purchased — how many additional square feet of space the business acquired, how many new drill presses it bought, and so on. (Some businesses do leave a clearer trail of their investments, though: For example, airlines describe how many new aircraft of each kind were purchased to replace old equipment or expand their fleets.)

*Note:* Typically, every year a business disposes of some of its fixed assets that have reached the end of their useful lives and will no longer be used. These fixed assets are sent to the junkyard, traded in on new fixed assets, or sold for relatively small amounts of money. The value of a fixed asset at the end of its useful life is called its *salvage value.* The disposal proceeds from selling fixed assets are reported as a source of cash in the investments section of the cash flow statement. Usually, these amounts are fairly small. In contrast, a business may sell off fixed assets because it's downsizing or abandoning a major segment of its business. These cash proceeds can be fairly large.

## Financing activities

Note that in the annual cash flow statement (refer to Figure 7-2) of the business example I've been using, the positive cash flow from profit is $1,100,000 and the negative cash flow from investing activities is $1,275,000. The result to this point, therefore, is a net cash outflow of $175,000 — which would have decreased the company's cash balance this much if the business did not go to outside sources of capital for additional money during the year. In fact, the business increased its short-term and long-term debt during the year, and its owners invested additional money in the business. The third section of the cash flow statement summarizes these financing activities of the business over the period.

The term *financing* generally refers to a business raising capital from debt and equity sources — from borrowing money from banks and other sources willing to loan money to the business and from its owners putting additional money in the business. The term also includes the flip side, that is, making payments on debt and returning capital to owners. The term *financing* also includes cash distributions (if any) from profit by the business to its owners.

Most businesses borrow money for a short-term (generally defined as less than one year), as well as for longer terms (generally defined as more than one year). In other words, a typical business has both short-term and long-term debt. (Chapter 6 explains that short-term debt is presented in the current liabilities section of the balance sheet.) The business in my example has both short-term and long-term debt. Although not a hard and fast rule, most cash flow statements report just the *net* increase or decrease in short-term debt, not the total amount borrowed and the total payments on short-term debt during the period. In contrast, both the total amount borrowed from and the total amount paid on long-term debt during the year are reported in the cash flow statement.

For the business I've been using as an example, no long-term debt was paid down during the year, but short-term debt was paid off during the year and replaced with new short-term notes payable. However, only the net increase ($200,000) is reported in the cash flow statement. The business also increased its long-term debt by $300,000 (refer to Figure 7-2).

The financing section of the cash flow statement also reports on the flow of cash between the business and its owners (who are the stockholders of a corporation). Owners can be both a *source* of a business's cash (capital invested by owners) and a *use* of a business's cash (profit distributed to owners). This section of the cash flow statement reports capital raised from its owners, if any, as well as any capital returned to the owners. In the cash flow statement (Figure 7-2), note that the business did issue additional stock shares for $60,000 during the year, and it paid a total of $400,000 cash dividends (distributions) from profit to its owners.

# Free Cash Flow: What the Devil Does That Mean?

A new term has emerged in the lexicon of accounting and finance: *free cash flow*. This piece of language is not — I repeat, *not* — an officially defined term by any authoritative accounting rule-making body. Furthermore, the term does *not* appear in the cash flow statements reported by businesses. Rather, free cash flow is street language, or slang, even though the term appears often in *The Wall Street Journal* and *The New York Times*. Securities brokers and investment analysts use the term freely (pun intended). Like most new words being tossed around for the first time, this one hasn't settled down into one universal meaning, although the most common usage of the term pivots on cash flow from profit.

The term *free cash flow* is used to mean any of the following:

- ✔ Net income plus depreciation (plus any other expense recorded during the period that does not involve the outlay of cash but rather the allocation of the cost of a long-term asset other than property, plant, and equipment — such as the intangible assets of a business)

✔ Cash flow from operating activities (as reported in the cash flow statement)

✔ Cash flow from operating activities minus some or all of the capital expenditures made during the year (such as purchases or construction of new, long-lived operating assets such as property, plant, and equipment)

✔ Cash flow from operating activities plus interest, and depreciation, and income tax expenses, or, in other words, cash flow before these expenses are deducted

In the strongest possible terms, I advise you to be very clear on which definition of *free cash flow* the speaker or writer is using. Unfortunately, you can't always determine what the term means in any given context. The reporter or investment professional should define the term.

One definition of free cash flow, in my view, is quite useful: cash flow from profit minus capital expenditures for the year. The idea is that a business needs to make capital expenditures in order to stay in business and thrive. And to make capital expenditures, the business needs cash. Only after paying for its capital expenditures does a business have "free" cash flow that it can use as it likes. In my example, the free cash flow is, in fact, negative: $1,100,000 cash flow from profit minus $1,275,000 capital expenditures for new fixed assets equals a *negative* $175,000.

This is a key point: In many cases, cash flow from profit falls short of the money needed for capital expenditures. So the business has to borrow more money, persuade its owners to invest more money in the business, or dip into its cash reserve. Should a business in this situation distribute some of its profit to owners? After all, it has a cash *deficit* after paying for capital expenditures. But many companies like the business in my example do, in fact, make cash distributions from profit to their owners.

# Scrutinizing the Cash Flow Statement

Analyzing a business's cash flow statement inevitably raises certain questions: What would I have done differently if I were running this business? Would I have borrowed more money? Would I have raised more money from the owners? Would I have distributed so much of the profit to the owners? Would I have let my cash balance drop by even such a small amount?

One purpose of the cash flow statement is to show readers what judgment calls and financial decisions the business's managers made during the period. Of course, management decisions are always subject to second-guessing and criticizing, and passing judgment based on a financial statement isn't totally fair because it doesn't reveal the pressures the managers faced during the period. Maybe they made the best possible decisions given the circumstances. Maybe not.

The business in my example (refer to Figure 7-2) distributed $400,000 cash from profit to its owners — a 25 percent *pay-out ratio* (which is the $400,000 distribution divided by $1.6 million net income). In analyzing whether the pay-out ratio is too high, too low, or just about right, you need to look at the broader context of the business's sources of, and needs for, cash.

First look at cash flow from profit: $1.1 million, which is not enough to cover the business's $1,275,000 capital expenditures during the year. The business increased its total debt $500,000. Given these circumstances, maybe the business should've hoarded its cash and not paid so much in cash distributions to its owners.

So does this business have enough cash to operate with? You can't answer that question just by examining the cash flow statement — or any financial statement, for that matter. Every business needs a buffer of cash to protect against unexpected developments and to take advantage of unexpected opportunities, as I explain in Chapter 10 on budgeting. This particular business has a $2 million cash balance compared with $25 million annual sales revenue for the period just ended, which probably is enough. If you were the boss of this business, how much working cash balance would you want? Not an easy question to answer! Don't forget that you need to look at all three primary financial statements — the income statement and the balance sheet as well as the cash flow statement — to get the big picture of a business's financial health.

You probably didn't count the number of lines of information in Figure 7-2, the cash flow statement for the business example. Anyway, the financial statement has 17 lines of information. Would you like to hazard a guess regarding the average number of lines in cash flow statements of publicly owned corporations? Typically, their cash flow statements have 30 to 40 lines of information by my reckoning. So it takes quite a while to read the cash flow statement — more time than the average investor probably has to read this financial statement. (Professional stock analysts and investment managers are paid to take the time to read this financial statement meticulously.) Quite frankly, I find that many cash flow statements are not only rather long, but also difficult to understand — even for a CPA. I won't get on my soapbox here, but I definitely think businesses could do a better job of reporting their cash flow statements by reducing the number of lines in this financial statement and making each line clearer.

# Chapter 8

# Getting a Financial Report Ready for Prime Time

C hapters 5, 6, and 7 explain the primary financial statements of a business:

✔ **Income statement:** Summarizes sales revenue inflows and expense outflows for the period and ends with the bottom-line profit, which is the net inflow for the period (a loss is a net outflow)

✔ **Balance sheet:** Summarizes financial condition at the end of the period, consisting of amounts for assets, liabilities, and owners' equity at that instant in time

✔ **Cash flow statement:** Summarizes the net cash inflow (or outflow) from profit for the period, plus the other sources and uses of cash during the period

An annual financial report of a business contains more than just these three financial statements. In the "more," the business manager plays an important role — which outside investors and lenders should understand. The manager should do certain critical things before the financial report is released to the outside world.

1. **The manager should review with a critical eye the *vital connections* between the items reported in all three financial statements** — all amounts have to fit together like the pieces of a puzzle. The net cash increase (or decrease) reported at the end of the cash flow statement, for instance, has to tie in with the change in cash reported in the balance sheet. Abnormally high or low ratios between connected accounts should be scrutinized carefully. For example, suppose accounts receivable increased substantially during the year but sales revenue was flat compared with last year. The manager should definitely look into this discrepancy before letting the financial statements go outside the business.

2. **The manager should carefully review the *disclosures* in the financial report** (all information in addition to the financial statements) to make sure that disclosure is adequate according to financial reporting standards, and that all the disclosure elements are truthful but not damaging to the interests of the business.

   This disclosure review can be compared with the notion of *due diligence,* which is done to make certain that all relevant information is collected, that the information is accurate and reliable, and that all relevant requirements and regulations are being complied with. This step is especially important for public corporations whose securities (stock shares and debt instruments) are traded on national securities exchanges.

3. **The manager should consider whether the financial statement numbers need *touching up*** to smooth the jagged edges off the company's year-to-year profit gyrations or to improve the business's short-term solvency picture. Although this can be described as putting your thumb on the scale, you can also argue that sometimes the scale is a little out of balance to begin with and the manager is adjusting the financial statements to jibe better with the normal circumstances of the business.

In discussing the third step later in the chapter, I walk on thin ice. Some topics are, shall I say, rather delicate. The manager has to strike a balance between the interests of the business on the one hand and the interests of the owners (investors) and creditors of the business on the other. The best analogy I can think of is the advertising done by a business. Advertising should be truthful, but as I'm sure you know, businesses have a lot of leeway in how to advertise their products and they have been known to engage in hyperbole. Managers exercise the same freedoms in putting together their financial reports.

## *Reviewing Vital Connections*

Business managers and investors read financial reports because these reports provide information regarding how the business is doing. The top managers of a business, in reviewing the annual financial report before releasing it outside the business, should keep in mind that a financial report is designed to answer certain basic financial questions:

✔ Is the business making a profit or suffering a loss, and how much?

✔ How do assets stack up against liabilities?

✔ Where did the business get its capital, and is it making good use of the money?

✔ Is profit generating cash flow?

✔ Did the business reinvest all its profit or distribute some of the profit to owners?

✔ Does the business have enough capital for future growth?

People read a financial report like a road map — to point the way and check how the trip is going. Managing and investing in a business is a financial journey. A manager is like the driver and must pay attention to all the road signs; investors are like the passengers who watch the same road signs. Some of the most important road signs are the vital connections between sales revenue and expenses and their related assets and operating liabilities in the balance sheet.

 As a hypothetical but realistic business example, Figure 8-1 highlights some of the vital connections — the lines connect one or more balance sheet accounts with sales revenue or an expense in the income statement. The savvy manager or investor checks these links to see whether everything is in order or whether some danger signals point to problems. (I should make clear that these lines of connection do not appear in actual financial reports.)

**Figure 8-1:**
Vital connections between the income statement and the balance sheet.

(Dollar amounts in thousands)

| Income Statement For Year | |
|---|---|
| Sales Revenue | $ 52,000 |
| Cost of Goods Sold Expense | 31,200 |
| Gross Margin | $ 20,800 |
| Sales, Administration, and General Expenses | 15,600 |
| Depreciation Expense | 1,650 |
| Earnings Before Interest and Income Tax | $ 3,550 |
| Interest Expense | 750 |
| Earnings Before Income Tax | $ 2,800 |
| Income Tax Expense | 900 |
| Net Income | $ 1,900 |

**Balance Sheet at End of Year**

| Assets | |
|---|---|
| Cash | $ 3,500 |
| Accounts Receivable | 5,000 |
| Inventory | 7,800 |
| Prepaid Expenses | 900 |
| Fixed Assets | 19,500 |
| Accumulated Depreciation | (6,825) |
| Total Assets | $ 29,875 |
| Liabilities | |
| Accounts Payable | $ 1,500 |
| Accrued Expenses Payable | 2,400 |
| Income Tax Payable | 75 |
| Short-term Notes Payable | 4,000 |
| Long-term Notes Payable | 6,000 |
| Owners' Equity | |
| Capital Stock | 4,000 |
| Retained Earnings | 11,900 |
| Liabilities and Owners' Equity | $ 29,875 |

## What to do if your income isn't coming in

After making credit sales, a business should closely monitor collections from customers to make sure that the money is coming in on time. In larger organizations, someone is assigned responsibility for credit and collections. This person (or department) screens first-time customers who ask for credit and keeps a close eye on actual collections of accounts receivable. When a customer does not pay on time, the business sends out a friendly reminder. If the customer doesn't respond to one or more of these requests for payment, the business follows up with a very unfriendly *dun letter which demands payment or else legal action will be taken, or at least threatens that the lack of payment will be reported to a credit rating agency.*

Eventually, the business may take legal action against deadbeats (customers whose accounts receivable are overdue by 60 to 90 days or longer). The business might hire a collection agency, even though the cost is high — usually half or more of the amount collected.

In the following list, I briefly explain these five connections mainly from the manager's point of view. Chapters 14 and 17 explain how investors and lenders read a financial report and compute certain ratios. (Investors and lenders are on the outside looking in; managers are on the inside looking out.)

*Note:* I cut right to the chase in the following brief comments, and I do not illustrate the calculations behind the comments. The purpose here is to emphasize why managers should pay attention to these important ratios. (Chapters 5 and 6 provide fuller explanations of these and other connections of operating assets and liabilities with sales revenue and expenses.)

1. **Sales Revenue and Accounts Receivable:** This business's ending balance of accounts receivable is five weeks of its annual sales revenue. The manager should compare this ratio to the normal credit terms offered to the business's customers. If the ending balance is too high, the manager should identify which customers' accounts are past due and take actions to collect these amounts, or perhaps shut off future credit to these customers. (Refer to the sidebar "What to do if your income isn't coming in" for more information.) An abnormally high balance of accounts receivable may signal that some of these customers' amounts owed to the business should be written off as uncollectible bad debts.

2. **Cost of Goods Sold Expense and Inventory:** This business's ending inventory is 13 weeks of its annual cost of goods sold expense. The manager should compare this ratio to the company's inventory policies and objectives regarding how long inventory should be held awaiting sale. If inventory is too large, the manager should identify which products have been in stock too long; further purchases (or manufacturing) should be curtailed. Also, the manager may want to consider sales promotions or cutting sales prices to move these products out of inventory faster.

3. **Sales, Administration, and General (SA&G) Expenses and Prepaid Expenses:** This business's ending balance of prepaid expenses is three weeks of the total of these annual operating expenses. The manager should know what the normal ratio of prepaid expenses should be relative to the annual SA&G operating expenses (excluding depreciation expense). If the ending balance is too high, the manager should investigate which costs have been paid too far in advance and take action to bring these prepaids back down to normal.

4. **Sales, Administration, and General (SA&G) Expenses and Accounts Payable:** This business's ending balance of accounts payable is five weeks of its annual operating expenses. Delaying payment of these liabilities is good from the cash flow point of view (refer to Chapter 7). But delaying too long may jeopardize the company's good credit rating with its key suppliers and vendors. If this ratio is too high, the manager should pinpoint which specific liabilities have not been paid and whether any of these are overdue and should be paid immediately. Or, the high balance may indicate that the company is in a difficult short-term solvency situation and needs to raise more money to pay the amounts owed to suppliers and vendors.

5. **Sales, Administration, and General (SA&G) Expenses and Accrued Expenses Payable:** This business's ending balance of this operating liability is eight weeks of the business's annual operating expenses. This ratio may be consistent with past experience and the normal lag before paying these costs. On the other hand, the ending balance may be abnormally high. The manager should identify which of these unpaid costs are higher than they should be. As with accounts payable, inflated amounts of accrued liabilities may signal serious short-term solvency problems.

These five key connections are very important ones, but the manager should scan all basic connections to see whether the ratios pass the common sense test. For example, the manager should make a quick eyeball test of interest expense compared with interest-bearing debt. In Figure 8-1, interest expense is $750,000 compared with $10 million total debt, which indicates a 7.5 percent interest rate. This seems okay. But if the interest expense were more than $1 million, the manager should investigate to determine why it's so high.

There's always the chance of errors in the accounts of a business. Reviewing the vital connections between the income statement items and the balance sheet items is a very valuable final check before the financial statements are approved for inclusion in the business's financial report. After the financial report is released to the outside world, it becomes the latest chapter in the official financial history of the business. If the financial statements are wrong, the business and its top managers are responsible.

# Statement of Changes in Owners' Equity and Comprehensive Income

In many situations, a business needs to prepare one additional financial statement — the *statement of changes in owners' equity.* Owners' equity consists of two fundamentally different sources — capital invested in the business by the owners, and profit earned by and retained in the business. The specific accounts maintained by the business for its total owners' equity depends on the legal organization of the business entity. One of the main types of legal organization of business is the *corporation*, and its owners are *stockholders* because the corporation issues ownership shares called *capital stock*. So, the title *statement of changes in stockholders' equity* is used for corporations. (Chapter 11 explains the corporation and other legal types of business entities.)

First, consider the situation in which a business does *not* need to report this statement — to make clearer why the statement is needed. Suppose a business corporation has only one class of capital stock (ownership shares), and it did not buy any of its capital stock shares during the year, and it did not record any gains or losses in owners' equity during the year due to *other comprehensive income* (explained below). This business does not need a statement of changes in stockholders' equity. In reading the financial report of this business you would see in its cash flow statement (Figure 7-2 shows an example) whether the business raised additional capital from its owners during the year, and how much *cash dividends* (distributions from profit) were paid to the owners during the year. The cash flow statement contains all the in the owners' equity accounts during the year.

In sharp contrast, larger businesses — especially publicly-traded corporations — generally have complex ownership structures consisting of two or more classes of capital stock shares; they usually buy some of their own capital stock shares; and, they have one or more technical types of gains or losses during the year. So, they prepare a statement of changes in stockholders' equity, to collect together in one place all the changes affecting the owners' equity accounts during the year. This particular "mini" statement (that focuses narrowly on changes in owners' equity accounts) is where you find certain gains and losses that increase or decrease owners' equity but which are *not* reported in the income statement. Basically, a business has the option to bypass the income statement and, instead, report these gains and losses in the statement of changes in owners' equity. In this way, the gains or losses do not affect the bottom-line profit of the business reported in its income statement. You have to read this financial summary of the changes in the owners' equity accounts to find out whether the business had any of these gains or losses, and the amounts of the gains or losses.

The special types of gains and losses that can be reported in the statement of owners' equity (instead of the income statement) have to do with foreign currency translations, unrealized gains and losses from certain types of securities investments by the business, and changes in liabilities for unfunded pension fund obligations of the business. *Comprehensive income* is the term used to describe the normal content of the income statement *plus* the additional layer of these special types of gains and losses. Being so technical in nature, these gains and losses fall in a "twilight zone," as it were, in financial reporting The gains and losses can be tacked on at the bottom of the income statement, or they can be put in the statement of changes in owners' equity — it's up to the business to make the choice. If you encounter these gains and losses in reading a financial report, you'll have to study the footnotes to the financial statements to learn more information about each gain and loss.

Keep on the lookout for the special types of gains and losses that are reported in the statement of changes in owners' equity. A business has the option to tack such gains and losses onto the bottom of its income statement — below the net income line. But, most businesses put these income gains and losses in their statement of changes in stockholders' equity. So, watch out for any large amounts of gains or losses that are reported in the statement of changes in owners' equity. Fortunately, the magnitude of these gains and losses usually is fairly small for most businesses — although you have to read the statement to be sure.

The general format of the statement of changes in stockholders' equity includes a column for each class of stock (common stock, preferred stock, and so on); a column for any *treasury stock* (shares of its own capital stock the business has purchased and not cancelled); a column for retained earnings; and, one or more columns for any other separate components of the business's owners' equity. Each column starts with the beginning balance and then shows the increases or decreases in the account during the year. For example, a comprehensive gain is shown as an increase in retained earnings, and a comprehensive loss as a decrease. The purchase of shares of its own capital stock is shown as an increase in the treasury stock column, and if the business reissued some of these shares (such as for stock options exercised by executives), the cost of the treasury shares reissued is shown as a decrease in the column.

I have to admit that reading the statement of changes in stockholders' equity can be heavy lifting. The professionals — stock analysts, money and investment managers, and so on — carefully read through and dissect this statement, or at least they should. The average, nonprofessional investor should focus on whether the business had a major increase or decrease in the number of stock shares during the year, whether the business changed its ownership structure by creating or eliminating a class of stock, and should consider the impact of stock options awarded to managers of the business.

# *Making Sure that Disclosure Is Adequate*

The primary financial statements (including the statement of changes in owners' equity, if reported) are the backbone of a financial report. In fact, a financial report is not deserving of the name if the primary financial statements are not included. But, as mentioned earlier, there's much more to a financial report than the financial statements. A financial report needs *disclosures.* Of course, the financial statements provide disclosure of the most important financial information about the business. The term disclosures, however, usually refers to additional information provided in a financial report. In a nutshell, a financial report has two basic parts: (1) the primary financial statements and (2) disclosures.

The chief officer of the business (usually the CEO of a publicly owned corporation, the president of a private corporation, or the managing partner of a partnership) has the primary responsibility to make sure that the financial statements have been prepared according to generally accepted accounting principles (GAAP) and that the financial report provides adequate disclosure. He or she works with the chief financial officer and Controller of the business to make sure that the financial report meets the standard of adequate disclosure. (Many smaller businesses hire an independent CPA to advise them on their financial statements and other disclosure in their financial reports.)

## *Types of disclosures in financial reports*

For a quick survey of disclosures in financial reports — that is to say, the disclosures in addition to the financial statements — the following distinctions are helpful:

- ✔ **Footnotes** that provide additional information about the basic figures included in the financial statements; virtually all financial statements need footnotes to provide additional information for the account balances in the financial statements.

- ✔ **Supplementary financial schedules and tables** to the financial statements provide more details than can be included in the body of financial statements.

- ✔ A wide variety of **other information** is included, some of which is required if the business is a public corporation subject to federal regulations regarding financial reporting to its stockholders, and other information that is voluntary and not strictly required legally or according to GAAP.

## *Footnotes: Nettlesome but needed*

Footnotes appear at the end of the primary financial statements. Within the financial statements, you see references to particular footnotes. And at the bottom of each financial statement, you find the following sentence (or words to this effect): "The footnotes are integral to the financial statements." You should read all footnotes for a full understanding of the financial statements.

Footnotes come in two types:

✔ One or more footnotes must be included to identify the **major accounting policies and methods** that the business uses. (Chapter 13 explains that a business must choose among alternative accounting methods for certain expenses, and for their corresponding operating assets and liabilities.) The business must reveal which accounting methods it uses for its major expenses. In particular, the business must identify its cost of goods sold expense (and inventory) method and its depreciation methods. Some businesses have unusual problems regarding the timing for recording sales revenue, and a footnote should clarify their revenue recognition method. Other accounting methods that have a material impact on the financial statements are disclosed in footnotes as well.

✔ Other footnotes provide **additional information and details** for many assets and liabilities. For example, during the asbestos lawsuits that went on for many years, the businesses that manufactured and sold these products included long footnotes describing the lawsuits. Details about stock option plans for key executives are the main type of footnote to the capital stock account in the owners' equity section of the balance sheet.

Some footnotes are always required; a financial report would be naked without some footnotes. Deciding whether a footnote is needed (after you get beyond the obvious ones disclosing the business's accounting methods) and how to write the footnote is largely a matter of judgment and opinion. Believe it or not, there is no official, comprehensive checklist for footnote disclosure in annual financial reports. On the other hand, many standards have been laid down by the Financial Accounting Standards Board (FASB) and the Securities & Exchange Commission (SEC) for publicly owned corporations that mandate disclosure of certain information — such as the recent FASB pronouncement regarding disclosure of the effects of stock options.

One problem that most investors face when reading footnotes — and, for that matter, many managers who should understand their own footnotes but find them a little dense — is that footnotes often deal with complex issues (such as lawsuits) and rather technical accounting matters. Let me offer you one footnote that brings out this latter point. This footnote is taken from the recent financial report of a well-known manufacturer that uses a very conservative accounting method for determining its cost of goods sold expense and inventory cost value. I know that I have not yet talked about these accounting methods; this is deliberate on my part. (Chapter 13 explains accounting methods.) I want you to read the following footnote from the 1999 Annual Report of Caterpillar, Inc. (available at its Web site) and try to make sense of it (dollar amounts are in thousands).

*D. Inventories: Inventories are valued principally by the LIFO (last-in, first-out) method. If the FIFO (first-in, first-out) method had been in use, inventories would have been $2,000 million and $1,978 million higher than reported at December 31, 1999 and 1998, respectively.*

Yes, these amounts are in *millions* of dollars. The company's inventory cost value at the end of 1999 would have been $2.0 billion higher if the FIFO method had been used. Of course, you have to have some idea of the difference between the two methods, which I explain in Chapter 13.

You may wonder how different the company's annual profits would have been if the alternative method had been in use. A manager can ask the accounting department to do this analysis. But, as an outside investor, you would have to compute these amounts. Businesses disclose which accounting methods they use, but they do not have to disclose how different annual profits would have been if the alternative method had been used — and very few do.

---

## Warren Buffett's annual letter to stockholders

I have to call your attention to one notable exception to the generally self-serving and slanted writing found in the letter to stockholders by the chief executive officer of the business in annual financial reports. The annual letter to stockholders of Berkshire Hathaway, Inc. is written by Warren Buffett, the Chairman and CEO. Mr. Buffett has become very well known; he's called the "Oracle of Omaha." In the annual ranking of the world's richest people by *Forbes* magazine he is near the top of the list — right behind people like Bill Gates, the cofounder of Microsoft. If you had invested $1,000 with him in 1960 your investment would be worth well over $1,000,000 today. Mr. Buffett's letters are the epitome of telling it like it is; they are very frank and quite humorous.

You can go the Web site of the company (www.berkshirehathaway.com) and download his most recent letter (and earlier ones if you like). You'll learn a lot about his investing philosophy, and the letters are a delight to read. By the way, his letters are copyrighted, which is very unusual — seldom do you see an annual financial report, or any part thereof, that's copyrighted. Therefore, be careful if you quote more than a line or two from Mr. Buffett's annual letters to stockholders.

## *Other disclosures in financial reports*

The following discussion includes a fairly comprehensive list of the various types of disclosures found in annual financial reports of larger, publicly owned businesses — in addition to footnotes. A few caveats are in order. First, not every public corporation includes every one of the following items, although the disclosures are fairly common. Second, the level of disclosure by private businesses — after you get beyond the financial statements and footnotes — is much less than in public corporations. Third, tracking the actual disclosure practices of private businesses is difficult because their annual financial reports are circulated only to their owners and lenders. A private business may include any or all of the following disclosures, but by and large it is not legally required to do so. The next section further explains the differences between private and public businesses regarding disclosure practices in their annual financial reports.

Public corporations typically include most of the following disclosures in their annual financial reports to their stockholders:

- ✔ **Cover (or transmittal) letter:** A letter from the chief executive of the business to the stockholders — which usually takes credit for good news and blames bad news on big government, unfavorable world political developments, a poor economy, or some other thing beyond management's control. (Refer to the sidebar "Warren Buffett's annual letter to stockholders.")

- ✔ **Highlights table:** A short table that presents key figures from the financial statements, such as sales revenue, total assets, profit, total debt, owners' equity, number of employees, and number of products sold (such as the number of vehicles sold by an automobile manufacturer, or the number of "revenue seat miles" flown by an airline, meaning one airplane seat occupied by a paying customer for one mile ). The idea is to give the stockholder a financial thumbnail sketch of the business.

- ✔ **Management discussion and analysis (MD&A):** Deals with the major developments and changes during the year that affected the financial performance and situation of the business. The SEC requires this disclosure to be included in the annual financial reports of publicly owned corporations.

- ✔ **Segment information:** The sales revenue and operating profits ( before interest and income tax, and perhaps before certain costs that cannot be allocated among different segments) are reported for the major divisions of the organization, or for its different markets (international versus domestic, for example).

- ✔ **Historical summaries:** Financial history that extends back beyond the years (usually three) included in the primary financial statements.

- ✔ **Graphics:** Bar charts, trend charts, and pie charts representing financial conditions; photos of key people and products.

- ✔ **Promotional material:** information about the company, its products, its employees, and its managers, often stressing an over-arching theme for the year.

- ✔ **Profiles:** Information about members of top management and the board of directors.

- ✔ **Quarterly summaries of profit performance and stock share prices:** Shows financial performance for all four quarters in the year and stock price ranges for each quarter (required by the SEC).

- ✔ **Management's responsibility statement:** A short statement that management has primary responsibility for the accounting methods used to prepare the financial statements, for writing the footnotes to the statements, and for providing the other disclosures in the financial report. Usually, this statement appears next to the independent auditor's report.

- ✔ **Independent auditor's report:** The report from the CPA firm that performed the audit, expressing an opinion on the fairness of the financial statements and accompanying disclosures. Chapter 15 discusses the nature of audits by CPAs and the audit reports that they present to the board of directors of the corporation for inclusion in the annual financial report. Public corporations are required to have audits; private businesses may or may not have their annual financial reports audited.

- ✔ **Company contact information:** Information on how to contact the company, the Web site address of the company, how to get copies of the reports filed with the SEC, the stock transfer agent and registrar of the company, and other information.

Managers of public corporations rely on lawyers, CPA auditors, and their financial and accounting officers to make sure that everything that should be disclosed in the business's annual financial reports is included, and that the exact wording of the disclosures is not misleading, inaccurate, or incomplete. This is a tall order. The field of financial reporting disclosure changes constantly. Both federal and state laws, as well as authoritative accounting standards, have to be observed. Inadequate disclosure in an annual financial report is just as serious as using wrong accounting methods for measuring profit and for determining values for assets, liabilities, and owners' equity. A financial report can be misleading because of improper accounting methods or because of inadequate or misleading disclosure. Both types of deficiencies can lead to nasty lawsuits against the business and its managers.

# *Keeping It Private versus Going Public*

Suppose you had the inkling (and the time!) to compare 100 annual financial reports of large, publicly owned corporations with 100 annual reports of small, privately held businesses.( More than two million private business entities file income tax returns each year.) You'd see many differences.

Compared with their big brothers and sisters, privately owned businesses provide very little additional disclosures in their annual financial reports. The primary financial statements and footnotes are pretty much the whole enchilada. Often, their financial reports may be typed on plain paper and stapled together. A privately held company may have very few stockholders, and typically one or more of the stockholders are active managers of the business.

The annual financial reports of publicly owned corporations include all or most all of the disclosure items listed earlier. Somewhere in the range of 10,000 corporations are publicly owned, and their stock shares are traded on the New York Stock Exchange, NASDAQ, or other stock exchanges. Publicly owned companies must file annual financial reports with the Securities & Exchange Commission (SEC), which is the federal agency that makes and enforces the rules for trading in securities and for the financial reporting requirements of publicly owned corporations. These filings are available to the public on the SEC's EDGAR database at the SEC's Web site — `www.sec.gov/edgar.htm`.

Annual reports published by large publicly owned corporations can run 30, 40, or 50 and more pages. A large number of public companies put their annual reports on-line at their Web sites. Generally their annual reports are very well done — the quality of the editorial work and graphics is excellent; the color scheme, layout, and design have very good eye appeal. But be warned that the volume of detail in their financial reports is overwhelming. (Refer to the last section of this chapter regarding how to deal with the information overload in annual financial reports.)

Both privately held and publicly owned businesses are bound by the same accounting rules for measuring profit, assets, liabilities, and owners' equity in annual financial reports to the owners of the business and in reports that are made available to others (such as the lenders to the business). These ground rules are called *generally accepted accounting principles* (GAAP) and are mentioned many times in this book. There aren't two different sets of accounting rules — one for private companies and a second set for public businesses. The accounting measurement and valuation rules are the same for all businesses. However, *disclosure* requirements and practices differ greatly between private and public companies.

Publicly owned businesses live in a fish bowl. When a company goes public with an *IPO* (initial public offering of stock shares), it gives up a lot of the privacy that a closely held business enjoys. Publicly owned corporations whose stock shares are traded on national stock exchanges live in glass houses. In contrast, privately owned business corporations lock their doors regarding disclosure. Whenever a privately-owned business releases a financial report — to its bank in seeking a loan, or to the outside nonmanagement investors in the business — it should include its three primary financial statements and footnotes. But beyond this, they have much more leeway and do not have to include the additional disclosure items listed in the preceding section.

A private business may have its financial statements audited by a CPA firm. If so, the audit report is included in the business's annual financial report. The very purpose of having an audit is to reassure stockholders and potential investors in the business that the financial statements can be trusted. But as I look up and down the preceding list of disclosure items, I don't see any other absolutely required disclosure item for a privately held business. The large majority of closely held businesses guard their financial information like Fort Knox.

The less information divulged in the annual financial report, the better — that's their thinking. And I don't entirely disagree. The stockholders don't have the liquidity for their stock shares that stockholders of publicly held corporations enjoy. The market prices of public corporations are everything, so information is made publicly available so that market prices are fairly determined. The stock shares of privately owned businesses are not traded, so there is not such an urgent need for a complete package of information.

A private corporation could provide all the disclosures given in the preceding list — there's certainly no law against this. But usually they don't. Investors in private businesses can request confidential reports from managers at the annual stockholders' meetings, but doing so is not practical for a stockholder in a large public corporation.

# Nudging the Numbers

This section discusses two accounting tricks that business managers and investors should know about. I don't endorse either technique, but you should be aware of both of them. In some situations, the financial statement numbers don't come out exactly the way the business wants. Accountants use certain tricks of the trade — some would say sleight of hand — to move the numbers closer to what the business prefers. One trick improves the appearance of the *short-term solvency* of the business, in particular the cash balance reported in the balance sheet at the end of the year. The other device shifts profit from one year to the next to make for a smoother trend of net income from year to year.

Not all businesses use these techniques, but the extent of their use is hard to pin down because no business would openly admit to using these manipulation methods. The evidence is fairly convincing, however, that many businesses use these techniques. I'm sure you've heard the term *loopholes* applied to income tax accounting. Well, some loopholes exist in financial statement accounting as well.

## *Fluffing up the cash balance by "window dressing"*

Suppose you manage a business and your accountant has just submitted to you a preliminary, or first draft, of the year-end balance sheet for your review. (Chapter 6 explains the balance sheet, and Figure 6-1 shows a complete balance sheet for a business.) Your preliminary balance sheet includes the following:

| Preliminary Balances, Before Window Dressing | | | |
|---|---|---|---|
| Cash | $0 | Accounts payable | $235,000 |
| Accounts receivable | $486,000 | Accrued expenses payable | $187,000 |
| Inventory | $844,000 | Income tax payable | $58,000 |
| Prepaid expenses | $72,000 | Short-term notes payable | $200,000 |
| Current assets | $1,402,000 | Current liabilities | $680,000 |

You start reading the numbers when something strikes you: a zero cash balance? How can that be? Maybe your business has been having some cash flow problems and you've intended to increase your short-term borrowing and speed up collection of accounts receivable to help the cash balance. But that plan doesn't help you right now, with this particular financial report that you must send out to your business's investors and your banker. Folks generally don't like to see a zero cash balance — it makes them kind of nervous, to put it mildly, no matter how you try to cushion it. So what do you do to avoid alarming them?

Your accountant is probably aware of a technique known as *window dressing,* a very simple method for making the cash balance look better. Suppose your fiscal year-end is October 31. Your accountant takes the cash receipts from customers paying their accounts receivable that are actually received on November 1, 2, and 3, and records them as if these cash collections had been received on October 31. After all, the argument can be made that the customers' checks were in the mail — that money is yours, as far as the customers are concerned, so your reports should reflect that cash inflow.

What impact does window dressing have? It reduces the amount in accounts receivable and increases the amount in cash by the same amount — it has absolutely no effect on the profit figure. It just makes your cash balance look a touch better. Window dressing can also be used to improve other accounts' balances, which I don't go into here. All of these techniques involve holding the books open — to record certain events that take place after the end of the fiscal year (the ending balance sheet date) to make things look better than they actually were at the close of business on the last day of the year.

Sounds like everybody wins, doesn't it? Your investors don't panic, and your job is safe. I have to warn you, though, that window dressing may be the first step on a slippery slope. A little window dressing today, and tomorrow who knows — maybe giving the numbers a nudge will lead to serious financial fraud. Anyway you look at it, window dressing is deceptive to your investors, who have every right to expect that the end of your fiscal year as stated on your financial reports is truly the end of your fiscal year. Think about it this way: If you've invested in a business that has fudged this data, how do you know what other numbers on the report are suspect?

## Smoothing the rough edges off of profit

You should not be surprised when I tell you that business managers are under tremendous pressure to make profit every year and to keep profit on the up escalator year after year. Managers strive to make their numbers, and to hit the milestone markers set for the business. Reporting a loss for the year, or even a dip below the profit trend line, is a red flag that investors view with alarm. Everyone likes to see a steady upward trend line for profit; no one likes to see a profit curve that looks like a roller coaster. Most investors want a smooth journey and don't like putting on their investment life preservers.

Managers can do certain things to deflate or inflate profit (the net income) recorded in the year, which are referred to as *profit smoothing* techniques. Profit smoothing is also called *income smoothing*. Profit smoothing is not nearly as serious as *cooking the books,* or *juggling the books,* which refers to deliber-ate, fraudulent accounting practices such as recording sales revenue that has not happened or not recording expenses that have happened. Cooking the books is very serious; managers can go to jail for fraudulent financial state-ments (although white-collar criminals seldom go to jail, to be truthful). Profit smoothing is more like a white lie that is told for the good of the business, and perhaps for the good of managers as well. Managers know that there is always some noise in the accounting system. Profit smoothing muffles the noise.

Managers of publicly owned corporations whose stock shares are actively traded are under intense pressure to keep profits steadily rising. Security analysts who follow a particular company make profit forecasts for the busi-ness, and their buy-hold-sell recommendations are based largely on these earnings forecasts. If a business fails to meet its own profit forecast or falls short of stock analysts' forecasts, the market price of its stock shares suffers. Stock option and bonus incentive compensation plans are also strong motiva-tions for achieving the profit goals set for the business.

The evidence is fairly strong that publicly owned businesses engage in some degree of profit smoothing. Frankly, it's much harder to know whether private businesses do so. Private businesses don't face the public scrutiny and expectations that public corporations do. On the other hand, key managers in a private business may have incentive bonus arrangements that depend on recorded profit. In any case, business investors and managers should know about profit smoothing and how it's done.

Most profit smoothing involves pushing revenue and expenses into other years than they would normally be recorded. For example, if the president of a business wants to report more profit for the year, he or she can instruct the chief accountant to accelerate the recording of some sales revenue that normally wouldn't be recorded until next year, or to delay the recording of some expenses until next year that normally would be recorded this year. The main reason for smoothing profit is to keep it closer to a projected trend line and make the line less jagged.

Chapter 13 explains that managers choose among alternative accounting methods for several important expenses. After making these key choices, the managers should let the accountants do their jobs and let the chips fall where they may. If bottom-line profit for the year turns out to be a little short of the forecast or target for the period, so be it. This hands-off approach to profit accounting is the ideal way. However, managers often use a hands-on approach — they intercede (one could say interfere) and override the normal accounting for sales revenue or expenses.

Both managers who do it and investors who rely on financial statements in which profit smoothing has been done should definitely understand one thing: These techniques have robbing-Peter-to-pay-Paul effects. Accountants refer to these as *compensatory effects.* The effects next year offset and cancel out the effects this year. Less expense this year is counterbalanced by more expense next year. Sales revenue recorded this year means less sales revenue recorded next year.

### Two profit histories

Figure 8-2 shows, side by side, the annual profit histories of two different companies over six years. Business X shows a nice steady upward trend of profit. Business Y, in contrast, shows somewhat of a roller coaster ride over the six years. Both businesses earned the same total profit for the six years — in this case, $1,050,449. Their total six-year profit performance is the same, down to the last dollar. Which company would you be more willing to risk your money in? I suspect that you'd prefer Business X because of the steady upward slope of its profit history.

Question: Does Figure 8-2 really show two different companies — or are the two profit histories actually alternatives for the same company? The year-by-year profits for Business X could be the company's *smoothed* profit, and the annual profits for Business Y could be the *actual* profit of the same business — the profit that would have been recorded if smoothing techniques had not been applied.

For the first year in the series, 1996, no profit smoothing occurred. Actual profit is on target. For each of the next five years, the two profit numbers differ. The under-gap or over-gap of actual profit compared with smoothed profit for the year is the amount of revenue or expenses manipulation that was done in the year. For example, in 1997, actual profit would have been too high, so the company moved some expenses that normally would be recorded the following year into 1997. In contrast, in 1998, actual profit was running too low, so the business took action to put off recording some expenses until 1999.

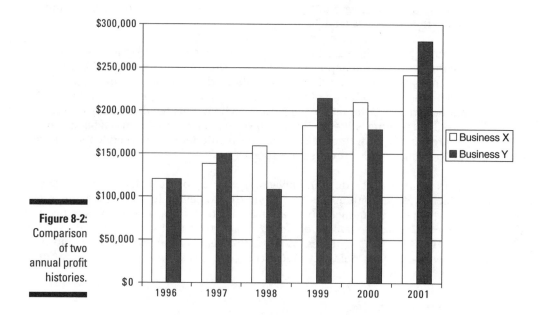

**Figure 8-2:**
Comparison of two annual profit histories.

A business can go only so far in smoothing profit. If a business has a particularly bad year, all the profit-smoothing tricks in the world won't close the gap. But several smoothing techniques are available for filling the potholes and straightening the curves on the profit highway.

### Profit-smoothing techniques

Most profit-smoothing techniques require one essential ingredient: *management discretion* in deciding *when* to record expenses or *when* to record sales. For example, when I was in public accounting, one of our clients was a contractor that used the *completed contract method* for recording its sales revenue. Not until the job was totally complete did the company book the sales revenue and deduct all costs to determine the gross margin from the job (in other words, from the contract). In most cases, the company had to return a few weeks later for final touch-up work or to satisfy minor customer complaints. In the past, the company waited for this final visit before calling a job complete. But the year

I was on the audit, the company was falling short of its profit goals. So the president decided to move up the point at which a job was called complete. The company decided not to wait for the final visit, which rarely involved more than a few minor expenses. Thus more jobs were completed during the year, more sales revenue and more gross margin were recorded in the year, and the company met its profit goals.

One common technique for profit smoothing is *deferred maintenance.* Many routine and recurring maintenance costs required for autos, trucks, machines, equipment, and buildings can be put off, or deferred until later. These costs are not recorded to expense until the actual maintenance is done, so putting off the work means that no expense is recorded. Likewise, a business may spend a fair amount of money for employee training and development. These programs can be delayed until next year, and this expense would be lower. Or a company can cut back on its current year's outlays for market research and product development. Keep in mind that most of these costs will be incurred next year, so the effect is to rob Peter (make next year absorb the cost) to pay Paul (let this year escape the cost).

A business can ease up on its rules regarding when slow-paying customers are decided to be bad debts (uncollectible accounts receivable). A business can put off recording some of its bad debts expense until next year. A fixed asset out of active use may have very little or no future value to a business. Instead of writing off the undepreciated cost of the *impaired asset* as a loss this year, the business may delay the write-off until next year.

## Into the future: On-line electronic financial reporting

A quick glance toward the future shows one thing for certain: Financial reports are going to become more and more available on the Internet. Increasing numbers of people are using computer-based means to gain access to financial reports. For many years, financial report information has been entered in large computer databases and has been accessible through the information superhighway, which includes the Internet and other commercial on-line services. The SEC has constructed EDGAR (Electronic Data Gathering, Analysis, and Retrieval), and this database of filings with the SEC probably will continue to expand and become more popular in the future. You can access the EDGAR database on the World Wide Web at the U.S. Securities and Exchange Commission Web site at www.sec.gov/edgar.htm.

Perhaps sometime in the future the traditional hard copy, or paper, annual report will be replaced by electronic equivalents. I doubt this, but you never know. On their Web sites, many companies already make available a PDF file (using Adobe Acrobat Reader) that is the exact replica of the hard copy of their annual report. My crystal ball is no better than yours, but it is fun to peer into the future the best I can.

So, managers have control over the timing of many expenses, and they can use this discretion for profit smoothing. Some amount of expenses can be accelerated into this year or deferred to next year in order to make for a smoother profit trend. Of course, a business does not divulge in its external financial report the extent to which it has engaged in profit smoothing. Nor does the independent auditor comment on the use of profit-smoothing techniques by the business — unless the auditor thinks that the company has gone too far in massaging the numbers and that its financial statements are misleading.

# Browsing versus Reading Financial Reports

I've seen annual financial reports of small, privately owned businesses that you could read in 30 minutes to an hour. But, as a general rule, the bigger the business the bigger its annual financial report. As mentioned earlier, the annual reports of large, publicly owned business corporations are typically 30, 40, or 50 and more pages. You would need at least two hours or more to do a quick read of the entire annual financial report, without trying to digest all the details in the report. Very few persons have the time to carefully read all the information in an annual financial report — even if the report is relatively short.

Annual financial reports are long and dense documents — like lengthy legal contracts in many ways. Pick up a typical annual financial report of a public corporation: You would need many hours (perhaps the whole day) to thoroughly read everything in the report. You would need at least an hour or two just to read and absorb the main points in the report. For one thing, there are many, many numbers in an annual financial report. I've never taken the time to count the number of numbers in an average annual financial report. But, without a doubt, there are hundreds of numbers in annual reports, and well over a thousand for large, diversified, global, conglomerate businesses.

How do investors in a business deal with the *information overload* of annual financial reports put out by businesses? Very, very few persons take the time to plough through every sentence, every word, every detail, and every number on every page — except for those professional accountants, lawyers, and auditors directly involved in the preparation and review of the financial report. It's hard to say how most managers, investors, creditors, and others interested in annual financial reports go about dealing with the massive amount of information in these reports. As a matter of fact, very little research has been done on this subject. But I have some observations to share with you.

An annual financial report is like the Sunday edition of a large city newspaper, such as *The New York Times* or the *Chicago Tribune*. Hardly anyone reads every sentence on every page of these Sunday papers — most people pick and choose what they want to read. They browse their way through the paper, stopping to read only the particular articles or topics they're interested in. Some people just skim through the paper. Some just glance at the headlines. Investors read annual financial reports like they read Sunday newspapers. The information is there if you really want to read it, but most readers pick and choose which information they have time to read.

Annual financial reports are designed for archival purposes, not for a quick read. Instead of addressing the needs of investors and others who want to know about the profit performance and financial condition of the business — but have only a very limited amount of time to do so — accountants produce an annual financial report that is a voluminous financial history of the business. Accountants leave it to the users of annual reports to extract the main points from an annual report. So, financial statement readers use a relatively few ratios and other tests to get a feel for the financial performance and position of the business. (Chapters 14 and 17 explain how readers of financial reports get a fix on the financial performance and position of a business.)

Some businesses (and nonprofit organizations in reporting to their members and other constituencies) don't furnish an annual financial report. They know that few persons have the time or the technical background to read through their annual financial reports. Instead, they provide relatively brief summaries that are boiled-down versions of their official financial statements. Typically these summaries do not provide footnotes or the other disclosures that are included in annual financial reports. These *condensed financial statements,* without footnotes, are provided by several nonprofit organizations: credit unions, for instance. If you really want to see the complete financial report of the organization, you can ask its headquarters to send you a copy. (My retirement fund manager, TIAA-CREF, puts out only financial summaries to its participants and retirees; I have to ask for the official financial reports.)

By the way, the Securities & Exchange Commission (SEC) has supported the idea that corporations should issue scaled-down summaries of their annual financial reports. But by and large, the business community has not been very receptive to this idea.

You should keep in mind that annual financial reports do not report everything of interest to owners, creditors, and others who have a financial interest in the business. *Annual* reports, of course, come out only once a year — usually two months or so after the end of the company's fiscal (accounting) year. You have to keep abreast of developments during the year by reading financial newspapers or through other means. Also, annual financial reports present the "sanitized" version of events; they don't divulge scandals or other negative news about the business.

Finally, not everything you may like to know as an investor is included in the annual financial report. For example, information about salaries and incentive compensation arrangements with the top-level managers of the business are disclosed in the *proxy statement,* not in the annual financial report of the business. A proxy statement is the means by which the corporation solicits the vote of stockholders on issues that stockholders must give their approval — one of which is compensation packages of top-level managers. Proxy statements are filed with the SEC and are available on its EDGAR data base, www.sec.gov/edgar.htm.

# Part III
# Accounting in Managing a Business

**The 5th Wave**     **By Rich Tennant**

I'm mathematically dyslexic. But it's not that unusual - 100 out of every 15 people are.

# In this part . . .

Business managers and owners depend on financial statements as well as other internal accounting reports to know how much profit they're making, where that profit is at the end of the period, and whether the business is in good financial shape or needs improvement. They also use financial statements to keep a close watch on the lifeblood of the business: cash flows. Managers must know how to read their financial statements. Also, they should take advantage of proven accounting tools and techniques to assist them in making profit, controlling cash flow, and keeping the business in good financial condition.

Managers need a good accounting model for analyzing profit; they can use budgeting to plan and achieve the financial goals of the business, which is the essence of management control. Business managers and owners must decide which ownership structure to use, especially from an income tax point of view. Finally, managers should clearly understand how the costs of the business are determined, and they should get involved in choosing the basic accounting methods for measuring profit and for recording values of their assets and liabilities. This part of the book, in short, explains how accounting helps managers achieve the financial goals of the business.

# Chapter 9

# Managing Profit Performance

A s a manager, you get paid to make profit happen. That's what separates you from the non-manager employees at your business. Of course, you have to be a motivator, innovator, consensus builder, lobbyist, and maybe sometimes a baby-sitter, too, but the real purpose of your job is to control and improve the profit of your business. No matter how much your staff loves you (or do they love those doughnuts you bring in every Monday?), if you don't meet your profit goals, you're facing the unemployment line.

You have to be relentless in your search for better ways to do things. Competition in most industries is fierce, and you can never take profit performance for granted. Changes take place all the time — changes initiated by the business and changes pressured by outside forces. Maybe a new super-store down the street is causing your profit to fall off, and you figure that you'll have a huge sale to draw customers, complete with splashy ads on TV and Dimbo the Clown in the store.

Whoa, not so fast. First make sure that you can afford to cut prices and spend money on advertising and still turn a profit. Maybe price cuts and Dimbo's balloon creations will keep your cash register singing and the kiddies smiling, but you need to remember that making sales does not guarantee that you make a profit. As all you experienced business managers know, profit is a two-headed beast: Profit comes from making sales *and* controlling expenses.

So how do you determine what effect price cuts and advertising costs may have on your bottom line? By turning to your beloved accounting staff, of course, and asking for some *what-if* reports (like "What if we offer a 15 percent discount and hire Dimbo for two days at $45 an hour?").

This chapter shows you how to identify the key variables that determine what your profit would be if you changed certain factors (such as prices) and whether Dimbo is really worth that kind of money.

# Redesigning the External Income Statement

To begin, Figure 9-1 presents the income statement of a business (the same example as is used in Chapter 8). Figure 9-1 shows an *external income statement* — the income statement that's reported to the outside investors and creditors of the business. The expenses in Figure 9-1 are presented as they are usually disclosed in an external statement. (Chapter 5 explains sales revenue, expenses, and the format of the external income statement.)

| (Dollar amounts in thousands) | |
| :--- | ---: |
| **External Income Statement For Year** | |
| Sales Revenue | $ 52,000 |
| Cost of Goods Sold Expense | 31,200 |
| Gross Margin | $ 20,800 |
| Sales, Administration, and General Expenses | 15,600 |
| Depreciation Expense | 1,650 |
| Earnings Before Interest and Income Tax | $ 3,550 |
| Interest Expense | 750 |
| Earnings Before Income Tax | $ 2,800 |
| Income Tax Expense | 900 |
| Net Income | $ 1,900 |

**Figure 9-1:** Example of a business's external income statement.

The managers of the business should understand this income statement, of course. But, the external income statement is not entirely adequate for management decision-making; this profit report falls short of providing all the information about expenses needed by managers. But, before moving on to the additional information managers need, take a quick look at the external income statement (Figure 9-1) before the train leaves the station.

For more information about the external income statement and all its sundry parts, see Chapter 5. Let me just point out the following here about this particular financial statement:

✔ The business represented by this income statement sells products and therefore has a *cost of goods sold expense.* In contrast, companies that sell services (airlines, movie theaters, law firms) don't have a cost of goods sold expense, as all their sales revenue goes toward meeting operating expenses and then providing profit.

✔ The external income statement shown in Figure 9-1 is prepared according to accounting methods and disclosure standards called *generally accepted accounting principles* (GAAP), but keep in mind that these financial reporting standards are designed for reporting information *outside* the business. Once an income statement is released to people outside the business, a business has no control over the circulation of its statement. The accounting profession, in deciding on the information for disclosure in external income statements, has attempted to strike a balance. On the one side are the needs of those who have invested capital in the business and have loaned money to the business; clearly they have the right to receive enough information to evaluate their investments in the business and their loans to the business. On the other side is the need of the business to keep certain information confidential and out of the hands of its competitors. What it comes down to is that certain information that outside investors and creditors might find interesting and helpful does not, in fact, have to be disclosed according to GAAP.

The SEC has mandated that certain information that is not required by GAAP for external financial reporting by businesses must be disclosed in filings under the federal securities laws . One such item of information, for example, is the amount of annual expense for repairs and maintenance of property, plant, equipment, and tools. This particular expense is seldom disclosed in external income statements or footnotes. Also, the SEC requires more disclosure regarding marketing and advertising expenses than most businesses reveal in their annual external financial reports.

✔ The income statement does not report the *financial effects* of the company's profit-making activities — that is, the increases and decreases in its assets and liabilities caused by revenue and expenses. Managers need to control these financial effects, for which purpose they need the complete financial picture provided by the two other primary financial statements (the balance sheet and the cash flow statement) in addition to the income statement. See Chapters 6 and 7 for more about these two other primary financial statements.

# Basic Model for Management Income Statement

Figure 9-2 presents a model for a *management* income statement, using the same business as the example whose external income statement is shown in

Figure 9-1. Many lines of information are exactly the same: sales revenue and cost of goods sold expense, and thus gross margin are the same. And, the last five lines in the two statements are the same, starting with operating profit (earnings before interest and income tax) down to the bottom line. In other respects, however, there are critical differences between the two profit reports.

First, note that total *unit sales volume* and *per unit amounts* are included in the management income statement (Figure 9-2). The business appears to sell only one product; the 520,000 units total sales volume is from sales of this product. In fact, most businesses sell a mix of many different products. The company's various managers need detailed sales revenue and cost information for each product, or product line, or segment of the business they are responsible for. To keep the illustration easy to follow I have collapsed the business's entire sales into one "average" product. Instead of grappling with 100 or 1,000 different products, I condense them all into one proxy product. The main purpose of Figure 9-2 is to show a basic template, or model, that can be used for the more detailed reports to different managers in the business organization.

## Variable versus fixed operating expenses

Another fundamental difference between the external profit report (Figure 9-1) and the internal profit report (Figure 9-2) is that the company's *operating expenses* (sales, administration, and general expenses plus depreciation expense) are separated into two different categories in the management report:

- ✔ **Variable expenses:** The *revenue-driven expenses* that depend directly on the total sales revenue amount for the period. These expenses move in lock step with changes in total sales revenue dollars. Commissions paid to sales persons based on a percent of the amount of sales are a common example of a variable operating expense.

- ✔ **Fixed expenses:** The operating expenses that are relatively fixed in amount for the period, regardless of whether the company's total unit sales (sales volume) had been substantially more or less than the 520,000 units that it actually sold during the year. An example of a fixed operating expense is the annual property tax on the company's real estate. Also, depreciation is a fixed expense; a certain amount of depreciation expense is recorded to the year regardless of actual sales volume.

The management income statement does not, I repeat, does *not* present different profit numbers for the year compared with the profit numbers reported in the company's external income statement. Note that operating profit for the year (or, earnings before interest and income tax expenses) is the same as reported outside the business — in Figures 9-1 and 9-2 this number is the same. And, in reading down the rest of the two income statements note that earnings before income tax and bottom-line net income are the same in both the external and internal reports. The external income statement of the business reports a broad, all-inclusive group of "sales, administration, and general expenses" and a separate expense for depreciation. In contrast, the management income statement reveals information about *how the operating expenses behave relative to the sales of the business*. The actual reporting of expenses in external income statements varies from business to business — but you never see income statements in which operating expenses are sorted between variable and fixed.

| Management Income Statement For Year | | |
| --- | --- | --- |
| (Dollar amounts in thousands) | **Totals for Period** | **Per Unit** |
| Unit Sales Volume = | 520,000 | |
| Sales Revenue | $52,000 | $100 |
| Cost of Goods Sold Expense | 31,200 | 60 |
| Gross Margin | $20,800 | $40 |
| Revenue-driven Operating Expenses | 4,160 | 8 |
| Contribution Margin | $16,640 | $32 |
| Fixed Operating Expenses | 13,090 | |
| Operating Profit, or Earnings Before Interest and Income Tax Expenses (EBIT) | $ 3,550 | |
| Interest Expense | 750 | |
| Earnings Before Income Tax | $ 2,800 | |
| Income Tax Expense | 900 | |
| Net Income | $ 1,900 | |

**Figure 9-2:** Management income statement model.

Virtually every business has *variable* operating expenses, which move up and down in tight proportion to changes in unit sales volume or sales revenue. Here are some examples of common variable operating expenses:

- Cost of goods sold expense, the cost of the products sold to customers.
- Commissions paid to salespeople based on their sales.
- Transportation costs of delivering products to customers.
- Fees that a business pays to a bank when a customer uses a credit card such as Visa, MasterCard, or American Express. (When a business deposits its copy of the credit card slip, the local bank deducts a certain percentage of the amount deposited as the bank's fee for handling the transaction, and a part of the fee is shared with the credit card issuer.)

The management income statement (Figure 9-2) can be referred to as the *internal profit report,* since it is for management eyes only and does not circulate outside the business — although, it may be the target of industrial intelligence gathering and perhaps even industrial espionage by competitors. Remember that in the external income statement only one lump sum for the category of sales, administrative, and general (SA&G) expenses is reported — a category for which some of the expenses are fixed but some are variable. What you need to do is have your accountant carefully examine these expenses to determine which are fixed and which are variable. (Some expenses may have both fixed and variable components, but I don't go into these technical details.)

Further complicating the matter somewhat is the fact that the accountant needs to divide variable expenses between those that vary with sales *volume* (total number of units sold) and those that vary with sales *revenue* (total dollars of sales revenue). This is an important distinction.

- An example of an expense driven by sales volume is the cost of shipping and packaging. This cost depends strictly on the *number* of units sold and generally is the same regardless of how much the item inside the box costs.

- An example of an expense driven by sales revenue are sales commissions paid to salespersons, which directly depend on the amounts of sales made to customers. Other examples are franchise fees based on total sales revenue of retailers, real estate rental contracts that include a clause that bases monthly rent on sales revenue, and royalties based on total sales revenue that are paid for the right to use a well-known name or a trademarked logo in selling the company's products.

The business represented in Figure 9-2 has just one variable operating expense: an 8 percent sales commission, resulting in an expense total of $4,160,000 ($52 million sales revenue × 8 percent). Of course, a real business probably would have many different variable operating expenses, some driven by unit sales volume and some driven by total sales revenue dollars. But the basic idea is the same for all of them and one variable operating expense serves the purpose here. Also, cost of goods sold expense is itself a sales volume driven expense (see Chapter 13 regarding different accounting methods for measuring this expense). The example shown in Figure 9-2 is a bit oversimplified — the business sells only one product and has only one variable operating expense — but, the main purpose is to present a general template that can be tailored to fit the particular circumstances of a business.

*Fixed operating expenses* are the many different costs that a business is obligated to pay and cannot decrease over the short run without major surgery on the human resources and physical facilities of the business. You definitely should distinguish fixed expenses from your variable operating expenses.

As an example of fixed expenses, consider the typical self-service car wash business — you know, the kind where you drive in, put some coins in a box, and use the water spray to clean your car. Almost all the operating costs of this business are fixed: Rent on the land, depreciation of the structure and the equipment, and the annual insurance premium cost don't depend on the number of cars passing through the car wash. The only variable expenses are probably the water and the soap.

If you want to decrease fixed expenses significantly, you need to downsize the business (lay off workers, sell off property, and so on). When looking at the various ways you have for improving your profit, significantly cutting down on fixed expenses is generally the last-resort option. Refer to "Improving profit" later in this chapter for the better options.

Better than anyone else, managers know that sales for the year could have been lower or higher. A natural question is how much different profit would have been at the lower or higher level of sales. If you'd sold 10 percent fewer total units during the year, what would your net income (bottom-line profit) have been? You might guess that profit would have slipped 10 percent, but that would *not* have been the case. In fact, profit would have slipped by much more than 10 percent. Are you surprised? Read on for the reasons.

Why wouldn't profit fall the same percent as sales? Because of the nature of fixed expenses — just because your sales are lower doesn't mean that your expenses are lower. *Fixed expenses* are the costs of doing business that, for all practical purposes, are stuck at a certain amount over the short term. Fixed expenses do not react to changes in the sales level. Here are some examples of fixed expenses:

- ✔ Interest on money that the business has borrowed
- ✔ Employees' salaries and benefits
- ✔ Property taxes
- ✔ Fire insurance

A business can downsize its assets and therefore reduce its fixed expenses to fit a lower sales level, but that can be a drastic reaction to what may be a temporary downturn. After deducting cost of goods sold, variable operating expenses, and fixed operating expenses, the next line in the management income statement is operating profit, which is also called *earnings before interest and income tax* (or *EBIT*). This profit line in the report is a critical juncture that managers need to fully appreciate.

## From operating profit (EBIT) to the bottom line

After deducting all operating expenses from sales revenue, you get to earnings before interest and tax (EBIT), which is $3,550,000 in the example. *Operating* is an umbrella term that includes cost of goods sold expense and all other expenses of making sales and operating your business — but not interest and income tax. Sometimes EBIT is called *operating profit*, or *operating earnings*, to emphasize that profit comes from making sales and controlling operating expenses. This business earned $3,550,000 operating profit from its $52 million sales revenue — which seems satisfactory. But is its $3,550,000 EBIT really good enough? What's the reference for answering this question?

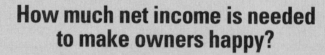

### How much net income is needed to make owners happy?

People who invest in a business usually aren't philanthropists who don't want to make any money on the deal. No, these investors want a business to protect their capital investment, earn a good bottom-line profit for them, and enhance the value of their investment over time. They understand that a business may not earn a profit but suffer a loss — that's the risk they take as owners.

As described in Chapters 6 and 11, how much of a business's net income (bottom-line profit) is distributed to the owners depends on the business and the arrangement that it made with the owners. But regardless of how much money the owners actually receive, they still have certain expectations of how well the business will do — that is, what the business's earnings before interest and income tax will be. After all, they've staked their money on the business's success.

One test of whether the owners will be satisfied with the net income (after interest and income tax) is to compute the *return on equity* (ROE), which is the ratio of net income to total owners' equity (net income ÷ owners' equity). In this chapter's business example, the bottom-line profit is $1.9 million. Suppose that the total owners' equity in the business is $15.9 million (as shown in Figure 8-1 for the business example). Thus, the ROE is 12 percent ($1.9 million ÷ $15.9 million). Is 12 percent a good ROE? Well, that depends on how much the owners could earn from an alternative investment. I'd say that a 12 percent ROE isn't bad.

**Note:** ROE does not imply that all the net income was distributed in cash to the owners. Usually, a business needs to retain a good part of its bottom-line net income to provide capital for growing the business. Suppose, in this example, that none of the net income is distributed in cash to its owners. The ROE is still 12 percent; ROE does not depend on how much, if any, of the net income is distributed to the owners. (Of course, the owners may prefer that a good part of the net income be distributed to them.)

The main benchmark for judging EBIT is whether this amount of profit is adequate to cover the *cost of capital* of the business. Chapter 6 explains the various assets that a business needs to make sales and earn profit. A business must secure money to invest in its various assets — and this capital has a cost. A business has to pay interest on its debt capital, and it should earn enough after-tax net income (bottom-line profit) to satisfy its owners who have put their capital in the business. See the sidebar "How much net income is needed to make owners happy?" in this chapter.

Nobody — not even the most die-hard humanitarian — is in business to make a zero EBIT. You simply can't do this, because profit is an absolutely necessary part of doing business — and recouping the cost of capital is why profit's needed.

Don't treat the word *profit* as something that's whispered in the hallways. Profit builds owners' value and provides the basic stability for a business. Earning a satisfactory EBIT is the cornerstone of business. Without earning an adequate operating profit, a business could not attract capital, and you can't have a business without capital.

# Traveling Two Trails to Profit

How is the additional information in the management income statement useful? Well, with this information you can figure out how the business earned its profit for the year. I'm not referring to how the company decided which products to sell, and the best ways to market and advertise its products, and how to set sales prices, and how to design an efficient and smooth running organization, and how to motivate its employees, and all the other things every business has to do to achieve its financial goals. I'm talking about an *accounting explanation of profit* that focuses on methods for calculating profit — going from the basic input factors of sales price, sales volume, and costs to arrive at the amount of profit that results from the interaction of the factors. Business managers should be familiar with these accounting calculations. They are responsible for each factor and for profit, of course. With this in mind, therefore: How did the business earn its profit for the year?

## First path to profit: Contribution margin minus fixed expenses

I can't read your mind. But, if I had to hazard a guess regarding how you would go about answering the profit question, I'd bet that, after you had the chance to study Figure 9-2, you would do something like the following, which is correct as a matter of fact:

| Computing profit before income tax | |
| --- | --- |
| Contribution margin per Unit | $32 |
| × Unit sales volume | 520,000 |
| Equals: Total contribution margin | $16,640,000 |
| Less: Total fixed operating expenses | $13,090,000 |
| Equals: Operating profit (EBIT) | $3,550,000 |
| Less: Interest Expense | $750,000 |
| Equals: Earnings before income tax | $2,800,000 |

Note that I stop at the earnings before income tax line in this calculation. You're aware, of course, that business profit is subject to federal income tax. Chapter 3 provides a general overview of the federal taxation of business profit. This chapter focuses on profit above the income tax expense line. Nevertheless, please keep in mind as a broad rule of thumb that taxable income of a regular business corporation is subject to a 34 or 35 percent federal income tax and perhaps state income tax as well — except small businesses whose taxable income is taxed at a lower rate. (Chapter 11 explains that some legal types of business entities do not pay income tax but act as conduits to their owners, who pick up their shares of the taxable income of the business in their individual tax returns.)

*Contribution margin* is what's left over after you subtract cost of goods sold expense and other variable expenses from sales revenue. On a *per unit* basis the business sells its product for $100, its variable product cost (cost of goods sold) is $60, and its variable operating cost per unit is $8 — which yields $32 contribution margin per unit. *Total* contribution margin for a period equals contribution margin per unit times the units sold during the period — in the business example, $32 × 520,000 units, which is $16,640,000 total contribution margin. Total contribution margin is a measure of profit *before fixed expenses are deducted.* To pay for its fixed operating expenses and its interest expense a business needs to earn a sufficient amount of total contribution margin. In the example, the business earned more total contribution margin than its fixed expenses, so it earned a profit for the year.

Here are some other concepts associated with the term *margin,* which you're likely to encounter:

   ✓ **Gross margin, also called gross profit:** Gross margin = sales revenue – cost of goods sold expense. Gross margin is profit from sales revenue *before* deducting the other variable expenses of making the sales. So gross margin is one step short of the final contribution margin earned on making sales. Businesses that sell products must report gross margin on their *external* income statements. However, GAAP standards do *not* require that you report other variable expenses of making sales on external income statements. In their external financial reports, very few businesses divulge other variable expenses of making sales. In other words, managers do not want the outside world and competitors to know their contribution margins. Most businesses carefully guard information about contribution margins because the information is very sensitive.

✔ **Gross margin ratio:** Gross margin ratio = gross margin ÷ sales revenue. In the business I use as an example in this chapter, the gross margin on sales is 40 percent. Gross margins of companies vary from industry to industry, from over 50 percent to under 25 percent — but very few businesses can make a bottom-line profit with less than a 20 percent gross margin.

✔ **Markup:** Generally refers to the amount added to the product cost to determine the sales price. For example, suppose a product that cost $60 is marked up (based on cost) by 66⅔ percent to determine its sales price of $100 — for a gross margin of $40 on the product. ***Note:*** The markup based on *cost* is 66⅔ percent ($40 markup ÷ $60 product cost). But the gross margin ratio is only 40 percent, which is based on *sales price* ($40 ÷ $100).

## *Second path to profit: Excess over breakeven volume × contribution margin per unit*

The second method of computing a company's profit starts with a particular sales volume as the point of reference. So, the first step is to compute this specific sales volume of the business (which is not its actual sales volume for the year) by dividing its total annual fixed expenses by its contribution margin per unit. Interest expense is treated as a fixed expense (because for all practical purposes it is more or less fixed in amount over the short-run). For the business in the example the interest expense is $750,000 (see Figure 9-2), which, added to the $13,090,000 fixed operating expenses, gives total fixed expenses of $13,840,000. The company's *breakeven point*, also called its *breakeven sales volume,* is computed as follows:

```
$13,840,000 total annual fixed expenses for year ÷ $32
        contribution margin per unit = 432,500 units
        breakeven point (or, breakeven sales volume) for
        the year
```

In other words, if you multiply $32 contribution margin per unit times 432,500 units you get a total contribution margin of $13,840,000, which exactly equals the company's total fixed expenses for the year. The business actually sold more than this number of units during the year. But, if it had sold only 432,500 units, the company's profit would have been exactly zero. Below this sales level the business suffers a loss, and above this sales level the business makes profit. The breakeven sales volume is the crossover point from the loss column to the profit column. Of course, a business's goal is to do better than just reaching its breakeven sales volume.

REAL WORLD EXAMPLE

# How variable expenses mow down your sales price

Consider a retail hardware store that sells, say, a Toro lawnmower to a customer. The purchase cost per unit that the retailer paid to Toro, the manufacturer, when the retailer bought its shipment of these lawnmowers is the *product cost* in the contribution margin equation. The retailer also provides one free servicing of the lawnmower after the customer has used it a few months (cleaning it and sharpening the blade) and also pays its salesperson a commission on the sale. These two additional expenses, for the service and the commission, are examples of variable expenses in the margin equation.

Calculating its breakeven point calls attention to the amount of fixed expenses hanging over a business. As explained earlier, a business is committed to its fixed expenses over the short-run and cannot do much to avoid these costs — short of breaking some of its contracts and taking actions to downsize the business that could have disastrous long-run effects. Some-times the total fixed expenses for the year are referred to as the "nut" of the business — which may be a hard nut to crack ( by exceeding its breakeven sales volume).

In the example (see Figure 9-2) the business actually sold 520,000 units during the year, which is 87,500 units more than its breakeven sales volume (520,000 units sold minus its 432,500 breakeven sales volume). Therefore, you can determine the company's earnings before income tax as follows:

### Second Way of Computing Profit

| | |
|---|---|
| Contribution margin per unit | $32 |
| × Units sold in excess of breakeven point | 87,500 |
| Equals: Earnings before income tax | $2,800,000 |

This second way of analyzing profit calls attention to the need of the business to achieve and exceed its breakeven point to make profit. The business makes no profit until it clears its breakeven hurdle, but once over this level of sales it makes profit hand over fist — because the units sold from here on are not burdened with any fixed costs, which have been covered by the first 432,500 of units sold during the year. Be careful in thinking that only the last 87,500 units sold during the year generate all the profit for the year. The first 432,500 units sold are necessary to get the business into position so that the next 87,500 units make profit.

The key point is that once the business has reached its breakeven sales volume (thereby covering its annual fixed expenses), each additional unit sold brings in pretax profit equal to the contribution margin per unit. Each additional unit sold brings in "pure profit" of $32 per unit, which is the company's contribution margin per unit. A business has to get into this upper region of sales volume to make a profit for the year.

## Calculating the margin of safety

The *margin of safety* is the excess of its actual sales volume over a company's break-even sales volume. This business sold 520,000 units, which is 87,500 units above its break-even sales volume — a rather large cushion against any downturn in sales. Only a major sales collapse would cause the business to fall all the way down to its breakeven point, assuming that it can maintain its $32 contribution margin per unit and that its fixed costs don't change. You may wonder what a "normal" margin of safety is for most businesses. Sorry, I can't give you a definitive answer on this. Due to the nature of the business or industry-wide problems, or due to conditions beyond its control, a business may have to operate with a smaller margin of safety than it would prefer.

# Doing What-If Analysis

Managing profit is like driving a car — you need to be glancing in the rearview mirror constantly as well as looking ahead through the windshield. You have to know your profit history to see your profit future. Understanding the past is the best preparation for the future.

The model of a *management income statement* shown in Figure 9-2 allows you to compare your actual profit with what it would've looked like if you'd done something differently — for example, raised prices and sold less units. With the profit model, you can test-drive adjustments before putting them into effect. It lets you plan and map out your profit strategy for the *coming* period. Also, you can analyze why profit went up or down from the *last* period, using the model to do hindsight analysis.

The management income statement profit model focuses on the key factors and variables that drive profit. Here's what you should know about these factors:

✔ Even a small decrease in the contribution margin per unit can have a drastic impact on profit because fixed expenses don't go down over the short run (and are hard to reduce even over the long run).

✔ Even a small increase in the contribution margin per unit can have a dramatic impact on profit because fixed expenses won't go up over the short run — although they may have to be increased in the long run.

> ✔ Compared with changes in contribution margin per unit, sales volume changes have secondary profit impact; sales volume changes are not trivial, but even relatively small margin changes can have a bigger effect on profit.
>
> ✔ You can, perhaps, reduce fixed expenses to improve profit, but you have to be very careful to cut fat and not muscle; reducing fixed expenses may very well diminish the capacity of your business to make sales and deliver high-quality service to customers.

The following sections expand on these key points.

## Lower profit from lower sales — but that much lower?

The management income statement shown in Figure 9-2 is designed for managers to use in profit analysis — to expose the critical factors that drive profit. Remember what information has been added that isn't included in the external income statement:

> ✔ **Unit sales volume** for the year
>
> ✔ **Per-unit values**
>
> ✔ **Fixed versus variable** operating expenses
>
> ✔ **Contribution margin** — total and per unit

Handle this information with care. The contribution margin per unit is confidential, for your eyes only. This information is limited to you and other managers in the business. Clearly, you don't want your competitors to find out your margins. Even within a business, the information may not circulate to all managers — just those who need to know.

The contribution margin per unit is one of the three most important determinants of profit performance, along with sales volume and fixed expenses — as shown in the upcoming sections.

With the information provided in the management income statement, you're ready to paint a what-if scenario. I'm making you the president and chief operating officer of the business in this example. What if you had sold 5 percent fewer units during this period? In this example, that would mean you had sold only 494,000 units rather than 520,000 units, or 26,000 units less. The following computation shows you how much profit damage this seemingly modest drop in sales volume would've caused.

**Impact of 5 Percent Lower Sales Volume on Profit**

| | |
|---|---|
| Contribution margin per unit | $32 |
| × 26,000 fewer units sold | 26,000 |
| Equals: Decrease in earnings before income tax | $832,000 |

By selling 26,000 fewer units you missed out on the $832,000 profit that these units would have produced — this is fairly straightforward. What is not so obvious, however, is that this $832,000 decrease in profit would have been a 30 percent drop in profit: ($832,000 decrease ÷ $2,800,000 profit = 30 percent decrease). Lose just 5 percent of your sales, and lose 30 percent of your profit? How can such a thing happen? The next section expands on how a seemingly small decrease in sales volume can cause a stunning decrease in profit. Read on.

## Violent profit swings due to operating leverage

First, the bare facts for the business in my example: the company's contribution margin per unit is $32; and, before making any changes, the company sold 520,000 units during the year, which is 87,500 units in excess of its breakeven sales volume. The company earned total contribution margin of $16,640,000 (see Figure 9-2), which is its contribution per unit times its total units sold during the year. If the company had sold 5 percent less during the year (26,000 fewer units), you'd expect its total contribution margin to decrease 5 percent, and you'd be absolutely correct — $832,000 decrease ÷ $16,640,000 = 5 percent decrease. Compared with its $2,800,000 profit before income tax, however, the $832,000 drop in total contribution margin equals a *30 percent* fall-off in profit.

The main focus of business managers and investors is on profit, which in this example is profit before income tax. Therefore, the 30 percent drop in profit would get more attention than the 5 percent drop in total contribution margin. The much larger percent of change in profit caused by a relatively small change in sales volume is the effect of *operating leverage*. Leverage means that there is a multiplier effect — that a relatively small percent of change in one factor can cause a much larger change in another factor. A small push can cause a large movement — this is the idea of leverage.

In the above scenario for the 5 percent, 26,000 units decrease in sales volume, note that the 5 percent is based on the total 520,000 units sales volume of the business. But, if the 26,000 units decrease in sales volume is divided by the 87,500 units in excess of the company's breakeven point — which are the units that generate profit for the business — the sales volume decrease equals 30 percent. In other words, the business lost 30 percent of its profit layer of sales volume and, thus, the company's profit would have dropped 30 percent. This dramatic drop is caused by the operating leverage effect.

*Note:* If the company had sold 5 percent *more* units, with no increase in its fixed expenses, its pretax profit would have *increased* by 30 percent, reflecting the operating leverage effect. The 26,000 additional units sold at a $32 contribution margin per unit would increase its total contribution margin by $832,000 and this increase would increase profit by 30 percent. You can see why businesses are always trying to increase sales volume.

## Cutting sales price, even a little, can gut profit

So, what effect would a 5 percent decrease in the sales price have caused? Around a 30 percent drop, similar to the effect of a 5 percent decrease in sales volume? Not quite. Check out the following computation for this 5 percent sales price decrease scenario:

| Impact of 5 Percent Lower Sales Price on Profit | |
| --- | --- |
| Contribution margin per unit decrease | $4.60 |
| × Units sold during year | 520,000 |
| Equals: Decrease in earnings before income tax | $2,392,000 |

Whoa! Earnings before income tax would drop from $2,800,000 at the $100 sales price (refer to Figure 9-2) to only $408,000 at the $95 sales price — a plunge of 85 percent. What could cause such a drastic dive in profit?

The sales price drops $5 per unit — a 5 percent decrease of the $100 sales price. But, contribution margin per unit does not drop by the entire $5 because the variable operating expense per unit (sales commissions in this example) would also drop 5 percent, or $.40 per unit — for a net decrease of $4.60 per unit in the contribution margin per unit. (This is one reason for identifying the expenses that depend on sales revenue — as shown in the management income statement in Figure 9-2.) For this what-if scenario that examines the case of the company selling all units at a 5 percent lower sales price than it did, the company's contribution margin would have been only $27.40 per unit. Such a serious reduction in its contribution margin per unit would have been intolerable.

At the lower sales price, the company's contribution margin would be $27.40 per unit ($32.00 in the original example minus the $4.60 decrease = $27.40). As a result, the breakeven sales volume would be much higher, and the company's 520,000 sales volume for the year would have been only 14,891 units over its breakeven point. So, the lower $27.40 contribution margin per unit would yield only $408,000 profit before income tax.

The moral of the story is to protect contribution margin per unit above all else. Every dollar of contribution margin per unit that's lost — due to decreased sales prices, increased product cost, or increases in other variable costs — has a tremendous negative impact on profit. Conversely, if you can increase the contribution margin per unit without hurting sales volume, you reap very large profit benefits, as described next.

## *Improving profit*

The preceding sections explore the downside of things — that is, what would've happened to profit if sales volume or sales prices had been lower. The upside — higher profit — is so much more pleasant to discuss and analyze, don't you think?

Profit improvement boils down to the three critical profit-making factors, listed in order from the most effective to the least effective:

✔ Increasing the contribution margin per unit

✔ Increasing sales volume

✔ Reducing fixed expenses

Say you want to improve your bottom-line profit from the $1,900,000 net income you earned the year just ended to $2,110,000 next year. How can you pump up your net income by $210,000? (By the way, this is the only place in the chapter I bring the income tax factor into the analysis.)

First of all, realize that to increase your net income *after taxes* by $210,000, you need to increase your before-tax profit by much more — to provide for the amount that goes to income tax. Your accountant calculates that you would need a $312,000 increase in earnings before tax next year, because your income tax increase would be about $102,000 on the $312,000 increase in pretax earnings. So, you have to find a way to increase earnings, before income tax, by $312,000.

You should also take into account the possibility that fixed costs and interest expense may rise next year, but for this example I'm assuming that they won't. I'm also assuming that the business can't cut any of its fixed operating expenses without hurting its ability to maintain and support its present sales level (and a modest increase in the sales level). Of course, in real life, every business should carefully scrutinize its fixed expenses to see if some of them can be cut.

Okay, so how can you increase your business's before-tax profit by $312,000? You have two choices (well, actually three choices). Take another look at Figure 9-2 and study these options:

- ✔ Increase your contribution margin per unit by $.60, which would raise the total contribution margin by $312,000, based on a 520,000 units sales volume ($.60 × 520,000 = $312,000).

- ✔ Sell 9,750 additional units at the current contribution margin per unit of $32, which would raise the total contribution margin by $312,000 (9,750 × $32 = $312,000).

- ✔ Use a combination of these two approaches: Increase both the margin per unit and the sales volume.

The second approach is obvious — you just need to set a sales goal of increasing the number of products sold by 9,750 units. (How you motivate your already overworked sales staff to accomplish that sales volume goal is up to you.) But how do you go about the first approach, increasing the contribution margin per unit by $.60?

The simplest way to increase contribution margin per unit by $.60 would be to decrease your product cost per unit by $.60. Or you could attempt to reduce sales commissions from $8 per $100 of sales to $7.40 per $100 — which may adversely affect the motivation of your sales force, of course. Or you could raise the sales price about $.65 (remember that 8 percent comes off the top for the sales commission, so only $.60 would remain from that $.65 to improve the unit contribution margin). Or you could combine two or more such changes so that your unit contribution next year would increase $.60. However you do it, the improvement would increase your earnings before income tax the desired amount:

### Impact of $.60 Higher Unit Contribution Margin on Profit

| | |
|---|---|
| Contribution margin per unit increase | $.60 |
| × Units sold during year | 520,000 |
| Equals: Increase in earnings before income tax | $312,000 |

# Cutting prices to increase sales volume: A very tricky game to play!

A word of warning: Be sure to *run the numbers* (accountant speak for using a profit model) before deciding to drop sales prices in an effort to gain more sales volume. Suppose, for example, you're convinced that if you decrease sales prices by 5 percent, your sales volume will increase by 10 percent. Seems like an attractive trade-off, one that would increase both profit performance and market share. But are you sure that those positive changes are the results you'll get?

The impact on profit may surprise you. Get a piece of scratch paper and do the computation for this lower sales price and higher sales volume scenario:

| Lower Sales Price & Higher Sales Volume Impact on Profit | |
|---|---|
| New sales price (lower) | $95.00 |
| Less: Product cost per unit (same) | $60.00 |
| Less: Variable operating expenses (lower) | $ 7.60 |
| Equals: New unit contribution margin (lower) | $27.40 |
| × Sales volume (higher) | 572,000 |
| Equals: Total contribution margin | $15,672,800 |
| Less: Previous total contribution margin | $16,640,000 |
| Equals: Decrease in total contribution margin | $967,200 |

Your total contribution margin would not go up; instead, it would go down $967,200! In dropping the sales price by $5, you would give up too much of your contribution margin per unit. The increase in sales volume would not make up for the big dent in unit contribution margin. You may gain more market share but would pay for it with a $967,200 drop in earnings before income tax.

To keep profit the same, you would have to increase sales volume more than 10 percent. By how much? Divide the total contribution margin for the 520,000 units situation by the contribution margin per unit for the new scenario:

```
$16,640,000 ÷ $27.40 = 607,300 units
```

In other words, just to keep your total contribution margin the same at the lower sales price, you would have to increase sales volume to 607,300 units — an increase of 87,300 units, or a whopping 17 percent. That would be quite a challenge, to say the least.

## Cash flow from improving profit margin versus improving sales volume

Chapter 9 discusses increasing profit margin versus increasing sales volume to improve bottom-line profit. Improving your profit margin is the better way to go, compared with increasing sales volume. Both actions increase profit, but the profit margin tactic is much better in terms of cash flow. When sales volume increases, so does inventory. On the other hand, when you improve profit margin (by raising the sales price or by lowering product cost), you don't have to increase inventory — in fact, reducing product cost may actually cause inventory to decrease a little. In short, increasing your profit margin yields a higher cash flow from profit than does increasing your sales volume.

# A Final Word or Two

Recently, some friends pooled their capital and opened an upscale liquor store in a rapidly growing area. The business has a lot of promise, I think. I can tell you one thing they should have done before going ahead with this new venture — in addition to location analysis and competition analysis, of course. They should have used the basic profit model (in other words, the management income statement) discussed in this chapter to figure out their breakeven sales volume — because I'm sure they have rather large fixed expenses. And they should have determined how much more sales revenue over their breakeven point that they will need to earn a satisfactory return on their investment in the business.

During their open house for the new store, I noticed the very large number of different beers, wines, and spirits available for sale in the store — to say nothing of the different sizes and types of containers many products come in. Quite literally, the business sells thousands of distinct products. The store also sells many products like soft drinks, ice, corkscrews, and so on. Therefore, the company does not have a single sales volume factor (meaning the number of units sold) to work with in the basic profit model? So, you have to adapt the profit model to get along without the sales volume factor.

The trick is to determine your *average contribution margin as a percent of sales revenue.* I'd estimate that a liquor store's average gross margin (sales revenue less cost of goods sold) is about 25 percent. The other variable operating expenses of the liquor store probably run about 5 percent of sales. So, the average contribution margin would be 20 percent of sales (25 percent gross margin less 5 percent variable operating expenses). Suppose the total fixed operating expenses of the liquor store are about $100,000 per month (for rent, salaries, electricity, and so on), which is $1.2 million per year. So, the store needs $6 million in sales per year just to break even:

```
$1.2 million fixed expenses ÷ 20% average contribution margin
           = $6 million annual sales to break even
```

Selling $6 million of product a year means moving a lot of booze. The business needs to sell another $1 million dollars to provide $200,000 of operating earnings (at the 20 percent average contribution margin) — to pay interest expense, income tax, and leave enough net income for the owners who invested capital in the business and who expect a good return on their investment.

By the way, some disreputable liquor store owners are known (especially to the Internal Revenue Service) to engage in *sales skimming.* This term refers to not recording all sales revenue; instead, some cash collected from customers is put in the pockets of the owners. They don't report the profit in their income tax returns or in the income statements of the business. My friends who started the liquor store are honest businessmen, and I'm sure they won't engage in sales skimming — but they do have to make sure that none of their store's employees skim off some sales revenue.

When sales skimming is being committed, not all of the actual sales revenue for the year is recorded even though the total cost of all products sold during the year is recorded. Obviously, this distorts the income statement and throws off normal ratios of gross profit and operating profit to sales revenue. If you have the opportunity to buy a business, please be alert to the possibility that some sales skimming has been done by the present owner. Indeed, I've been involved in situations in which the person selling the business bragged about how much he was skimming off the top.

# Chapter 10

# Business Budgeting

## In This Chapter

▶ Discovering the benefits of budgeting

▶ Designing accounting reports for managers

▶ Budgeting in action: developing a profit plan and projecting cash flow from profit

▶ Staying flexible with budgets

*A* business can't open its doors each day without having some idea of what to expect. And it can't close its doors at the end of the day not knowing what happened. When I was in the Boy Scouts, the motto was "Be Prepared." Likewise, a business should plan and be prepared for its future, and should control its actual performance to reach its financial goals. The only question is how.

*Budgeting* is one answer. Please be careful with this term. Budgeting does *not* refer to putting a financial straitjacket on a business. Instead, business budgeting refers to setting specific goals and having the detailed plans necessary to achieve the goals. Business budgeting is built on realistic forecasts for the coming period, and demands that managers develop a thorough understanding of the profit blueprint of the business as well as the financial effects of the business's profit-making activities. A business budget is an integrated plan of action — not simply a few trend lines on a financial chart. Business managers have two broad options. They can wait for results to be reported to them on a "look back" basis. Or, they can look ahead and plan what profit and cash flow should be, and then compare actual results against the plan. Budgeting is the method used to enact this second option.

The financial statements included in the annual financial report of a business are prepared *after the fact;* that is, the statements are based on actual transactions that have already taken place. Budgeted financial statements, on the other hand, are prepared *before the fact,* and are based on future transactions that you expect to take place based on the business's profit and financial strategy and goals. These forward-looking financial statements are referred to as *pro forma,* which is Latin for "provided in advance." ***Note:*** Budgeted financial statements are not reported outside the business; they are strictly for internal management use.

You can see a business's budget most easily in its set of *budgeted financial statements* — its budgeted income statement, balance sheet, and cash flow statement. Preparing these three budgeted financial statements requires a lot of time and effort; managers do detailed analysis to determine how to improve the financial performance of the business. The vigilance required in budgeting helps to maintain and improve profit performance and to plan cash flow.

Budgeting is much more than slap-dashing together a few figures. A budget is an integrated financial plan put down on paper, or these days I should say entered in computer spreadsheets. Planning is the key characteristic of budgeting. The budgeted financial statements encapsulate the financial plan of the business for the coming year.

# The Reasons for Budgeting

Managers don't just look out the window and come up with budget numbers. Budgeting is not pie-in-the-sky wishful thinking. Business budgeting — to have real value — must start with a critical analysis of the most recent actual performance and position of the business by the managers who are responsible for the results. Then the managers decide on specific and concrete goals for the coming year. (Budgets can be done for more than one year, but the key stepping-stone into the future is the budget for the coming year — see the sidebar "Taking it one game at a time.")

In short, budgeting demands a fair amount of management time and energy. Budgets have to be worth this time and effort. So why should a business go to the trouble of budgeting? Business managers do budgeting and prepare budgeted financial statements for three quite different reasons — distinguishing them from each other is useful.

## The modeling reasons for budgeting

To construct budgeted financial statements, you need good models of the profit, cash flow, and financial condition of your business. Models are blueprints, or schematics of how things work. A business budget is, at its core, a financial blueprint of the business.

*Note:* Don't be intimidated by the term *model.* It simply refers to an explicit, condensed description of how profit, cash flow, and assets and liabilities behave. For example, Chapter 9 presents a model of a management income statement. A model is analytical, but not all models are mathematical. In fact, none of the financial models in this book is the least bit mathematical — but you do have to look at each factor of the model and how it interacts with one or more other factors. The simple accounting equation — assets = liabilities + owners' equity — is a model of the balance sheet, for example. And, as Chapter 9 explains, profit = contribution margin per unit × units sold in excess of the breakeven point.

Budgeting relies on financial models, or blueprints that serve as the foundation for each budgeted financial statement. These blueprints are briefly explained, as follows:

- ✔ **Budgeted management income statement:** Chapter 9 presents a design for the internal income statement that provides the basic information that managers need for making decisions and exercising control. This internal (for managers only) profit report contains information that is not divulged outside the business. The management income statement shown in Figure 9-2 serves as a hands-on profit model — one that highlights the critical variables that drive profit. This management income statement separates variable and fixed expenses and includes sales volume, contribution margin per unit, as well as other factors that determine profit performance. The management income statement is like a schematic that shows the path to the bottom line. It reveals the factors that must be improved in order to improve profit performance in the coming period.

- ✔ **Budgeted balance sheet:** The key connections and ratios between sales revenue and expenses and their related assets and liabilities are the elements of the basic model for the budgeted balance sheet. These vital connections are explained throughout Chapters 5 and 6; Chapter 8 (specifically Figure 8-1) also presents an overview of these connections.

- ✔ **Budgeted cash flow statement:** The changes in assets and liabilities from their balances at the end of the year just concluded and the balances at the end of the coming year determine cash flow from profit for the coming year. These changes constitute the basic model of cash flow from profit, which Chapter 7 explains (see Figure 7-3 in particular). The other sources and uses of cash depend on managers' strategic decisions regarding capital expenditures that will be made during the coming year, and how much new capital will be raised by increased debt and from owners' additional investment of capital in the business.

In short, budgeting requires good working models of profit performance, financial condition (assets and liabilities), and cash flow from profit. Constructing good budgets is a strong incentive for businesses to develop financial models that not only help in the budgeting process but also help managers make day-to-day decisions.

## Taking it one game at a time

A company generally prepares one-year budgets, although many businesses also develop
budgets for two, three, and five years. However,
reaching out beyond a year becomes quite ten-
tative and very iffy. Making forecasts and estimates for the next 12 months is tough enough.
A one-year budget is much more definite and
detailed in comparison to longer-term budgets.

As they say in the sports world, a business
should take it one game (or year) at a time.

Looking down the road beyond one year is a
good idea, to set long-term goals and to develop
long-term strategy. But long-term planning is
different than long-term budgeting.

### *Planning reasons for budgeting*

One main purpose of budgeting is to develop a definite and detailed financial
plan for the coming period. To do budgeting, managers have to establish
explicit financial objectives for the coming year and identify exactly what has
to be done to accomplish these financial objectives. Budgeted financial statements and their supporting schedules provide clear destination points — the
financial flight plan for a business.

The process of putting together a budget directs attention to the specific
things that you must do to achieve your profit objectives and to optimize
your assets and capital requirements. Basically, budgets are a form of planning, and planning pushes managers to answer the question "How are we
going to get there from here?"

Budgeting also has other planning-related benefits:

✔ **Budgeting encourages a business to articulate its vision, strategy,
and goals.** A business needs a clearly-stated strategy guided by an
over-arching vision, and should have definite and explicit goals. It is
not enough for business managers to have strategy and goals in their
heads — and nowhere else. Developing budgeted financial statements
forces managers to be explicit and definite about the objectives of the
business, and to formulate realistic plans for achieving the business
objectives.

✔ **Budgeting imposes discipline and deadlines on the planning process.**
Many busy managers have trouble finding enough time for lunch, let alone
planning for the upcoming financial period. Budgeting pushes managers
to set aside time to prepare a detailed plan that serves as a road map for
the business. Good planning results in a concrete course of action that
details how a company plans to achieve its financial objectives.

# *Management control reasons for budgeting*

Budgets can be and usually are used as a means of *management control,* which involves comparing budgets against actual performance and holding individual managers responsible for keeping the business on schedule in reaching its financial objectives. The board of directors of a corporation focus their attention on the master budget for the whole business: the budgeted management income statement, the budgeted balance sheet, and the budgeted cash flow statement for the coming year.

The chief executive officer and the president of the business focus on the master budget. They also look at how each manager in the organization is doing on his or her part of the master budget. As you move down the organization chart of a business, managers have narrower responsibilities — say, for the business's northeastern territory or for one major product line — therefore, the master budget is broken down into parts that follow the business's organizational structure. In other words, the master budget is put together from many pieces, one for each separate organizational unit of the business. So, for example, the manager of one of the company's far-flung warehouses has a separate budget for expenses and inventory levels for his or her bailiwick.

By using budget targets as benchmarks against which actual performance is compared, managers can closely monitor progress toward (or deviations from) the budget goals and timetable. You use a budget plan like a navigation chart to keep your business on course. Significant variations from budget raise red flags, in which case you can determine that performance is off course or that the budget needs to be revised because of unexpected developments.

For management control, the annual budgeted management income statement is divided into months or quarters. The budgeted balance sheet and budgeted cash flow statement are also put on a monthly or quarterly basis. The business should not wait too long to compare budgeted sales revenue and expenses against actual performance (or to compare actual cash flows and asset levels against the budget timetable). You need to take prompt action when problems arise, such as a divergence between budgeted expenses and actual expenses. Profit is the main thing to pay attention to, but accounts receivable and inventory can get out of control (become too high relative to actual sales revenue and cost of goods sold expense), causing cash flow problems. (Chapter 7 explains how increases in accounts receivable and inventory are negative factors on cash flow from profit.) A business cannot afford to ignore its balance sheet and cash flow numbers until the end of the year.

## *Other benefits of budgeting*

Budgeting has advantages and ramifications that go beyond the financial dimension and have more to do with business management in general. These points are briefly discussed as follows:

- ✔ **Budgeting forces managers to do better forecasting.** Managers should constantly scan the business environment to identify sea changes that can impact the business. Vague generalizations about what the future might hold for the business are not quite good enough for assembling a budget. Managers are forced to put their predictions into definite and concrete forecasts.

- ✔ **Budgeting motivates managers and employees by providing useful yardsticks for evaluating performance and for setting managers' compensation when goals are achieved.** The budgeting process can have a good motivational impact on employees and managers by involving managers in the budgeting process (especially in setting goals and objectives) and by providing incentives to managers to strive for and achieve the business's goals and objectives. Budgets can be used to reward good results. Budgets provide useful information for superiors to evaluate the performance of managers. Budgets supply baseline financial information for incentive compensation plans. The profit plan (budget) for the year can be used to award year-end bonuses according to whether designated goals are achieved.

- ✔ **Budgeting is essential in writing a business plan.** New and emerging businesses must present a convincing *business plan* when raising capital. Because these businesses may have little or no history, the managers and owners of a small business must demonstrate convincingly that the company has a clear strategy and a realistic plan to make money. A coherent, realistic budget forecast is an essential component of a business plan. Venture capital sources definitely want to see the budgeted financial statements of the business.

In larger businesses, budgets are typically used to hold managers accountable for their areas of responsibility in the organization; actual results are compared against budgeted goals and timetables, and variances are highlighted. Managers do not mind taking credit for *favorable* variances, or when actual comes in better than budget. Beating the budget for the period, after all, calls attention to outstanding performance. But *unfavorable* variances are a different matter. If the manager's budgeted goals and targets are fair and reasonable, the manager should carefully analyze what went wrong and what needs to be improved. But if the manager perceives the budgeted goals and targets to be arbitrarily imposed by superiors and not realistic, serious motivational problems can arise.

In reviewing the performance of their subordinates, managers should handle unfavorable variances very carefully. Stern action may be called for, but managers should recognize that the budget benchmarks may not be entirely fair and should make allowances for unexpected developments that occur after the budget goals and targets are established.

# Budgeting and Management Accounting

What I say earlier in the chapter can be likened to a commercial for budgeting — emphasizing the reasons for and advantages of budgeting by a business. So every business does budgeting, right? Nope. Smaller businesses generally do little or no budgeting — and, even many larger businesses avoid budgeting. The reasons are many, and mostly practical in nature.

Some businesses are in relatively mature stages of their life cycle or operate in an industry that is mature and stable. These companies do not have to plan for any major changes or discontinuities. Next year will be a great deal like last year. The benefits of going through a formal budgeting process do not seem worth the time and cost to them. At the other extreme, a business may be in a very uncertain environment; attempting to predict the future seems pointless. A business may lack the expertise and experience to prepare budgeted financial statements, and it may not be willing to pay the cost for a CPA or outside consultant to help them.

In applying for a loan the lender may be impressed that your business plan includes a well-thought-out budget. I served on a local bank's board of directors for several years, and I reviewed many loan requests. Our bank did not expect a business to include a set of budgeted financial statements in the loan request package. Of course, we did demand to see the latest financial statements of the business. Very few of our smaller business clients prepared budgets. Although many businesses do not prepare budgets, they do establish detailed goals and performance objectives that serve as good benchmarks for management control.

Every business — whether it does budgeting or not — should design internal accounting reports that provide the information managers need to control the business. Obviously, managers should keep close tabs on what's going on throughout the business. Some years ago, in one of my classes, I asked students for a short definition of management control. One student answered that management control means "watching everything." That's not bad.

A business may not do any budgeting, and thus it does not prepare budgeted financial statements. But its managers should receive regular income statements, balance sheets, and cash flow statements — and these key internal financial statements should contain detailed management control information. Other specialized accounting reports may be needed as well.

Most business managers, in my experience, would tell you that the accounting reports they get are reasonably good for management control. Their accounting reports provide the detailed information they need for keeping a close watch on the thousand and one details about the business (or their particular sphere of responsibility in the business organization). Their main criticisms are that too much information is reported to them and all the information is flat, as if all the information is equally relevant. Managers are very busy people, and have only so much time to read the accounting reports coming to them. Managers have a valid beef on this score, I think. Ideally, significant deviations and problems should be highlighted in the accounting reports they receive — but separating the important from the not-so-important is easier said than done.

If you were to ask a cross section of business managers how useful their accounting reports are for making decisions, you would get a different answer than how good the accounting reports are for management control. Business managers make many decisions affecting profit: setting sales prices, buying products, determining wages and salaries, hiring independent contractors, and purchasing fixed assets are just a few that come to mind. Managers should carefully analyze how their actions would impact profit before reaching final decisions. Managers need internal income statements that are good profit models — that make clear the critical variables that affect profit (see Figure 9-2 for an example). Well designed management income statements are absolutely essential for helping managers make good decisions.

Keep in mind that almost all business decisions involve nonfinancial and nonquantifiable factors that go beyond the information included in management accounting reports. For example, the accounting department of a business can calculate the cost savings of a wage cut, or the elimination of overtime hours by employees, or a change in the retirement plan for employees — and the manager would certainly look at this data. But such decisions must consider many other factors such as effects on employee morale and productivity, the possibility of the union going out on strike, legal issues, and so on. In short, accounting reports provide only part of the information needed for business decisions, though an essential part for sure.

Needless to say, the internal accounting reports to managers should be clear and straightforward. The manner of presentation and means of communication should be attention getting. A manager should not have to call the accounting department for an explanation. Designing management accounting reports is a separate topic — one beyond the limits of this book.

In the absence of budgeting by a business, the internal accounting reports to its managers become the major — often the only — regular source of financial information to them. Without budgeting, the internal accounting reports have to serve a dual function — both for control and for planning. The managers use the accounting reports to critically review what's happened (control), and use the information in the reports to make decisions for the future (planning).

Before leaving the topic, I have one final observation to share with you. Many management accounting reports that I've seen could be improved. Accounting systems, unfortunately, give so much attention to the demands of preparing external financial statements and tax returns that the needs managers have for good internal reports are too often overlooked or ignored. The accounting reports in many businesses do not speak to the managers receiving them — the reports are too voluminous and technical, and are not focused on the most urgent and important problems facing the managers. Designing good internal accounting reports for managers is a demanding task, to be sure. Every business should take a hard look at its internal management accounting reports and identify what needs to be improved.

# Budgeting in Action

Suppose you're the general manager of one of a large company's several divisions. You have broad authority to run this division, as well as the responsibility for meeting the financial expectations for your division. To be more specific, your profit responsibility is to produce a satisfactory annual operating profit, or earnings before interest and tax (EBIT). (Interest and income tax expenses are handled at a higher level in the organization.)

The CEO has made clear to you that she expects your division to increase EBIT during the coming year by about 10 percent ($256,000, to be exact). In fact, she has asked you to prepare a budgeted management income statement showing your plan for increasing your division's EBIT by this target amount. She also has asked you to prepare a budgeted cash flow from profit based on your profit plan for the coming year.

Figure 10-1 presents the management income statement of your division for the year just ended. The format of this accounting report follows the profit model discussed in Chapter 9, which explains profit behavior and how to increase profit. Note that fixed operating expenses are separated from the two variable operating expenses. To simplify the discussion, I've significantly condensed your management income statement. (Your actual reports would include much more detailed information about sales and expenses.) Also, I assume that you sell only one product to keep the number crunching to a minimum.

| | Totals for Period | Per Unit |
|---|---|---|
| Unit Sales Volume = | 26,000 | |
| Sales Revenue | $ 26,000,000 | $1,000.00 |
| Cost of Goods Sold Expense | 14,300,000 | 550.00 |
| Gross Margin | $ 11,700,000 | $450.00 |
| Revenue-driven Operating Expenses | 2,080,000 | 80.00 |
| Volume-driven Operating Expenses | 1,300,000 | 50.00 |
| Contribution Margin | $ 8,320,000 | $320.00 |
| Fixed Operating Expenses | 5,720,000 | |
| Operating Profit | $ 2,600,000 | |

**Figure 10-1:** Management income statement for year just ended.

Most businesses, or the major divisions of a large business, sell a mix of several different products. General Motors, for example, sells many different makes and models of autos and light trucks, to say nothing about its other products. The next time you visit your local hardware store look at the number of products on the shelves. The assortment of products sold by a business and the quantities sold of each that make up its total sales revenue is referred to as its *sales mix*. As a general rule, certain products have higher profit margins than others. Some products may have extremely low profit margins, which are called *loss leaders*. The marketing strategy for loss leaders is to use them as magnets to get customers to buy your higher profit margin products along with their purchase of the loss leaders. Shifting the sales mix to a higher proportion of higher profit margin products has the effect of increasing the average profit margin on all products sold. (A shift to lower profit margin products would have the opposite effect, of course.) Budgeting sales revenue and expenses for the coming year must include any planned shifts in the company's sales mix.

## Developing your profit strategy and budgeted income statement

Being an experienced manager, you know the importance of protecting your unit contribution margins (see Chapter 9). Your division's total sales volume was 26,000 units for the year (see Figure 10-1). Your contribution margin per unit is $320 (see Figure 10-1 again). If all your costs were to remain the same next year (you wish!), you could simply sell 800 more units at a $320 contribution margin per unit to add $256,000 to your total contribution margin and EBIT (800 units × $320 per unit = $256,000). This relatively small increase in your sales volume would achieve your profit increase goal. However, costs seldom remain constant year to year.

Suppose that you and your managers, with the assistance of your accounting staff, have analyzed your fixed operating expenses line by line for the coming year. Some of these fixed expenses will actually be reduced or eliminated next year. But the large majority of these costs will continue next year, and most are subject to inflation. Based on careful studies and estimates, you and your staff forecast your total fixed operating expenses for next year will be $6,006,000 (including $835,000 depreciation expense, compared with the $780,000 depreciation expense for last year).

Thus, you will need to earn $8,862,000 total contribution margin next year:

| | |
|---|---|
| $2,856,000 | EBIT goal ($2,600,000 last year plus $256,000 budgeted increase) |
| + 6,006,000 | Budgeted fixed operating expenses next year |
| $8,862,000 | Total contribution margin goal next year |

This is your main profit budget goal for next year, assuming that fixed operating expenses are kept in line. Fortunately, your volume-driven variable operating expenses should not increase next year. These are mainly transportation costs, and the shipping industry is in a very competitive, hold-the-price-down mode of operations that should last through the coming year. The cost per unit shipped should not increase, but if you sell and ship more units next year, the expense will increase in proportion.

You have decided to hold the revenue-driven operating expenses at 8 percent of sales revenue during the coming year, the same as for the year just ended. These are sales commissions, and you have already announced to your sales staff that their sales commission percentage will remain the same during the coming year. On the other hand, your purchasing manager has told you to plan on a 4 percent product cost increase next year — from $550 per unit to $572 per unit, or an increase of $22 per unit. Thus, your unit contribution margin would drop from $320 to $298 (if the other factors that determine margin remain the same).

One way to attempt to achieve your total contribution margin objective next year is to load all the needed increase on sales volume and keep sales price the same. (I'm not suggesting that this strategy is a good one, but it's a good point of departure.) At the lower unit contribution margin your sales volume next year would have to be 29,738 units:

```
$8,862,000 total contribution margin goal ÷ $298 contribution
       margin per unit = 29,738 units sales volume
```

Compared with last year's 26,000 units sales volume, you would have to increase your sales by over 14 percent. This may not be feasible.

After discussing this scenario with your sales manager, you conclude that sales volume cannot be increased 14 percent. You'll have to raise the sales price to provide part of the needed increase in total contribution margin and to offset the increase in product cost. After much discussion, you and your sales manager decide to increase the sales price by 3 percent. Based on the 3 percent sales price increase and the 4 percent product cost increase your unit contribution margin next year is determined as follows:

### Unit Contribution Margin Next Year

| | |
|---|---|
| Sales price | $1,030.00 |
| Less: Product cost | 572.00 |
| Less: Revenue-driven operating expenses | 82.40 |
| Less: Volume-driven variable operating expenses | 50.00 |
| Equals: Contribution margin per unit | $325.60 |

At this $325.60 budgeted contribution margin per unit, you determine the total sales volume needed next year to reach your profit goal as follows:

```
$8,862,000 total contribution margin goal next year ÷ $325.60
          contribution margin per unit = 27,217 units sales
          volume
```

This sales volume is about 5 percent higher than last year (1,217 additional units over the 26,000 sales volume last year = about 5 percent increase).

If you don't raise the sales price, your division has to increase sales volume by 14 percent (as calculated above). If you increase the sales price by just 3 percent, the sales volume increase you need to achieve your profit goal next year is only 5 percent. Does this make sense? Well, this is just one of many alternative strategies for next year. Perhaps you could increase sales price by 4 percent. But, you know that most of your customers are sensitive to a sales price increase, and your competitors may not follow with their own sales price increase.

After lengthy consultation with your sales manager you finally decide to go with the 3 percent sales price increase combined with the 5 percent sales volume growth as your official budget strategy. Accordingly, you forward your budgeted management income statement to the CEO. Figure 10-2 summarizes this profit budget for the coming year. This summary-level budgeted management income statement is supplemented with appropriate schedules to provide additional detail about sales by types of customers and other relevant information. Also, your annual profit plan is broken down into quarters (perhaps months) to provide benchmarks for comparing actual performance during the year against your budgeted targets and timetable.

| | Totals for Period | Per Unit |
|---|---|---|
| Unit Sales Volume = | 27,217 | |
| Sales Revenue | $ 28,033,968 | $1,030.00 |
| Cost of Goods Sold Expense | 15,568,378 | 572.00 |
| Gross Margin | $ 12,465,590 | $458.00 |
| Revenue-driven Operating Expenses | 2,242,717 | 82.40 |
| Volume-driven Operating Expenses | 1,360,872 | 50.00 |
| Contribution Margin | $ 8,862,000 | $325.60 |
| Fixed Operating Expenses | 6,006,000 | |
| Operating Profit | $ 2,856,000 | |

**Figure 10-2:** Budgeted income statement for coming year.

## Budgeting cash flow from profit for the coming year

The budgeted profit plan (refer to Figure 10-2) is the main focus of attention, but the CEO also requests that all divisions present a *budgeted cash flow from profit* for the coming year. **Remember:** The profit you're responsible for as general manager of the division is earnings before interest and tax (EBIT) — not net income after interest and income tax.

Chapter 7 explains that increases in accounts receivable, inventory, and prepaid expenses *hurt* cash flow from profit and that increases in accounts payable and accrued liabilities *help* cash flow from profit. You should compare your budgeted management income statement for the coming year (Figure 10-2) with your actual statement for last year (Figure 10-1). This side-by-side comparison (not shown here) reveals that sales revenue and all expenses are higher next year.

Therefore, your short-term operating assets, as well as the liabilities that are driven by operating expenses, will increase at the higher sales revenue and expense levels next year — unless you can implement changes to prevent the increases.

For example, sales revenue increases from $26,000,000 last year to the budgeted $28,033,968 for next year — an increase of $2,033,968. Your accounts receivable balance was five weeks of annual sales last year. Do you plan to tighten up the credit terms offered to customers next year — a year in which you will raise the sales price and also plan to increase sales volume? I doubt it. More likely, you will keep your accounts receivable balance at five weeks of annual sales. Assume that you decide to offer your customers the same credit terms next year. Thus, the increase in sales revenue will cause accounts receivable to increase by $195,574 ($\frac{5}{52}$ × $2,033,968 sales revenue increase).

Last year, inventory was 13 weeks of annual cost of goods sold expense. You may be in the process of implementing inventory reduction techniques. f you really expect to reduce the average time inventory will be held in stock before being sold, you should inform your accounting staff so that they can include this key change in the balance sheet and cash flow models. Otherwise, they will assume that the past ratios for these vital connection will continue next year.

Figure 10-3 presents a summary of your budgeted cash flow from profit (the EBIT for your division) based on the information given for this example and using the ratios explained in Chapter 7 for short-term operating assets and liabilities. For example, accounts receivable increases by $195,574, as just explained. And, inventory increases by $317,095 ($\frac{13}{52}$ × $1,268,378 cost of goods sold expense increase). *Note:* Increases in accrued interest payable and income tax payable are not included in your budgeted cash flow. Your profit responsibility ends at the operating profit line, or earnings before interest and income tax expenses.

| | |
|---|---|
| Budgeted Operating Profit (See Figure 10-2) | $2,856,000 |
| Accounts Receivable Increase | (195,574) |
| Inventory Increase | (317,095) |
| Prepaid Expenses Increase | (26,226) |
| Depreciation Expense | 835,000 |
| Accounts Payable Increase | 34,968 |
| Accrued Expenses Payable Increase | 52,453 |
| Budgeted Cash Flow From Operating Profit | $3,239,526 |

**Figure 10-3:** Budgeted cash flow from profit statement for coming year.

You submit this budgeted cash flow from profit statement (Figure 10-3) to top management. Top management expects you to control the increases in your short-term assets and liabilities so that the actual cash flow generated by your division next year comes in on target. The cash flow from profit of your division (minus the small amount needed to increase the working cash balance held by your division for operating purposes) will be transferred to the central treasury of the business.

## Beyond profit and cash flow from profit

This chapter focuses on profit budgeting for the coming year, and budgeting the cash flow from that profit. These two are hardcore components of business budgeting — but not the whole story. Another key element of the budgeting process is to prepare a *capital expenditures budget* for top management review and approval. A business has to take a hard look at its long-term operating assets — in particular, the capacity, condition, and efficiency of these resources — and decide whether it needs to expand and modernize its fixed assets. In most cases, a business would have to invest substantial sums of money in purchasing new fixed assets or retrofitting and upgrading its old fixed assets. These long-term investments require major cash outlays. So, a business (or each division of the business) prepares a formal list of the fixed assets to be purchased or upgraded. The money for these major outlays comes from the central treasury of the business. Accordingly, the capital expenditures budget goes to the highest levels in the organization for review and final approval. The chief financial officer, the CEO, and the board of directors of the business go over a capital expenditure budget request with a fine-toothed comb.

At the company-wide level, the financial officers merge the profit and cash flow budgets of all divisions. The budgets submitted by one or more of the divisions may be returned for revision before final approval is given. One main concern is whether the collective total of cash flow from all the units provides enough money for the capital expenditures that have to be made during the coming year for new fixed assets — and to meet the other demands for cash, such as for cash distributions from profit. The business may have to raise more capital from debt or equity sources during the coming year to close the gap between cash flow from profit and its needs for cash. This is a central topic in the field of business finance, beyond the coverage of this book.

# Staying Flexible with Budgets

One thing never to lose sight of is that budgeting is a *means to an end*. It's a tool for doing something better than you could without the tool. Preparing budgeted financial statements is not the ultimate objective; a budget is not an end in itself. The budgeting process should provide definite benefits, and businesses should use their budgeted financial statements to measure progress toward their financial objectives — and not just file them away someplace.

Budgets are not the only tool for management control. Control, in my mind, means accomplishing your financial objectives. Many businesses do not use budgeting and do not prepare budgeted financial statements. But they do lay down goals and objectives for each period and compare actual performance against these targets. Doing at least this much is essential for all businesses.

## Business budgeting versus government budgeting: Only the name is the same

Business and government budgeting are more different than alike. Government budgeting is preoccupied with allocating scarce resources among many competing demands. From federal agencies down to local school districts, government entities have only so much revenue available. They have to make very difficult choices regarding how to spend their limited tax revenue.

Formal budgeting is legally required for almost all government entities. First, a budget request is submitted. After money is appropriated, the budget document becomes legally binding on the government agency. Government budgets are legal straitjackets; the government entity has to stay within the amounts appropriated for each expenditure category. Any changes from the established budgets need formal approval and are difficult to get through the system.

A business is not legally required to use budgeting. A business can use its budget as it pleases and can even abandon its budget in midstream. Unlike the government, the revenue of a business is not constrained; a business can do many things to increase sales revenue. In short, a business has much more flexibility in its budgeting. Both business and government should apply the general principle of cost/benefits analysis to make sure that they are getting the most bang for every buck spent. But a business can pass its costs to its customers in the sales prices it charges. In contrast, government has to raise taxes to spend more (except for federal deficit spending, of course, but efforts are being made to balance the federal budget and generate budget surpluses).

Keep in mind that budgets are not the only means for controlling expenses. Actually, I shy away from the term *controlling* because I've found that, in the minds of most people, *controlling* expenses means minimizing them. The *cost/benefits* idea captures the better view of expenses. Spending more on advertising, for example, may have a good payoff in the additional sales volume it produces. In other words, it's easy to cut advertising to zero if you really want to minimize this expense — but the impact on sales volume may be disastrous.

Business managers should eliminate any *excessive* amount of an expense — the amount that really doesn't yield a benefit or add value to the business. For example, it's possible for a business to spend too much on quality inspection by doing unnecessary or duplicate steps, or by spending too much time testing products that have a long history of good quality. But this doesn't mean that the business should eliminate the expense entirely. Expense control means trimming the cost down to the right size. In this sense, expense control is one of the hardest jobs that business managers do, second only to managing people, in my opinion.

# Chapter 11

# Choosing the Right Ownership Structure

· · · · · · · · · · · · · · · · · · · · · · · · · · · · · · · · · · · · · · · · · ·

· · · · · · · · · · · · · · · · · · · · · · · · · · · · · · · · · · · · · · · · · ·

The obvious reason for investing in a business as an owner rather than a safer kind of investment is the potential for greater rewards. As one of the partners or shareholders of a business, you're entitled to part of the business's profit — and you're also subject to the risk that the business will go down the tubes, taking your money down with it.

But ignore the risks for a moment and look at just the rosy side of the picture: Suppose the doohickeys that this business sells become the hottest products of the year. Business is great, and you start looking at five-bedroom riverfront houses. Don't jump into that down payment just yet, though — you may not get as big a piece of the profit pie as you're expecting. First of all, profit is at the bottom of the list of what the business needs to use its sales revenue to pay for. You may not see any of that profit at all. And even if you do, the way the profit is divided among owners depends on the business's ownership structure, which can be pretty simple or extremely complex.

This chapter shows you how ownership structure affects your share of the profit — especially how changes beyond your control can make your share less valuable. It also explains how the ownership structure has a dramatic impact on the income taxes paid by the business and its owners.

# *From the Top Line to the Bottom Line*

Chapter 5 explains the business profit-making process and the accounting profit report for a period, which is called the *income statement*. The chapter focuses on the financial effects on the various operating assets and operating liabilities of a business of its sales revenue and expense activities. To make sense of a company's *balance sheet* (its statement of financial condition at the end of the profit period), which is explained in Chapter 6, you need to understand how its sales revenue and expenses propel the company's operating assets and operating liabilities. And, to round out the financial picture of a business you need to look at its sources and uses of cash flows for the period, which are presented in its *cash flow statement* — see Chapter 7.

Whew! These three business financial statements present a lot of information. But, if you're a manager or owner of a business you should have a good grip on these three *accounting sheets* (as they're sometimes called). Accounting often is called the language of business, and learning the basic vocabulary of accounting is extraordinarily helpful, if not downright essential, for business managers and owners.

One aspect of the business profit-making process is easy to lose sight of when reading an income statement. How does a business get from the top line in its income statement (sales revenue) down to its bottom line (net income)? Business managers set sales prices and make sales of products and services that generate cash inflow in the form of sales revenue. *And,* business managers set prices that the business pays for many of its expenses. Profit depends on the successful efforts of managers in setting both kinds of prices — for the things the business sells and for the things the business buys.

In our free enterprise, largely unregulated, and nongovernment controlled economy, business managers have the responsibility of negotiating the prices paid for labor and most of the other services, supplies, and other factors used in the profit-making process. This book isn't the place to delve into the fields of labor economics and political economy. But, I would point out that business income statements are one key source of information for scholars who do research in these areas. In particular, the financial statements prepared by accountants report how sales revenue is divided among the different parties in a business's profit-making process.

A business collects money from its customers and then redistributes that sales revenue to the many parties clamoring for their fair share. You may think that the second part of this process would be the easy part, but business managers sometimes have a tough time deciding what constitutes a "fair share" for each claimant. For example, in deciding how much to pay employees in regular wages and fringe benefits, business managers have to ask what value each employee adds to the business, whether to raise sales prices in order to pay higher wages, and so on.

The distribution of total sales revenue among the various claimants on the revenue is a *zero-sum game*. This means that if one party gets a bigger piece of the revenue pie then some other party gets a smaller piece, keeping the size of the pie (total sales revenue) the same. (The alternative is for the business to increase the size of its sales revenue pie — by raising its sales prices or selling more units.) If a business increases compensation to its employees, for instance, without changing the prices paid for all other services and supplies, then the shares of total sales revenue going to Uncle Sam in income tax and to owners as after-tax net income decrease. (Note that a business may increase wages expecting that labor productivity gains will offset the wage gains.) Business managers must constantly calculate how changes in the prices they charge customers and changes in the prices they pay for labor, materials, products, utilities, and many other expenses affect bottom-line profit.

*Net income* is the bottom-line profit that the business earned this period (or, to be more precise, the period just concluded, which often is called "this period" to mean the most recent period). This figure is the starting point for determining how much cash — if any — to distribute to the owners. Businesses are not legally required to distribute any of their profit for the period, but if they do distribute some or all of their profit, the amounts distributed to each owner depend on the business's ownership structure, as described in the following section, "What Owners Expect for Their Money."

The owners of a business, in a real sense, stand at the end of the line for their piece of the sales revenue pie. How can you tell whether a business is doing well for its owners? What's a good net income figure? One test is to compare bottom-line profit with sales revenue. Dividing profit by sales revenue gives the *profit ratio,* which is expressed as a percent. Many people don't really know what's a typical profit ratio for a businesses. They think it's high — 20, 30, or even 50 percent of sales revenue. In fact, the large majority of businesses earn profit ratios of less than 10 percent.

Although profit ratio is a useful test of profit performance, it ignores the amount of capital the owners have tied-up in the business. Every business needs owners' capital to invest in the assets needed for making profit. The ratio of profit over owners' equity is called *return on equity.* To calculate a business's return on equity (ROE) you divide net income by total owners' equity (you can find owners' equity listed on the business's balance sheet). Compare the ROE of a business with the ROEs of investment alternatives that have the same kinds of risks and advantages when you're deciding whether to invest in a business. Business managers keep a close watch on their ROE in order to judge their business's profit performance relative to the amount of its owners' capital being used to make that profit

Usually, managers have an ownership interest in the business — although in large, public corporations, managers usually own only a small percentage of total owners' equity. For a small business, the two or three chief managers may be the only owners. But many small businesses have outside, non-manager investors who put money in the business and share in the profit that the business earns. Chapter 14 explains more about ROE and other ways outside investors interpret the information in a business's external financial report.

# What Owners Expect for Their Money

Every business — regardless of how big it is and whether it's publicly or privately owned — has owners; no business can get all the financing it needs just by borrowing. An *owner* is someone who

- ✓ Invested money in the business when it originally raised capital from its owners (for instance, when IBM issued shares of stock to persons who invested money in the company when it started up many years ago) — or, who bought ownership shares from one of the existing owners of the business (for instance, when you buy IBM stock shares from a stockholder who wants to unload IBM shares)

- ✓ Expects the business to earn profit on the owners' capital and expects to share in that profit by receiving cash distributions from profit and by benefiting from increases in the value of the ownership shares — with no guarantee of either

- ✓ Directly participates in the management of the business or hires others to manage the business — in smaller businesses an owner may be one of the managers or may sit on the board of directors of the business, but in very large businesses you are just one of thousands of owners who elect a representative board of directors to oversee the managers of the business and to protect the interests of the owners

- ✓ Receives a proportionate share of the proceeds if the business is sold or if the business sells off its assets

When owners invest money in a business the accountant records the amount of money received as an increase in the company's *cash* account (note the account is not called "money"). And, to keep things in balance, the amount invested in the business is recorded as an increase in an *owners' equity* account. (This is one example of *double entry accounting*, which is explained in Chapter 2.) Owners' equity also increases when a business makes profit. Because of the two different reasons for increases, the owners' equity of a business is divided into two separate accounts:

- ✓ **Invested capital:** Represents the amounts of money that owners have invested in the business, which could have been many years ago. Owners may invest additional capital from time to time, but generally speaking they cannot be forced to put additional money in a business.

✔ **Retained earnings:** Represents the profit earned by a business over the years that has not been distributed to its owners. If all profit had been distributed every year, retained earnings would have a zero balance. (If a business has never made a profit, its accumulated loss would cause retained earnings to have a negative balance, called a *deficit.*) If none of the annual profits of a business had been distributed to its owners, the balance in retained earnings would be the cumulative profit earned by the business since it opened its doors.

The account title *retained earnings* for the profit that a business earns and does not distribute to its owners is appropriate for any type of business entity. Business corporations — the most common type of business entities — use this title. The other types of business entities discussed in this chapter may use this title, but they may collapse both sources of owners' equity into just one account for each owner. Corporations are legally required to distinguish between the two sources of owners' equity: invested capital versus retained earnings. The other types of business entities are not.

Whether to retain some or all of annual net income is one of the most important decisions that a business makes; distributions from profit have to be decided at the highest level of a business. A growing business needs additional capital for expanding its assets, and increasing the debt load of the business usually cannot supply all the additional capital. So, the business *ploughs back* some of its profit for the year — it keeps some (perhaps all) of the profit, rather than giving it out to the owners. In the long run this may be the best course of action, a step back before a leap forward.

As mentioned earlier, most businesses borrow money because their owners are not able or not willing to supply all the capital needed to invest in its various assets. Banks are one major source of loans to businesses. Of course, banks charge interest on the loans; a business and its bank negotiate an interest rate acceptable to both. Also, many other terms and conditions are negotiated, such as the term (time period) of the loan, whether collateral is required to secure the loan, and so on. The loan contract between a business and its lender may prohibit the business from distributing profit to owners during the period of the loan. Or, the loan agreement may require that the business maintain a minimum cash balance — which could mean that money the business would like to distribute to owners from profit has to stay in its cash account instead.

The president or other appropriate officer of the business signs the note payable to the bank. In addition, the bank may ask the major investors in the business to sign the note payable *as individuals*, in their personal capacities — and perhaps ask their spouses to sign the note payable as well. You should definitely understand your personal obligations if you are inclined to sign a note payable of a business. You take the risk that you may have to pay some part or perhaps all the loan out of your personal assets.

Now, who are the owners and how do they organize themselves? A business may have just one owner, or two or more owners. A one-owner business may choose to operate as a *sole proprietorship;* a multiowner business must choose to be a *corporation,* a *partnership,* or a *limited liability company.* The most common type of business is a corporation.

No ownership structure is inherently better than another; which one is right for a particular business is something that the business's managers and owners need to decide (or should consult a tax advisor about, as discussed later in this chapter). The following discussion focuses on how ownership structure affects profit distribution to owners. Later, this chapter explains how the ownership structure determines the income tax paid by the business and its owners — which is always an important consideration.

## Corporations

The law views a *corporation* as a real, live person. Like an adult, a corporation is treated as a distinct and independent individual who has rights and responsibilities. A corporation's "birth certificate" is the legal form that is filed with the Secretary of State of the state in which the corporation is created. A corporation must have a legal name, of course, like an individual. Just as a child is separate from his or her parents, a corporation is separate from its owners. The corporation is responsible for its own debts, just like a person is. The bank can't come after you if your neighbor defaults on his or her loan, and the bank can't come after you if the corporation you have invested money in goes belly up. If a corporation doesn't pay its debts, its creditors can seize only the corporation's assets, not the assets of the corporation's owners.(But, see the sidebar "Be careful what you sign.")

---

### Be careful what you sign

In making loans to business, a bank or other lender may ask the principal officers of the business (and perhaps all its principal owners as well) to sign the note payable as individuals, meaning that the lender can reach into the individuals' pockets if the business can't pay off the loan. The corporate and limited liability company forms of business organization protect the business's managers by limiting creditors' rights to reach through to these individuals' personal assets. But these individuals give up this protection when they sign loan agreements as individuals.

If I sign a $10,000,000 note payable to the bank as "John A. Tracy, President of Best-selling Books, Inc.," then only the business (Best-selling Books, Inc.) is liable for the debt. But if I also add my personal signature, "John A. Tracy," below my signature as chief officer of the business, the bank can come after my personal assets in the event that the business can't pay the note payable. A good friend of mine once did this; only later did he learn, to his chagrin, of his legal exposure by signing as an individual. In fact, the bank made his wife sign the note as well, even though she was not an officer or employee of the business.

This important legal distinction between the obligations of the business entity and its individual owners is known as *limited liability* — that is, the limited liability of the owners. Even if the owners have deep pockets (are wealthy) they have no legal liability for the unpaid debts of the corporation (unless they've used the corporate shell to defraud creditors). So, when you invest money in a corporation as an owner you know that the most you can lose is the same amount you put in. You may lose every dollar you put in, but that's the most you can lose. The corporation's creditors cannot reach through the corporate entity to grab your assets to pay off the liabilities of the business.

### Stock shares

A corporation issues ownership shares to persons who invest money in the business. These ownership shares are documented by *stock certificates,* which state the name of the owner and how many shares are owned. The corporation has to keep an *register* (list) of how many shares everyone owns, of course. (An owner can be another corporation, or any other legal entity.) The owners of a corporation are called its *stockholders* because they own *stock shares* issued by the corporation. The stock shares are fully *negotiable*, which means the owner can sell them at any time to anyone willing to buy themwithout having to get the approval of the corporation or the other stockholders to sell the shares. *Publicly-owned corporations* are those whose stock shares are traded in public markets, most notably the New York Stock Exchange and NASDAQ.

One share of stock is one unit of ownership; how much one share is worth with respect to the value of the whole business depends on the total number of stock shares that the business issues. If a business has issued 400,000 shares and you own 40,000 of them, you own 1/10 of the business. But suppose that the business issues an additional 40,000 shares; you now have 40,000 of 440,000, giving you a 1/11 interest in the business. The more shares a business issues, the smaller the percentage of total owners' equity each share represents. Issuing additional shares may dilute, or decrease the value of each share of stock. A good example is when a publicly-owned corporation doubles the number of its shares by issuing a two-for-one stock split. Each shareholder gets one new share for each share presently owned, without investing any additional money in the business. As you would expect, the market value of the stock drops in half — which is exactly the purpose of the split because the lower stock price is better for stock market trading (according to conventional wisdom).

If new shares are issued at a price equal to the going value of the stock shares, the value of the existing shares should not be adversely affected. But if new shares are issued at a discount from the going value, the value of each stock share after the additional shares are issued may decline. For example, assume you own stock shares in a business and the stock is selling for $100 per share. Suppose the corporation issues some stock for $50 per share. Each new share adds only $50 value to the business, which drags down the average value of all shares of the corporation. I quickly admit here that the valuation of corporation stock shares is not nearly so simple — but, my purpose is to emphasize that stockholders should pay attention to the issue of additional shares for less than the going market price of a corporation's stock shares. Management stock options are the prime example of issuing stock shares at below market prices.

Many publicly-owned corporations give their managers stock options in addition to their salaries and other benefits. A *stock option* gives a manager the legal right to buy a certain number of shares at a fixed price starting at some time in the future — assuming conditions of continued employment and other requirements are satisfied. Usually the *exercise price*(also called the *strike price*) of a management stock option is set equal to or higher than the present market value of the stock shares. So, granting the manager the stock option does not produce any immediate gain to the manager — and these options can't be exercised for some time anyway. If the market price of the stock shares rises above the exercise price of the stock option sometime in the future the stock options become valuable — indeed, many managers have become multimillionaires from their stock options.

Suppose that the market value of a corporation's stock shares has risen to, say, $100 and that the exercise price of the stock options awarded to several managers a few years ago was set at $50 per share. And, assume that all the other conditions of the stock options are satisfied. The managers' stock options surely will be exercised, to realize their gains. It would seem, therefore, that the management stock options would have a negative impact on the market price of the corporation's stock shares — because the total value of the business has to be divided over a larger number of stock shares and this results in a smaller value per share. On the other hand, it can be argued that the total value of the business is higher than it would have been without the management stock options because better qualified managers were attracted to the business or that the managers performed better because of their options. Even with the decrease in the value per share, it is argued, the stockholders are better off than they would have been if no stock options had been awarded to the managers. The stock's market value may have been only $90 or $80 without the management stock options — so the story goes.

### Classes of stock shares

Before you invest in stock shares, you should ascertain whether the corporation has issued just one *class* of stock shares. A class is one group, or type of stock shares all having have identical rights; every share is the same as every other share. A corporation can issue two or more different classes of stock shares. For example, a business may offer Class A and Class B stock shares, where Class A stockholders are given the vote in elections for the board of directors but Class B stockholders do not get a vote. Of course, if you want to vote in the annual election of directors you should buy Class A stock shares. State laws generally are very liberal regarding the different classes of stock shares that can be issued by corporations. For a whimsical example, one class could get the best seats at the annual meetings of the stockholders. To be serious, differences between classes of stock shares are very significant and affect the investment value of the shares of each class of stock.

Two classes of corporate stock shares are fundamentally different: *common stock* and *preferred stock*. Preferred stockholders are promised a certain amount of cash dividends each year (note I said "promised," not "guaranteed") — but the corporation makes no such promises to its common stockholders. If the business ends up liquidating its assets and after paying off its liabilities returns money to its owners, the preferred stockholders have to be paid before any money goes to the common stockholders. The common stockholders are at the top of the risk chain: A business that ends up in deep financial trouble is obligated to pay off its liabilities first, and then its preferred stockholders, and by the time the common stockholders get their turn the business may have no money left to pay them. So, preferred stock has the promise of annual dividends and stands ahead of common stock in the liquidation of the business. What's the attraction of common stock, therefore? The main advantage of common stock is that it has unlimited upside potential. After obligations to its preferred stock are satisfied, the rest of the profit earned by the corporation accrues to the benefit of its common stock.

The main difference between preferred stock and common stock concerns *cash dividends* — what the business pays its owners from its profit. Here are the key points:

- A business must pay dividends to its preferred stockholders, because it has a contractual obligation to do so, whereas each year the board of directors must decide how much, if any, cash dividends to distribute to its common stockholders.

- Preferred stock shares usually are promised a fixed (limited) dividend per year and typically don't have a claim to any profit beyond the stated amount of dividends. (Some corporations issue *participating* preferred stock, which give the preferred stockholders a contingent right to more than just their basic amount of dividends, which gets too technical for this book.)

- Preferred stockholders don't have voting rights — unless they don't receive dividends for one period or more. In other words, preferred stock shareholders usually do not have voting rights in electing the corporation's board of directors or on other critical issues facing the corporation. Needless to say, these matters can become complex, and they vary from corporation to corporation — no wonder there are so many corporate lawyers! If you need more information I recommend *Investing For Dummies* by Eric Tyson (published by the same outfit that publishes this book).

Here are some other general things to know about common stock shares:

✔ Each stock share is equal to every other stock share in its class. This way, ownership rights are standardized, and the main difference between two stockholders in how many shares each owns.

✔ The only way a business has to return stockholders' capital (composed of invested capital and retained earnings) is if the majority of stockholders vote to liquidate the business in part or in total. Other than that, the business's managers don't have to worry about losing the stockholders' capital. Of course, stockholders are free to sell their shares at any time, as noted next.

✔ A stockholder can sell his or her shares at any time, without the approval of the other stockholders. However, stockholders of a privately-owned business may have agreed to certain restrictions on this right when they invested in the business.

✔ Stockholders can either put themselves in key management positions or delegate the task of selecting top managers and officers to a *board of directors,* which is a small group of persons selected by the stockholders to set the business's policies and represent stockholders' interests. Now don't get the impression that if you buy 100 shares of IBM, you can get yourself elected to its board of directors. On the other hand, if Warren Buffett bought 100,000,000 shares of IBM, he could very well get himself on the board. The *relative size* of your ownership interest is the key factor. If you put up more than half the money in a business, you can put yourself on the board and elect yourself president of the business. The stockholders who own 50 percent plus one share constitute the controlling group that decides who goes on the board of directors.

*Note:* The all-stocks-are-created-equal aspect of corporations is a practical and simple way to divide ownership, but its inflexibility can be a hindrance, too. Suppose the stockholders want to delegate to one person extraordinary power, or to give one person a share of profit out of proportion to his or her stock ownership. The business can make special compensation arrangements for key executives and ask a lawyer for advice on the best way to implement the stockholders' intentions. Nevertheless, state corporation laws require that certain voting matters be settled by a majority vote of stockholders. If enough stockholders oppose a certain arrangement, the other stockholders may have to buy them out to gain a controlling interest in the business. (The business can be organized as a limited liability company, which permits more flexibility in these matters; I talk about this type of legal structure later in the chapter.)

If you want to sell your stock shares, how much can you get for them? You can check any daily financial newspaper — such as *The Wall Street Journal* — for the market trading prices of thousands of publicly-owned corporations. But stock shares in privately-owned businesses aren't publicly traded, so how can you determine the value of your stock shares in such a business?

To be frank, you can't really. Until you actually sell your shares for a certain price per share you simply don't know their market value for sure. On the other hand, you can use certain benchmarks, or valuation methods to estimate market value. For example, you could look to the *book value per share,* which is based on values reported on the business's latest balance sheet:

```
Total stockholders' equity ÷ total number of shares = book
          value per share
```

Book values are historical — based on the past transactions of the business — whereas market pricing looks to how the business is likely to do in the future. The past is important, but the future prospects of the business are more important in setting a value on the business. Market value depends on forecast profit performance (future earnings), which in many cases is much more important than book value per share. One way of estimating the value of your stock shares in a private business corporation is the *earnings multiple* method, in which you calculate the theoretical value of a stock share by using a certain multiple of the business's earnings (net income) per share.

For example, suppose a privately owned business corporation earned $3.20 net income per share last year. You calculate the book value per share at the end of the year, which is $20.00, assume. You may be able to sell your shares at ten times earnings per share, or $32.00, which is considerably more than the book value per share. If someone paid $32.00 for the stock shares and the business earned $3.20 again per share next year, the new stockholder might be satisfied to earn 10 percent on his or her $32.00 investment — calculated by dividing the $3.20 earnings per share by the $32.00 cost of the stock share. (Not all of the $3.20 may be paid out as a cash dividend, so part of the 10 percent earnings on the investment consists of the increase in retained earnings of the business.)

Keep in mind that the $32.00 market value is only an estimate and just a theoretical price — although these days it would be a reasonable, and probably conservative, value for many businesses. However, you don't know the market price until you sell the stock. As a potential investor in the business, I may be willing to offer you $35.00 or $40.00 per share — or I may offer less than the book value per share.

Business valuation is highly dependent on the specific circumstances of each business: The valuation is not governed by one or two simple ratios. The present owners may be very eager to sell out and they may be willing to accept a lower price instead of waiting and driving a better bargain. The potential buyers of the business may see opportunities that the present owners don't see or aren't willing to pursue. Even Warren Buffett, who has a well-earned reputation for knowing how to value a business, admits that he's made some real blunders along the way.

### Stockholders and managers

Stockholders (including managers who own stock shares in the business) are concerned, first and foremost, with the profit performance of their business. The dividends they receive and the value of their stock shares depend on profit. Managers, too, are concerned with profit — their jobs depend on living up to the business's profit goals. But even though stockholders and managers strive toward the common goal of making the business profitable, they have an inherent conflict of interest that revolves around money and power:

- The more money that managers make in wages and benefits, the less stockholders see in the bottom-line net income. Stockholders obviously want the best managers for the job, but they don't want to pay any more than they have to. In many corporations, top-level managers, for all practical purposes, set their own salaries and compensation packages.

  The best solution is often to have outside directors (with no management position in the business) set the compensation of the top-level managers instead.

- Who should control the business: the managers, who were hired for their competence and are intimately familiar with the business, or the stockholders, who probably have no experience relevant to running this particular business but who put up the money that the business is running on? In ideal situations, the two sides respect each other's importance to the business and use this tension constructively. Of course, the real world is far from ideal, and you have situations in which managers are controlling the board of directors rather than the other way around. But this book isn't the proper place to get into all that.

As an investor, be aware of these issues and how they affect your profit. If you don't like the way your business is being run, you have the right to sell your shares and invest your money elsewhere.

In particular, watch out for actions that cause a *dilution effect* on the value of your stock shares — that is, cause each stock share to drop in value. Now, the dilution effect may be the result of a good business decision, so even though your share of the business has decreased in the short-term, the long-term profit performance of the business (and, therefore, your investment) may benefit. But you need to watch these decisions closely. The following situations cause a dilution effect:

- A business issues additional stock shares at the going market value, but doesn't really need the additional capital — the business is in no better profit-making position than it was before issuing the new stock shares. For example, a business may issue new stock shares in order to let a newly hired chief executive officer buy them. The immediate effect may be a dilution in the market value per share. Over the long-term, however, the new CEO may turn the business around and lead it to higher levels of profit performance that increase the stock's value.

✔ A business issues new stock shares at a discount below its stock shares' current value. For example, the business may issue a new batch of stock shares at a price lower than the current market value to employees who take advantage of an employee stock-purchase plan. Selling stock shares at a discount, by itself, has a dilution effect on the market value of the shares. But in the grand scheme of things the stock-purchase plan may motivate its employees to achieve higher productivity levels, which leads to superior profit performance of the business.

## Where profit goes in a corporation

Suppose that your business earned $1.32 million in net income for the year just ended and has issued a total of 400,000 shares of capital stock. Divide net income by the number of shares, and you come up with an earnings per share of $3.30.

The cash flow statement reports that the business paid $400,000 total cash dividends during the year, or $1.00 per share. (Cash dividends are usually paid quarterly, so the business most likely paid $0.25 dividends per share each of the four quarters.) The rest of the net income — $920,000 — remains in the retained earnings account. (**Remember:** Net income is first entered as an increase in the retained earnings account, and distributions are taken out of this account.) The retained earnings account thus increased by $2.30 per share (the difference between the net income, or earnings per share, and the dividends per share).

Although stockholders don't have the cash to show for it, their investment is better off by $2.30 per share — which shows up in the balance sheet as an increase in the retained earnings account in owners' equity. They can just hope that the business will use the cash flow provided from profit this year to make more profit in the future, which should lead to higher cash dividends.

If the business is a publicly-owned corporation whose stock shares are actively traded, its stockholders look to the change in the *market price* of the stock shares during the year. Did the market value go up or down during the year? You may think that the market value should increase $2.30 per share, because the business earned this much per share that it kept in the business and did not distribute to its shareholders. Your thinking is quite logical: Profit is an increase in the net assets of a business (assets less liabilities). The business is $2.30 per share "richer" at the end of the year than it was at the start of the year, due to profit earned and retained.

Yet it's entirely possible that the market price of the stock shares actually *decreased* during the year. Market prices are governed by psychological, political, and economic factors that go beyond the information in the financial reports of a business. Financial statements are one — but only one — of the information sources that stock investors use in making their buy-and-sell decisions. Chapter 14 explains how stock investors use the information in financial reports.

# Partnerships and limited liability companies

Suppose you're starting a new business with one or more other owners, but you do not want it to be a corporation. You can choose to form a *partnership* or a *limited liability company,* which are the main alternatives to the corporate form of a business. **Note**: A partnership is also called a *firm.* (You don't see this term used to refer to a corporation or limited liability company nearly as often as you do to a partnership.) The term firm connotes an association of a group of individuals working together in a business or professional practice.

Compared with the relatively rigid structure of corporations, partnership and limited liability company ownership structures allow the division of management authority, profit sharing, and ownership rights among the owners to be very flexible. Here are the key features of these two ownership structures:

✔ **Partnerships:** Partnerships avoid the double-taxation feature that corporations are subject to (see "Choosing the Right Legal Structure for Income Tax," later in this chapter, for details). Partnerships also differ from corporations with respect to liability. A partnership's owners fall into two categories:

- **General partners** are subject to *unlimited liability.* If a business can't pay its debts, its creditors can reach into general partners' personal assets. General partners have the authority and responsibility to manage the business. They are roughly equivalent to the president and other high-level managers of a business corporation. The general partners usually divide authority and responsibility among themselves, and often they elect one member of their group as the senior general partner or elect a small executive committee to make major decisions.

- **Limited partners** escape the unlimited liability that the general partners have hanging around their necks. Limited partners are not responsible, as individuals, for the liabilities of the partnership entity. These junior partners have ownership rights to the business's profit, but they don't generally participate in the management of the business. A partnership must have one or more general partners; not all partners can be limited partners.

Many large partnerships copy some of the management features of the corporate form — for example, a senior partner who serves as chair of the general partners' executive committee acts in much the same way as the chair of a corporation's board of directors. Generally, a partner can't sell his or her interest to an outsider without the consent of all the other partners. You can't just buy your way into a partnership; the other partners have to approve your joining the partnership. In contrast, you can buy stock shares and thereby become part owner of a corporation; you don't need the approval of the other stockholders.

✔ **Limited liability company (LLC):** The LLC is a relatively new but increasingly popular type of business creature. An LLC is like a corporation regarding limited liability, and it's like a partnership regarding the flexibility of dividing profit among the owners. The IRS treats an LLC like a partnership for income tax purposes (which means that an LLC is not subject to the potential double taxation on corporations, which is discussed later in this chapter). An LLC's key advantage is flexibility — especially regarding how profit and management authority are determined. For example, an LLC permits the founders of the business to put up, say, only 10 or 20 percent of the money to start a business venture, but to keep all management authority in their hands. The other investors share in profit, but not necessarily in proportion to their invested capital.

LLCs have a lot more flexibility than corporations, but flexibility is not all good. The owners must enter into a very detailed agreement that spells out the division of profit, the division of management authority and responsibility, their rights to withdraw capital, and their responsibilities to contribute new capital as needed. These schemes can get very complicated and difficult to understand, and they may end up requiring a lawyer to untangle them. If the ownership structure of an LLC is too complicated and too far off the beaten path, the business may have difficulty explaining itself to a lender when applying for a loan, and it may have difficulty convincing new shareholders to put capital into the business.

A partner or a shareholder in an LLC who participates in running the business — that is, who contributes more than just money — may receive a salary in addition to a share of the profit. The bottom-line profit is after deducting for all expenses *except* salaries to owners; these salaries are *not* deducted to determine bottom-line profit. The salaries are viewed as distributions from profit. I should warn you that the accounting for compensation and services provided by owners in an LLC and partners in a partnership gets rather technical and is beyond the scope of this book.

*Caution:* I would advise you as a member of a partnership or as a shareholder in an LLC to get up to speed on the special accounting practices of the business regarding how salaries and other payments for services to owners and partners are accounted for in the entity's financial statements and how they are treated in determining annual taxable income. Don't take anything for granted; investigate first. Call a tax professional if you have questions or need advice in this area.

Professional partnerships — physicians, CPAs, lawyers, and so on — may choose to become *professional corporations (PCs),* which are a special type of legal structure that states offer to professionals who otherwise would have to operate under the specter of unlimited partnership liability. States also permit *limited liability partnerships (LLPs)* for qualified professionals (such as doctors, lawyers, CPAs, and dentists), in which all the partners have limited liability. These types of legal entities were created mainly as the result of large damage awards in malpractice lawsuits against professional partnerships during the last three decades. The professionals pleaded for protection from the unlimited liability of the partnership form of organization, which they had traditionally used. Until these new types of professional legal entities came along, the code of professional ethics of the various professions required that practitioners operate as a partnership (or as sole practitioners). Today, almost all professional associations are organized as PCs or LLPs. They function very much as a partnership does, but without the unlimited liability feature of the partnership form of business organization.

The partnership or LLC agreement specifies how to divide profit among the owners. Whereas owners of a corporation receive a portion of profit that's directly proportional to the number of shares they own and, therefore, how much they invested, a partnership or LLC does not have to divide profit according to how much each owner invested. Invested capital is only one of three factors that generally play into profit allocation in partnerships and LLCs:

- ✔ **Treasure:** Owners may be rewarded according to how much of the "treasure" — invested capital — they contributed; they get back a certain percentage (return) on their investment. So if Joe invested twice as much as Jane did, his cut of the profit may be set at twice as much as Jane's.

- ✔ **Time:** Owners who invest more time in the business may receive more of the profit. In some businesses, a partner may not contribute much more than capital and his or her name, whereas other partners work long hours. This way of allocating profit works like a salary.

- ✔ **Talent:** Regardless of capital or time, some partners bring more to the business than others. Maybe they have better business contacts, or they have a knack for making deals happen, or their celebrity status makes their names alone worth a special share of the profit. Whatever it is that they do for the business, they contribute much more to the business's success than their capital or time suggests.

**Note:** A partnership needs to maintain a separate capital (or *ownership*) account for each partner. The total profit of the entity is allocated into these capital accounts, as spelled out in the partnership agreement. The agreement also specifies how much money each partner can withdraw from his capital account — for example, partners may be limited to withdrawing no more than 80 percent of their anticipated share of profit for the coming year, or they may be allowed to withdraw only a certain amount until they've built up their capital accounts.

## Sole proprietorships

A *sole proprietorship* is, basically, the business arm of an individual who has decided *not* to carry on his or her business activity as a separate legal entity (as a corporation, or partnership, or limited liability company) — it's the default option. This kind of business is not a separate entity; it's like the front porch of a house — attached to the house but a separate and distinct area of the house. You may be a sole proprietor of a business without knowing it! An individual may do house repair work for homeowners on a part-time basis, or be a full-time barber who operates on his own. Both are sole proprietorships. Anytime you regularly provide services for a fee, or sell things at a flea market, or engage in any business activity whose primary purpose is to make profit, you are a sole proprietor. If you carry on business activity to make profit or income, the IRS requires that you file a separate Schedule C "Profit or Loss From Business" with your annual individual income tax return. Schedule C summarizes your income and expenses from your sole proprietorship.

As the sole owner (proprietor), you have *unlimited liability,* meaning that if your business can't pay all its liabilities, the creditors to whom your business owes money can come after your personal assets. Many part-time entrepreneurs may not know this or may put it out of their minds, but this is a big risk to take. I have friends who are part-time business consultants, and most operate their consulting businesses as sole proprietorships. If they are sued for giving bad advice, all their personal assets are at risk — though they may be able to buy malpractice insurance to cover these losses.

Obviously, a sole proprietorship has no other owners to prepare financial statements for — although the proprietor should still prepare these statements as a check on how his or her business is doing. (Also, banks usually require financial statements of sole proprietors who apply for loans.)

One other piece of advice for sole proprietors: Although you don't have to separate invested capital from retained earnings like corporations do, you should still keep these two separate accounts for owners' equity — not only for the purpose of tracking the business but for the benefit of any future buyers of the business as well.

---

# Spreading the joy of profit to your customers: Business cooperatives

A business that shares its profit with its customers? Nobody can be *that* generous!

Actually, one type of business does just that: A *cooperative* pays its customers *patronage dividends* based on its profit for the year — each customer receives a year-end refund based on his or her purchases from the business over the year. Imagine that.

Oh, did I mention that in a cooperative, the customers are the owners? To shop in the cooperative, a customer must invest a certain amount of money in the business. (You knew there had to be a catch somewhere!) I grew up in the Midwest. You see the silos of grain co-ops (cooperative associations) in most towns and cities. They are owned by the farmers who use the co-ops to store and deliver their crops.

Business cooperatives deduct patronage dividends in determining their taxable income for the year. If the business returns all profit to customers as patronage dividends, taxable income is zero.

# Choosing the Right Legal Structure for Income Tax

In deciding which type of ownership structure is best for securing capital and managing their business, owners should also consider the income tax factor. They should know the key differences between two basic types of business entities from the income tax point of view:

- ✔ **Taxable-entity C corporations:** These corporations pay income tax on their annual taxable income amounts. Their stockholders pay a second income tax on cash dividends that the business distributes to them from profit, making C corporations and their owners subject to double taxation. The owners (stockholders) of a C corporation include in their individual income tax returns the cash distributions from profit paid to them by the business.

- ✔ **Pass-through entities — partnerships, S corporations, and LLCs:** This type of tax entity does not pay income tax on its annual taxable income; instead, it hands off its taxable income to its owners, who pick up their shares of the taxable income on their individual tax returns. Pass-through entities still have to file tax returns with the IRS, even though they don't pay income tax on their taxable income. In their tax returns, they also inform the IRS how much taxable income is allocated to each owner and send each owner a copy of this information to include with his or her individual income tax return.

*Note:* Most LLCs opt to be treated as a pass-through entity for income tax purposes, although under the tax law they can choose to be taxed as a C corporation and pay income tax on their taxable income for the year, with their individual shareholders paying a second tax on cash distributions of profit from the LLC. Read on to find out why they may choose to be treated as a C corporation.

The following sections illustrate the differences between the two types of tax entities for structuring a business. In these examples, I assume that the business uses the same accounting methods in preparing its income statement that it uses for determining its taxable income — a realistic assumption. To keep it simple, I consider just the federal income tax, which is much larger than any state income tax that might apply.

## C corporations

The regular type of corporation is called a *C corporation* in the tax law (no, not an R corporation for "regular" corporation). Unless you qualify as a small, or S, corporation (I explain the rules later in the chapter), your business corporation is assumed to be type C, which means that it pays income tax on its taxable income for the year.

Suppose you have a C corporation with the following abbreviated income statement (see Chapter 5 for details on income statements):

| | |
|---|---|
| Sales revenue | $26,000,000 |
| Expenses, except income tax | (23,800,000) |
| Earnings before income tax | $2,200,000 |
| Income tax | (748,000) |
| Net income | $1,452,000 |

The $748,000 income tax is determined by the fact that this business's $2.2 million taxable income puts it in the 34 percent income tax bracket (based on corporate taxable income rates effective in 2000, which have been stable for several years):

```
$2,200,000 taxable income × 34% income tax rate = $748,00
               income tax
```

That's a big chunk of the business's hard-earned profit. You must also consider the so-called *double taxation* of corporate profit — a most unpleasant topic if you're a stockholder in a C corporation. Not only does the C corporation have to pay $748,000 income tax on its profit (as I just calculated), but when the business distributes some of its after-tax profit to its stockholders as their just rewards for investing capital in the business, the stockholders include these cash dividends as income in their individual income tax returns and pay a second tax.

For a rather dramatic example, suppose that this business distributed its entire after-tax net income as cash dividends to its stockholders. (Even though most businesses don't pay 100 percent cash dividends from their net incomes.) Its stockholders must include the cash dividends in their individual income tax returns. How much each individual pays in taxes depends on his or her total taxable income for the year, but let me make an arbitrary (but reasonable) assumption that the stockholders are, on average, in the marginal 31 percent tax bracket. In this example, the stockholders would combine to pay $450,120 total individual income tax on their dividend incomes:

```
$1,452,000 dividends × 31% income tax rate = $450,120 total
           individual income tax paid by stockholders
```

You can calculate the total tax paid by both the corporation and its stockholders as follows:

| | |
|---|---|
| $748,000 | paid by the corporation on its $2,200,000 taxable income |
| 450,120 | paid by its stockholders on $1,452,000 in cash dividends |
| $1,198,120 | total income tax paid by both the corporation and its stockholders |

Compare this to the corporation's $2,200,000 of taxable income. Out of the $2,200,000 pretax profit that the business earned, $1,198,120 is quite a bit of total income tax to pay — more than half. On the other hand, if the corporation had retained all of its after-tax profit and paid no cash dividends, then at least for now the individual stockholders would not have to pay the second tax. Distributing no cash dividends may not go down well with all the stockholders, however. If you had persuaded your Aunt Hilda to invest some of her money in your business, but you don't pay any cash dividends, she may be very upset. Most corporations — but by no means all corporations — pay part of their after-tax net income as cash dividends to their stockholders.

## S corporations

A business that meets the following criteria can file IRS Form 2553 to be treated as an S corporation:

- ✔ It has issued only one class of stock.
- ✔ It has 75 or fewer people holding its stock shares.
- ✔ It has received approval for becoming an S corporation from all its stockholders.

Suppose that an S corporation has allocated its $2.2 million of taxable income among its owners (stockholders) in proportion to how much stock each owner holds. The business's total number of stock shares is 400,000, so a stockholder is allocated $5.50 taxable income for each share:

```
$2,200,000 taxable income ÷ 400,000 shares = $5.50 taxable
                income per share
```

So if you own 10,000 shares, you pick up $55,000 of the business's taxable income and include this amount in your individual income tax return for the year. *Caution:* I haven't yet said anything about how much cash dividends the corporation has paid. With $2,200,000 pretax profit, the business probably has enough cash flow from profit to make a distribution to its stockholders (Chapter 7 explains cash flow from profit.) But the point is that, as an S corporation stockholder, you have to pay income tax on your share of the taxable income *whether or not* the business distributes any of its profit to its stockholders.

Assume again that the stockholders pay an average of 31 percent income tax rate. Thus, as a group, they pay $682,000 total income tax:

```
$2,200,000 taxable income × 31% income tax rate = $682,000
                total income tax
```

Compare this total income tax paid by the stockholders of an S corporation with the two-tax total paid by the C corporation and its stockholders, in which all its after-tax net income is distributed to its stockholders. In that scenario, the total income tax bill is $1,198,120 — which is a lot more than what the stockholders of the S corporation with the same taxable income would pay. Shouldn't the business therefore elect to be an S corporation? Not necessarily — don't jump the gun. The stockholders of an S corporation have to include their shares of the company's total taxable income in their individual tax returns whether or not any of the company's profit is distributed to them. If the business doesn't intend to distribute any of its profit, or only a small part of its profit, the choice between being a C corporation or an S corporation gets rather complicated.

**_Note:_** I would need to know a lot more about the individual tax situations of every major stockholder — as well as other factors — before I would even consider giving tax advice in this situation. This discussion is limited to a simple comparison of a C corporation example and an S corporation example regarding who pays income tax on the business's taxable income and how the cash dividends paid by the corporation are taxed. Again, I have to advise you to consult a CPA or other income tax professional.

## *Partnerships and limited liability companies*

The LLC type of business entity borrows some features from the corporate form and some features from the partnership form. The LLC is neither fish nor fowl; it's an unusual blending of those features that have worked well for corporations and of those features that have worked well for partnerships. A business organized as an LLC has the option to be a pass-through tax entity, instead of paying income tax on its taxable income. A partnership doesn't have an option; it is a pass-through tax entity by virtue of being a partnership. The income tax features of partnerships and LLCs are summarized as follows:

- ✔ A partnership is a pass-through tax entity, just like an S corporation. **_Note:_** When two or more owners join together and invest money to start a business and don't incorporate and don't file legal papers to form an LLC, the tax law treats the business as a de facto partnership. Most partnerships are based on written agreements among the owners — but even without a formal, written agreement, a partnership exists in the eyes of the income tax law.

- ✔ An LLC has the choice between being treated as a pass-through tax entity, or as a taxable entity (like a regular C corporation). All you need to do is check off a box in the business's tax return to make the choice. (It's hard to believe that anything related to taxes and the IRS is as simple as that!) Many businesses that organize as LLCs organize that way because they want to be pass-through tax entities (although the flexible structure of the LLC is also a strong advantage of this type of type of business organization).

The partners in a partnership and the shareholders of an LLC pick up their shares of the business's taxable income in the same manner as the stockholders of an S corporation. They include their shares of the entity's taxable income in their individual income tax returns for the year. For example, suppose your share of the annual profit as a partner, or as one of the LLC's shareholders, is $150,000. You include this amount in your personal income tax return. So what's the difference between these two types of business entities and an S corporation?

In a word, flexibility. Whereas an S corporation must allocate profit based on one factor — the number of shares owned by each stockholder — partnerships and LLCs can use a number of factors in allocating profit among its owners. In an S corporation, if you own 10 percent of the stock, you pick up 10 percent of the business's total taxable income. But in a partnership or LLC, you might get 5 percent of the taxable income, or maybe 60 percent, or whatever.

Partners don't actually get paid salaries, although partners may take monthly draws (withdrawals from the partnership) that may look like salaries. Partners are not employees, but rather owners whose compensation consists of sharing in the profit of the partnership. A partner's share of profit may be disproportionately large as a substitute for a salary, if that partner puts in more hours at the business or otherwise makes a disproportionate contribution. But the amount paid out is a withdrawal of profit by the partner and not a true salary.

Another thing to keep in mind is that a partnership's general partners and an LLC's owners who actively manage the LLC are covered under the social security and Medicare law. That's the good news. The bad news is that they are required to pay for social security and Medicare as a *self-employment tax.* This means that these particular individuals have to pay both halves of these two taxes. I explain in Chapter 3 that employees of a business pay half of these taxes and the employer pays the other half. (On the plus side, anyone paying self-employment taxes gets a special deduction on their tax returns which mitigates the effect of having to pay both halves of the social security and Medicare taxes.)

Once more, I must mention that choosing the best ownership structure for a business is a complicated affair that goes beyond the income tax factor. You need to consider many other factors. After you select a particular ownership structure, changing it later is not easy. Asking the advice of a qualified professional is well worth the money and can prevent costly mistakes.

Sometimes the search for the ideal ownership structure that minimizes income tax and maximizes other benefits is like the search for the Holy Grail. Business owners should not expect to find the perfect answer — they have to make compromises and choose among advantages and disadvantages.

# Chapter 12

# Cost Conundrums

• • • • • • • • • • • • • • • • • • • • • • • • • • • • • • • • • • • • • • • • • • • • • •

## In This Chapter

▶ Determining costs: The second most important thing accountants do

▶ Comprehending the different needs for cost information

▶ Contrasting costs to understand them better

▶ Determining product cost for manufacturers

▶ Padding profit by manufacturing too many products

• • • • • • • • • • • • • • • • • • • • • • • • • • • • • • • • • • • • • • • • • • • • • •

*M*easuring costs is the second most important thing accountants do, right after measuring profit. But really, can measuring a cost be very complicated? You just take numbers off a purchase invoice and call it a day, right? Not if your business manufactures the products you sell — that's for sure! Even your favorite coffee shop has cost accounting problems (although the coffee shop's problems are not as serious as the manufacturer's).

To take an example close to home: Suppose you just returned from the grocery store with several items in the bag. What's the cost of the loaf of bread you bought? Should you include the sales tax? Should you include the cost of gas you used driving to the store? Should you include some amount of depreciation expense on your car? Suppose you returned some aluminum cans for recycling while you were at the grocery store, and were paid a small amount for the cans. Should you subtract this amount against the total cost of your purchases? Or, should you subtract the amount directly against the cost of only the sodas in aluminum cans that you bought? And, to repeat a point from Chapter 4: Is total cost the before-tax cost? In other words, is your cost equal to the amount of income you had to earn before income tax so that you have enough after-tax income to buy the items?

These questions about the cost of your groceries are interesting (well, interesting to me at least). But, you don't really have to come up with definite answers for such questions in managing your personal financial affairs. Individuals don't have to keep cost records of their personal expenditures, other than what's needed for their annual income tax returns. In contrast, businesses must carefully record all their costs correctly so that profit can be determined each period, and so that managers have the information they need to make decisions and to control profit performance.

# Previewing What's Coming Down the Pike

One main function of accounting for a manufacturing business is measuring *product cost*. Examples are the cost of a new Cadillac just rolling off the assembly line at General Motors or the cost of my book, *Accounting For Dummies*. Most production (manufacturing) processes are fairly complex, so measuring product cost is also fairly complex in most cases. Every step in the production process has to be tracked very carefully from start to finish. One major problem is that many manufacturing costs cannot be directly matched with particular products; these are called *indirect costs*. To arrive at the *full cost* of each separate product manufactured, accountants devise methods for allocating the indirect production costs to specific products. Different accountants use different allocation methods. In other respects, as well, product cost accounting is characterized by a diversity of methods. Generally accepted accounting principles provide very little guidance for measuring product cost. Manufacturing businesses have a lot of leeway in how their product costs are determined; even businesses in the same industry use different product cost accounting methods.

In addition to measuring product costs of manufacturers, accountants in all businesses determine many other costs: the costs of the departments and other organizational units of the business; the cost of the retirement plan for the company's employees; the cost of marketing initiatives and advertising campaigns; and, on occasion the cost of restructuring the business or the cost of a major recall of products sold by the business. A common refrain among accountants is "different costs for different purposes." True enough, but at its core cost accounting serves two broad purposes — measuring profit and providing relevant information to managers.

If you're running your business based on inaccurate or misleading cost figures, you likely have inadequate sales prices, misleading profit figures, and misstated asset values — not to mention that you're more vulnerable to lawsuits. In my experience, managers too often are inclined to take cost numbers for granted. The phrase *actual cost* gets tossed around too loosely, without a clear definition.

One thing business managers need to know is that putting a number on a cost is an accounting problem without an obvious answer. There's no one-size-fits-all definition of cost, and there's no one correct method of measuring cost. The conundrum is that, in spite of this ambiguity, you need exact amounts for costs. In order to understand the income statement and balance sheet that your accountant churns out for you to base business decisions on, you need to understand a little bit about the choices an accountant has to make in measuring costs. Some cost accounting methods result in conservative profit numbers; other methods boost profit, at least in the short run.

This chapter covers cost concepts and cost measurement methods that are used by both retail and manufacturing businesses, along with additional stuff for manufacturers to worry about. I also discuss how having a good handle on cost issues can help you recognize when a business is monkeying around with product cost to deliberately manipulate its profit figure. Service businesses — which sell a service such as transportation or entertainment — have a break here. They do not encounter the cost-accounting problems of manufacturers, but they have plenty of cost allocation issues to deal with in assessing the profitability of each of their separate sales revenue sources.

# What Makes Cost So Important?

Without good cost information, a business operates in the dark. Cost data is needed for different purposes in business, including the following:

- **Setting sales prices:** The common method for setting sales prices (known as *cost-plus* or *markup on cost*) starts with cost and then adds a certain percentage. If you don't know exactly how much a product costs, you can't be as shrewd and competitive in your pricing as you need to be. Even if sales prices are dictated by other forces and not set by managers, managers need to compare sales prices against product costs and other costs that should be matched against each sales revenue source.

- **Formulating a legal defense against charges of predatory pricing practices:** Many states have laws prohibiting businesses from selling below cost except in certain circumstances. And a business can be sued under federal law for charging artificially low prices intended to drive its competitors out of business. Be prepared to prove that your lower pricing is based on lower costs and not some illegitimate purpose.

- **Measuring gross margin:** Investors and managers judge business performance by the bottom-line profit figure. This profit figure depends on the *gross margin* figure you get when you subtract your cost of goods sold expense from your sales revenue. Gross margin (also called *gross profit*) is the first profit line in the income statement (see Figure 9-1 and 12-1 for examples). If gross margin is wrong, bottom-line net income is wrong — no two ways about this. The cost of goods sold expense depends on correct product costs — which are tricky costs for manufacturers in particular to compute (see "Putting Together the Pieces of Product Cost for Manufacturers" later in this chapter).

- **Valuing assets:** The balance sheet reports cost values for many assets, and these values are, of course, included in the overall financial position of your business. See Chapter 6 for more about assets and how asset values are reported in the balance sheet (also called the *statement of financial condition*).

# Accounting versus economic costs

Accountants record *actual costs* (though they disagree regarding how exactly to measure these costs). Actual costs are rooted in the actual, historical transactions of a business. Accountants also determine *budgeted costs* for businesses that prepare budgets (see Chapter 10), and they develop *standard costs* that serve as yardsticks to compare with the actual costs of a business. Other types of cost are found in economic theory. No, you don't have to become an economic theorist to understand these economic theory definitions of cost. The point is that you encounter a variety of accounting and economic cost terms when reading *The Wall Street Journal* and in many business discussions and deliberations. Don't squint your eyes and reveal your ignorance of the following cost terms:

✔ **Opportunity cost:** The amount of income given up when you follow a better course of action. For example, say that you quit your $50,000 job, invest $200,000 to start a new business, and end up netting $80,000 in your new business for the year. Suppose also that you would have earned 7 percent on the $200,000 (a total of $14,000) if you'd kept the money in whatever investment you took it from. So you gave up a $50,000 salary and $14,000 in investment income with your course of action; your opportunity cost is $64,000. Subtract that figure from what your actual course of action netted you — $80,000 — and you end up with a "real" economic profit of $16,000.

✔ **Marginal cost:** The *incremental*, out-of-pocket outlay required for taking a particular course of action. Generally speaking, it's the same thing as a *variable* cost (see "Fixed versus variable costs," later in this chapter). To maximize profit, you should keep moving in one direction until marginal cost equals marginal revenue. This sounds good in theory, but in actual practice managers cannot ignore

the need to recover fixed costs as well as marginal costs through sales revenue in order to remain in business over the long run.

✔ **Replacement cost:** The estimated amount it would take today to purchase an asset that the business already owns. The longer ago an asset was acquired, the more likely its current replacement cost is higher than its original cost. Economists are of the opinion that current replacement costs are relevant in making rational economic decisions. For insuring assets against fire, theft, and natural catastrophes the current replacement costs of the assets are clearly relevant. Beyond insurance, however, replacement costs play a minor role in business decisions — except in those situations in which one alternative being seriously considered is actually replacing assets.

✔ **Imputed cost:** An ideal, or hypothetical, cost figure that is used as a *benchmark or yardstick against which actual costs are compared.* Two examples are *standard costs* and the *cost of capital.* Standard costs are set in advance for the manufacture of products during the coming period, and then actual costs are compared against standard costs to identify significant variances. The cost of capital is the weighted average of the interest rate on debt capital and a minimum rate of return that should be earned on equity capital. The *economic value added* (EVA) method compares a business's cost of capital against its actual return on capital, to determine whether the business did better or worse than the benchmark.

For the most part, these types of cost aren't reflected in external financial reports. I've included them here to familiarize you with terms you're likely to see in the financial press and hear on financial talk shows. And, business managers toss these terms around a lot.

✔ **Making optimal choices:** You often must choose one alternative over others in making business decisions. The best alternative depends heavily on cost factors, and you have to be careful to distinguish *relevant* costs from *irrelevant* costs, as described in the section "Relevant versus irrelevant (sunk) costs," later in this chapter.

In most situations, the book value of a fixed asset is an *irrelevant* cost. Say book value is $35,000 for a machine used in the manufacturing operations of the business. This is the amount of original cost that has not yet been charged to depreciation expense since it was acquired, and it may seem quite relevant. However, in deciding between keeping the old machine or replacing it with a newer, more efficient machine, the *disposable value* of the old machine is the relevant amount, not the undepreciated cost balance of the asset. Suppose the old machine has only a $20,000 salvage value at this time; this is the relevant cost for the alternative of keeping it for use in the future — not the $35,000 that hasn't been depreciated yet. In order to keep using it, the business forgoes the $20,000 it could get by selling the asset, and this $20,000 is the relevant cost in this decision situation. Making decisions involves looking at the future cash flows of each alternative — not looking back at historical-based cost values.

# Sharpening Your Sensitivity to Costs

The following sections explain important distinctions between costs that managers should understand in making decisions and exercising control. Also, these cost distinctions help managers better appreciate the cost figures that accountants attach to products that are manufactured or purchased by the business. In a later section I focus on the special accounting methods and problems of computing product costs of *manufacturers*. Retailers (such as Wal-Mart) purchase products in a condition ready for sale to their customers — although the products have to be removed from shipping containers and a retailer does a little work making the products presentable for sale and putting the products on display.

Manufacturers don't have it so easy; their product costs have to be "manufactured" in the sense that the accountants have to compile production costs and compute the cost per unit for every product manufactured. I cannot exaggerate the importance of correct product costs (for businesses that sell products, of course). The total cost of goods (products) sold is the first, and usually the largest, expense deducted from sales revenue in measuring profit. The bottom-line profit amount reported the income statement of a business for the period depends heavily on whether its product costs have been measured properly. Also, keep in mind that product cost is the value for the inventory asset reported in the balance sheet of a business.

## Direct versus indirect costs

- ✔ **Direct costs:** Can be clearly attributed to one product or product line, or one source of sales revenue, or one organizational unit of the business, or one specific operation in a process. An example of a direct cost in the book publishing industry is the cost of the paper that a book is printed on; this cost can be squarely attached to one particular phase of the book production process.

- ✔ **Indirect costs:** Are far removed from and cannot be obviously attributed to specific products, organizational units, or activities. A book publisher's phone bill is a cost of doing business but can't be tied down to just one step in the book editorial and production process. The salary of the purchasing officer who selects the paper for all the books is another example of a cost that is indirect to the production of particular books.

Indirect costs are allocated according to some method to different products, sources of sales revenue, organizational units, and so on. Most allocation methods are far from perfect, and in the last analysis end up being rather arbitrary. Business managers should always keep an eye on the allocation methods used for indirect costs, and take the cost figures produced by these methods with a grain of salt. If I were called in as an expert witness in a court trial involving costs, the first thing I'd do is to critically analyze the cost allocation methods used by the business. If I were on the side of the defendant, I'd do my best to defend the allocation methods. But, if I were on the side of the plaintiff, I'd do my best to discredit the allocation methods. There's always grounds for criticism.

The cost of filling the gas tank in driving my car from Denver to San Diego and back is a direct cost of making the trip. The annual license plate that Colorado charges me for is an indirect cost of the trip, although it is a direct cost of having the car available during the year.

## Fixed versus variable costs

- ✔ **Fixed costs** remain the same over a relatively broad range of sales volume or production output. For example, the cost of renting office space doesn't change regardless of how much a business's sales volume increases or decreases, until the increase or decrease reaches the point where the business needs to either hire more people and obtain more office space or lay off employees and reduce its office space. Fixed costs are like a dead weight on the business. Its total fixed costs is the hurdle that the business must overcome by selling enough units at high enough profit margins per unit in order to avoid a loss and move into the profit zone. (Chapter 9 explains the break-even point, which is the level of sales needed to cover fixed costs for the period.)

- ✔ **Variable costs** increase and decrease in proportion to changes in sales or production level. If you increase the number of books that your business produces, the cost of the paper and ink also goes up.

# Relevant versus irrelevant (sunk) costs

- ✔ **Relevant costs:** Costs that should be considered when deciding on a future course of action. Relevant costs are *future* costs — costs that you would incur, or bring upon yourself, depending on which course of action you take. For example, say that you want to increase the number of books that your business produces next year in order to increase your sales revenue, but the cost of paper has just shot up. Should you take the cost of paper into consideration? Absolutely; that cost will affect your bottom-line profit and may negate any increases in sales volume that you experience (unless you increase the sales price). The cost of paper is a relevant cost.

- ✔ **Irrelevant (or sunk) costs:** Costs that should be disregarded when deciding on a future course of action; if brought into the analysis, these costs could cause you to make the wrong decision. An irrelevant cost is a vestige of the past; that money is gone, so get over it. For example, suppose that your supervisor tells you to expect a slew of new hires next week. All your staff members use computers now, but you have a bunch of typewriters gathering dust in the supply room. Should you consider the cost paid for those typewriters in your decision to buy computers for all the new hires? Absolutely not; that cost should have been written off and is no match for the cost you'd pay in productivity (and morale) for new employees who are forced to use typewriters.

Generally speaking, fixed costs are irrelevant when deciding on a future course of action, assuming that they're truly fixed and can't be increased or decreased over the short term. Most variable costs are relevant because they depend on which alternative is decided on.

Fixed costs are usually irrelevant in decision making because these costs will be the same no matter which course of action you decide upon. Looking behind these costs, you usually find that the costs provide *capacity* of one sort or another — so much building space, so many machine-hours available for use, so many hours of labor that will be worked, and so on. Managers have to figure out the best overall way to utilize these capacities. For example, suppose your retail business pays an annual building rent of $200,000, which is a fixed cost (unless the rental contract with the landlord has a rent escalation clause based on sales revenue). The rent, which gives the business the legal right to occupy the building, provides 15,000 square feet of retail and storage space. You should figure out which sales mix of products will generate the highest total contribution margin — equal to total sales revenue less total variable costs of making the sales including the costs of the goods sold and any other costs driven by sales revenue and sales volume.

# Separating between actual, budgeted, and standard costs

✔ **Actual costs:** Historical costs, based on actual transactions and operations for the period just ended, or going back to earlier periods. Financial statement accounting is based on a business's actual transactions and operations; the basic approach to determining annual profit is to record the financial effects of actual transactions and allocate historical costs to the periods benefited by the costs.

✔ **Budgeted costs:** Future costs, for transactions and operations expected to take place over the coming period, based on forecasts and established goals. Note that fixed costs are budgeted differently than variable costs — for example, if sales volume is forecast to increase by 10 percent, variable costs will definitely increase accordingly, but fixed costs may or may not need to be increased to accommodate the volume increase (see "Fixed versus variable costs," earlier in this chapter). Chapter 10 explains the budgeting process and budgeted financial statements.

✔ **Standard costs:** Costs, primarily in manufacturing, that are carefully engineered based on detailed analysis of operations and forecast costs for each component or step in an operation. Developing standard costs for variable production costs is relatively straightforward because many of these are direct costs, whereas most fixed costs are indirect, and standard costs for fixed costs are necessarily based on more arbitrary methods (see "Direct versus indirect costs," earlier in this chapter). *Note:* Some variable costs are indirect and have to be allocated to specific products in order to come up with a full (total) standard cost of the product.

# Product versus period costs

✔ **Product costs:** Costs attached to particular products. The cost is recorded in the inventory asset account until the product is sold, at which time the cost goes into the cost of goods sold expense account. (See Chapters 5 and 6 for more about these accounts; also, see Chapter 13 for alternative methods for selecting which product costs are first charged to the cost of goods sold expense). One key point to keep in mind is that product cost is deferred and not recorded to expense until the product is sold.

For example, the cost of a new Ford Taurus sitting on a car dealer's showroom floor is a product cost. The dealer keeps the cost in the inventory asset account until you buy the car, at which point the dealer charges the cost to the cost of goods sold expense.

✔ **Period costs:** Costs that are *not* attached to particular products. These costs do not spend time in the "waiting room" of inventory. Period costs are recorded as expenses immediately; unlike product costs, period costs don't pass through the inventory account first. Advertising costs, for example, are accounted for as period costs and recorded immediately in an expense account. Also, research and development costs are treated as a period cost.

Separating between product costs and period costs is particularly important for manufacturing businesses, as you find out in the following section.

# Putting Together the Pieces of Product Cost for Manufacturers

Businesses that manufacture products have several additional cost problems to deal with. I use the term *manufacture* in the broadest sense: Automobile makers assemble cars, beer companies brew beer, automobile gasoline companies refine oil, DuPont makes products through chemical synthesis, and so on. *Retailers* (also called *merchandisers*), on the other hand, buy products in a condition ready for resale to the end consumer. For example, Levi Strauss manufactures clothing, and the Gap is a retailer that buys from Levi Strauss and sells the clothes to the public.

The following sections describe costs that are unique to manufacturers and address the issue of determining the cost of products that are manufactured.

## Minding manufacturing costs

Manufacturing costs consist of four basic types:

✔ **Raw materials:** What a manufacturer buys from other companies to use in the production of its own products. For example, General Motors buys tires from Goodyear (an other tire manufacturers) that then become part of GM's cars.

✔ **Direct labor:** The employees who work on the production line.

✔ **Variable overhead:** Indirect production costs that increase or decrease as the quantity produced increases or decreases. An example is the cost of electricity that runs the production equipment: You pay for the electricity for the whole plant, not machine by machine, so you can't attach this cost to one particular part of the process. But if you increase or decrease the use of those machines, the electricity cost increases or decreases accordingly.

✔ **Fixed overhead:** Indirect production costs that do *not* increase or decrease as the quantity produced increases or decreases. These fixed costs remain the same over a fairly broad range of production output levels (see "Fixed versus variable costs," earlier in this chapter). Three significant fixed manufacturing costs are

- Salaries for certain production employees who don't work directly on the production line, such as a vice president, safety inspectors, security guards, accountants, and shipping and receiving workers

- Depreciation of production buildings, equipment, and other manufacturing fixed assets

- Occupancy costs, such as building insurance, property taxes, and heating and lighting charges

Figure 12-1 shows a sample management income statement for a manufacturer, including supplementary information about its manufacturing costs. Notice that the cost of goods sold expense depends directly on the product cost from the manufacturing cost summary that appears below the management income statement. A business may manufacture 100 or 1,000 different products, or even more. To keep the example easy to follow, Figure 12-1 presents a scenario for a one-product manufacturer. The example is realistic yet avoids the clutter of too much detail. The multi-product manufacturer has some additional accounting problems, but these are too technical for a book like this. The fundamental accounting problems and methods of all manufactures are illustrated in the example.

The information in the manufacturing cost summary schedule below the income statement (see Figure 12-1) is highly confidential and for management eyes only. Competitors would love to know this information. A company may enjoy a significant cost advantage over its competitors and definitely would not want its cost data to get into the hands of its competitors. As just mentioned, the example shown in Figure 12-1 is for a one-product manufacturer — to keep the presentation easy to follow. In practice, most manufacturers sell many products and such a schedule is prepared for each product. The company does not want its competitors to know any of its product costs, of course.

Unlike a retailer, a manufacturer does not *purchase* products but begins by buying the raw materials needed in the production process. Then the manufacturer pays workers to operate the machines and equipment and to move the products into warehouses after they've been produced. All this is done in a sprawling plant that has many indirect overhead costs. All these different production costs have to be funneled into the product cost so that the product cost can be entered in the inventory account, and then to cost of goods sold expense when products are sold.

**Management Income Statement For Year**

| Sales Volume | 110,000 | Units |
| --- | --- | --- |

| | Per Unit | Totals |
| --- | --- | --- |
| Sales Revenue | $1,400 | $154,000,000 |
| Cost of Goods Sold Expense | (760) | (83,600,000) |
| Gross Margin | $640 | $70,400,000 |
| Variable Operating Expenses | (300) | (33,000,000) |
| Contribution Margin | $340 | $37,400,000 |
| Fixed Operating Expenses | (195) | (21,450,000) |
| Earnings Before Interest and Income Tax (EBIT) | $145 | $15,950,000 |
| Interest Expense | | (2,750,000) |
| Earnings Before Income Tax | | $13,200,000 |
| Income Tax Expense | | (4,488,000) |
| Net Income | | $8,712,000 |

**Manufacturing Cost Summary For Year**

| Annual Production Capacity | 150,000 | Units |
| --- | --- | --- |
| Actual Output | 120,000 | Units |

| Production Cost Components | Per Unit | Totals |
| --- | --- | --- |
| Raw Materials | $215 | $25,800,000 |
| Direct Labor | 125 | 15,000,000 |
| Variable Overhead | 70 | 8,400,000 |
| Total Variable Manufacturing Costs | $410 | $49,200,000 |
| Fixed Overhead | 350 | 42,000,000 |
| Total Manufacturing Costs | $760 | $91,200,000 |
| To 10,000 Units Inventory Increase | | (7,600,000) |
| To 110,000 Units Sold | | $83,600,000 |

**Figure 12-1:**
Example for determining product cost of a manufacturer.

# Allocating costs properly: Not easy!

Two vexing issues rear their ugly heads in determining product cost for a manufacturer:

> ✔ **Drawing a bright line between manufacturing costs and nonmanufacturing operating costs:** The key difference here is that manufacturing costs are categorized as product costs, whereas nonmanufacturing operating costs are categorized as period costs (refer to "Product versus period costs," earlier in this chapter). In calculating product cost, you

factor in only manufacturing costs and not other costs. Period costs are recorded right away as an expense — either in variable operating expenses or fixed operating expenses for the example shown in Figure 12-1.

Wages paid to production line workers are a clear-cut example of a manufacturing cost. Salaries paid to salespeople is a marketing cost and are not part of product cost; marketing costs are treated as period costs, which means these costs are recorded immediately to expense of the period. Depreciation on production equipment is a manufacturing cost, but depreciation on the warehouse in which products are stored after being manufactured is a period cost. Moving the raw materials and works-in-progress through the production process is a manufacturing cost, but transporting the finished products from the warehouse to customers is a period cost. In short, product cost stops at the end of the production line — but every cost up to that point should be included as a manufacturing cost. In short, the accumulation of direct and variable production costs starts at the beginning of the manufacturing process and stops at the end of the production line. All fixed and indirect manufacturing costs during the year are allocated to the actual production output during the year.

If you misclassify some manufacturing costs as operating costs, your product cost calculation will be too low (refer to "Calculating product cost," later in this chapter).

✔ **Whether to allocate indirect costs among different products, or organizational units, or assets:** Indirect *manufacturing* costs must be allocated among the products produced during the period. The full product cost includes both direct and indirect manufacturing costs. Coming up with a completely satisfactory allocation method is difficult and ends up being somewhat arbitrary — but must be done to determine product cost. For nonmanufacturing operating costs, the basic test of whether to allocate indirect costs is whether allocation helps managers make better decisions and exercise better control. Maybe, maybe not. In any case, managers should understand how manufacturing indirect costs are allocated to products and how indirect nonmanufacturing costs are allocated, keeping in mind that every allocation method is arbitrary and that a different allocation method may be just as convincing. (See the sidebar "Allocating indirect costs is as simple as ABC — not!")

## Calculating product cost

The basic equation for calculating product cost is as follows (using the example of the manufacturer from Figure 12-1):

```
$91.2 million total manufacturing costs ÷ 120,000 units
    production output = $760 product cost per unit
```

# Allocating indirect costs is as simple as ABC — not!

Accountants for manufacturers have developed loads of different methods and schemes for allocating indirect overhead costs, many based on some common denominator of production activity, such as direct labor hours. The latest method to get a lot of press is called *activity-based costing* (ABC).

With the ABC method, you identify each necessary, supporting activity in the production process and collect costs into a separate pool for each identified activity. Then you develop a *measure* for each activity — for example, the measure for the engineering department may be hours, and the measure for the maintenance department may be square feet. You use the activity measures as *cost drivers* to allocate cost to products. So if Product A needs 200 hours of the engineering department's time and Product B is a simple product that needs only 20 hours of engineering, you allocate ten times as much of the engineering cost to Product A.

The idea is that the engineering department doesn't come cheap — including the cost of their slide rules and pocket protectors as well as their salaries and benefits, the total cost per hour for those engineers could be $100 to $200. The logic of the ABC cost-allocation method is that the engineering cost per hour should be allocated on the basis of the number of hours (the driver) required by each product. In similar fashion, suppose the cost of the maintenance department is $10 per square foot per year. If Product C uses twice as much floor space as Product D, it would be charged with twice as much maintenance cost.

The ABC method has received much praise for being better than traditional allocation methods, especially for management decision making, but keep in mind that it still requires rather arbitrary definitions of cost drivers — and having too many different cost drivers, each with its own pool of costs, is not too practical. Cost allocation always involves arbitrary methods. Managers should be aware of which methods are being used and should challenge a method if they think that it's misleading and should be replaced with a better (though still somewhat arbitrary) method. I don't mean to put too fine a point on this, but to a large extent, cost allocation boils down to a "my arbitrary method is better than your arbitrary method" argument.

**Note:** Cost allocation methods should be transparent to managers who use the cost data provided to them by accountants. Managers should never have to guess about what methods are being used, or have to call upon the accountants to explain the allocation methods.

Looks pretty straightforward, doesn't it? Well, the equation itself may be simple, but the accuracy of the results depends directly on the accuracy of your manufacturing cost numbers. And because manufacturing processes are fairly complex, with hundreds or thousands of steps and operations, your accounting systems must be very complex and detailed to keep accurate track of all the manufacturing costs.

As I explain earlier, when introducing the example, this business manufactures just one product. Also, its product cost per unit is determined for the entire year. In actual practice, manufacturers calculate their product costs monthly or quarterly. The computation process is the same, but the frequency of doing the computation varies from business to business.

In this example the business manufactured 120,000 units and sold 110,000 units during the year. As just computed, its product cost per unit is $760. The 110,000 total units sold during the year is multiplied by the $760 product cost to compute the $83,600,000 cost of goods sold expense, which is deducted against the company's revenue from selling 110,000 units during the year. The company's total manufacturing costs for the year were $91,200,000, which is $7,600,000 more than the cost of goods sold expense. This remainder of the total annual manufacturing costs is recorded as an increase in the company's inventory asset account, to recognize the 10,000 units increase of units awaiting sale in the future. In Figure 12-1, note that the $760 product cost per unit is applied both to the 110,000 units sold and to the 10,000 units added to inventory.

*Note:* As just mentioned, most manufacturers determine their product costs monthly or quarterly rather than once a year (as in the example). Product costs likely will vary each successive period the costs are determined. Because the product costs vary from period to period the business must choose which cost of goods sold and inventory cost method to use — unless product cost remains absolutely flat and constant period to period, in which case the different methods would yield the same results. Chapter 13 explains the alternative accounting methods for determining cost of goods sold expense and inventory cost value.

## Fixed manufacturing costs and production capacity

Product cost consists of two very distinct components: *variable manufacturing costs* and *fixed manufacturing costs*. In Figure 12-1, note that the company's variable manufacturing costs are $410 per unit, and that its fixed manufacturing costs are $350 per unit. Now, what if the business had manufactured just one more unit? Its total variable manufacturing costs would have been $410 higher; these costs are driven by the actual number of units produced, so even one more unit would have caused the variable costs to increase. But, the company's total fixed costs would have been the same if it had produced one more unit, or 10,000 more units for that matter. Variable manufacturing costs are bought on a per unit basis, as it were, whereas fixed manufacturing costs are bought in bulk for the whole period.

Fixed manufacturing costs are needed to provide *production capacity* — the people and physical resources needed to manufacture products — for the period. Once the business has the production plant and people in place for the year, its fixed manufacturing costs cannot be easily scaled down. The business is stuck with these costs over the short run. It has to make the best use it can from its production capacity.

Production capacity is a critical concept for business managers to grasp. You need to plan your production capacity well ahead of time because you need plenty of lead time to assemble the right people, equipment, land, and buildings. When you have the necessary production capacity in place, you want to make sure that you're making optimal use of that capacity. The fixed costs of production capacity remain the same even as production output increases or decreases, so you may as well make optimal use of the capacity provided by those fixed costs. For example, you're recording the same depreciation amount on your machinery regardless of how you actually use those machines, so you should be sure to optimize the use of those machines (within limits, of course — overworking the machines to the point where they break down won't do you much good).

The fixed cost component of product cost is called the *burden rate*. In my manufacturing example the burden rate is computed as follows (see Figure 12-1 for data):

```
$42.0 million total fixed manufacturing costs for period ÷
         120,000 units production output for period = $350
         burden rate
```

Note that the burden rate depends on the number divided into total fixed manufacturing costs for the period; that is, the production output for the period. Now, here's a very important twist on my example: Suppose the company had manufactured only 110,000 units during the period — equal exactly to the quantity sold during the year. Its variable manufacturing cost per unit would have been the same, or $410 per unit. But, its burden rate would have been $381.82 per unit (computed by dividing the $42.0 million total fixed manufacturing costs by the 110,000 units production output). Each unit sold, therefore, would have cost $31.82 more simply because the company produced fewer units ($381.82 burden rate at the 110,000 output level compared with the $350 burden rate at the 120,000 output level).

In this alternative scenario (in which only 110,000 units are produced), the company's product cost would have been $791.82 ($410 variable costs plus the $381.82 burden rate). The company's cost of goods sold, therefore, would have been $3,500,000 higher for the year ($31.82 higher product cost × 110,000 units sold). This rather significant increase in its cost of goods sold expense is caused by the company producing fewer units, although it did produce all the units that it needed for sales during the year. The same total amount of fixed manufacturing costs would be spread over fewer units of production output.

Shifting the focus back to the example shown in Figure 12-1, the company's cost of goods sold benefited from the fact that it produced 10,000 more units than it sold during the year — these 10,000 units absorbed $3.5 million of its total fixed manufacturing costs for the year, and until the units are sold this $3.5 million stays in the inventory asset account. It's entirely possible that the higher production level was justified — to have more inventory on hand for sales growth next year. But, production output can get out of hand — see the following section, "Excessive production output for puffing-up profit."

Managers (and investors as well) should understand the inventory increase effect caused by manufacturing more units than are sold during the year. In the example shown in Figure 12-1, cost of goods sold expense escaped from $3.5 million of fixed manufacturing costs because the company produced 10,000 more units than it sold during the year, thus pushing down the burden rate. The company's cost of goods sold expense would have been $3.5 million higher if it had produced just the number of units it sold during the year. The lower output level would have increased cost of goods sold expense, and would have caused a $3.5 million drop in gross margin and earnings before income tax. Indeed, earnings before income tax would have been 27 percent lower ($3.5 million ÷ $13.2 million = 27 percent decrease).

For the example illustrated in Figure 12-1, the business's production capacity for the year is 150,000 units. However, this business produced only 120,000 units during the year, which is 30,000 units fewer than it could have. In other words, it operated at 80 percent of production capacity, which is 20 percent *idle capacity* (which isn't unusual — the average U.S. manufacturing plant normally operates at 80 to 85 percent of its production capacity):

```
120,000 units output ÷ 150,000 units capacity = 80 percent
               utilization
```

Running at 80 percent of production capacity, this business's burden rate for the year is $350 per unit ($42 million total fixed manufacturing costs ÷ 120,000 units output). As explained earlier, the burden rate would have been higher if the company had produced, say, only 110,000 units during the year. The burden rate, in other words, is sensitive to the number of units produced. This can lead to all kinds of mischief, as explained next.

## *Excessive production output for puffing-up profit*

Whenever production output is higher than sales volume, be on guard. Excessive production can puff up the profit figure. How? Until a product is sold, the product cost goes in the inventory asset account rather than the cost of goods sold expense account, meaning that the product cost is counted as a *positive* number (an asset) rather than a *negative* number (an expense). The burden rate is included in product cost, which means that this cost component goes into inventory and is held there until the products are sold later. In short, when you overproduce, more of your fixed manufacturing costs for the period are moved to the inventory asset account and less are moved into cost of goods sold expense, which is based on the number of units sold.

# The actual costs/actual output method and when not to use it

To determine its product cost, the business in the Figure 12-1 example uses the *actual cost/actual output method,* in which you take your actual costs — which may have been higher or lower than the budgeted costs for the year — and divide by the actual output for the year.

The actual cost/actual output method is appropriate in most situations. However, this method is not appropriate and would have to be modified in two extreme situations:

- **Manufacturing costs are grossly excessive or wasteful due to inefficient production operations:** For example, suppose that the business represented in Figure 12-1 had to throw away $1.2 million of raw materials during the year. The $1.2 million is included in the total raw materials cost, but should be removed from the calculation of the raw material cost per unit. Instead, you treat it as a period cost — meaning that you take it directly into expense. Then the cost of

goods sold expense would be based on $750 per unit instead of $760, which lowers this expense by $1.1 million (based on the 110,000 units sold). But you still have to record the $1.2 million expense for wasted raw materials, so EBIT would be $100,000 lower.

- **Production output is significantly less than normal capacity utilization:** Suppose that the Figure 12-1 business produced only 75,000 units during the year but still sold 110,000 units because it was working off a large inventory carryover from the year before. Then its production capacity would be 50 percent instead of 80 percent. In a sense, the business wasted half of its production capacity, and you can argue that half of its fixed manufacturing costs should be charged directly to expense on the income statement and not included in the calculation of product cost.

You need to judge whether an inventory increase is justified. Be aware that an unjustified increase may be evidence of profit manipulation or just good old-fashioned management bungling. Either way, the day of reckoning will come when the products are sold and the cost of inventory becomes cost of goods sold expense — at which point the cost subtracts from the bottom line.

Recapping the example shown in Figure 12-1: The business manufactured 10,000 more units than it sold during the year. With variable manufacturing costs at $410 per unit, the business took on $4.1 million more in manufacturing costs than it would have if it had produced only the 110,000 units needed for its sales volume. In other words, if the business had produced 10,000 fewer units, its variable manufacturing costs would have been $4.1 million less. That's the nature of variable costs. In contrast, if the company had manufactured 10,000 fewer units, its *fixed* manufacturing costs would not have been any less — that's the nature of fixed costs.

Of its $42 million total fixed manufacturing costs for the year, only $38.5 million ended up in the cost of goods sold expense for the year ($350 burden rate × 110,000 units sold). The other $3.5 million ended up in the inventory asset account ($350 burden rate × 10,000 units inventory increase). Let me be very clear here: I'm not suggesting any hanky-panky. But the business did help its pretax profit to the amount of $3.5 million by producing 10,000 more units than it sold. If the business had produced only 110,000 units, equal to its sales volume for the year, then all the fixed manufacturing costs would have gone into cost of goods sold expense. As explained above, the expense would have been $3.5 million higher, and EBIT would have been that much lower.

Now suppose that the business manufactured 150,000 units during the year and increased its inventory by 40,000 units — which may be a legitimate move if the business is anticipating a big jump in sales next year. On the other hand, an inventory increase of 40,000 units in a year in which only 110,000 units were sold may be the result of a serious overproduction mistake, and the larger inventory may not be needed next year. In any case, Figure 12-2 shows what happens to production costs and — more importantly — what happens to profit at the higher production output level.

The additional 30,000 units (over and above the 120,000 units manufactured by the business in the original example) cost $410 per unit. (The precise cost may be a little higher than $410per unit because as you start crowding your production capacity, some variable costs may increase a little.) The business would need about $12.3 million more for the additional 30,000 units of production output:

```
$410 variable manufacturing cost per unit x 30,000 additional
       units produced = $12,300,000 additional variable
          manufacturing costs invested in inventory
```

Again, its fixed manufacturing costs would not have increased, given the nature of fixed costs. Fixed costs stay put until capacity is increased. Sales volume, in this scenario, also remains the same.

But check out the business's EBIT in Figure 12-2: $23.65 million, compared with $15.95 million in Figure 12-1 — a $7.70 million increase, even though sales volume, sales prices, and operating costs all remain the same. Whoa! What's going on here? The simple answer is that the cost of goods sold expense is $7.70 million less than before. But how can cost of goods sold expense be less? The business sells 110,000 units in both scenarios. And, variable manufacturing costs are $410 per unit in both cases.

### Management Income Statement For Year

| Sales Volume | 110,000 | Units |
| --- | --- | --- |

| | Per Unit | Totals |
| --- | --- | --- |
| Sales Revenue | $1,400 | $154,000,000 |
| ➤ Cost of Goods Sold Expense | (690) | (75,900,000) |
| Gross Margin | $710 | $78,100,000 |
| Variable Operating Expenses | (300) | (33,000,000) |
| Contribution Margin | $410 | $45,100,000 |
| Fixed Operating Expenses | (195) | (21,450,000) |
| Earnings Before Interest and Income Tax (EBIT) | $215 | $23,650,000 |
| Interest Expense | | (2,750,000) |
| Earnings Before Income Tax | | $20,900,000 |
| Income Tax Expense | | (7,106,000) |
| Net Income | | $13,794,000 |

### Manufacturing Cost Summary For Year

| Annual Production Capacity | 150,000 | Units |
| --- | --- | --- |
| Actual Output | 150,000 | Units |

| **Production Cost Components** | **Per Unit** | **Totals** |
| --- | --- | --- |
| Raw Materials | $215 | $32,250,000 |
| Direct Labor | 125 | 18,750,000 |
| Variable Overhead | 70 | 10,500,000 |
| Total Variable Manufacturing Costs | $410 | $61,500,000 |
| Fixed Overhead | 280 | 42,000,000 |
| Total Manufacturing Costs | $690 | $103,500,000 |
| To 40,000 Units Inventory Increase | | (27,600,000) |
| To 110,000 Units Sold | | $75,900,000 |

**Figure 12-2:**
Example in which production output greatly exceeds sales volume, thereby boosting profit for the period.

The burden rate component of product cost in the first case is $350 (see Figure 12-1). In the second case the burden rate is only $280 (see Figure 12-2). Recall that the burden rate is computed by dividing total fixed manufacturing costs for the period by the production output during the period. Dividing by 150,000 units compared with 120,000 units reduces the burden rate from $350 to $280. The $70 lower burden rate multiplied by the 110,000 units sold results in a $7.7 million smaller cost of goods sold expense for the period, and a higher pretax profit of the same amount.

In the first case the business puts $3.5 million of its total annual fixed manufacturing costs into the increase in inventory (10,000 units increase × $350 burden rate). In the second case, in which the production output is at capacity, the business puts $11.2 million of its total fixed manufacturing costs into the increase in inventory (40,000 units increase × $280 burden rate). Thus, $7.7 million more of its fixed manufacturing costs go into inventory rather than cost of goods sold expense. But don't forget that inventory increased 40,000 units, which is quite a large increase compared with the annual sales of 110,000 during the year just ended.

Who was responsible for the decision to go full blast and produce up to production capacity? Do the managers really expect sales to jump up enough next period to justify the much larger inventory level? If they prove to be right, they'll look brilliant. But if the output level was a mistake and sales do not go up next year . . . they'll have you-know-what to pay next year, even though profit looks good this year. An experienced business manager knows to be on guard when inventory takes such a big jump.

# A View from the Top Regarding Costs

The CEO of a business gets paid to take the big picture point of view. Using the business example in the chapter (refer to Figure 12-1 again), a typical CEO would study the management income statement and say something like the following:

*Not a bad year. Total costs were just about 90 percent of sales revenue. EBIT per unit was a little more than 10 percent of sales price ($145 per unit ÷ $1,400 sales price). I was able to spread my fixed operating expenses over 110,000 units of sales, for an average of $195 per unit. Compared with the $340 contribution margin per unit this yielded $145 EBIT per unit. I can live with this.*

*I'd like to improve our margins, of course, but even if we don't, we should be able to increase sales volume next year. In fact, I notice that we produced 10,000 units more than we sold this year. So, I'll put pressure on the sales manager to give me her plan for increasing sales volume next year.*

*I realize that cost numbers can be pushed around by my sharp-pencil accountants. They keep reminding me about cost classification problems between manufacturing and nonmanufacturing costs — but, what the heck, it all comes out in the wash sooner or later. I watch the three major cost lines in my income statement — cost of goods sold, variable operating expenses, and fixed operating expenses.*

*I realize that some costs can be classified in one or another of these groupings. So, I expect my accountants to be consistent period to period, and I have instructed them not to make any changes without my approval. Without consistency of accounting methods, I can't reliably compare my expense numbers from period to period. In my view, it's better to be arbitrary in the same way, period after period, rather than changing cost methods to keep up with the latest cost allocation fads.*

The CEO has a good understanding of the importance of the cost data in the company's profit report, as well as the inherent limitations of cost measurement. The late economist Kenneth Boulding is well known for one of his quips: "Accountants are people who would rather be precisely wrong than approximately correct." His point is well taken, and one that is especially true when it comes to calculating costs.

# Chapter 13

# Choosing Accounting Methods

● ● ● ● ● ● ● ● ● ● ● ● ● ● ● ● ● ● ● ● ● ● ● ● ● ● ● ● ● ● ● ● ● ● ● ● ● ● ● ● ● ● ● ● ●

### In This Chapter

▶ Having a choice of accounting methods

▶ Understanding the alternatives for calculating cost of goods sold expense and inventory cost

▶ Dealing with depreciation

▶ Writing down inventory and accounts receivable

▶ Keeping two sets of books

● ● ● ● ● ● ● ● ● ● ● ● ● ● ● ● ● ● ● ● ● ● ● ● ● ● ● ● ● ● ● ● ● ● ● ● ● ● ● ● ● ● ● ● ●

$S$ome people put a great deal of faith in numbers: 2 + 2 = 4, and that's the end of the story. They see a number reported to the last digit on an accounting report, and they get the impression of exactitude. But accounting isn't just a matter of adding up numbers. It's not an exact science. Some even argue that accounting is more like an art, although I wouldn't go that far (and I certainly wouldn't trust any numbers that Picasso came up with — would you?). Accounting involves a whole lot more judgment and choice than most people think, especially in measuring expenses.

Accountants *do* have plenty of rules that they must follow. The official rule book of generally accepted accounting principles (GAAP) laid down by the Financial Standards Board (and its predecessors) is more than 1,000 pages long, to say nothing of the rules and regulations issued by the federal regulatory agency that governs financial reporting and accounting methods by publicly owned corporations: the Securities & Exchange Commission (SEC). Also, the American Institute of Certified Public Accountants (AICPA) plays a role in setting accounting standards. Actually there's a hierarchy, or pecking order, in making GAAP — but, I won't go into that.

Although we're still in the early stages, standards are going *international* — the goal being to establish worldwide accounting standards. With the advent of the European Union and the ever-increasing amount of international trade and investing, business and political leaders in many nations recognize the need to iron out differences in accounting methods and disclosure standards from country to country. Whether accountants in the United States and other countries will accept and abide by new international accounting standards that require changing some of their long-held views on certain accounting matters is difficult to predict. In any case, you can keep alert about what's going on at the International Accounting Standards Committee Web site, www.iasc.org.uk.

Perhaps the most surprising thing — considering that formal rule-making activity has been going on since the 1930s — is that a business still has options for choosing among alternative accounting methods. For example, in recording certain expenses two or more methods are equally acceptable, even though they give different results. You can compare choosing between accounting methods to choosing which side of the road to drive on. It doesn't matter which side people drive on, as long as everyone is in agreement. In traffic, different choices lead to accidents; in accounting, different choices lead to inconsistent profit measures from company to company. The often-repeated goal for standardizing accounting methods is to make like things look alike and different things look different — but, the accounting profession hasn't reached this stage of nirvana yet. In addition, accounting methods change over the years, as the business world changes. GAAP are, to one degree or another, in a state of flux.

Because the choice of accounting methods directly affects the profit figure for the year and the values reported in the ending balance sheet, business managers (and investors) need to know the difference between accounting methods. You don't need to probe into these accounting methods in excruciating, technical detail, but you should at least know whether one method versus another yields higher or lower profit measures and higher or lower asset values in financial statements. This chapter explains accounting choices for measuring cost of goods sold, depreciation, and other expenses. Get involved in making these important accounting decisions — it's your business, after all.

# Decision-Making behind the Scenes in Income Statements

Chapter 5 introduces the conventional format for presenting income statements in *external* financial reports. (Also see Figure 9-1 for another example.) Figure 13-1 presents another income statement for a business — with certain modifications that you won't see in actual external income statements. For explaining the choices between alternative accounting methods, certain specific expenses are broken down under the company's sales, administrative, and general expenses (SA&G) category in Figure 13-1. Of these particular expenses only depreciation is disclosed in external income statements. Don't expect to find in external income statements the other expenses shown under the SA&G category in Figure 13-1. Businesses are a very reluctant to divulge such information to the outside world.

Here's a quick overview of the accounting matters and choices relating to each line in the income statement shown in Figure 13-1, from the top line to the bottom line.

| Income Statement For Year | | |
| --- | --- | --- |
| Sales Revenue | | $26,000,000 |
| Cost of Goods Sold Expense | | 14,300,000 |
| Gross Margin | | $11,700,000 |
| Sales, Administrative & General Expenses: | | |
| Inventory Shrinkage and Write-downs | $378,750 | |
| Bad Debts | 385,000 | |
| Asset Impairment Write-downs | 287,000 | |
| Depreciation | 780,000 | |
| Warranty and Guarantee Expenses | 967,250 | |
| All Other SA&G Expenses | 6,302,000 | |
| Total | | 9,100,000 |
| Earnings Before Interest and Income Tax | | $2,600,000 |
| Interest Expense | | 400,000 |
| Earnings Before Income Tax | | $2,200,000 |
| Income Tax Expense | | 880,000 |
| Net Income | | $1,320,000 |

**Figure 13-1:** An income statement including certain expenses that are not reported outside the business.

✔ **Sales revenue:** Timing the recording of sales is something to be aware of. Generally speaking, sales revenue timing is not a serious accounting problem, but businesses should be consistent from one year to the next. For some businesses, however, the timing of recording sales revenue is a major problem — such as software and other high-tech companies, and companies in their early start-up phases. A footnote to the company's financial statements should explain its revenue recognition method if there is anything unusual about it.

*Note:* If products are returnable and the deal between the seller and buyer does not satisfy normal conditions for a completed sale, then recognition of sales revenue should be postponed until the return privilege no longer exists. For example, some products are sold *on approval,* which means the customer takes the product and tries it out for a few days or longer to see if the customer really wants it.

✔ **Cost of goods sold expense:** Whether to use the first-in, first-out (FIFO) method, or the last-in, first-out (LIFO) method, or the average cost method, each of which is explained in the section "Calculating Cost of

Goods Sold and Cost of Inventory," later in this chapter. Cost of goods sold is a big expense for companies that sell products, naturally; the choice of method can have a real impact.

✔ **Gross margin:** Can be dramatically affected by the method used for calculating cost of goods sold expense (and the method of revenue recognition, if this is a problem).

✔ **Inventory write-downs:** Whether to count and inspect inventory very carefully to determine loss due to theft, damage, and deterioration, and whether to apply the lower-of-cost-or-market (LCM) method strictly or loosely are the two main questions that need to be answered. See "Identifying Inventory Losses: Lower of Cost or Market (LCM)" in this chapter. Inventory is a high-risk asset that's subject to theft, damage, and obsolescence.

✔ **Bad debts expense:** When to conclude that the debts owed to you by customers who bought on credit (accounts receivable) are not going to be paid — the question is really when to *write down* these debts (that is, remove the amounts from your asset column). You can wait until after you've made a substantial effort at collecting the debts, or you can make your decision before that time. See "Collecting or Writing Off Bad Debts," later in this chapter.

✔ **Asset impairment write-downs:** Whether (and when) to *write down* or *write off* an asset — that is, remove it from the asset column. Inventory shrinkage, bad debts, and depreciation by their very nature are asset write-downs. Other asset write-downs are required when any asset becomes *impaired,* which means that it has lost some of all of its economic utility to the business and has little or no disposable value. An asset write-down reduces the book (recorded) value of an asset (and at the same time records an expense or loss of the same amount). A *write-off* reduces the asset's book value to zero and removes it from the accounts, and the entire amount becomes an expense or loss.

For example, your delivery truck driver had an accident. The repair of the truck was covered by insurance, so no write-down is necessary. But the products being delivered had to be thrown away and were not insured while in transit. You write off the cost of the inventory lost in the accident.

✔ **Depreciation expense:** Whether to use a short-life method and load most of the expense over the first few years, or a longer-life method and spread the expense evenly over the years. Refer to "Appreciating Depreciation Methods," later in this chapter. Depreciation is a big expense for some businesses, making the choice of method even more important.

✔ **Warranty and guarantee (post-sales) expenses:** Whether to record an expense for products sold with warranties and guarantees in the same period that the goods are sold (along with the cost of goods sold expense, of course) or later, when customers actually return products for repair or replacement. Businesses usually can forecast the percent of products sold that will be returned for repair or replacement under the guarantees and warranties offered to customers — although a new product with no track record can be a problem in this regard.

✔ **All other SA&G expenses**: Whether to disclose separately one of more of the specific expenses included in this conglomerate total. For example, the SEC requires that *advertising* and *repairs and maintenance* expenses be disclosed in the documents businesses file with the SEC, but you hardly ever see these two expenses reported in external income statements. Nor do you find top management compensation revealed in external income statements. GAAP does not require such disclosures — much less revealing things like bribes or other legally questionable payments by a business.

✔ **Earnings before interest and tax (EBIT):** This profit measure equals sales revenue less all the expenses above this line; therefore, EBIT depends on the particular choices made for recording sales revenue and expenses. Having a choice of accounting methods means that an amount of wiggle is inherent in recording sales revenue and many expenses. How much wiggle effect do all these accounting choices have on the EBIT profit figure? This is a very difficult question to answer. The business itself may not know. I would guess (and it's no more than a conjecture on my part) that the EBIT for a period reported by most businesses could easily be 10 to 20 percent lower or higher if different accounting choices had been made.

✔ **Interest expense:** Usually a cut-and-dried calculation, with no accounting problems. (Well, I can think of some really hairy interest accounting problems, but I won't go into them here.)

✔ **Income tax expense:** You can use different accounting methods for some of the expenses reported in your income statement than you use for calculating taxable income. Oh, boy! The hypothetical amount of taxable income, if the accounting methods used in the income statement were used in the tax return, is calculated; then the income tax based on this hypothetical taxable income is figured. This is the income tax expense reported in the income statement. This amount is reconciled with the actual amount of income tax owed based on the accounting methods used for income tax purposes. A reconciliation of the two different income tax amounts is provided in a rather technical footnote to the financial statements. See "Reconciling Income Tax," later in this chapter.

✔ **Net income:** Like EBIT, can vary considerably depending on which accounting methods you use for measuring expenses. (See also Chapter 8 on *profit smoothing,* which crosses the line from choosing acceptable accounting methods from the laundry list of GAAP into the gray area of "earnings management" through means of accounting manipulation.)

Whereas bad debts, post-sales expenses, and asset write-downs vary in importance from business to business, cost of goods sold and depreciation methods are so important that a business must disclose which methods it uses for these two expenses in the footnotes to its financial statements. (Chapter 8 explains footnotes to financial statements.) The Internal Revenue Code requires that a company actually record in its cost of goods sold expense and inventory asset accounts the amounts determined by the accounting method they use to determine taxable income — a rare requirement in the income tax law.

Considering how important the bottom-line profit number is and that different accounting methods can cause a major difference on this all-important number, you'd think that accountants would have developed clear-cut and definite rules so that only one accounting method would be correct for a given set of facts. No such luck. The final choice boils down to an arbitrary decision, made by top-level accountants with consultation and consent of managers. If you own a business or are a manager in a business, I strongly encourage you to get involved in choosing which accounting methods to use for measuring your profit and for presenting your balance sheet. Chapter 17 explains that a manager has to answer questions about his or her financial reports on many occasions, and so should know which accounting methods are used to prepare the financial statements.

Accounting methods vary from business to business more than you'd probably suspect, even though all of them stay within the boundaries of GAAP. Accounting methods may even vary within an organization, although most larger businesses prefer to have consistency across the board. The rest of this chapter expands on the methods available for measuring certain expenses. Sales revenue accounting can be a challenge as well, but profit accounting problems lie mostly on the expense side of the ledger.

# Calculating Cost of Goods Sold and Cost of Inventory

One main accounting problem of companies that sell products is how to measure their *cost of goods sold expense,* which is the sum of the costs of the products sold to customers during the period. You deduct cost of goods sold from sales revenue to determine *gross margin* — the first profit line on the income statement (see Chapter 5 for more about income statements, and Figure 9-1 for a typical income statement). Cost of goods sold is therefore a very important figure, because if gross margin is wrong, bottom-line profit (net income) is wrong.

First a business acquires products, either by buying them (retailers) or by producing them (manufacturers). Chapter 12 explains how manufacturers determine product cost; for retailers, product cost is simply the purchase cost. (Well, it's not entirely this simple, but you get the point.) Product cost is entered in the inventory asset account and is held there until the products are sold. Then, but not before, product cost is taken out of inventory and recorded in the cost of goods sold expense account. You must be absolutely clear on this point. Suppose that you clear $700 from your salary for the week and deposit this amount in your checking account. The money stays in your bank account and is an asset until you spend it. You don't have an expense until you write a check.

Likewise, not until the business sells products does it have a cost of goods sold expense. When you write a check, you know how much it's for — you have no doubt about the amount of the expense. But when a business withdraws products from its inventory and records cost of goods sold expense, the expense amount is in some doubt. The amount of expense depends on which accounting method the business selects.

The essence of this accounting issue is that you have to divide the total cost of your inventory between the units sold (cost of goods sold expense, in the income statement) and the unsold units that remain on hand waiting to be sold next period (inventory asset, in the balance sheet).

For example, say you own a store that sells antiques. Every time an item sells, you need to transfer the amount you paid for the item from the inventory asset account into the cost of goods sold expense account. At the start of a fiscal period, your cost of goods sold expense is zero, and if you own a medium-sized shop selling medium-quality antiques, your inventory asset account may be $20,000. Over the course of the fiscal period, your cost of goods sold expense should increase (hopefully rapidly, as you make many sales).

You probably want your inventory asset account to remain fairly static, however. If you paid $200 for a wardrobe that sells during the period, the $200 leaves the inventory asset account and finds a new home in the cost of goods sold expense account. However, you probably want to turn around and replace the item you sold, ultimately keeping your inventory asset account at around the same level — although more complicated businesses have more complicated strategies for dealing with inventory and more perplexing accounting problems.

You have three methods to choose from when you measure cost of goods sold and inventory costs: You can follow a first-in, first-out (FIFO) cost sequence, follow a last-in, first-out cost sequence (LIFO), or compromise between the two methods and take the average costs for the period. Other methods are acceptable, but these three are the primary options. *Caution:* Product costs are entered in the inventory asset account in the order acquired, but they are not necessarily taken out of the inventory asset account in this order. The different methods refer to the order in which product costs are *taken out* of the inventory asset account. You may think that only one method is appropriate — that the sequence in should be the sequence out. However, generally accepted accounting principles (GAAP) permit other methods.

In reality, the choice boils down to FIFO versus LIFO; the average cost method runs a distant third in popularity. If you want my opinion, FIFO is better than LIFO, for reasons that I explain in the next two sections. You may not agree, and that's your right. For your business, you make the call.

## The FIFO method

With the FIFO method, you charge out product costs to cost of goods sold expense in the chronological order in which you acquired the goods. The procedure is that simple. It's like the first people in line to see a movie get in the theater first. The ticket-taker collects the tickets in the order in which they were bought.

I think that FIFO is the best method for both the expense and the asset amounts. I hope that you like this method, but also look at the LIFO method before making up your mind. You should make up your mind, you know. Don't just sit on the sidelines. Take a stand.

Suppose that you acquire four units of a product during a period, one unit at a time, with unit costs as follows (in the order in which you acquire the items): $100, $102, $104, and $106. By the end of the period, you have sold three of those units. Using FIFO, you calculate the cost of goods sold expense as follows:

```
$100 + $102 + $104 = $306
```

In short, you use the first three units to calculate cost of goods sold expense. (You can see the benefit of having such a standard method if you sell hundreds or thousands of different products.)

The ending inventory asset, then, is $106, which is the cost of the most recent acquisition. The $412 total cost of the four units is divided between $306 cost of goods sold expense for the three units sold and the $106 cost of the one unit in ending inventory. The total cost has been taken care of; nothing fell between the cracks.

FIFO works well for two reasons:

- ✔ In most businesses, products actually move into and out of inventory in a first-in, first-out sequence: The earlier acquired products are delivered to customers before the later acquired products are delivered, so the most recently purchased products are the ones still in ending inventory to be delivered in the future. Using FIFO, the inventory asset reported on the balance sheet at the end of the period reflects the most recent purchase cost and therefore is close to the current *replacement cost* of the product.

- ✔ When product costs are steadily increasing, many (but not all) businesses follow a first-in, first-out sales price strategy and hold off on raising sales prices as long as possible. They delay raising sales prices until they have sold all lower-cost products. Only when they start selling from the next batch of products, acquired at a higher cost, do they raise sales prices. I strongly favor using the FIFO cost of goods sold expense method when the business follows this basic sales pricing policy, because both the expense and the sales revenue are better matched for determining gross margin. I realize that sales pricing is complex and may not follow such a simple process, but the main point is that many businesses do use a FIFO-based sales pricing approach. If your business is one of them, I urge you to use the FIFO expense method to be consistent with your sales pricing.

## The LIFO method

Remember the movie ticket-taker I mentioned earlier? Think about that ticket-taker going to the *back* of the line of people waiting to get into the next showing and letting them in from the rear of the line first. In other words, the later you bought your ticket, the sooner you get into the theater. This is the LIFO method, which stands for *last-in, first-out*. The people in the front of a movie line wouldn't stand for it, of course, but the LIFO method is quite acceptable for determining the cost of goods sold expense for products sold during the period. The main feature of the LIFO method is that it selects the *last* item you purchased first and then works backward until you have the total cost for the total number of units sold during the period. What about the ending inventory, the products you haven't sold by the end of the year? Using the LIFO method, you never get back to the cost of the first products acquired (unless you sold out your entire stock of inventory); the earliest cost remains in the inventory asset account.

Using the same example from the preceding section, assume that the business uses the LIFO method instead of FIFO. The four units, in order of acquisition, had costs of $100, $102, $104, and $106. If you sell three units during the period, LIFO gives you the following cost of goods sold expense:

```
$106 + $104 + $102 = $312
```

The ending inventory cost of the one unit not sold is $100, which is the oldest cost. The $412 total cost of the four units acquired less the $312 cost of goods sold expense leaves $100 in the inventory asset account. Determining which units you actually delivered to customers is irrelevant; when you use the LIFO method, you always count backward from the last unit you acquired.

If you really want to argue in favor of using LIFO — and I gotta tell you that I won't back you up on this one — here's what you can say:

✔ Assigning the most recent costs of products purchased to the cost of goods sold expense makes sense because you have to replace your products to stay in business, and the most recent costs are closest to the amount you will have to pay to replace your products. Ideally, you should base your sales prices not on original cost but on the cost of replacing the units sold.

✔ During times of rising costs, the most recent purchase cost maximizes the cost of goods sold expense deduction for determining taxable income, and thus minimizes the taxable income. In fact, LIFO was invented for income tax purposes. True, the cost of inventory on the ending balance sheet is lower than recent acquisition costs, but the income statement effect is more important than the balance sheet effect.

The more product cost you take out of the inventory asset to charge to cost of goods sold expense, the less product cost you have in the ending inventory. In maximizing cost of goods sold expense, you minimize the inventory cost value.

But here are the reasons why LIFO, in my view, is usually the wrong choice (the following sections of this chapter go into more details about these issues):

✔ Unless you base your sales prices on the most recent purchase costs or you raise sales prices as soon as replacement costs increase — and most businesses don't follow either of these pricing policies — using LIFO depresses your gross margin and, therefore, your bottom-line net income.

✔ The LIFO method can result in an ending inventory cost value that's seriously out of date, especially if the business sells products that have very long lives. For example, for several years, the equipment manufacturer Caterpillar's LIFO-based inventory has been about $2 billion less that what it would have been under the FIFO method (sources: Caterpillar's annual financial reports from 1995 through 1999).

✔ Unscrupulous managers can use the LIFO method to manipulate their profit figures if business isn't going well. Refer to "Manipulating LIFO inventory levels to give profit a boost," later in the chapter.

*Note:* In periods of rising product costs, it's true that FIFO results in higher taxable income than LIFO does — something you probably want to avoid, I'm sure. Nevertheless, even though LIFO may be preferable in some circumstances, I still say that FIFO is the better choice in the majority of situations, for the reasons discussed earlier, and you may come over to my way of thinking after reading the following sections. By the way, if the products are intermingled such that they cannot be identified with particular purchases, then the business has to use FIFO for in its income tax returns.

### The graying of LIFO inventory cost

If you sell products that have long lives and for which your product costs rise steadily over the years, using the LIFO method has a serious impact on the ending inventory cost value reported on the balance sheet and can cause the balance sheet to look misleading. Over time, the cost of replacing products becomes further and further removed from the LIFO-based inventory costs. Your 2000 balance sheet may very well report inventory based on 1985, 1975, or 1965 product costs. As a matter of fact, the product costs used to value inventory can go back even further.

Suppose that a major manufacturing business (read "Caterpillar") has been using LIFO for more than 45 years. The products that this business manufactures and sells have very long lives — in fact, the business has been making and selling many of the same products for many years. Believe it or not, the difference between its LIFO and FIFO cost values for its ending inventory is about $2 *billion,* because some of the products are based on costs going back to the 1950s, when the company first started using the LIFO method. The FIFO cost value of its ending inventory is disclosed in a footnote to its financial statements; this disclosure is how you can tell the difference between a business's LIFO and FIFO cost values. The gross margin ( before income tax) over the business's 45 years would have been $2 billion higher if the business had used the FIFO method — and its total taxable income over the 45 years would have been this much higher as well.

Of course, the business's income taxes over the years would have been correspondingly higher as well. That's the trade-off.

*Note:* A business must disclose the difference between its inventory cost value according to LIFO and its inventory cost value according to FIFO in a footnote on its financial statements — but, of course, not too many people outside of stock analysts and professional investment managers read footnotes. Business managers get involved in reviewing footnotes in the final steps of getting annual financial reports ready for release (refer to Chapter 8). If your business uses FIFO, your ending inventory is stated at recent acquisition costs, and you do not have to determine what the LIFO value may have been. Annual financial reports do not disclose the estimated LIFO cost value for a FIFO-based inventory.

Many products and raw materials have very short lives; they're regularly replaced by new models ( you know, with those "New and Improved!" labels) because of the latest technology or marketing wisdom. These products aren't around long enough to develop a wide gap between LIFO and FIFO, so the accounting choice between the two methods doesn't make as much difference as with long-lived products.

### Manipulating LIFO inventory levels to give profit a boost

The LIFO method opens the door to manipulation of profit — not that you would think of doing this, of course. Certainly, most of the businesses that choose LIFO do so to minimize current taxable income and delay paying income taxes as long as possible — a legitimate (though perhaps misguided in some cases) goal. However, some unscrupulous managers know that they can use the LIFO method to "create" some profit when business isn't going well.

So if a business that uses LIFO sells more products than it purchased (or manufactured) during the period, it has to reach back into its inventory account and pull out older costs to transfer to the cost of goods sold expense. These costs are much lower than current costs, leading to an artificially low cost of goods sold expense, which in turn leads to an artificially high gross margin figure. This dipping into old cost layers of LIFO-based inventory is called a *LIFO liquidation gain*.

This unethical manipulation of profit is possible for businesses that have been using LIFO for many years and have inventory cost values far lower than the current purchase or manufacturing costs of products. By not replacing all the quantities sold, they let inventory fall below normal levels.

Suppose that a retailer sold 100,000 units during the year and normally would have replaced all units sold. Instead, it purchased only 90,000 replacement units. Therefore, the other 10,000 units were taken out of inventory, and the accountant had to reach back into the old cost layers of inventory to record some of the cost of goods sold expense. To see the impact of LIFO liquidation gain on the gross margin, check out what the gross margin would look like if this business had replaced all 100,000 units versus the gross margin for replacing only 90,000. In this example, the old units in inventory carry a LIFO-based cost of only $30, and the current purchase cost is $65. Assume that the units have a $100 price tag for the customer.

#### Gross margin if the business replaced all 100,000 of the units sold

| | |
|---|---|
| Sales revenue (100,000 units at $100 per unit) | $10,000,000 |
| Cost of goods sold expense (100,000 units at $65 per unit) | 6,500,000 |
| Gross margin | $3,500,000 |

#### Gross margin if the business replaced only 90,000 of the units sold

| | | |
|---|---|---|
| Sales revenue (100,000 units at $100 per unit) | | $10,000,000 |
| Cost of goods sold expense: | | |
| Units replaced (90,000 units at $65 per unit) | $5,850,000 | |
| Units from inventory (10,000 units at $30 per unit) | 300,000 | 6,150,000 |
| Gross margin | | $3,850,000 |

The LIFO liquidation gain (the difference between the two gross margins) in this example is $350,000 — the $35 difference between the old and the current unit costs multiplied by 10,000 units. Just by ordering fewer replacement products, this business padded its gross margin — but in a very questionable way.

Of course, this business may have a good, legitimate reason for trimming inventory by 10,000 units — to reduce the capital invested in that asset, for example, or to anticipate lower sales demand in the year ahead. LIFO liquidation gains may also occur when a business stops selling a product and that inventory drops to zero. Still, I have to warn investors that when you see a financial statement reporting a dramatic decrease in inventory and the business uses the LIFO method, you should be aware of the possible profit manipulation reasons behind the decrease.

*Note:* A business must disclose in the footnotes to its financial statement s any substantial LIFO liquidation gains that occurred during the year. The outside CPA auditor should make sure that the company includes this disclosure. (Chapter 15 discusses audits of financial statements by CPAs.)

## *The average cost method*

Although not nearly as popular as the FIFO and LIFO methods, the average cost method seems to offer the best of both worlds. The costs of many things in the business world fluctuate; business managers focus on the average product cost over a time period. Also, the averaging of product costs over a period of time has a desirable smoothing effect that prevents cost of goods sold from being overly dependent on wild swings of one or two purchases.

To many businesses, the compromise aspect of the method is its *worst* feature. Businesses may want to go one way or the other and avoid the middle ground. If they want to minimize taxable income, LIFO gives the best effect during times of rising prices. Why go only halfway with the average cost method? Or if the business wants its ending inventory to be as near to current replacement costs as possible, FIFO is better than the average cost method. Even using computers to keep track of averages, which change every time product costs change, is a nuisance. No wonder the average cost method is not popular! But it *is* an acceptable method under GAAP and for income tax purposes.

# *Identifying Inventory Losses: Lower of Cost or Market (LCM)*

Regardless of which method you use to determine inventory cost, you should make sure that your accountants apply the *lower-of-cost-or-market* (LCM) test to inventory. A business should go through the LCM routine at least once a year, usually near or at year-end. The process consists of comparing the cost of every product in inventory — meaning the cost that's recorded for each product in the inventory asset account according to the FIFO or LIFO method (or whichever method the company uses) — with two benchmark values:

 ✔ The product's *current replacement cost* (how much the business would pay to obtain the same product right now)

 ✔ The product's *net realizable value* (how much the business can sell the product for)

If a product's cost on the books is higher than either of these two benchmark values, your accountant should decrease product cost to the lower of the two. In other words, inventory losses are recognized *now* rather than *later,* when the products are sold. The drop in the replacement cost or sales value of the product should be recorded now, on the theory that it's better to take your medicine now than to put it off. Also, the inventory cost value on the balance sheet is more conservative because inventory is reported at a lower cost value.

Buying and holding inventory involves certain unavoidable risks. Asset write-downs, explained in the "Decision-Making behind the Scenes in Income Statements" section of this chapter, are recorded to recognize the consequences of two of those risks — inventory shrinkage and losses to natural disasters not fully covered by insurance. LCM records the losses from two other risks of holding inventory:

 ✔ **Replacement cost risk:** After you purchase or manufacture a product, its replacement cost may drop permanently below the amount you paid (which usually also affects the amount you can charge customers for the products, because competitors will drop their prices).

 ✔ **Sales demand risk:** Demand for a product may drop off permanently, forcing you to sell the products below cost just to get rid of them.

Determining current replacement cost values for every product in your inventory isn't easy! When I worked for a CPA firm many years ago, we tested the ways clients applied the LCM method to their ending inventories. I was surprised by how hard market values were to pin down — vendors wouldn't quote current prices or had gone out of business, prices bounced around from day to day, suppliers offered special promotions that confused matters, and on and on. Applying the LCM test leaves much room for interpretation.

Keeping accurate track of your inventory costs is important to your bottom line, both now and in the future, so don't fall into the trap of doing a quick LCM scan and making a snap judgment that you don't need an inventory write-down.

Some shady characters abuse LCM to cheat on their income tax returns. They *knock down* their ending inventory cost value — decrease ending inventory cost more than can be justified by the LCM test — to increase the deductible expenses on their income tax returns and thus decrease taxable income. A product may have proper cost value of $100, for example, but a shady character may invent some reason to lower it to $75 and thus record a $25 inventory write-down expense in this period for each unit — which is not justified by the facts. But, even though the person can deduct more this year, he or she will have a lower inventory cost to deduct in the future. Also, if the person is selected for an IRS audit and the Feds discover an unjustified inventory knockdown, the person may end up with a felony conviction for income tax evasion.

# Appreciating Depreciation Methods

In theory, depreciation expense accounting is straightforward enough: You divide the cost of a fixed asset among the number of years that the business expects to use the asset. In other words, instead of having a huge lump-sum expense in the year that you make the purchase, you charge a fraction of the cost to expense for each year of the asset's lifetime. Using this method is much easier on your bottom line in the year of purchase, of course.

But theories are rarely as simple in real life as they are on paper, and this one is no exception. Do you divide the cost *evenly* across the asset's lifetime, or do you charge more to certain years than others? Furthermore, when it eventually comes time to dispose of fixed assets, the assets may have some disposable, or *salvage,* value. Only cost minus the salvage value should be depreciated, right? Or, should salvage value estimates be ignored and the total cost of a fixed asset be depreciated? And how do you estimate how long an asset will last in the first place? Do you consult an accountant psychic hot line?

As it turns out, the IRS runs its own little psychic business on the side, with a crystal ball known as the Internal Revenue Code. Okay, so the IRS can't tell you that your truck is going to conk out in another five years, seven months, and two days. The Internal Revenue Code doesn't give you predictions of how long your fixed assets will *last;* it only tells you what kind of time line to use for income tax purposes, as well as how to divide the cost along that time line.

Hundreds of books have been written on depreciation, but the only book that counts is the Internal Revenue Code. Most businesses adopt the useful lives allowed by the income tax law for their financial statement accounting; they don't go to the trouble of keeping a second depreciation schedule for financial reporting. Why complicate things if you don't have to? Why keep one depreciation schedule for income tax and a second for preparing your financial statements?

By the way, keeping two depreciation schedules is an example of *keeping two sets of books.* In some situations a person using this term is referring to the illegal tactic of keeping one set of accounts for the actual amounts of sales revenue and expenses and keeping a second set of fictional accounts for income tax purposes. (I've never seen two sets of books in actual practice — although, I have seen cases of skimming sales revenue and inflating expenses on the books to minimize the taxable income of a business.)

*Note:* The tax law can change at any time and can get extremely technical. Please use the following information for a basic understanding of the procedures (as they exist in early 2000) and *not* as tax advice. The annual income tax guides, such as *Taxes For Dummies* by Eric Tyson and David Silverman (IDG Books), go into the more technical details of calculating depreciation.

The part of the present federal income tax law that regulates the rules of depreciation is known as the *modified accelerated cost recovery system* (MACRS) — which is quite a mouthful. These regulations specify the depreciation life spans that can be used for specific fixed assets. They also specify the percentage of the cost to charge as depreciation expense each year. (Fixed assets acquired before 1986 are subject to different rules).

The IRS rules tell you which of two depreciation methods to use for particular types of assets:

- ✔ **Straight-line depreciation method:** With this method, you divide the cost evenly among the years of the asset's estimated lifetime. So if a new building owned and used by a business costs $390,000 and its useful life — according to the appropriate section of MACRS — is 39 years, the depreciation expense is $10,000 ($\frac{1}{39}$ of the cost) for each of the 39 years. You must use straight-line depreciation for buildings and may choose to use it for other types of assets; once you start using this method for a particular asset, you can't change your mind and switch to another method later.

- ✔ **Accelerated depreciation method:** Actually, this term is a generic catchall for several different kinds of methods. What they all have in common is that they're *front-loading* methods, meaning that you charge a larger amount of depreciation expense in the early years and a smaller amount in the later years. *Accelerated depreciation method* also refers to adopting useful lives that are shorter than realistic estimates (very few automobiles are useless after five years, for example, but they can be fully depreciated over five years for income tax purposes).

One popular accelerated method is the *double-declining balance* (DDB) depreciation method. With this method, you calculate the straight-line depreciation *rate* and then you double that percentage. You apply that doubled percentage to the declining balance over the course of the asset's depreciation time line. After a certain number of years, you switch back to the straight-line method for the remainder of the asset's depreciation years to ensure that you depreciate the full cost by the end of the predetermined number of years. See the sidebar "The double-declining balance depreciation method" for an example.

*TIP*

By the way, the salvage value of fixed assets (the estimated disposal values when the assets are taken to the junkyard or sold off at the end of their useful lives) is ignored in the calculation of depreciation for income tax. Put another way, if a fixed asset is held to the end of its entire depreciation life, then its original cost will be fully depreciated, and the fixed asset from that time forward will have a zero book value. (Recall that book value is equal to the cost minus the balance in the accumulated depreciation account.) Fully depreciated fixed assets are grouped with all other fixed assets in external balance sheets. All these long-term resources of a business are reported in one asset account called *property, plant, and equipment* (instead of fixed assets). If all its fixed assets were fully depreciated the balance sheet of a company would look rather peculiar — the cost of its fixed assets would be completely offset by its accumulated depreciation. I've never seen this, but would be possible for a business that hasn't replaced any of its fixed assets for a long time.

The straight-line method has strong advantages: It's easy to understand and it stabilizes the depreciation expense from year to year. But many business managers and accountants favor the accelerated depreciation method in order to minimize the size of the checks they have to write to the IRS in the early years of using fixed assets. This lets the business keep the cash, for the time being, instead of paying more income tax. Keep in mind, however, that the depreciation expense in the annual income statement is higher in the early years when you use an accelerated depreciation method, and so bottom-line profit is lower until later years. Nevertheless, many accountants and businesses like accelerated depreciation because it paints a more conservative (a lower, or a more moderate) picture of profit performance in the early years. Who knows? Fixed assets may lose their economic usefulness to a business sooner than expected. If this happens, using the accelerated depreciation method would look good in hindsight.

Minimizing taxable income and income tax in the early years to hang on to as much cash as possible is very important to many businesses, and they pay the price of reporting lower net income in order to defer paying income tax as long as possible. Or they may use the straight-line method in their financial statements even though they use an accelerated method in their annual income tax returns, which complicates matters. (Refer to the section "Reconciling Income Tax" for more information.)

# The double-declining balance depreciation method

Suppose that a business pays $100,000 for a fixed asset that has a five-year useful life (according to its MACRS classification) and for which the double-declining balance depreciation method is used. The annual depreciation expense by the straight-line method is $\frac{1}{5}$, or 20 percent, of cost per year — which in this example would be $20,000 per year. With the DDB method, you double that percentage to 40 percent, which gives $40,000 depreciation for the first year. After the first year, however, the 40 percent rate of depreciation is applied to the declining balance of the fixed asset. For example, in the second year depreciation equals the $60,000 undepreciated balance of the fixed asset ($100,000 cost less the $40,000 first year depreciation) multiplied by the 40 percent rate — which gives $24,000 depreciation for the second year. The third year's depreciation is 40 percent of $36,000 ($100,000 cost minus the $64,000 accumulated depreciation balance).

You then switch to the straight-line method on the remaining amount of undepreciated cost for the last two years in this example (the exact number of years depends on the number of years in the asset's depreciation time line) — meaning that you divide the remaining balance by the number of remaining years. In this example, you need to use the straight-line method after the third year because if you applied the 40 percent rate to the undepreciated balance of the fixed asset at the start of the fourth year and again in the following year on the declining balance, the fixed asset's cost would not be completely depreciated by the end of five years.

Got all that? Good, because things get even more technical and complicated in income tax law. For example, businesses that buy fixed assets in the later part of a year must follow the *half-year* convention, which requires that the business use a midpoint date in the year that an asset is acquired and placed in service. I don't want to get into all the details here; suffice it to say that you need a good tax-law accountant to get the most out of your depreciation expense deduction.

Except for brand-new enterprises, a business typically has a mix of fixed assets — some in their early years of depreciation, some in their middle years, and some in their later years. So, the overall depreciation expense for the year may not be that different than if the business had been using straight-line depreciation for all its fixed assets. A business does *not* have to disclose in its external financial report what its depreciation expense would have been if it had been using an alternative method. Readers of the financial statements cannot tell how much difference the choice of depreciation method made in that year.

# *Collecting or Writing Off Bad Debts*

A business that allows its customers to pay on credit granted by the business is always subject to *bad debts* — debts that some customers never pay off.

You may have heard of the *allowance method,* which a business uses to esti-mate how much of its accounts receivable (that is, the amounts owed to the business by customers who paid on credit) at year-end will turn out to be uncollectible in the future. Based on this estimate, the business records a bad debts expense. However, the IRS no longer allows anyone but certain finan-cial institutions (such as banks with big loans) to use the allowance method. Although the allowance method was based on solid accounting theory — recording an expense in the same period as the sales revenue that generated the uncollectible accounts receivable — it was too easy to abuse and too hard for the IRS to audit. Estimating how much of your accounts receivable will turn out to be uncollectible is difficult and arbitrary, to put it mildly.

Instead of estimating the amount of future uncollectible accounts receivable, the income tax law requires businesses use the *direct write-off method* for timing the recording of bad debts expense. Under this method, you don't record a bad debts expense until you put serious effort into collecting on the debt and then actually write off the debt (that is, record in your books that the debt will not be paid). By the end of the year (though preferably at regu-lar times throughout the year) businesses should take a hard look at their overdue accounts receivable, identify the ones they have no hope of collect-ing, and make a write-off entry decreasing accounts receivable and recording a bad debts expense. But look at the bright side: The expense is deductible for income tax. Most businesses adopt certain guidelines for pulling the plug and writing off a customer's account receivable, such as more than 90 days overdue and after two serious efforts of collecting the debt.

*Note:* You still see the allowance method used on financial statements (which is perfectly legitimate and in accordance with GAAP), but because a business can't use that method for income tax purposes, many businesses have given up on it altogether. A business may use the allowance method for its financial statements, but it has to use the direct write-off method in its income tax returns. This is one more reason why the income tax amount figured on a business's annual tax return has to be reconciled with the income tax expense reported in its annual financial statements — which I turn to next.

# *Reconciling Income Tax*

Income tax is a heavy influence on a business's choice of accounting meth-ods. Many a business decides to minimize its current taxable income by recording the maximum amount of deductible expenses. Thus, taxable income is lower, income tax paid to the Treasury Department is lower, and the business's cash balance is higher. Using these expense maximization methods to prepare the income statement of the business has the obvious effect of minimizing the profit that's reported to the owners of the business. So, you may ask whether you can use one accounting method for income tax but an alternative method for preparing your financial statements. Can a business eat its cake (minimize income tax), and have it too (report more profit in its income statement)?

The answer is yes, you can — except for cost of goods sold expense. If you use LIFO for income tax, you must use LIFO in your financial statements. But you can use an accelerated depreciation method in your tax returns and use the straight-line method in your financial statements. You may decide that using two different accounting methods is not worth the time and effort. Then again, you may very well use the straight-line method if it weren't for income tax. You may, therefore, want your financial statements to be prepared using the straight-line depreciation method. In other areas of accounting for profit, businesses use one method for income tax and an alternative method in the financial statements (but I don't want to go into the details here).

If the income tax accounting method is different than the financial statement accounting method, GAAP require that the income tax expense amount reported in the income statement be consistent with the expense methods used to prepare that income statement. So the income tax amount owed to the IRS (based on taxable income for the year) is not the correct amount of expense to report in the income statement for that year. The income tax return amount has to be adjusted to make the income tax expense consistent with the accounting methods used to prepare the income statement.

Illustrating how accountants reconcile the two income tax amounts — the income tax owed for the year from the tax return and the amount of income tax expense to put in the annual income statement — can get rather technical. I'll keep it simple. Refer to the double-declining balance depreciation method example presented earlier (see the sidebar "The double-declining balance depreciation method"). Your business uses the five-year accelerated depreciation method explained there, but, for your financial statements, you decide to use the straight-line method over seven years (which is longer than the five-year accelerated method useful life).

Assume that your business is a regular C corporation — Chapter 11 explains the income tax on this type of ownership structure — and that your income tax rate is 34 percent.

In the first year, you deduct $40,000 depreciation to determine your taxable income. In your income statement for the first year, however, you include only ½ of the fixed asset's cost, or $14,286 depreciation expense. Thus, your earnings before income tax is $25,714 higher than your taxable income because of the difference in the two depreciation methods. So the amount owed to the IRS is $8,743 lower ($25,714 additional depreciation × 34 percent tax rate = $8,743). Starting with the amount owed to the IRS, the accountant records an $8,743 increase in the income tax expense to raise it to the amount that it would have been if the straight-line method had been used for income tax.

When recording an expense, either an asset is decreased or a liability is increased. In this example, a special type of liability is increased to record the full amount of income tax expense: *deferred income tax payable.* This unique liability account recognizes the special contingency hanging over the head of the business — to anticipate the time in the future when the business exhausts the higher depreciation amounts deducted in the early years by accelerated depreciation, and moves into the later years when annual depreciation amounts are less than amounts by the straight-line depreciation method. This liability account does not bear interest. Be warned that the accounting for this liability can get very complicated. The business provides information about this liability in a footnote to its financial statements, as well as reconciling the amount of income tax expense reported in its income statement with the income tax owed the government based on its income tax return for the year. These footnotes are a joy to read — just kidding.

# Two Final Issues to Consider

I think that you have been assuming all along that *all* its expenses should be recorded by a business. Of course, you're correct on this score. Many accountants argue that two expenses, in fact, are not recorded by businesses, but should be. A good deal of controversy surrounds both items. Many think one or both expenses should be recognized in measuring profit and in presenting the financial statements of a business:

✔ **Stock options:** As part of their compensation packages, many public corporations award their high-level executives stock options, which give them the right to buy a certain number of stock shares at fixed prices after certain conditions are satisfied (years of service and the like). If the market price of the corporation's stock shares in the future rises above the exercise (purchase) prices of the stock options — assuming the other conditions of these contracts are satisfied — the executives use their stock options to buy shares below the going market price of the shares.

Should the difference between the going market price of the stock shares and the exercise prices paid for the shares by the executives be recognized as an expense? Generally accepted accounting principles (GAAP) do not require that such an expense be recorded (unless the exercise price was below the market price at the time of granting the stock option). However, the business must present a footnote disclosing the number of shares and exercise prices of its stock options, the theoretical cost of the stock options to the business, and the dilution effect on earnings per share that exercising the stock options will have. But, this is a far cry from recording an expense in the income statement. Many persons, including Warren Buffett, who is Chair of Berkshire Hathaway, Inc., are strongly opposed to stock options — thinking that the better alternative is to pay the executives in cash and avoid diluting earnings per share, which depresses the market value of the stock shares.

In brief, the cost to stockholders of stock options is off the books. The dilution in the market value of the stock shares of the corporation caused by its stock options is suffered by the stockholders, but does not flow through the income statement of the business.

✔ **Purchasing power of dollar loss caused by inflation:** Most people — and this certainly includes Alan Greenspan, presently the Chair of the Federal Reserve System — worry about inflation. As the prices of things we buy inflate, the purchasing value of our dollar deflates. Due to inflation, the purchasing power of one dollar today is less than it was one year ago, two years ago, and so on back in time. Yet, accountants treat all dollars the same, regardless of when the dollar amounts were recorded on the books. The cost balance in a fixed asset account (a building, for instance) may have been recorded 10 or 20 years ago; in contrast, the cost balance in a current asset account (inventory, for instance) may have been recorded only one or two months ago (assuming the business uses the FIFO method). So, depreciation expense is based on very old dollars that had more purchasing power back then, and cost of goods sold expense is based on current dollars that have less purchasing power than in earlier years.

Over the years, attempts have been made to measure and report the effects of general price inflation in the financial statements of a business. But, for all practical purposes, the general price level accounting argument is dead and buried. The loss of purchasing power of the dollar due to inflation is not recognized in a company's financial statements. I doubt if anyone will go to the trouble of resurrecting this proposal — but, if inflation gets out of control in the future, you never know what may happen.

Stay tuned for what might develop in the future regarding these two expenses. If I had to hazard a prediction, I would say that the pressure for recording the expense of stock options will continue and might conceivably succeed — although I would add that powerful interests oppose recording stock options expense. On the other hand, the loss of purchasing power of the dollar caused by inflation has had its day in court; only an enormous increase in the rate of inflation would resurrect this argument.

# Part IV
# Financial Reports in the Outside World

The 5th Wave          By Rich Tennant

"COOKED BOOKS? LET ME JUST SAY YOU COULD SERVE THIS PROFIT AND LOSS STATEMENT WITH A FRUITY ZINFANDEL AND NOT BE OUT OF PLACE."

# In this part . . .

This part looks at accounting and financial reporting from the outside investor's, or non-manager's point of view. Outside investors in a business — the owners who are not on the inside managing the business — depend on the financial reports from the business as their main source of information about the business. Investors should know how to read and interpret the financial statements and what to look for in the footnotes to the statements. Their main concerns are the business's profit and cash flow performance and its financial health. Lenders to the business have similar interests in how the business is doing. Key ratios are calculated to test the success of the business in making profit and keeping its financial affairs in order.

Investors should also read the independent CPA auditor's report, which provides additional assurance that the financial statements have been prepared properly. The auditor's report reveals serious shortcomings in the statements (if there are any) and warns investors in the event that the business is standing on thin financial ice and may not be able to continue as a going concern.

# Chapter 14

# How Investors Read a Financial Report

## In This Chapter

▶ Looking after your investments

▶ Keeping financial reports private versus making them public

▶ Using ratios to interpret profit performance

▶ Using ratios to interpret financial condition and cash flow

▶ Scanning footnotes and identifying the important ones

▶ Paying attention to what the auditor has to say

few years ago, I invested some money in a private, closely held business that needed additional capital to continue its rapid growth. The stockholders of the corporation could not provide the additional capital, and they invited several people to buy stock shares in the company. (Chapter 11 explains corporations and the stock shares they issue when owners invest capital in the business.) After studying its most recent financial report, I concluded that the profit prospects of the business looked good and that I would receive reasonable cash dividends on my investment. And maybe the business would be bought out by a bigger business someday, and I would make a capital gain on my investment. In fact, this did happen a few years later; I doubled my money, plus earned dividends along the way. (Not all investment stories have a happy ending, of course.)

You may not have an opportunity like I did to invest in a private business. However, if you make it known that you have money to invest as an equity shareholder, you may be surprised at how many offers come your way. You can certainly invest your money in publicly traded *securities,* those stocks and bonds listed every day in *The Wall Street Journal.* Your broker would be delighted to execute a buy order for 100 shares of, say, General Motors (GM) for you. Keep in mind that your money does not go to GM; GM already has all the money it needs. Your money goes to the seller of the 100 shares. You're investing in the *secondary capital market* — the trading in stocks after the shares were issued some time ago — whereas I invested in the *primary capital market,* in which the money goes directly to the business.

You may not invest *directly* in securities. Instead, you can place your money with an investment management firm (who typically require portfolios of $500,000 or more), or you can put your money in one of the 8,000 mutual funds available today (who generally accept $1,000 or less to start). You'll have to read other books for the choices you have for investing your money and managing your investments — such as the excellent book by Eric Tyson, *Investing For Dummies* (IDG Books Worldwide).

In reading financial reports, investors need to know how to navigate through the financial statements to find the vital signs of progress and problems. The financial statement ratios explained in this chapter point the way — these ratios are signposts on the financial information highway. Also, investors read financial newspapers and investment magazines, and investment newsletters are very popular. These sources of investment information refer to the ratios discussed in this chapter, on the premise that you know what the ratios mean.

So you get a copy of the financial report of a business you're interested in. You wade through page after page of numbers, looking to your well-worn copy of *Accounting For Dummies* for help in decoding all those numbers. Even though you end up with a fair understanding of what most of the numbers mean, you still aren't sure that this business is a good one to invest in. What do you do? You take the time-honored, all-American path of having someone else do the work for you.

No, I'm not being facetious. Most individual stock investors in public companies don't have the time or expertise to study a financial report thoroughly enough to make decisions based on the report, so they rely on stockbrokers, investment advisors, and publishers of credit ratings (like *Standard & Poor's*) for interpretations of financial reports. The fact is that the folks who prepare financial reports have this kind of expert audience in mind; they don't include explanations or mark passages with icons to help *you* understand the report.

Why should you bother reading this chapter if you rely on others to interpret financial reports anyway? Investors in private businesses have no choice in most situations; they study the financial reports of the companies they invest in. When you invest in securities of public businesses, you shouldn't ignore their financial statements entirely. At least browse through a financial report if you don't read every item in the entire booklet. (Refer to Chapter 8 for more information.)

The more you understand the factors that go into interpreting a financial report, the better prepared you are to evaluate the commentary and advice of stock analysts and other investment experts. If you can at least nod intelligently while your stockbroker talks about a business's P/E and EPS, you'll look like a savvy investor — and therefore get more favorable treatment. (P/E and EPS, by the way, are two of the key ratios explained later in the chapter.)

You may regularly watch financial news on television or listen to one of today's popular radio financial talk shows. The ratios explained in this chapter are frequently mentioned on television and radio shows.

This chapter gives you the basics for comparing companies' financial reports, including the points of difference between private and public companies, the important ratios that you should know about, and the warning signs to look out for on audit reports. Part II of this book explains the three primary financial statements that are the core of every financial report: the income statement, the balance sheet, and the cash flow statement. In this chapter, I also suggest how to sort through the footnotes that are an integral part of every financial report to identify those that have the most importance to you. Believe me, the pros read the footnotes with a keen eye.

# Financial Reporting by Private versus Public Businesses

The main impetus behind the continued development of generally accepted accounting principles (GAAP) has been the widespread public ownership and trading in the securities (stocks and bonds) issued by thousands of corporations. The 1929 stock market crash and its aftermath plainly exposed the lack of accounting standards, as well as many financial reporting abuses and frauds. Landmark federal securities laws were passed in 1933 and 1934, and a federal regulatory agency with broad powers — the Securities & Exchange Commission (SEC) — was created and given jurisdiction over trading in corporate securities. Financial reports and other information must be filed with the SEC and made available to the investing public.

GAAP are not limited to public corporations whose securities are traded on public exchanges, such as the New York Stock Exchange and NASDAQ. These financial accounting and reporting standards apply with equal force and authority to private businesses whose ownership shares are not traded in any open market. When the shareholders of a private business receive its periodic financial reports, they are entitled to assume that the company's financial statements and footnotes are prepared in accordance with GAAP. If not, the president or other chief officer of the business should clearly warn the shareholders that GAAP have not been followed in one or more respects. Of course, such a warning might be like waving a red flag and cause the owners to demand an explanation.

The bare-bones content of a private business's annual financial report includes the three primary financial statements (balance sheet, income statement, and cash flow statement) plus a few footnotes. I've seen many private company financial reports that don't even have a letter from the president — just the three financial statements plus a few footnotes, and nothing more.

In fact, I've seen financial reports of private businesses (mostly small companies) that don't even include a cash flow statement; only the balance sheet and income statement are presented. Omitting a cash flow statement violates GAAP — but the company's stockholders and its lenders may not demand to see the cash flow statement, so the company can get away with violating the GAAP rules.

Publicly owned businesses must comply with an additional layer of rules and requirements that don't apply to privately owned businesses. These rules are issued by the SEC, the federal agency that regulates financial reporting and trading in stocks and bonds of publicly owned businesses. The SEC has no jurisdiction over private businesses; those businesses need only worry about GAAP, which don't have many hard-and-fast rules about financial report formats. Public businesses have to file financial reports and other forms with the SEC that are made available to the public. The SEC maintains a Web site for these filings at www.sec.gov/edgarhp.htm. The best known of these forms is the annual 10-K, which includes the business's annual financial statements in prescribed formats, with all the supporting schedules and detailed disclosures that the SEC requires.

Here are some (but not all) of the main financial reporting requirements that publicly owned businesses must adhere to. (Private businesses may include these items as well if they want, but they generally don't.)

- **Management discussion and analysis (MD&A) section:** Presents the top managers' interpretation and analysis of a business's profit performance and other important financial developments over the year.

- **Earnings per share (EPS):** The only ratio that a public business is *required* to report, although most public businesses do report a few other ratios as well. See "Earnings per share (EPS)," later in this chapter. Note that private businesses' reports generally don't include any ratios (but you can, of course, compute the ratios yourself).

- **Three-year comparative income statement:** See Chapter 5 for more information about income statements.

*Note:* A publicly owned business can make the required filings with the SEC and then prepare a different annual financial report for its stockholders, thus preparing two sets of financial reports. This is common practice. However, the financial information in the two documents can't differ in any material way. A typical annual financial report to stockholders is a glossy booklet with excellent art and graphic design, including high-quality photographs. The company's products are promoted and its people are featured in glowing terms that describe teamwork, creativity, and innovation — I'm sure you get the picture. In contrast, the reports to the SEC look like legal briefs — nothing fancy in these filings. The core of financial statements and footnotes (plus certain other information) is the same in both the SEC filings and the annual reports to stockholders. The SEC filings contain more information about certain expenses and require much more disclosure about the history of the business, its main markets and competitors, its principal officers, any major changes on the horizon, and so on. Professional investors and investment managers read the SEC filings.

Most public corporations solicit their stockholders' votes in the annual election of persons to the board of directors (whom the business has nominated) and on other matters that must be put to a vote at the annual stockholders' meeting. The method of communication for doing so is called a *proxy statement* — the reason being that the stockholders give their votes to a *proxy,* or designated person, who actually casts the votes at the annual meeting. The SEC requires many disclosures in proxy statements that are not found in annual financial reports issued to stockholders or in the business's annual 10-K. For example, compensation paid to the top-level officers of the business must be disclosed, as well as their stock holdings. If you own stock in a public corporation, take the time to read through the annual proxy statement you receive.

One difference you're sure to notice between the financial reports issued by private and public companies concerns the graphics — pictures of products, colorful charts, and even photos of top executives (unless the business had a bad year, in which case those photos may be mysteriously omitted).

You may think, then, that the financial reports of private businesses tend to be a bit on the dull and dry side. To be honest, I haven't seen enough private business financial reports to make a fair judgment — they're not easy to come by — but I think I can get away with saying that these reports are much *skinnier* than public businesses' (which isn't necessarily a bad thing!).

# Analyzing Financial Reports with Ratios

Financial reports have lots of numbers in them. (Duh!) The significance of many of these numbers is not clear unless they are compared with other numbers in the financial statements to determine the relative size of one number to another number. One very useful way of interpreting financial reports is to compute *ratios* — that is, to divide a particular number in the financial report by another. Financial report ratios are also useful because they enable you to compare a business's current performance with its past performance or with another business's performance, regardless of whether sales revenue or net income was bigger or smaller for the other years or the other business. In other words, using ratios cancels out size differences.

You may be surprised when I point out that you don't find too many ratios in financial reports. Publicly owned businesses are required to report just one ratio (earnings per share, or EPS), and privately owned businesses generally don't report any ratios. Generally accepted accounting principles (GAAP) don't demand that any ratios be reported (except EPS for publicly owned companies). However, you still see and hear about ratios all the time, especially from stockbrokers and other financial experts, so you should know what the ratios mean, even if you never go to the trouble of computing them yourself.

Ratios do not provide final answers — they're helpful indicators, and that's it. For example, if you're in the market for a house, you may consider cost per square foot (the total cost divided by the total number of square feet) as a way of comparing the prices of the houses you're looking at. But you have to put that ratio in context: Maybe one neighborhood is nicer than another, and maybe one house will need more repairs than another. In short, the ratio isn't the only factor in your decision — and the same should hold true for financial report ratios.

The following sections explain the ten financial statement ratios that you're most likely to run into. Here's a general overview of why these ratios are important:

- **Gross margin ratio and profit ratio:** You use these ratios to measure a business's profit performance with respect to its sales revenue. Sales revenue is the starting point for making profit; these ratios measure the percentage of total sales revenue that is left over as profit.

- **Earnings per share (EPS), price/earnings (P/E) ratio, and dividend yield:** These three ratios revolve around the market price of stock shares, and anyone who invests in publicly owned businesses should be intimately familiar with them. As an investor, your main concern is the return you receive on your invested capital. Return on capital consists of two elements:

  - Periodic **cash dividends** distributed by the business

  - Increase (or decrease) in the **market price** of the stock shares

  Dividends and market prices depend on earnings — and there you have the relationship among these three ratios and why they're so important to you, the investor. Major newspapers report P/E ratios and dividend yields in their stock market activity tables; stockbrokers' investment reports focus mainly on forecasts of EPS and dividend yield.

- **Book value per share and return on equity (ROE):** Stock shares for private businesses have no ready market price, so investors in these businesses use the ROE ratio, which is based on the value of their ownership equity reported in the balance sheet, to measure investment performance. Without a market price for the stock shares of a private business, the P/E ratio cannot be determined. EPS can easily be determined for a private business but does not have to be reported in its income statement.

- **Current ratio and acid-test ratio:** These ratios indicate whether a business should have enough cash to pay its liabilities.

- **Return on assets (ROA):** This ratio is the first step in determining how well a business is using its capital and whether it's earning more than the interest rate on its debt, which causes financial leverage gain (or loss).

## Hold on — it's a bumpy ride!

If you selected, say, 100 annual financial reports and read all their income statements, you might be surprised to find that so many report *extra-ordinary gains* or *losses* for the year. These big numbers are out-of-the-ordinary bumps and detours along the profit highway, but they're far from uncommon. Not too many businesses have the luxury of a noninterrupted, even-keel performance year after year.

These kinds of discontinuities certainly make analyzing profit performance difficult. A business

that has reported good annual profits for five or ten years suddenly gets clobbered with some huge loss — how should you interpret that loss? By itself, or in the context of the business's historical performance? What does it mean for the coming year? You'll find none of these questions answered in a business's financial report; you have to look elsewhere. See Chapter 5 for more about the reporting of nonrecurring gains and losses.

The income statement and balance sheet of the business example that I first use in Chapter 8 are repeated here so that you have a financial statement to reference — see Figures 14-1 (income statement) and 14-2 (balance sheet). Notice that a cash flow statement is not presented here — mainly because no ratios are calculated from data in the cash flow statement. (Refer to the sidebar "The temptation to compute cash flow per share: Don't give in!") The footnotes to the company's financial statements are not presented here, but the use of footnotes is discussed in the following sections.

| (Dollar amounts in thousands, except per share amounts) | |
|---|---|
| **Income Statement For Year** | |
| Sales Revenue | $ 52,000 |
| Cost of Goods Sold Expense | 31,200 |
| Gross Margin | $ 20,800 |
| Sales, Administration, and General Expenses | 15,600 |
| Depreciation Expense | 1,650 |
| Earnings Before Interest and Income Tax | $ 3,550 |
| Interest Expense | 750 |
| Earnings Before Income Tax | $ 2,800 |
| Income Tax Expense | 900 |
| Net Income | $ 1,900 |
| Earnings Per Share | $ 2.39 |

**Figure 14-1:**
A sample income statement.

| (Dollar amounts in thousands) | | |
|---|---|---|
| **Balance Sheet at End of Year** | | |
| **Assets** | | |
| Cash | $ 3,500 | |
| Accounts Receivable | 5,000 | |
| Inventory | 7,800 | |
| Prepaid Expenses | 900 | |
| Current Assets | | $ 17,200 |
| Fixed Assets | $ 19,500 | |
| Accumulated Depreciation | (6,825) | 12,675 |
| Total Assets | | $ 29,875 |
| **Liabilities** | | |
| Accounts Payable | $ 1,500 | |
| Accrued Expenses Payable | 2,400 | |
| Income Tax Payable | 75 | |
| Short-term Notes Payable | 4,000 | |
| Current Liabilities | | $ 7,975 |
| Long-term Notes Payable | | 6,000 |
| **Owners' Equity** | | |
| Capital Stock (795,000 shares) | $ 4,000 | |
| Retained Earnings | 11,900 | 15,900 |
| Total Liabilities and Owners' Equity | | $ 29,875 |

**Figure 14-2:**
A sample balance sheet.

# Gross margin ratio

Making bottom-line profit begins with making sales and earning enough gross margin from those sales, as explained in Chapters 5 and 9. In other words, a business must set its sales prices high enough over product costs to yield satisfactory gross margins on its products, because the business has to worry about many more expenses of making sales and running the business, plus interest expense and income tax expense. You calculate the *gross margin ratio* as follows:

```
Gross margin ÷ sales revenue = gross margin ratio
```

So a business with a $20.8 million gross margin and $52 million in sales revenue (refer to Figure 14-1) ends up with a 40 percent gross margin ratio. Now, if the business had only been able to earn a 41 percent gross margin, that one additional point (one point is 1 percent) would have caused a jump in its gross margin of $520,000 (1 percent × $52 million sales revenue) — which would have trickled down to earnings before income tax. Earnings before income tax would have been 19 percent higher (a $520,000 bump in gross margin ÷ $2.8 million income before income tax). Never underestimate the impact of even a small improvement in the gross margin ratio!

Outside investors know only the information disclosed in the external financial report that the business releases. They can't do much more than compare the gross margin for the two or three yearly income statements included in the annual financial report. Although publicly owned businesses are required to include a management discussion and analysis (MD&A) section that should comment on any significant change in the gross margin ratio, corporate managers have wide latitude in deciding what exactly to discuss and how much detail to go into. You definitely should read the MD&A section, but it may not provide all the answers you're looking for. You have to search further in stockbroker releases, in articles in the financial press, or at the next professional business meeting you attend.

As explained in Chapter 9, managers focus on *contribution margin per unit* and *total contribution margin* to control and improve profit performance business. Contribution margin equals sales revenue minus product cost and other variable operating expenses of the business. Contribution margin is profit before the company's total fixed costs for the period are deducted. Changes in the contribution margins per unit of the products sold by a business and changes in its total fixed costs are extremely important information in managing profit.

However, businesses do not disclose contribution margin information in their *external* financial reports — they wouldn't even think of doing so. This information is considered to be proprietary in nature; it should be kept confidential and out of the hands of its competitors. In short, investors do not have access to information about the business's contribution margin. Neither GAAP nor the SEC requires that such information be disclosed. The external income statement discloses gross margin and operating profit, or earnings before interest and income tax expenses. However, the expenses between these two profit lines in the income statement are not separated between variable and fixed (refer to Figure 14-1).

## Profit ratio

Business is motivated by profit, so the *profit ratio* is very important, to say the least. The profit ratio indicates how much net income was earned on each $100 of sales revenue:

```
Net income ÷ sales revenue = profit ratio
```

For example, the business in Figure 14-1 earned $1.9 million net income from its $52 million sales revenue, so its profit ratio is 3.65 percent, meaning that the business earned $3.65 net income for each $100 of sales revenue.

A seemingly small change in the profit ratio can have a big impact on the bottom line. Suppose that this business had earned a profit ratio of 5 percent instead of 3.65 percent. That increase in the profit ratio translates into a $700,000 increase in bottom-line profit (net income) on the same sales revenue.

Profit ratios vary widely from industry to industry. A 5 to 10 percent profit ratio is common in most industries, although some high-volume retailers, such as supermarkets, are satisfied with profit ratios around 1 or 2 percent.

You can turn any ratio upside down and come up with a new way of looking at the same information. If you flip the profit ratio over to be sales revenue divided by net income, the result is the amount of sales revenue needed to make $1 profit. Using the same example, $52 million sales revenue ÷ $1.9 million net income = 27.37 to 1 upside-down profit ratio, which means that this business needs $27.37 in sales to make $1 profit. So you can say that net income is 3.65 percent of sales revenue, or you can say that sales revenue is 27.37 times net income — but the standard profit ratio is expressed as net income divided by sales revenue.

## Earnings per share, basic and diluted

Publicly owned businesses, according to generally accepted accounting principles (GAAP), must report *earnings per share (EPS)* below the net income line in their income statements — giving EPS a certain distinction among the ratios. Why is EPS considered so important? Because it gives investors a means of determining the amount the business earned on their stock share investments: EPS tells you how much net income the business earned for each stock share you own. The essential equation for EPS is as follows:

```
Net income ÷ total number of capital stock shares = EPS
```

For the example in Figures 14-1 and 14-2, the company's $1.9 million net income is divided by the 795,000 shares of stock the business has issued to compute its $2.39 EPS.

*Note:* Private businesses do not have to report EPS if they don't want to. Considering the wide range of issues covered by GAAP, you find surprisingly few distinctions between private and public businesses — these authoritative accounting rules apply to all businesses. But EPS is one area where GAAP makes an exception for privately owned businesses. EPS is extraordinarily important to the stockholders of businesses whose stock shares are publicly traded. These stockholders focus on market price *per share.* They want the total net income of the business to be communicated to them on a per share basis so that they can easily compare it with the market price of their stock shares. The stock shares of privately owned corporations are not actively traded, so there is no readily available market value for the stock shares. The thinking behind the rule that privately owned businesses should not have to report EPS is that their stockholders do not focus on per share values and are more interested in the business's total net income performance.

The business in the example is too small to be publicly owned. So I turn here to a larger public corporation example. This publicly owned corporation reports that it earned $1.32 billion net income for the year just ended. At the end of the year, this corporation has 400 million stock shares *outstanding*, which refers to the number of shares that have been issued and are owned by its stockholders. Thus its EPS is $3.30 ($1.32 billion net income ÷ 400 million stock shares). But here's a complication: The business is committed to issuing additional capital stock shares in the future for stock options that the company has granted to its managers, and it has borrowed money on the basis of debt instruments that give the lenders the right to convert the debt into its capital stock. Under terms of its management stock options and its convertible debt, the business could have to issue 40 million additional capital stock shares in the future. Dividing net income by the number of shares outstanding plus the number of shares that could be issued in the future gives the following computation of EPS:

```
$1.32 billion net income ÷ 440 million capital stock shares =
        $3.00 EPS
```

This second computation, based on the higher number of stock shares, is called the *diluted* earnings per share. (*Diluted* means thinned out or spread over a larger number of shares.) The first computation, based on the number of stock shares actually outstanding, is called *basic* earnings per share. Publicly owned businesses have to report two EPS figures — unless they have a *simple capital structure* that does not require the business to issue additional stock shares in the future. Generally, publicly owned corporations have *complex capital structures* and have to report two EPS figures. Both are reported at the bottom of the income statement. So the company is this example reports $3.30 basic EPS and $3.00 diluted EPS. Sometimes it's not clear which of the two EPS figures is being used in press releases and in articles giving investment advice. Fortunately, *The Wall Street Journal* and most other major financial publications leave a clear trail of both EPS figures.

Calculating basic and diluted EPS isn't always as simple as my examples may suggest. An accountant would have to adjust the EPS equation for the following complicating things that a business may do:

- ✔ Issue additional stock shares during the year and buy back some of its stock shares (shares of its stock owned by the business itself that are not formally cancelled are called *treasury stock*)

- ✔ Issue more than one class of stock, causing net income to be divided into two or more pools — one pool for each class of stock

- ✔ Go through a merger (business combination) in which a large number of stock shares are issued to acquire the other business

# Price/earnings (P/E) ratio

The *price/earnings (P/E) ratio* is another ratio that's of particular interest to investors in public businesses. The P/E ratio gives you an idea of how much you're paying in the current price for the stock shares for each dollar of earnings, or net income being earned by the business. Remember that earnings prop up the market value of stock shares, not the book value of the stock shares that's reported in the balance sheet. (Read on for the book value per share discussion.)

The P/E ratio is, in one sense, a reality check on just how high the current market price is in relation to the underlying profit that the business is earning. Extraordinarily high P/E ratios are justified only when investors think that the company's EPS has a lot of upside potential in the future.

The P/E ratio is calculated as follows:

```
Current market price of stock ÷ most recent trailing 12
          months diluted EPS* = P/E ratio
```

*If the business has a simple capital structure and does not report a diluted EPS, its basic EPS is used for calculating its P/E ratio. (See the earlier section "Earnings per share, basic and diluted.")

Assume that the stock shares of a public business with a $3.65 diluted EPS are selling at $54.75 in the stock market. **Note:** From here forward, I will use the briefer term EPS in reference to P/E ratios; I assume you understand that it refers to diluted EPS for businesses with complex capital structures and to basic EPS for businesses with simple capital structures.

The actual share price bounces around day to day and is subject to change on short notice. To illustrate the P/E ratio, I use this price, which is the closing price on the latest trading day in the stock market. This market price means that investors trading in the stock think that the shares are worth 15 times diluted EPS ($54.75 market price ÷ $3.65 diluted EPS = 15). This value may be below the broad market average that values stocks at, say, 20 times EPS. The outlook for future growth in its EPS is probably not too good.

In recent years, average stock market P/E ratios have been at historically high levels, although they vary quite a bit from business to business, industry to industry, and year to year. One dollar of EPS may command only a $12 market value for a mature business in a nongrowth industry, whereas a dollar of EPS for dynamic businesses in growth industries may be rewarded with a $35 market value or more.

---

## Market cap — not a cap on market value

One investment number you see a lot in the financial press is the *market cap.* No, this does not refer to a cap, or limit, on the market value of a corporation's capital stock shares. The term is shorthand for *market capitalization,* which refers to the total market value of the business that is determined by multiplying the stock's current market price times the total number of stock shares issued by the corporation.

Suppose a company's stock is selling at $50 per share in the stock market and it has 200 million shares outstanding. Its market cap is $10 billion. Another business may be willing to pay higher than $50 per share for the company. Indeed, many acquisitions and mergers involve the acquiring company paying a hefty premium over the going market price of the stock shares of the company being acquired.

---

## Dividend yield

The *dividend yield* tells investors how much *cash flow income* they're receiving on their investment. (The dividend is the cash flow income part of investment return; the other part is the gain or loss in the market value of the investment over the year.)

Suppose that a stock of a public corporation that is selling for $60 paid $1.20 cash dividends per share over the last year. You calculate dividend yield as follows:

```
$1.20 annual cash dividend per share ÷ $60 current market
          price of stock = 2% dividend yield
```

You use dividend yield to compare how your stock investment is doing to how it would be doing if you'd put that money in corporate or U.S. Treasury bonds and notes or other debt securities that pay interest. The average interest rate of high-grade debt securities has recently been three to four times the dividend yields on most public corporations; in theory, market price appreciation of the stock shares over time makes up for that gap. Of course, stockholders take the risk that the market value will not increase enough to make their total return on investment rate higher than a benchmark interest rate.

Assume that long-term U.S. Treasury bonds are currently paying 6 percent annual interest, which is 4 percent higher than the business's 2 percent dividend yield in the example just discussed. If this business's stock shares don't increase in value by at least 4 percent over the year, its investors would have been better off investing in the debt securities instead. (Of course, they wouldn't have gotten all the perks of a stock investment, like those heartfelt letters from the president and those glossy financial reports.) The market price of publicly traded debt securities can fall or rise, so things get a little tricky in this sort of investment analysis.

## Book value per share

*Book value per share* is one measure, but it's certainly not the only amount used for determining the value of a privately owned business's stock shares. As discussed in Chapter 6, book value is not the same thing as market value. The asset values that a business records in its books (also known as its *accounts*) are *not* the amounts that a business could get if it put its assets up for sale. Book values of some assets are generally lower than what the cost would be for replacing the assets if a disaster (such as a flood or a fire) wiped out the business's inventory or equipment. Recording current market values in the books is really not a practical option. Until a seller and a buyer meet and haggle over price, trying to determine the market price for a privately owned business's stock shares is awfully hard.

You can calculate book value per share for publicly owned businesses, too. However, market value is readily available, so stockholders (and investment advisors and managers) do not put much weight on book value per share. EPS is the main factor that affects the market prices of stock shares of public corporations — not the book value per share. I should add that some investing strategies, known as *value investing,* search out companies that have a high book value per share compared to their going market prices. But by and large, book value per share plays a secondary role in the market values of stock shares issued by public corporations.

Although book value per share is generally not a good indicator of the market value of a private business's stock shares, you do run into this ratio, at least as a starting point for haggling over a selling price. Here's how to calculate book value per share:

```
Total owners' equity ÷ total number of stock shares = book
          value per share
```

The business shown in Figure 14-2 has issued 795,000 capital stock shares: Its $15.9 million total owners' equity divided by its 795,000 stock shares gives a book value per share of $20. If the business sold off its assets exactly for their book values and paid all its liabilities, it would end up with $15.9 million left for the stockholders, and it could therefore distribute $20 per share. But the company will not go out of business and liquidate its assets and pay off its liabilities. So book value per share is a theoretical value. It's not totally irrelevant, but it's not all that definitive, either.

## Return on equity (ROE) ratio

The *return on equity (ROE) ratio* tells you how much profit a business earned in comparison to the book value of stockholders' equity. This ratio is useful for privately owned businesses, which have no way of determining the current value of owners' equity (at least not until the business is actually sold).

ROE is also calculated for public corporations, but, just like book value per share, it plays a secondary role and is not the dominant factor driving market prices. (Earnings are.) Here's how you calculate this key ratio:

```
Net income ÷ owners' equity = ROE
```

The owners' equity figure is at book value, which is reported in the company's balance sheet. Chapter 6 explains owners' equity and the difference between invested capital and retained earnings, which are the two components of owners' equity.

The business whose income statement and balance sheet are shown in Figures 14-1 and 14-2 earned $1.9 million net income for the year just ended and has $15.9 million owners' equity. Therefore, its ROE is 11.95 percent ($1.9 million net income ÷ $15.9 million owners' equity = 11.95 percent). ROE is net income expressed as a percentage of the amount of total owners' equity of the business, which is one of the two sources of capital to the business — the other being borrowed money, or interest-bearing debt. (A business also has non-interest-bearing operating liabilities, such as accounts payable.) The cost of debt capital (interest) is deducted as an expense to determine net income. So net income "belongs" to the owners; it increases their equity in the business, so it makes sense to express net income as the percentage of improvement in the owners' equity.

## Current ratio

The *current ratio* is a test of a business's *short-term solvency* — its capability to pay off its liabilities that come due in the near future (up to one year). The ratio is a rough indicator of whether cash on hand plus the cash flow from collecting accounts receivable and selling inventory will be enough to pay off the liabilities that will come due in the next period.

As you can imagine, lenders are particularly keen on punching in the numbers to calculate the current ratio. Here's how they do it:

```
Current assets ÷ current liabilities = current ratio
```

***Note:*** Unlike with most of the other ratios, you don't multiply the result of this equation by 100 and represent it as a percentage.

Businesses are expected to maintain a minimum current ratio (2.0, meaning a 2-to-1 ratio, is the general rule) and may be legally required to stay above a minimum current ratio as stipulated in their contracts with lenders. The business in Figure 14-2 has $17.2 million in current assets and $7,975,000 in current liabilities, so its current ratio is 2.16, and it shouldn't have to worry about lenders coming by in the middle of the night to break its legs. Chapter 6 discusses current assets and current liabilities and how they are reported in the balance sheet.

## Acid-test ratio

Most serious investors and lenders don't stop with the current ratio for an indication of the business's short-term solvency — its capability to pay the liabilities that will come due in the short term. Investors also calculate the *acid-test ratio* (also known as the *quick ratio* or the *pounce ratio*), which is a more severe test of a business's solvency than the current ratio. The acid-test ratio excludes inventory and prepaid expenses, which the current ratio includes, and limits assets to cash and items that the business can quickly convert to cash. This limited category of assets is known as *quick* or *liquid* assets.

You calculate the acid-test ratio as follows:

```
Liquid assets ÷ total current liabilities = acid-test ratio
```

***Note:*** Unlike most other financial ratios, you don't multiply the result of this equation by 100 and represent it as a percentage.

For the business example shown in Figure 14-2, the acid test ratio is as follows:

| | |
|---|---|
| Cash | $3,500,000 |
| Marketable securities | none |
| Accounts receivable | 5,000,000 |
| Total liquid assets | $8,500,000 |
| Total current liabilities | $7,975,000 |
| Acid-test ratio | 1.07 |

A 1.07 acid-test ratio means that the business would be able to pay off its short-term liabilities and still have a little bit of liquid assets left over. The general rule is that the acid-test ratio should be at least 1.0, which means that liquid assets equal current liabilities. Of course, falling below 1.0 doesn't mean that the business is on the verge of bankruptcy, but if the ratio falls as low as 0.5, that may be cause for alarm.

This ratio is also known as the *pounce ratio* to emphasize that you're calculating for a worst-case scenario, where a pack of wolves (more politely known as *creditors*) has pounced on the business and is demanding quick payment of the business's liabilities. But don't panic. Short-term creditors do not have the right to demand immediate payment, except under unusual circumstances. This is a very conservative way to look at a business's capability to pay its short-term liabilities — too conservative in most cases.

# *Return on assets (ROA) ratio*

As discussed in Chapter 6 (refer to the sidebar "Trading on the equity: Taking a chance on debt"), one factor affecting the bottom-line profit of a business is whether it used debt to its advantage. For the year, a business may have realized a *financial leverage gain* — it earned more profit on the money it borrowed than the interest paid for the use of that borrowed money. So a good part of its net income for the year may be due to financial leverage. The first step in determining financial leverage gain is to calculate a business's *return on assets (ROA) ratio,* which is the ratio of EBIT (earnings before interest and income tax) to the total capital invested in operating assets.

Here's how to calculate ROA:

```
EBIT ÷ net operating assets = ROA
```

***Note:*** This equation calls for *net operating assets,* which equals total assets less the non-interest-bearing operating liabilities of the business. Actually, many stock analysts and investors use the total assets figure because deducting all the non-interest-bearing operating liabilities from total assets to determine net operating assets is, quite frankly, a nuisance. But I strongly recommend using net operating assets because that's the total amount of capital raised from debt and equity.

Compare ROA with the interest rate: If a business's ROA is 14 percent and the interest rate on its debt is 8 percent, for example, the business's net gain on its debt capital is 6 percent more than what it's paying in interest. There's a favorable spread of 6 points (one point = 1 percent), which can be multiplied times the total debt of the business to determine how much its total earnings before income tax is traceable to financial leverage gain.

In Figure 14-2, notice that the company has $10 million total interest-bearing debt ($4 million short-term plus $6 million long-term). Its total owners' equity is $15.9 million. So its net operating assets total is $25.9 million (which excludes the three short-term non-interest-bearing operating liabilities). The company's ROA, therefore, is

```
$3.55 million earnings before interest and income tax ÷ $25.9
        million net operating assets = 13.71% ROA
```

The business earned $1,371,000 (rounded) on its total debt — 13.71 percent ROA times $10 million total debt. The business paid only $750,000 interest on its debt. So the business had $621,000 financial leverage gain before income tax ($1,371,000 less $750,000). Put another way, the business paid 7.50 percent interest on its debt but earned 13.71 percent on this money for a favorable spread of 6.21 points — which, when multiplied by the $10 million debt, yields the $621,000 pretax financial gain for the year.

# The temptation to compute cash flow per share: Don't give in!

Now that you've gotten a taste of ratios, you can't get enough — you're devouring all the numbers on the financial report, sandwiching any two numbers that look good together to make a ratio. You start eyeing the cash flow statement, licking your lips over cash flow from profit (from *operating activities,* as it's called in the cash flow statement). You chew on that number and then reach for the total number of capital stock shares.

Stop right there! Businesses are prohibited from reporting a *cash flow per share* number on their financial reports. The accounting rule book (principally the standards set by the Financial Accounting Standards Board, or FASB) specifically prohibits very few things, and cash flow per share is on this small list of contraband. Why? Because — and this is somewhat speculative on my part — the FASB was worried that the cash flow number would usurp net income as the main measure for profit performance. Indeed, many writers in the financial press were talking up the importance of cash flow from profit, so I see the FASB's concern on this

matter. Knowing how important EPS is for market value of stocks, the FASB declared a similar per share amount for cash flow out of bounds and prohibited it from being included in a financial report. Of course, you could compute it quite easily — the FASB's rule doesn't apply to how financial statements are interpreted, only to how they are reported.

Actually, none of the popular ratios involves the cash flow statement, probably because that statement has been a required part of financial reports since only 1987, making it a baby compared to the much older balance sheet and income statement. Some technical reference books mention a few cash flow ratios, but these ratios really haven't gained a foothold in the investment and credit communities.

But the temptation is just too great! Should I dare give you an example of cash flow per share? Here goes: A business with $42 million cash flow from profit and 4.2 million total capital stock shares would end up with $10 cash flow per share. Shhh.

ROA is a useful earnings ratio, aside from determining financial leverage gain (or loss) for the period. ROA is a *capital utilization* test — how much profit before interest and income tax was earned on the total capital employed by the business. The basic idea is that it takes money (assets) to make money (profit); the final test is how much profit was made on the assets. If, for example, a business earns $1 million EBIT on $20 million assets, its ROA is only
5 percent. Such a low ROA signals that the business is making poor use of its assets and will have to improve its ROA or face serious problems in the future.

# *Frolicking through the Footnotes*

Reading the footnotes in annual financial reports is no picnic. The investment pros have to read them because in providing consultation to their clients they are required to comply with due diligence standards or because of their legal duties and responsibilities of managing other peoples' money. When I was an accounting professor, I had to stay on top of financial reporting; every year I read a sample of annual financial reports to keep up with current practices. I had to struggle through many, many footnotes. But beyond the group of people who get paid to read financial reports, does anyone read footnotes? The footnotes in the annual financial reports of Berkshire Hathaway, Inc. (Warren Buffet's company) are pretty well written for footnotes. However, even these footnotes are heavy reading, to say the least.

What I suggest is that you should do a quick read-through of the footnotes and identify the ones that seem to have the most significance. Generally, the most important footnotes are those dealing with the following matters:

- ✔ **Stock options awarded by the business to its executives:** The additional stock shares issued under stock options dilute (thin out) the earnings per share of the business, which in turn puts downside pressure on the market value of its stock shares, everything else being the same.

- ✔ **Pending lawsuits, litigation, and investigations by government agencies:** These intrusions into the normal affairs of the business can have enormous consequences.

- ✔ **Segment information for the business:** Most public businesses have to report information for the major segments of the organization — sales and operating profit by territories or product lines. This gives a better glimpse of the different parts making up the whole business. (However, segment information may be reported elsewhere in an annual financial report than in the footnotes.)

These are just three of the many important pieces of information you should look for in footnotes. But you have to stay alert for other critical matters that a business may disclose in its footnotes — scan each and every footnote for potentially important information. Finding a footnote that discusses a major lawsuit against the business, for example, may make the stock too risky for your stock portfolio.

## Financial reports on the Web

No reliable count of all the businesses that have put their annual reports on their Web sites exists, but it must be in the thousands. Each one seems to be a little different. Generally, the glossy annual financial report of a company is available on its Web site, but after downloading it you need Adobe Acrobat Reader to open the file. No problem; Adobe Acrobat Reader is free, and you can easily download it from many Web sites. One very handy feature is the ability to search for key words in the annual report. Find a company's Web site by searching for the company name on a search engine. Each company's Web site has a different look and feel, but navigating to where you want to go and what you want to do is fairly straightforward.

Also, the SEC maintains the EDGAR database of financial filings the SEC has received — go to the Web site at `www.sec.gov/edgarhp.htm`.

# Checking for Ominous Skies on the Audit Report

The value of analyzing a financial report depends directly and entirely on the accuracy of the report's numbers. Top management wants to present the best possible picture of the business in its financial report (which is understandable, of course). The managers have a vested interest in the profit performance and financial condition of the business. Their yearly bonuses usually depend on recorded profit, for instance. As mentioned several times in the book, the top managers and their accountants prepare the financial statements of the business and write the footnotes. This is somewhat like the batter in a baseball game calling the strikes and balls. (As you know, in a baseball game an umpire calls strikes and balls.)

Independent CPA auditors are like umpires in the financial reporting process. The CPA comes in, does an audit of the business's accounting system and procedures, and gives a report that is attached to the company's financial statements. You should check the audit report included with the financial report. Publicly owned businesses are required to have their annual financial reports audited by an independent CPA firm, and many privately owned businesses have audits done, too, because they know that an audit report adds credibility to the financial report.

What if a private business's financial report doesn't include an audit report? Well, you have to trust that the business prepared accurate financial statements that follow generally accepted accounting principles and that the footnotes to the financial statements provide adequate disclosure.

Unfortunately, the audit report gets short shrift in financial statement analysis, maybe because it's so full of technical terminology and accountant doublespeak. But even though audit reports are a tough read, anyone who reads and analyzes financial reports should definitely read the audit report. Chapter 15 provides a lot more information on audits and the auditor's report.

The auditor judges whether the business used accounting methods and procedures in accordance with generally accepted accounting principles (GAAP). In most cases, the auditor's report confirms that everything is hunky-dory, and you can rely on the financial report. However, sometimes an auditor waves a yellow flag — and in extreme cases, a red flag. Here are the two most important warnings to watch out for in an audit report:

✔ The business's capability to continue normal operations is in doubt because of what are known as *financial exigencies,* which may mean a low cash balance, unpaid overdue liabilities, or major lawsuits that the business doesn't have the cash to cover.

✔ One or more of the methods used in the report are not in complete agreement with GAAP, leading the auditor to conclude that the numbers reported are misleading or that disclosure is inadequate.

Although auditor warnings don't necessarily mean that a business is going down the tubes, they should turn on that light bulb in your head and make you more cautious and skeptical about the financial report. The auditor is questioning the very information on which the business's value is based, and you can't take that kind of thing lightly.

Just because a business has a clean audit report doesn't mean that the financial report is completely accurate and aboveboard. As discussed in Chapter 15, auditors don't necessarily catch everything. Keep in mind that the rules of GAAP are pretty flexible, leaving a company's accountants with room for interpretation and creativity that's just short of *cooking the books* (deliberately defrauding and misleading readers of the financial report). Some massaging of the numbers is tolerated, which may mean that what you see on the financial report isn't exactly an untarnished picture of the business. Window dressing and profit smoothing — two common examples of massaging the numbers — are explained in Chapter 8.

## Looking beyond financial statements

Investors can't rely solely on the financial report when making investment decisions. Analyzing a business's financial statements is just one part of the process. You may need to consider these additional factors, depending on the business you're thinking about investing in:

✔ Industry trends and problems

✔ National economic and political developments

✔ Possible mergers, friendly acquisitions, and hostile takeovers

✔ Turnover of key executives

✔ Labor problems

✔ International markets and currency exchange ratios

✔ Supply shortages

✔ Product surpluses

Whew! This kind of stuff goes way beyond accounting, obviously, and is just as significant as financial statement analysis when you're picking stocks and managing investment portfolios. A good book for new investors to read is *Investing For Dummies* by Eric Tyson (and I'm not just saying that because IDG Books publishes both that book and this book).

# Chapter 15

# CPAs: Auditors and Advisors

*I*f I had written this chapter 50 years ago, I would have talked almost exclusively about the role of the certified public accountant (CPA) as the *auditor* of the financial statements and footnotes presented in a business's annual financial report to its owners and lenders. Back then, in the "good old days," audits were a CPA firm's bread-and-butter service — audit fees were a large share of a CPA firm's annual revenue. Audits were the core function that CPAs performed then. In addition to audits, CPAs provided accounting and tax advice to their clients — and that was pretty much all CPAs did.

Today, CPAs do a lot more than auditing. In fact, the profession has shifted away from the term *auditing* in favor of broader descriptors like *assurance* and *attest.* More important, CPAs have moved aggressively into consulting and advising clients on matters other than accounting and tax matters. The movement into the consulting business while continuing to do audits — often for the same clients — has caused all sorts of problems, which this chapter looks at after discussing audits by CPAs.

## Why Audits?

When I graduated from college, I went to work for a Big 8 national CPA firm (now down to the Big 5). The transition from textbook accounting theory to real-world accounting practice came as a shock. Some of our clients dabbled in window dressing (refer to Chapter 8), and more than a few used earnings management tactics (see profit smoothing in Chapter 8). A few of our clients were engaged in accounting fraud, but just a very few. I was surprised how many businesses cut corners to get things done. Sometimes they were close to acting illegally, and some went over the edge. I soon realized that I had been rather naïve, and I came to tolerate most of the questionable practices in the rough and tumble world of business.

I mention my early experience in public accounting to remind you that the world of business is not like Sunday school. Not everything is pure and straight. Nevertheless, legal and ethical lines of conduct separate what is tolerated and what isn't. If you cross the lines, you are subject to legal sanctions and can be held liable to others. For instance, a business can deliberately deceive its investors and lenders with false or misleading numbers in its financial report. Instead of "What You See Is What You Get" in its financial statements, you get a filtered and twisted version of the business's financial affairs — more of a "What I Want You to See Is What You Get" version. That's where audits come in.

Audits are the best practical means for keeping fraudulent and misleading financial reporting to a minimum. In a sense, CPA auditors are like highway patrol officers who enforce traffic laws and issue tickets to keep speeding to a minimum. A business having an independent accounting professional come in once a year to check up on its accounting system is like a person getting a physical exam once a year — the audit exam may uncover problems that the business was not aware of, and knowing that the auditors come in once a year to take a close look at things keeps the business on its toes.

The basic purpose of an annual financial statement audit is to make sure that a business has followed the accounting methods and disclosure requirements of generally accepted accounting principles (GAAP) — in other words, to make sure that the business has stayed in the ballpark of accounting rules. After completing an audit examination, the CPA prepares a short auditor's report stating that the business has prepared its financial statements according to GAAP — or has not, as the case may be. In this way, audits are an effective means of enforcing accounting standards.

An audit by an independent CPA provides assurance ( but not an ironclad guarantee) that the business's financial statements follow accepted accounting methods and provide adequate disclosure. This is the main reason why CPA firms are paid to do annual audits of financial reports. The CPA auditor must be *independent* of the business being audited. The CPA can have no financial stake in the business or any other relationship with the client that may compromise his or her objectivity. However, the independence of auditors has come under scrutiny of late. See the section "From Audits to Advising," later in the chapter.

The core of a business's financial report is its three primary financial statements — the income statement, the cash flow statement, and the balance sheet — and the necessary footnotes to these statements. A financial report may consist of just these statements and footnotes and nothing more. Usually, however, there's more — in some cases, a lot more. Chapter 8 explains the additional content of financial reports of public business corporations, such as the transmittal letter to the owners from the chief executive of the business, historical summaries, supporting schedules, and listings of directors and top-level managers — items not often included in the financial reports of private businesses.

The CPA auditor's opinion covers the financial statements and the accompanying footnotes. The auditor, therefore, does not express an opinion of whether the president's letter to the stockholders is a good letter — although if the president's claims contradicted the financial statements, the auditor would comment on the inconsistency. In short, CPAs audit the financial statements and their footnotes but do not ignore the additional information included in annual financial reports.

Although the large majority of audited financial statements are reliable, a few slip through the audit net. Auditor approval is not a 100 percent guarantee that the financial statements contain no erroneous or fraudulent numbers or that the statements and their footnotes provide all required disclosures.

# Who's Who in the World of Audits

Chapter 1 explains that to be a licensed CPA, a person has to hold a college degree, pass a rigorous national exam, have audit experience, and satisfy continuing education requirements. Many CPAs operate as sole practitioners, but many CPAs form partnerships (also called firms). A CPA firm has to be large enough to assign enough staff auditors to the client so that all audit work can be completed in a relatively short period — financial reports are generally released about four to six weeks after the close of the fiscal year. Large businesses need large CPA firms, and very large global business organizations need very large international CPA firms. The public accounting profession consists of five very large international firms, several good-sized second-tier national firms, many regional firms, small local firms, and sole practitioners.

All businesses whose ownership units (stock shares) are traded in public markets in the United States are required to have annual audits by independent CPAs. Every stock you see listed on the NYSE (New York Stock Exchange), NASDAQ (National Association of Securities Dealers Automated Quotations), and other stock-trading markets must be audited by an outside CPA firm. (The federal securities laws of 1933 and 1934 require audits.)

The Big Five international CPA firms are household names in the business world

- ✔ **Arthur Andersen** (spelled Andersen, not Anderson)
- ✔ **Ernst & Young**
- ✔ **PricewaterhouseCoopers** (all one word, with the C capitalized, being the result of the merger of two firms)
- ✔ **Deloitte & Touche**
- ✔ **KPMG** (the only one of the five firm names having only letters; the PM in the name derives from an earlier time when "Peat Marwick" was part of the firm's name)

The firms are legally organized as limited liability partnerships, so you see LLP after their names. These five international CPA firms audit almost all of the large, public corporations in the United States. For these companies, the annual audit is a cost of doing business; it's the price they pay for going into public markets for their capital and for having their shares traded in a public marketplace — which provides liquidity for their stock shares.

Banks and other lenders to closely held businesses whose ownership shares are not traded in any public marketplace may insist on audited financial statements. I would say that the amount of a bank loan, generally speaking, has to be more than $5 or $10 million before a lender will insist that the business pay for the cost of an audit. If outside, non-manager investors have this much invested in a business, they may also insist on an annual audit.

Instead of an audit, which they couldn't realistically afford, many smaller businesses have an outside CPA come in regularly to look over their accounting methods and give advice on their financial reporting. Unless a CPA has done an audit, he or she has to be very careful not to express an opinion of the external financial statements. Without a careful examination of the evidence supporting the account balances, the CPA is in no position to give an opinion on the financial statements prepared from the accounts of the business.

In the grand scheme of things (as a good friend of mine was fond of saying), most audits are a necessary evil that do not uncover anything seriously wrong with a business's accounting system and the accounting methods it uses to prepare its financial statements. Overall, the financial statements end up looking virtually the same as they would have looked without an audit. Still, an audit has certain side benefits. In the course of doing an audit, a CPA watches for business practices that could stand some improvement and is alert to potential problems.

The CPA auditor usually recommends ways in which the client's *internal controls* can be strengthened. For example, a CPA auditor may discover that accounting employees are not required to take vacations and let someone else do their jobs while they're gone. The auditor would recommend that the internal control requiring vacations away from the office be strictly enforced. Chapter 2 explains that good internal controls are extremely important in an accounting system. Also, in many audits that I worked on, we caught several technical errors that were corrected, and we suggested minor improvements that were made — the end result being that the financial statements were marginally better than they would have been without the audit.

# What an Auditor Does Before Giving an Opinion

A CPA auditor does two basic things: *examines evidence* and *gives an opinion* about the financial statements. The lion's share of audit time is spent on examining evidence supporting the transactions and accounts of the business. A very small part of the total audit time is spent on writing the auditor's report, in which the CPA expresses an opinion of the financial statements and footnotes.

This list gives you an idea of what the auditor does "in the field" — that is, on the premises of the business being audited:

- ✔ Evaluates the design and operating dependability of the business's accounting system and procedures

- ✔ Evaluates and tests the business's internal accounting controls that are established to deter and detect errors and fraud

- ✔ Identifies and critically examines the business's accounting methods — especially whether the methods conform to generally accepted accounting principles (GAAP), which are the touchstones for all businesses

- ✔ Inspects documentary and physical evidence for the business's revenues, expenses, assets, liabilities, and owners' equities — for example, the auditor counts products held in inventory, observes the condition of those products, and confirms checking account balances directly with the banks

The purpose of all the audit work (examining evidence) is to provide a convincing basis for expressing an opinion of the business's financial statements, attesting that the company's financial statements and footnotes (as well as any directly supporting tables and schedules) can be relied on — or not, in some cases. The CPA auditor puts that opinion in the auditor's report.

The auditor's report is the only visible part of the audit process to financial statement readers — the tip of the iceberg. All the readers see is the auditor's one-page report (which is based on the evidence examined during the audit process, of course). For example, Deloitte & Touche spends thousands of hours auditing General Motors, but the only thing that GM's stockholders see is the final, one-page audit report.

# What's in an Auditor's Report

The audit report, which is included in the financial report near the financial statements, serves two useful purposes:

- ✔ It reassures investors and creditors that the financial report can be relied upon or calls attention to any serious departures from established financial reporting standards and generally accepted accounting principles (GAAP).

- ✔ It prevents (in the large majority of cases, anyway) businesses from issuing sloppy or fraudulent financial reports. Knowing that your report will be subject to an independent audit really keeps you on your toes!

The large majority of audit reports on financial statements give the business a clean bill of health, or a *clean opinion*. At the other end of the spectrum, the auditor might state that the financial statements are misleading and should not be relied upon. This negative audit report is called an *adverse opinion*. That's the big stick that auditors carry: They have the power to give a company's financial statements an adverse opinion, and no business wants that. Notice that I say here that the CPA firms "have the power" to give an adverse opinion. In fact, the threat of an adverse opinion almost always motivates a business to give way to the auditor and change its accounting or disclosure in order to avoid getting the kiss of death of an adverse opinion. An adverse audit opinion, if it were actually given, states that the financial statements of the business are misleading, and by implication fraudulent. The SEC does not tolerate adverse opinions; it would stop trading in the company's stock shares if the company received an adverse opinion from its CPA auditor.

Between the two extremes of a clean opinion and an adverse opinion, an auditor's report may point out a flaw in the company's financial statements — but not a fatal flaw that would require an adverse opinion. These are called *qualified opinions*. The following section looks at the most common type of audit report: the clean opinion, in which the auditor certifies that the business's financial statements conform to GAAP and are presented fairly.

# A clean opinion

If the auditor finds no serious problems, the CPA firm gives the financial report an *unqualified opinion,* which is the correct technical name. But most people call it a *clean opinion.* The clean-opinion audit report runs about 200 words and three paragraphs, with enough defensive, legalistic language to make even a seasoned accountant blush. Figure 15-1 shows the audit report by Deloitte & Touche on the 1999 financial statements of Berkshire Hathaway Inc. This is a clean, or unqualified, opinion in the standard three-paragraph format.

---

**INDEPENDENT AUDITORS' REPORT**

To the Board of Directors and Shareholders
Berkshire Hathaway Inc.

We have audited the accompanying consolidated balance sheets of Berkshire Hathaway Inc. and subsidiaries as of December 31, 1999 and 1998, and the related consolidated statements of earnings, changes in shareholders' equity, and cash flows for each of the three years in the period ended December 31, 1999. These financial statements are the responsibility of the Company's management. Our responsibility is to express an opinion on these financial statements based on our audits.

We conducted our audits in accordance with auditing standards generally accepted in the United States of America. Those standards require that we plan and perform the audit to obtain reasonable assurance about whether the financial statements are free of material misstatement. An audit includes examining, on a test basis, evidence supporting the amounts and disclosures in the financial statements. An audit also includes assessing the accounting principles used and significant estimates made by management, as well as evaluating the overall financial statement presentation. We believe that our audits provide a reasonable basis for our opinion.

In our opinion, such consolidated financial statements present fairly, in all material respects, the financial position of Berkshire Hathaway Inc. and subsidiaries as of December 31, 1999 and 1998, and the results of their operations and their cash flows for each of the three years in the period ended December 31, 1999 in conformity with accounting principles generally accepted in the United States of America.

DELOITTE & TOUCHE LLP
March 3, 2000
Omaha, Nebraska

---

**Figure 15-1:**
A standard three-paragraph audit report.

Figure 15-2 presents a clean opinion but in a *one*-paragraph format — given by PricewaterhouseCoopers on Caterpillar's 1999 financial statements. For many years, Price Waterhouse (as it was known before its merger with Coopers) was well known for its maverick one-paragraph audit report, and the new firm (PricewaterhouseCoopers) evidently intends to continue using the one-paragraph audit report. Which one do you like best? I tend to favor the one-paragraph audit report.

REPORT OF INDEPENDENT ACCOUNTANTS

**PRICEWATERHOUSE(COPERS** 🏢

**To the Board of Directors and Stockholders of Caterpillar Inc.:** We have audited, in accordance with auditing standards generally accepted in the United States, the consolidated financial position of Caterpillar Inc. and its subsidiaries as of December 31, 1999, 1998 and 1997, and the related consolidated results of their operations and their consolidated cash flow for each of the three years in the period ended December 31, 1999, (not presented herein); and in our report dated January 21, 2000, we expressed an unqualified opinion on those consolidated financial statements.

In our opinion, the information set forth in the accompanying condensed consolidated financial statements is fairly stated, in all material respects, in relation to the consolidated financial statements from which it has been derived.

*PricewaterhouseCoopers* LLP

**Peoria, Illinois**
January 21, 2000

**Figure 15-2:**
A one-paragraph audit report.

The following summary cuts through the jargon and shows you what the audit report really says.

| | |
|---|---|
| *1st paragraph* | We did the audit, but the financial statements are the responsibility of management; we just express an opinion of them. |
| *2nd paragraph* | We carried out audit procedures that provide us a reasonable basis for expressing our opinion, but we don't necessarily catch everything. |
| *3rd paragraph* | The company's financial statements conform to GAAP and are not misleading. |

## Other kinds of audit opinions

An audit report that does *not* give a clean opinion may look very similar to a clean-opinion audit report to the untrained eye. Some investors see the name of a CPA firm next to the financial statements and assume that everything is okay — after all, if the auditor had seen a problem, the Feds would have pounced on the business and put everyone in jail, right? Well, not exactly.

How do you know when an auditor's report may be something other than a straightforward, no-reservations clean opinion? *Look for a fourth paragraph;* that's the key. Many audits require the CPA firm to add additional, explanatory language to the standard, unqualified (clean) opinion.

One modification to an auditor's report is very serious — when the CPA firm expresses that it has substantial doubts about the capability of the business to continue as a going concern. A *going concern* is a business that has sufficient financial wherewithal and momentum to continue its normal operations into the foreseeable future and would be able to absorb a bad turn of events without having to default on its liabilities. A going concern does not face an imminent financial crisis or any pressing financial emergency. A business could be under some financial distress, but overall still be judged a going concern. Unless there is evidence to the contrary, the CPA auditor assumes that the business is a going concern.

But in some cases, the auditor may see unmistakable signs that a business is in deep financial waters and may not be able to convince its creditors and lenders to give it time to work itself out of its present financial difficulties. The creditors and lenders may force the business into involuntary bankruptcy, or the business may make a preemptive move and take itself into voluntary bankruptcy. The equity owners (stockholders of a corporation) may end up holding an empty bag after the bankruptcy proceedings have concluded. (This in one of the risks that stockholders take.) If an auditor has serious concerns about whether the business is a going concern, these doubts are spelled out in the auditor's report.

Auditors also point out any accounting methods that are inconsistent from one year to the next, whether their opinion is based in part on work done by another CPA audit firm, on limitations on the scope of their audit work, on departures from GAAP (if they're not serious enough to warrant an adverse opinion), or on one of several other more technical matters. Generally, businesses — and auditors, too — want to end up with a clean opinion; anything less is bound to catch the attention of the people who read the financial statements. Every business wants to avoid that sort of attention if possible.

# Do Audits Always Catch Fraud?

Business managers and investors should understand one thing: Having an audit of a business's financial statements does not guarantee that all fraud, embezzlement, theft, and dishonesty will be detected. Audits have to be cost-effective; auditors can't examine every transaction that occurred during the year. Instead, auditors carefully evaluate businesses' internal controls and rely on sampling — they examine only a relatively small portion of transactions closely and in depth. The sample may not include the transactions that would tip off the auditor that something is wrong, however. Perpetrators of fraud and embezzlement usually are clever in concealing their wrongdoing and often prepare fake evidence to cover their tracks.

## *Looking for errors and fraud*

Auditors look in the high-risk areas where fraud and embezzlement are most likely to occur and in areas where the company's internal controls are weak. But again, auditors can't catch everything. High-level management fraud is extraordinarily difficult to detect because CPA auditors rely a great deal on management explanations and assurances about the business. Top-level executives may lie to auditors, deliberately mislead them, and conceal things that they don't want auditors to find out about. Auditors have a particularly difficult time detecting management fraud.

Under tougher auditing standards adopted in 1997, CPA auditors have to develop a detailed and definite plan to search for indicators of fraud, and they have to document the search procedures and findings in their audit working papers. Searching is one thing, but actually finding fraud is quite another. There had been many cases in which high-level management fraud went on for some time before it was discovered, usually not by auditors. The new auditing standard was expected to lead to more effective audit procedures that would reduce undetected fraud.

Unfortunately, it does not appear that things have improved. Articles in the financial press since then have exposed many cases of accounting and management fraud that were not detected or, if known about, were not objected to by the auditors. This is most disturbing. It's difficult to understand how these audit failures and breakdowns happened. The trail of facts is hard to follow in each case, especially by just reading what's reported in the press. Nevertheless, I would say that two basic reasons explain why audits fail to find fraud.

First, business managers are aware that an audit relies on a very limited sampling from the large number of transactions. They know that there is only a needle-in-the-haystack chance of fraudulent transactions being selected for an in-depth examination by the auditor. Second, managers are in a position to cover their tracks — to conceal evidence and to fabricate false evidence. In short, well-designed and well-executed management fraud is extraordinarily difficult to uncover by ordinary audit procedures. Call this *audit evidence failure;* the auditor didn't know about the fraud.

In other situations, the auditor did know what was going on but didn't act on it — call this an *audit judgment failure.* In these cases, the auditor was overly tolerant of wrong accounting methods used by the client. The auditor may have had serious objections to the accounting methods, but the client persuaded the CPA to go along with the methods.

Take note of an article in *The Wall Street Journal* in late 1999, on the SEC's stepped-up activity in dealing with financial statement fraud. This article used the following terms: "busted audits," "bend the accounting rules," "fake numbers," "doctoring the books," "weak-kneed auditors," and "went soft on companies' books." Even allowing for journalistic hype, these are rather harsh words for an article in such a respected newspaper as *The Wall Street Journal.* The tone of the article says a lot about the state of affairs today in the world of auditing.

# What happens when auditors spot fraud

In the course of doing an audit, the CPA firm may make the following discoveries:

- ✔ **Errors in recording transactions:** These honest mistakes happen from time to time because of inexperienced bookkeepers, or poorly trained accountants, or simple failure to pay attention to details. No one is stealing money or other assets or defrauding the business. Management wants the errors corrected and wants to prevent them from happening again.

- ✔ **Theft, embezzlement, and fraud against the business:** This kind of dishonesty takes advantage of weak internal controls or involves the abuse of positions of authority in the organization that top management did not know about and was not involved in. Management may take action against the guilty parties.

- ✔ **Accounting fraud** (also called **financial fraud** or **financial reporting fraud**): This refers to top-level managers who know about and approve the use of misleading and invalid accounting methods for the purpose of disguising the business's financial problems or artificially inflating profit. Often, managers benefit from these improper accounting methods — by propping up the market price of the company's stock shares to make their stock options more valuable, for example.

- ✔ **Management fraud:** In the broadest sense, this includes accounting fraud, but in a more focused sense, it refers to high-level business managers engaging in illegal schemes to line their pockets at the business's expense, or knowingly violating laws and regulations that put the business at risk of large criminal or civil penalties. A manager may conspire with competitors to fix prices or divide the market, for example. Accepting kickbacks or bribes from customers is an example of management fraud — although most management fraud is more sophisticated than taking under-the-table payments.

When the first two types of problems are discovered, the auditor's follow-up is straightforward. Errors are corrected, and the loss from the crime against the business is recorded. (Such a loss may be a problem if it were so large that the auditor thinks it should be disclosed separately in the financial report, but the business disagrees and does not want to call attention to the loss.) In contrast, the CPA auditor is between a rock and a hard place when accounting or management fraud is uncovered.

When auditors spot accounting and management fraud, they report it to one level higher in the organization than the level at which the fraud took place — all the way to the board of directors if necessary. But auditors don't blow the whistle outside the client business. They don't take out an ad in *The Wall Street Journal* saying that they caught management fraud at XYZ Corporation, and they don't report the fraud to the SEC. Everything the CPA auditor learns during the course of the audit must be held in the *strictest confidence,* according to the professional standards and ethics of the CPA profession.

When an auditor discovers accounting or management fraud, the business has to clean up the fraud mess as best it can — which often involves recording a loss. Of course, the business should make changes to prevent the fraud from occurring again. And it may request the resignations of those responsible or even take legal action against those employees. Assuming that the fraud loss is recorded and reported correctly in the financial statements, the auditor then issues a clean opinion on the financial statements. But auditors can withhold a clean opinion and threaten to issue a qualified or adverse opinion if the client does not deal with the matter in a satisfactory manner in its financial statements. That's the auditor's real clout.

The most serious type of accounting fraud occurs when profit is substantially overstated with the result that the market value of the corporation's stock shares was based on inflated profit numbers. Another type of accounting fraud occurs when a business is in deep financial trouble but its balance sheet disguises the trouble and makes things look more sound than they really are. The business may be on the verge of financial failure, but the balance sheet gives no clue. When the fraud comes out into the open, the market value takes a plunge, and the investors call their lawyers and sue the business and the CPA auditor.

Investing money in a business or stock shares issued by a public business involves many risks. The risk of misleading financial statements is just one of many dangers that investors face. A business may have accurate and truthful financial statements but end up in the tank because of bad management, bad products, poor marketing, or just bad luck.

All in all, audited financial statements that carry a clean opinion (the best possible auditor's report) are reliable indicators for investors to use — especially because auditors are held accountable for their reports and can be sued for careless audit procedures. (In fact, CPA firms have had to pay many millions of dollars in malpractice lawsuit damages over the past 30 years.) Make sure that you don't overlook the audit report as a tool for judging the reliability of a business's financial statements. When I read the auditor's report on the annual financial statements from my pension fund manager, believe me, I'm very reassured! That's my retirement money they're talking about, after all.

# CPA Auditors and GAAP

In the course of doing an audit, the CPA often catches certain accounting methods used by the client that violate GAAP, the approved and authoritative methods and standards that businesses must follow in preparing and reporting financial statements. All businesses are subject to these ground rules. An auditor calls to the attention of the business any departures from GAAP, and he or she helps the business make adjustments to put its financial statements back on the GAAP track. Sometimes, a business may not want to make the changes that the auditor suggests because its profit numbers would be deflated. Professional standards demand that the auditor secure a change (assuming that the amount involved is material). If the client refuses to make a change to an acceptable accounting method, the CPA warns the financial report reader in the auditor's report.

CPA auditors do not allow their good names to be associated with financial reports that they know are misleading. Every now and then, I read in the financial press about a CPA firm walking away from a client ("withdraws from the engagement" is the official terminology). As mentioned earlier in this chapter, everything the CPA auditor learns in the course of an audit is confidential and cannot be divulged beyond top management and the board of directors of the business. A *confidential relationship* exists between the CPA auditor and the client — although it is not equal to the privileged communication between lawyers and their clients.

If a CPA auditor discovers a problem, he or she has the responsibility to move up the chain of command in the business organization to make sure that one level higher than the source of the problem is informed of the problem. But the board of directors is the end of the line. The CPA does not inform the SEC or another regulatory agency of any confidential information learned during the audit. If a CPA resigns from the audit of a public corporation, the CPA must file an information report with the SEC, but no confidential information is included. Even so, these notices to the SEC (which are public information) draw attention to what happened, and stock analysts and investment managers inquire as to why the CPA firm pulled off the audit.

I can't exaggerate the importance of reliable financial statements that are prepared according to uniform standards and methods for measuring profit and putting values on assets, liabilities, and owners' equity. Not to put too fine a point on it, but the flow of capital into businesses and the market prices of stock shares traded in the public markets (the New York Stock Exchange and over the NASDAQ network) depend on the information reported in financial statements.

Also, smaller, privately owned businesses would have a difficult time raising capital from owners and borrowing money from banks if no one could trust their financial statements. Generally accepted accounting principles, in short, are the gold standard for financial reporting. The sidebar "Setting accounting and financial reporting standards: The FASB and the SEC" presents a brief overview of how financial reporting standards are established.

Once financial reporting standards have been put into place, how are the standards enforced? To a large extent, the role of CPA auditors is to do just that — to enforce GAAP. The main purpose of having annual audits by CPAs, in other words, is to keep businesses on the straight-and-narrow path of GAAP and to prevent businesses from issuing misleading financial statements. CPAs are the guardians of the financial reporting rules. I think most business managers and investors agree that financial reporting would be in a sorry state of affairs if auditors weren't around.

# From Audits to Advising

If Rip van Winkle, CPA, woke up today after his 20-year sleep, he would be shocked to find that CPA firms make most of their money not from doing audits but from advising clients. A recent advertisement by one of the Big 5 international CPA firms listed the following services: "assurance, business consulting, corporate finance, eBusiness, human capital, legal services, outsourcing, risk consulting, and tax services." (Now, if the firm could only help me with my back problems!) Do you see audits in this list? No? Well, it's under the first category — assurance. Why have CPA firms moved so far beyond audits into many different fields of consulting?

I suspect that many businesses do not view audits as adding much value to their financial reports. True, having a clean opinion by a CPA auditor on financial statements adds credibility to a financial report. At the same time, managers tend to view the audit as an intrusion into and override on their prerogatives regarding how to account for profit and how to present the financial report of the business. Most audits, to be frank about it, involve a certain amount of tension between managers and the CPA firm. After all, the essence of an audit is to second-guess the business's accounting methods and financial reporting decisions. So it's quite understandable that CPA firms have looked to other types of services they can provide to clients that are more value-added and less adversarial — and that are more lucrative.

Nevertheless, many people argue that CPA firms should get out of the consulting and advising business — at least to the same clients they audit. Things seem to be moving in this direction. At the time of this writing, two of the Big 5 CPA firms have split-off their consulting arms. On the other hand, smaller CPA firms are refocusing their practices on providing personal financial advice and other non-audit services. Sometimes I take the pessimistic view that in the long run CPAs will abandon audits and do only taxes and consulting. Who will do audits then? Well, a cadre of governmental auditors could take over the task — but I don't think this would be too popular.

# Part V
# The Part of Tens

The 5th Wave                    By Rich Tennant

ORIGINAL VAN-GOGH OF THE MONTH CLUB

"SINCE WE BEGAN ON-LINE SHOPPING, I JUST DON'T KNOW WHERE THE MONEY'S GOING."

## In this part . . .

The Part of Tens contains two shorter chapters: one directed to business managers and the other to business investors. The former presents ten tools and techniques that are useful in running a business and getting the most from your accounting system. These top ten topics are summarized and condensed, and constitute a compact accounting tool kit for managers. The latter chapter provides investors with a checklist of the top ten things they should look for when reading a financial report in order to gain the maximum amount of information in the minimum amount of time.

# Chapter 16

# Ten Ways Savvy Business Managers Use Accounting

So how can accounting help make you a better business manager? This is the bottom-line question. Speaking of the bottom line, that's exactly the place to start. Accounting provides the financial information and analysis tools you need for making insightful profit decisions — and stops you from plunging ahead with gut decisions that may feel right but that don't hold water after due-diligent analysis.

## Make Better Profit Decisions

Making profit starts with earning margin on each unit sold and then selling enough units to overcome your total fixed expenses for the period (the basic concept that I explain more fully in Chapter 9). I condense the accounting model of profit into the following equation:

```
(Margin per unit × sales volume) - fixed expenses = profit
```

*Note:* Profit here is *before* income tax. Some businesses are organized as *pass-through* tax entities that do not pay income tax; their owners pick up the taxable income of the business in their individual tax returns. Regular corporations pay income tax based on the amount of their taxable income; different rates apply to different brackets of taxable income. The bottom-line net income in the income statement of a business is after-tax income. A business — whether a pass-through entity or a taxable corporation — may distribute all, part, or none of its profit for the year to its owners.

Insist that your accountant determine the margin per unit for all products you sell. The margin is also called the *contribution margin* to emphasize that it contributes toward the business's fixed expenses. Here's an example for determining the *margin per unit* for a product:

| Margin Factors | Amount |
|---|---|
| Sales price | $100.00 |
| Less product cost | 60.00 |
| Equals gross margin | $40.00 |
| Less sales revenue-driven expenses | 8.00 |
| Less sales volume-driven expenses | 5.00 |
| Equals margin per unit | $27.00 |

I'd bet you dollars to donuts that your accountant provides the gross margin (also called *gross profit*) on your products. So far, so good. But don't stop at the gross margin line. Push your accountant to determine the two variable expenses for each product. In this example, you don't make $40 per unit sold; you make only $27 from selling the product. Two products may have the same $40 gross profit, but one could provide a $27 margin and the other a $32 margin because the second one's variable expenses are lower.

Have your accountant differentiate between *revenue*-driven and *volume*-driven variable expenses for each product. Suppose you raise the sales price to $110.00, a 10 percent increase. The sales revenue-driven expense increases by 10 percent as well, to $8.80, because these expenses (such as sales commission) are a certain *percentage* of the sales price. Your margin increases not $10.00, but only $9.20 (the $10.00 sales price increase minus the $0.80 expense increase). In contrast, the higher sales price by itself does not increase the sales volume-driven expenses (such as shipping costs); these expenses remain at $5.00 per unit unless other factors cause them to increase.

You earn profit (or to be precise, profit before income tax) by selling enough products that your total margin is higher than your total fixed expenses for the period. The excess of total margin over fixed expenses is profit before income tax. Setting sales prices to generate an adequate total contribution margin is one of the most important functions of managers.

When thinking about changing sales price, focus on what happens to the _margin per unit._ Suppose, for example, that you're considering dropping the sales price 10 percent, from $100.00 to $90.00. You predict that your product cost and variable expenses will remain unchanged. Here's what would happen to your margin:

| Margin Factors | After | Before |
|---|---|---|
| Sales price | $90.00 | $100.00 |
| Less product cost | 60.00 | 60.00 |
| Equals gross margin | $30.00 | $40.00 |
| Less sales revenue-driven expenses | 7.20 | 8.00 |
| Less sales volume-driven expenses | 5.00 | 5.00 |
| Equals margin per unit | $17.80 | $27.00 |

Your margin would plunge $9.20 per unit — more than one-third!

Suppose you sold 100,000 units of this product during the year just ended. These sales generated $2.7 million total margin. If you drop the sales price, you give up $920,000 total margin. Where will the replacement come from for this $920,000 contribution margin? Higher sales volume? Sales volume would have to increase more than 50 percent to offset the drastic drop in the contribution margin per unit. You'd better have a good answer. The profit model directs attention to this critical question and gives you the amount of margin sacrificed by dropping the sales price.

# Understand That a Small Sales Volume Change Has a Big Effect on Profit

Is that big push before year-end for just 5 percent more sales volume really that important? You understand that more sales mean more profit, of course. But what's the big deal? Five percent more sales volume means just 5 percent more profit, doesn't it? Oh no. If you think so, you need to read Chapter 9. Because fixed expenses are just that — fixed and unchanging over the short run. Seemingly small changes in sales volume cause large swings in profit. This effect is called operating leverage.

The following example illustrates operating leverage. Suppose your $12.5 million annual fixed expenses provide the personnel and physical resources to sell 625,000 units over the year. However, you didn't hit capacity; your company's actual sales volume was 500,000 units for the year, or 80 percent of sales capacity — which isn't bad. Your average margin across all products is $30 per unit. Using the basic profit equation, you determine profit before income tax as follows:

$$[\$30 \text{ margin per unit} \times 500{,}000 \text{ units}] = \quad \$15{,}000{,}000 \quad \text{contribution margin}$$

$$\underline{-\ 12{,}500{,}000} \quad \text{fixed expenses}$$

$$=\ \$2{,}500{,}000 \quad \text{pretax profit}$$

Now, what if you had sold 25,000 more units, which is just 5 percent more sales volume? Your fixed expenses would have been the same because sales volume would still be well below the sales capacity provided by your fixed expenses. Therefore, the profit increase would have been the $30 margin per unit times the 25,000 additional units sold, or $750,000. This is a 5 percent gain in contribution margin. But compared to the $2,500,000 pretax profit, the additional $750,000 is a 30 percent gain — from only a 5 percent sales volume gain, which is a 6-to-1 payoff!

*Operating leverage* refers to the wider swing in profit than the smaller swing in sales volume. In this example, a 5 percent increase in sales volume would cause a 30 percent increase in profit. Unfortunately, operating leverage cuts both ways. If your sales volume had been 5 percent less, your profit would have been $750,000 less, which would have resulted in 30 percent less profit.

Here's a quick explanation of operating leverage. In this example, total contribution margin is 6 times profit: $15 million contribution margin ÷ $2.5 million profit = 6. So a 5 percent swing in contribution margin has a 6-times effect, or a 30 percent impact, on profit. Suppose a business had no fixed expenses (highly unlikely). In this odd situation, there is no operating leverage. The percentage gain or loss in profit would equal the percentage gain or loss in sales volume.

The fundamental lesson of operating leverage is to make the best use you can of your fixed expenses — that is, take advantage of the capacity provided by the resources purchased with your fixed expenses. If your sales volume is less than your sales capacity, the unsold quantity would have provided a lot more profit. Most businesses are satisfied if their actual sales volume is 80 to 90 percent of their sales capacity. But keep in mind one thing: That last 10 or 20 percent of sales volume would make a dramatic difference in profit!

# *Fathom Profit and Cash Flow from Profit*

Profit equals sales revenue minus expenses — you don't need to know much about accounting to understand this definition. However, business managers should dig a little deeper. First, you should be aware of the accounting problems in measuring sales revenue and expenses. Because of these problems, profit is not a clear-cut and precise number. Second, you should know the real stuff of profit and know where to find profit in your financial statements.

*Profit* is not a politically correct term. Instead, business financial reports call profit *net income* or *net earnings*. So don't look for the term *profit* in external financial statements. Remember, net income (or net earnings) = bottom-line profit after income tax.

## Profit accounting methods are like hemlines

Profit is not a hard-and-fast number but is rather soft and flexible on the edges. For example, profit depends on which accounting method is selected to measure the cost-of-goods-sold expense, which is usually the largest expense for businesses that sell products. The rules of the game, called *generally accepted accounting principles* (or GAAP for short), permit two or three alternative methods for measuring cost of goods sold and for other expenses as well. (Chapter 13 discusses accounting methods.)

When evaluating the profit performance of your own business or when sizing up the net income record of a business you're considering buying, look carefully at whether profit measurement is based on stingy (conservative) or generous (liberal) accounting methods. You can assume that profit is in the GAAP ballpark, but you have to determine whether profit is in the right field or the left field (or perhaps in center field). Businesses are not required to disclose how different the profit number would have been for the period if different accounting methods had been used, but they do have to reveal their major accounting methods in the footnotes to their annual financial statements.

## The real stuff of profit

Most people know that, in the general sense of the word, *profit* is a gain, or an increase in wealth, or how much better off you are. But managers and investors hit the wall when asked to identify the real stuff of profit earned by a business. To make my point, suppose that your business's latest annual income statement reports $10 million sales revenue and $9.4 million expenses, which yields $600,000 bottom-line net income. Your profit ratio is 6 percent of sales revenue, which is about typical for many businesses. But I digress.

My question is this: *Where is that $600,000 of profit?* Can you find and locate the profit earned by your business? Is it in cash? If not, where is it? If you can't answer this question, aren't you a little embarrassed? Quick — go read Chapter 5!

Profit accounting is more complicated than simple cash-in, cash-out book-keeping. Sales for cash increase cash, of course, but sales on credit initially increase an asset called accounts receivable. So *two* assets are used in recording sales revenue. Usually, a minimum of four assets and two liabilities are used in recording a business's expenses. To locate profit, you have to look at all the assets and liabilities that are changed by revenue and expenses. The *measure* of profit is found in the income statement. But the *substance* of profit is found in assets and liabilities, which are reported in the *balance sheet*.

As your accountant, I have determined that your $600,000 net income consists of the following three components:

```
$600,000 profit = $420,000 cash + $290,000 net increase in
           other assets - $110,000 increase in liabilities
```

This is a typical scenario for the makeup of profit — I don't mean the dollar amounts but rather the three components of profit. The dollar amounts of the increases or decreases in assets and liabilities vary from business to business, of course, and from year to year. But rarely would the profit equation be

```
$600,000 profit = $600,000 cash
```

Cash is only one piece of the profit pie. Business managers need accounting to sort out how profit is divided among the three components — in particular, you need to know the cash flow generated from profit.

# Govern Cash Flow Better

My youngest son, Tage, a successful business consultant, has a favorite saying: "If we're in the black, where's the green?" Being *in the black* means making a profit, as you probably have heard. By "green," Tage means, "Where's the cash? Where's the money to show for the profit?" Making profit does not generate immediate cash flow. Seldom does $1 of profit equal $1 of immediate cash flow, as Chapter 7 describes in detail.

A business wants to make profit, of course, but equally important, a business must convert its profit into *usable cash flow*. Profit that is never turned into cash or is not turned into cash for a long time is not very helpful. A business needs cash flow from profit to provide money for three critical uses:

   ✔ To distribute some of its profit to its equity (owner) sources of capital —
      to provide a cash income to them as compensation for their capital
      investment in the business

✔ To grow the business — to invest in new fixed (long-term) operating assets and to increase its inventory and other short-term operating assets

✔ To meet its debt payment obligations and to maintain the general liquidity and solvency of the business

One expense, depreciation, is not a cash outlay in the period it's recorded as an expense. Rather, depreciation expense for a period is an allocated amount of the original cost of the business's fixed assets that were bought and paid for in previous years. More importantly, the sales revenue collected by the business includes money for its depreciation expense. Thus the business converts back into cash some of the money that it put in its fixed assets years ago. Understanding how depreciation works in cash flow analysis is very important.

In one sense, you can say that depreciation generates cash flow. But please be careful here. This does *not* mean that if you had recorded more depreciation expense, you would have had more cash flow. What it means is that through making sales at prices that include recovery of some of the cost of fixed assets, your sales revenue (to the extent that it is collected by year-end) includes cash flow to offset the depreciation expense.

To illustrate this critical point, suppose a business did not make a profit for the year but did manage to break even. In this zero-profit situation, there is cash flow from profit because of depreciation. The company would realize cash flow equal to its depreciation for the year — assuming that it collected its sales revenue. Depreciation is a process of recycling fixed assets back into cash during the year, whether or not the business makes a profit.

In the example in the preceding section, the business earned $600,000 net income (profit). But its cash increased only $420,000. Why? The *cash flow statement* provides the details. In addition to reporting the depreciation for the year, the first section of the cash flow statement reports the short-term operating asset and liability changes caused by the business's sales and expenses. These changes either help or hurt cash flow from profit (from operating activities, to use the correct technical accounting term).

An increase in accounts receivable hurts cash flow from profit because the business did not collect all its sales on credit for the year. An increase in inventory hurts cash flow from profit because the business replaces the products sold and spends more money to increase its inventory of products. On the other hand, an increase in accounts payable or accrued expenses payable helps cash flow from profit. These two liabilities are, basically, unpaid expenses. When these liabilities increase, the business did not pay all its expenses for the year — and its cash outflows for expenses were less than its expenses.

Generally speaking, growth hurts cash flow from profit. To grow its sales and profit, a business usually has to increase its accounts receivable and inventory. Some of this total increase is offset by increases in the business's short-term operating liabilities. Usually, the increase in assets is more than the increase in liabilities, and therefore cash flow from profit suffers. When a business suffers a decline in sales revenue, its bottom-line profit usually goes down — but its cash flow from profit may not drop as much as net income, or perhaps not at all. A business should decrease its accounts receivable and inventory at the lower sales level; these decreases help cash flow from profit. Even if a business reported a loss for the year, its cash flow from profit could be positive because of the depreciation factor and because the business may have reduced its accounts receivable and inventory.

# Call the Shots on Your Accounting Methods

Business managers too often defer to their accountants — who are not called "bean counters" and "digitheads" for nothing — in choosing accounting methods for measuring sales revenue and expenses. You should get involved in making these decisions. The best accounting method is the one that best fits the operating methods and strategies of your business. As a business manager, you know these operating methods and strategies better than your accountant. Chapter 13 gives you the details on various accounting methods.

For example, consider sales prices. How do you set your sales prices? Many factors affect your sales prices, of course. What I'm asking here concerns your general sales pricing policy relative to product cost changes. For example, if your product cost goes up, do you allow your "old" stock of these products to sell out before you raise the sales price? In other words, do you generally wait until you start selling the more recently acquired, higher-cost products before you raise your sales price? If so, you're using the first-in, first-out (FIFO) method. You might prefer to keep your cost-of-goods-sold expense method consistent with your sales pricing method. But the accountant may choose the last-in, first-out (LIFO) expense method, which would mismatch the higher-cost products with the lower-sales-price products.

The point is this: Business managers formulate a basic strategy regarding expense recovery. Sales revenue has to recoup your expenses to make a profit. How do you pass along your expenses to your customers in the sales prices you charge them? Do you attempt to recover the cost of your fixed assets as quickly as possible and set your sales prices on this basis? Then you should use a fast, or *accelerated,* depreciation method. On the other hand, if you take longer to recover the cost of your fixed assets through sales revenue, then you should probably use the longer-life *straight-line* depreciation method.

In short, I encourage you to take charge and choose the accounting methods that best fit your strategic profit plan. You need to speak some of the accounting language and know which accounting methods are available. This is comparable to deciding which type of retirement income plan to provide for your employees — a traditional pension (defined benefit) plan, a 401(k) (defined contribution) plan, or perhaps a cash balance plan. You'd carefully compare the alternatives, listen to the experts, and make a decision. You should do the same in deciding the key accounting methods for measuring profit. The bonus is that you will have a much better appreciation of how your profit measure depends on which accounting methods are used to measure sales revenue and expenses.

In short, business managers should take charge of the accounting function just like they take charge of marketing and other key functions of the business.

# Build Better Budgets

Budgeting (explained in Chapter 10) provides important advantages — first, for understanding the profit dynamics and financial structure of your business, and second, for planning for changes in the coming period. Budgeting forces you to focus on the factors that have to improve in order to increase profit and helps you prepare for the future. The basic profit model provides the framework for the profit budget. A good profit model is the essential starting point for budgeting. To develop your profit plan for the coming year, focus on

- Margins
- Sales volume
- Fixed expenses

The profit budget, in turn, lays the foundation for changes in your operating assets and liabilities that are driven by sales revenue and expenses. Suppose you project a 10 percent rise in sales revenue. How much will your accounts receivable asset increase? Suppose your sales volume target for next year is 15 percent higher than this year. How much will your inventory increase? The budgeted changes in sales revenue and expenses for next year lead directly to the budgeted changes in operating assets and operating liabilities. These changes, in turn, direct attention to two other key issues.

First, if things go according to plan, how much cash flow from profit will be generated? Second, will you need more capital, and where will you get this money? You need the budgeted cash flow from profit (operating activities) for the coming year for three basic financial planning decisions:

- ✔ **Cash distributions from profit to owners** (cash dividends to stockholders of corporations and cash distributions to the shareholders of LLCs and to partners)

- ✔ **Capital expenditures** (purchases of new fixed assets to replace and upgrade old fixed assets and to expand the business's capacity)

- ✔ **Raising capital** from borrowing on debt and, possibly, raising new equity capital from owners

The higher your budgeted cash flow from profit, the more flexibility you have in having money available for cash distributions from profit and for capital expenditures, and the less pressure to go out and raise new capital from debt and equity sources of capital.

To sum up, your profit budget is dovetailed with the assets and liabilities budget and the cash flow budget. Your accountant takes your profit budget (your strategic plan for improving profit) and builds the budgeted balance sheet and the budgeted cash flow statement. This information is essential for good planning — focusing in particular on how much cash flow from profit will be realized and how much capital expenditures will be required, which in turn lead to how much additional capital you have to raise and how much cash distribution from profit you will be able to make.

# Optimize Capital Structure and Financial Leverage

My friend Ron, who works part-time at the local Greyhound dog track and owns a florist business, made this point one night: "To make profit, you must make sales." I quickly added that you also must invest in operating assets, which means that you must raise capital. Where do you get this money? Debt and equity are the two basic sources. *Equity* refers to the money that owners invest in a business with the hopes that the business will turn a profit. Profit builds the value of owner's equity; profit fundamentally is an increase in assets that accrues to the benefit of the owners. Chapter 11 discusses ownership structures; Chapter 6 covers debt and equity.

The return on the owners' equity interest in the business consists of two quite distinct parts:

- ✔ Cash distributions from profit to the owners
- ✔ Increases in the value of their ownership interest in the business

In contrast, lenders are paid a *fixed* rate of interest on the amount borrowed. This fixed nature of interest expense causes a *financial leverage* effect that either benefits or hurts the amount of profit remaining for the equity investors in the business.

Financial leverage refers in general to using debt in addition to equity capital. A financial leverage gain (or loss) refers to the difference between the earnings before interest and tax (EBIT) that a business can make on its debt capital versus the interest paid on the debt. The following example illustrates a case of financial leverage gain.

Your business earned $2.1 million EBIT for the year just ended. Your net operating assets are $12 million — recall that net operating assets equal total assets less non-interest-bearing operating liabilities (mainly accounts payable and accrued expenses payable). Thus your total capital sources equal $12 million. Suppose you have $4 million debt. The other $8 million is owners' equity. You paid 8 percent annual interest on your debt, or $320,000 total interest. Debt furnishes one-third of your capital, so one-third of EBIT is attributed to this capital source. One-third of EBIT is $700,000. But you paid only $320,000 interest for this capital. You earned $380,000 more than the interest. This is the amount of your pretax *financial leverage gain*.

Three factors determine financial leverage gain (or loss):

- ✔ Proportion of total capital provided from debt
- ✔ Interest rate
- ✔ Return on assets (ROA), or the rate of EBIT the business can earn on its total capital invested in its net operating assets

In the example, your business earned 17.5 percent on its net operating assets ($2.1 million EBIT ÷ $12 million total net operating assets). You used $4 million debt capital for the investment in your net operating assets, and you paid 8 percent annual interest on the debt, which gives a favorable 9.5 percent spread (17.5 percent – 8 percent). The 9.5 percent favorable spread times $4 million debt equals the $380,000 leverage gain for the year (before income tax).

Business managers should watch how much financial leverage gain contributes to the earnings for owners each year. In this example, the after-interest earnings for owners is $1,780,000 (equal to EBIT less interest expense). The $380,000 financial leverage gain provided a good part of this amount. Next year, one or more of the three factors driving the financial leverage gain may change. Savvy business managers sort out each year how much financial leverage impacts the earnings available for owners.

A financial leverage gain enhances the earnings on owners' equity capital. The conventional wisdom is that a business should take advantage of debt that charges a lower interest rate than it can earn on the debt capital. Looking at the bigger picture, however, the long-run success of a business depends mainly on maintaining and improving the factors that determine its profit from operations (EBIT) — rather than going overboard and depending too much on financial leverage.

# Develop Better Financial Controls

Experienced business managers can tell you that they spend a good deal of time dealing with problems. Things don't always go according to plan. Murphy's Law (if something can go wrong, it will, and usually at the worst possible time) is all too true. To solve a problem, you first have to know that you have one. You can't solve a problem if you don't know about it. Managers are problem-solvers; they need to get on top of problems as soon as possible. In short, business managers need to develop good *financial controls*.

Financial controls act like trip wires that sound alarms and wave red flags for a manager's attention. Many financial controls are accounting-based. For example, actual costs are compared with budgeted costs or against last period's costs; serious variances are highlighted for immediate management attention. Actual sales revenue for product lines and territories are compared with budgeted goals or last period's numbers. Cash flow from profit period by period is compared with the budgeted amount of cash flow for the period from this source. These many different financial controls don't just happen. You should identify the handful of critical factors that you need to keep a close eye on and insist that your internal accounting reports highlight these operating ratios and numbers.

Only you, the business manager, can single out the most important numbers that you must closely watch to know how things are going. Your accountant can't read your mind. If your regular accounting reports do not include the exact types of control information you need, sit down with your accountant and spell out in detail what you want to know. Don't take no for an answer. Don't let your accountant argue that the computer doesn't keep track of this information. Computers can be programmed to spit out any type of information you want.

The accounting profit model discussed in Chapter 9 is an excellent place to start. You must closely watch the margins on your products. Any deviation from the norm — even a relatively small deviation — needs your attention immediately. Remember that the margin per unit is multiplied by sales volume. If you sell 100,000 units of a product, a slippage of just 50 cents causes your total margin to fall $50,000. Of course, sales volume must be closely watched, too; that goes without saying. Fixed expenses should be watched in the early months of the year to see whether these costs are developing according to plan — and through the entire year.

Accounts receivable collections should be monitored closely. Average days before collection is a good control ratio to keep your eye on, and you should definitely get a listing of past-due customers' accounts. Inventory is always a problem area. Watch closely the average days in stock before products are sold, and get a listing of slow-moving products. Experience is the best teacher. Over time, you learn which financial controls are the most important to highlight in your internal accounting reports. The trick is to make sure that your accountants provide this information.

# Minimize Income Tax

The first decision regarding income tax concerns which type of legal owner-ship structure to use for carrying on the activities of the business, which is discussed in Chapter 11. When two or more owners provide capital for the business, you have four basic choices:

- ✔ A *partnership* — a specific contractual agreement among the owners regarding division of management authority, responsibilities, and profit

- ✔ A *limited liability company* (LLC), which has many characteristics of a partnership but is a separate legal entity, like a corporation

- ✔ An *S corporation,* which has 75 or fewer stockholders (owners)

- ✔ A *regular* or *C corporation* that cannot qualify as an S corporation or that could qualify but its stockholders do not elect to do so

Partnerships, LLCs, and S corporations are *pass-through* tax entities. A pass-through business entity pays no tax on its taxable income but passes the obligation to its owners, who pick up their shares of the total taxable income in their individual income tax returns. In contrast, the individual stockhold-ers of regular (C) corporations pay tax only on the amount of actual cash div-idends from profit distributed by the corporation. Keep in mind here that the corporation pays an income tax based on its taxable income. Except for very small and very large businesses, the basic corporate tax rate in 2000 is 34 percent of taxable income. Factors other than income tax affect the choice of ownership structure. You need the advice of tax professionals and financial consultants.

Regardless of the ownership structure, you should understand how accounting methods determine taxable income. Basically, the choice of accounting methods enables you to shift the timing of expenses — such as depreciation and cost of goods sold — between early years and later years. Do you want more expense deductions this year? Then choose the last-in, first-out (LIFO) method for cost-of-goods-sold expense and an accelerated method for depreciation. But keep in mind that what you gain today, you lose tomorrow. Higher expense deductions in early years cause lower deductions in later years. Also, these income-tax-driven accounting choices make the inventory and fixed assets in your balance sheet look anemic. Remember that expenses are asset decreases. You want more expense? Then lower asset values are reported in your balance sheet.

Think twice before jumping on the income tax minimization bandwagon. Knowing about accounting methods and their effects in both the income statement and the balance sheet helps you make these important decisions.

# Explain Your Financial Statements to Others

On many occasions, as a business manager you have to explain your financial statements to others:

✔ When applying for a loan — especially when the loan officer asks specific questions about your accounting methods and items in your financial statements

✔ When talking with people or other businesses who may be interested in buying your business — and they ask questions about the book values of your assets and your accounting methods to measure profit

✔ When dealing with the press — large corporations, of course, but even smaller businesses are profiled in local news stories

✔ When dealing with unions or other employee groups in setting new wages and benefit packages, who may think that your profits are very high, so you can afford to increase wages and benefits, and who generally have little appreciation for the need to earn a fair rate of return on equity capital

✔ When explaining the profit-sharing plan to your employees — who may take a close interest in how profit is determined

✔ When putting a value on an ownership interest for divorce or estate tax purposes — a difficult time, but the lawyer or executor of the estate needs these values, which are based on the financial statements of the business (and other factors)

✔ When reporting financial statement data to national trade associations that collect this information from their members — you should make sure that you're reporting the financial information consistent with the definitions used in the industry

✔ When presenting the annual financial report before the annual meeting of owners, who ask penetrating questions and expect you to be very familiar with the financial statements and basic accounting methods used to prepare them

Knowledge of financial statement reporting and accounting methods is also extremely useful when you sit on a bank's board of directors, or a hospital board, or any of several other types of oversight boards (university regents, for example). In the preceding list, you're the explainer, the one who has to do the explaining. As a board member, you're the explainee, the person who has to make sense of the financial statements and accounting methods being presented. A good accounting foundation is invaluable.

Part II of this book shows you how to understand financial reports. In brief, you need a good grip on the purpose, nature, and limitations of each of the three primary financial statements reported by a business:

✔ **The income statement:** Many people think that bottom-line profit is cash in the bank, but you know better.

✔ **The cash flow statement:** Many people just add back depreciation to net income to determine cash flow from profit, but you know better.

✔ **The balance sheet:** Many people think that this financial statement reports the current values for assets, but you know better.

I'll tell you one disadvantage of knowing some accounting: The other members of the board will be very impressed with your accounting smarts and may want to elect you chairperson.

# A short word on massaging the numbers: Don't!

For 39 years at Berkeley and Boulder, I taught accounting to future business managers and CPAs. I didn't encourage profit smoothing, window dressing, and other techniques for manipulating accounting numbers to make a company's financial statements look better — no more than my marketing professor colleagues encouraged their students to engage in deceptive advertising tactics. Yet these things go on, and I felt obligated to expose my students to these practices as a warning that accountants face difficult moral decisions. In a similar vein, I caution you, a business manager, that you will surely face pressures from time to time to massage the accounting numbers — to make profit look smoother from year to year, or to make the short-term solvency of the business look better (by window dressing).

# Chapter 17

# Ten Questions Investors Should Ask When Reading a Financial Report

· · · · · · · · · · · · · · · · · · · · · · · · · · · · · · · · · · · · · · · · · · · · · · · · · · · ·

### In This Chapter

▶ Analyzing sales and profit performance

▶ Evaluating earnings per share performance

▶ Investigating changes in assets and liabilities

▶ Interpreting cash flow from profit

▶ Looking for signs of financial distress

▶ Examining asset utilization and return on capital investment

· · · · · · · · · · · · · · · · · · · · · · · · · · · · · · · · · · · · · · · · · · · · · · · · · · · ·

You have only so much time to search for the most important signals in a business's financial report. You could read a financial report like a book, from the first page to the last, but this approach is not very practical. (See "Browsing versus Reading Financial Reports" in Chapter 8.) For a quick read through a financial report — one that allows you to decode the critical signals in the financial statements — you need a checklist of key questions to ask. I advise you to look for answers to the following basic questions, which help you understand what sort of investment you may be getting into — or, if you already have money invested in the business, the answers tell you how the company is doing and whether you should consider pulling your hard-earned money out of the business and putting it in another investment.

Before you read a business's annual financial report, get up to speed on which products and services the business sells — automobiles, computers, airlines, and heavy equipment manufacturers are quite different businesses, for example — and learn about the history of the business and any current problems it's facing. Is the business presently the target of a hostile takeover attempt? Is the business looking for a new CEO? Has the company recently shifted its strategy? One place to find much of this information is the company's annual 10-K filed with the Securities & Exchange Commission, which is a public document available to everyone. (For 10-Ks and other filings with the SEC, go to www.sec.gov/edgarhp.htm.) Company profiles are prepared by securities brokers and investment advisors, and they're very useful. *The Wall Street Journal* and other national newspapers, such as *The New York Times,* are good sources of information about public corporations. Last but not least, many annual financial reports often present an overview of the products and services sold by the business, although some businesses are stingy in presenting this information.

# Did Sales Grow?

Ron, that friend of mine who owns a flower business in Denver and whom I quote in Chapter 16, hit the nail on the head: He said that a business makes profit by making sales (although you do have to take controlling expenses into account). Sales growth is the key to long-run sustained profit growth. Even if profit is up, investors get worried when sales revenue is flat.

 Start reading a financial report by comparing this year's sales revenue with last year's, and with all prior years included in the financial report. A company's sales trend is the most important factor affecting its profit trend. I dare you to find a business that has had a steady downward sales trend line but a steady upward profit line — you'd be looking for a long time.

# Did the Profit Ratios Hold?

Higher sales from one year to the next don't necessarily mean higher profit. You also need to look at whether the business was able to maintain its profit ratio at the higher sales level. Recall that the *profit ratio* is net income divided by sales revenue. If the business earned, say, a 6 percent profit ratio last year, did it maintain or perhaps improve this ratio on its higher sales revenue this year?

Also compare the company's *gross margin ratios* from year to year. Cost-of-goods-sold expense is reported by companies that sell products. Recall that gross margin equals sales revenue less cost of goods sold. Any significant slippage in a company's gross margin ratio (gross margin divided by sales revenue) is a very serious matter. Suppose that a company gives up two or three points (one point = 1 percent) of its gross margin ratio. How can it make up for this loss? Decreasing its other operating expenses isn't easy or very practical — unless the business has allowed its operating expenses to become bloated.

In most external financial reports, profit ratios are *not* discussed openly and frankly, especially when things have not gone well for the business. You usually have to go digging for these important ratios and use your calculator. Articles in the financial press on the most recent earnings of public corporations focus on gross margin and profit ratios — for good reason. I always keep an eye on profit as a percentage of sales revenue, even though I have to calculate this key ratio for most businesses. I wish that all businesses would provide this ratio.

# Were There Any Unusual, Extraordinary Gains or Losses?

Every now and then, a business records an *unusual* or *extraordinary* gain or loss. The first section of the income statement reports sales revenue and the expenses of making the sales and operating the business. Also, interest and income tax expenses are deducted. Be careful: The profit down to this point may *not* be the final bottom line. The profit down to this point is from the business's ongoing, normal operations before any unusual, one-time gains or losses are recorded. The next layer of the income statement reports these extraordinary, nonrecurring gains or losses that the business recorded during the period.

These gains or losses are called extraordinary because they do not recur — or at least should not recur, although some companies report these gains and losses on a regular basis. These gains and losses are caused by a *discontinuity* in the business — such as a major organizational restructuring involving a reduction in the workforce and paying substantial severance packages to laid-off employees, selling off major assets and product lines of the business, retiring a huge amount of debt at a big gain or loss, and settling a huge lawsuit against the business. Generally, the gain or loss is reported on one line net of the income tax effect for each extraordinary item, and a brief explanation can be found in the footnotes to the financial statements.

Investors have to watch the pattern of these items over the years. An extraordinary gain or loss now and then is a normal part of doing business and is nothing to be alarmed about. However, a business that reports one or two of these gains or losses every year or every other year is suspect. These gains or losses may be evidence of past turmoil and future turbulence. I classify these businesses as high-risk investments — because you don't know what to expect in the future.

In any case, I advise you to consider whether an unusual loss is the cumulative result of inadequate accounting for expenses in previous years. A large legal settlement, for example, may be due to the business refusing to admit that it is selling unsafe products year after year; its liability finally catches up with it.

Many businesses use the occasion of recording extraordinary losses to take a "big bath." In addition to the losses that have to recorded, a business also records every kind of loss it can think up, plus an extra amount for good measure. Of course, the huge amount of losses for the period draws adverse attention to the business. Because the business has to endure bad publicity anyway, management decides that the company may as well pile it on and record extra losses, which won't make the adverse attention any worse than it would be otherwise. The motive for taking a big bath is to record losses now, in the period just ended, and get these losses behind you — thereby relieving future periods of having to report the losses. In other words, the business takes a big hit this period and in doing so clears the decks for future periods.

# Did Earnings Per Share Keep Up with Profit?

Chapter 14 explains that a publicly owned business with a simple capital structure — meaning that the business is not required to issue additional stock shares in the future — reports just one earnings per share (EPS) for the period, which is called *basic* EPS. You calculate basic EPS by using the actual number of shares owned by stockholders. However, many publicly owned businesses have complex capital structures that require them to issue additional stock shares in the future. These businesses report *two* EPS numbers — basic EPS and *diluted* EPS. The diluted EPS figure is based on a larger number of stock shares that includes the additional number of shares that will be issued under terms of management stock options, convertible debt, and other contractual obligations that require the business to issue stock shares in the future.

In analyzing earnings per share, therefore, you may have to put on your bifocals, as it were. For many businesses, you have to look at both basic EPS and diluted EPS. I suppose you could invest only in companies that report only basic EPS, but this investment strategy would eliminate a large number of businesses from your stock investment portfolio. Odds are, your stock investments include companies that report both basic and diluted EPS. The two EPS figures may not be too far apart, but then again, diluted EPS may be substantially less than basic EPS for some businesses.

Suppose you own stock in a public corporation that reports bottom-line net income that is 10 percent higher than last year's. So far, so good. But you know that the market price of your stock shares depends on earnings per share (EPS). Ask what happened to basic and diluted EPS. Did both EPS figures go up 10 percent? Not necessarily — the answer is often "no," in fact. You have to check.

Public corporations whose stock shares are traded on one of the national stock exchanges (New York Stock Exchange, NASDAQ, American Stock Exchange, and so on) are required to report EPS in their income statements, so you don't have to do any computations. (Private businesses whose shares are not traded do not have to report EPS.)

You often find that a business increased (or perhaps decreased) its total number of stock shares during the year. For example, some executives may have exercised stock options during the year and bought some shares. Or employees may have bought shares under the company's stock purchase plan. Or the business may have issued stock shares in the acquisition of other businesses during the year. Or the holders of convertible securities previously issued by the business may have converted their holdings into stock shares during the year.

EPS increases exactly the same percentage that net income increases only if the total number of stock shares remains constant. Usually, this is not the case. Many public corporations have a fair amount of activity in their stock shares during the year. So they include a schedule of changes in stockholders' equity during the year. (Chapter 8 discusses this financial summary of changes in stockholders' equity.) Look at this schedule to find out how many shares were issued during the year. Also, corporations may purchase some of their own stock during the year, which is reported in this schedule.

Suppose net income increased, say, 10.0 percent, but basic EPS increased only 6.8 percent because the number of stock shares issued by the business increased 3.0 percent during the year. (You can check the computation if you like.) You should definitely look into why additional shares were issued. And if diluted EPS does not keep pace with the company's earnings increase, you should pinpoint why the number of shares included in the calculation of diluted EPS increased during the period. (Maybe more management stock options were awarded during the year.)The number of stock shares may increase again next year and the year after. Businesses do not comment on why the percent change in their EPS is not the same as the percent change in their net income. I wish that companies were required to leave a clear explanation of any difference in the percent of change in EPS compared with the percent of change in net income. However, this is just wishful thinking on my part. You have to ferret out this information on your own, which I advise you to do.

An increase in EPS may not be due entirely to an increase in net income, but rather to a *decrease* in the number of stock shares. Cash-rich companies often buy their stock shares to reduce the total number of shares that is divided into net income, thereby increasing basic and diluted EPS. You should pay close attention to increases in EPS that result from decreases in the number of stock shares. The long-run basis of EPS growth is profit growth, although a decrease in the number of stock shares helps EPS and, hopefully, the market price of the stock shares.

# Did the Profit Increase Generate a Cash Flow Increase?

Increasing profit is all well and good, but you also should ask: Did *cash flow from profit* increase? Cash flow from profit is found in the first section of the cash flow statement, which is one of the three primary financial statements included in a financial report. The cash flow statement begins with an explanation of cash flow from profit.

Accountants use the term *cash flow from operating activities* — which, in my opinion, is not nearly as descriptive as *cash flow from profit.* The term *profit* is avoided like the plague in external financial reports; it's not a politically correct word. So you may think that accountants would use the phrase *cash flow from net income.* But no, the official pronouncement on the cash flow statement mandated the term *cash flow from operating activities. Operating activities* refers simply to sales revenue and expenses, which are the profit-making operations of a business. I'll stick with *cash flow from profit* — please don't report me to the accounting authorities.

Almost all expenses are bad for cash flow, except one: depreciation. Depreciation expense is actually good for cash flow. Each year, a business converts part of the cost of its fixed assets back into cash through the cash collections from sales made during the year. Over time, fixed assets are gradually used up, so each year is charged with part of the fixed assets' cost by recording depreciation expense. And each year, a business retrieves cash for part of the cost of its fixed assets. Thus depreciation expense decreases profit but increases cash flow. But net income plus depreciation does not equal cash flow from profit — except in the imaginary scenario in which all the company's other operating assets (mainly accounts receivable and inventory) and all its operating liabilities (mainly accounts payable and accrued expenses payable) don't increase or decrease during the year.

For example, a company's higher sales revenue for the year usually causes its accounts receivable to increase, so its cash collections from customers are less than its sales revenue. The business may have increased its inventory, which uses up cash. A business may have run up the balances of its unpaid expenses at year-end, which conserves cash. The first section of the cash flow statement summarizes these changes that affect cash flow from profit.

The key question is: Should cash flow from profit change about the same amount as net income changed, or is it normal for the change in cash flow to be higher or lower than the change in net income?

As a general rule, sales growth penalizes cash flow from profit in the short run. A business has to build up its accounts receivable and inventory, and these increases hurt cash flow — although, during growth periods, a business also increases its accounts payable and accrued expenses payable, which helps cash flow. The asset increases, in most cases, dominate the liability increases, and cash flow from profit suffers.

I strongly advise you to compare cash flow from operating activities (see, I use the officially correct term here) with net income for each of the past two or three years. Is cash flow from profit about the same percentage of net income each year? What does the trend look like? For example, last year, cash flow from profit may have been 90 percent of net income, but this year it may have dropped to 50 percent. (You have to pull out your calculator and divide cash flow from profit by net income; businesses do not report this ratio.) In this situation, the company's profit is not being converted into cash flow at the same pace as it was the preceding year. Don't hit the panic button just yet.

A dip in cash flow from profit in one year actually may be good from the long-run point of view — the business may be laying a good foundation for supporting a higher level of sales. But then again, the slowdown in cash flow from profit could present a short-term cash problem that the business has to deal with.

A company's cash flow from profit may be a trickle instead of a stream. In fact, cash flow from profit could be *negative;* in making a profit, the company could be draining its cash reserves. The business may have to curtail its cash distributions to owners. And it may have to raise capital from debt and equity to provide money for replacing and expanding its fixed assets. Low cash flow from profit, in an extreme case, may even raise questions about the *quality of earnings,* which refers to the credibility and soundness of the net income reported by a business. Cash flow from profit is low, in most cases, because accounts receivable from sales haven't been collected and because the business has made large increases in its inventories. These large increases raise questions about whether all the receivables will be collected and whether all the inventory will be sold at regular prices. Only time can tell. But generally speaking, you should be cautious and take the net income number that the business reports with a grain of salt.

Analyzing cash flow from *loss* (instead of from profit) is very important. When a company reports a loss for the year — instead of a profit — an immediate question is whether the company's cash reserve will buy it enough time to move out of the loss column into the profit column. When a business is in a loss situation (the early years of a start-up business, for example) and its cash flow from operating activities is negative, focus on the company's cash balance and how long the business can keep going until it turns the corner and becomes profitable. Stock analysts use the term *burn rate* to refer to how much cash outflow the business is using up each period. They compare this measure of how much cash the business is hemorrhaging each period to its present cash balance. The key question is this: Does the business have enough cash on hand to tide it over until it starts to generate positive cash flow from profit, and if not, where will it get more money to burn until it can record a profit?

# Are Increases in Assets and Liabilities Consistent with the Business's Growth?

Publicly owned businesses present their financial statements in a three-year comparative format (or sometimes a two-year comparative format). Strictly speaking, the language of GAAP does not require comparative financial statements — although all businesses, private and public, are encouraged to present comparative financial statements. Filings with the SEC require three-year comparative financial statements. Furthermore, business stock investors and lenders demand comparative financial statements. Thus three columns of numbers are reported in income statements, balance sheets, and cash flow statements — for the years 2001, 2000, and 1999, for instance. To keep financial statement illustrations in this book as brief as possible, I present only one year; I do not include two additional columns for the two previous years. Please keep this point in mind.

Presenting financial statements in a three-year comparative format, as may be obvious, helps the reader make year-to-year comparisons. Of course, you have to deal with three times as many numbers in a three-year comparative financial statement compared with a one-year financial statement. And I should point out that the *amounts of changes* are not presented; you either eyeball the changes or use a calculator to compute the amounts of changes during the year. For example, the ending balances of a business's property, plant, and equipment asset account may be reported as follows (in millions of dollars): $4,097, $4,187, and $3,614 for the fiscal years ending in 2001, 2000, and 1999. Only these ending balances are presented in the company's comparative balance sheet — the increase or decrease during the year is not presented.

A three-year comparative format enables you to see the general trend of sales revenue and expenses from year to year and the general drift in the amounts of the company's assets, liabilities, and owners' equity accounts. You can easily spot any major differences in each line of the cash flow statement across the years. Whether you just cast a glance at adjacent amounts or actually calculate changes, ask yourself whether the increases of a company's assets and liabilities reported in its balance sheet are consistent with the sales growth of the business from year to year.

Suppose a company's sales grew 10 percent over last year. This doesn't mean that every asset and liability should increase precisely 10 percent. But then again, if the increase is too far off 10 percent, you should look more closely. Check to see whether the company's accounts receivable are growing at a faster rate than its sales revenues. If so, the company may be having trouble getting its customers to pay up, possibly because the customers aren't happy with the company's products or services. Or a big blimp in accounts receivable might mean that the business gave its customers more liberal credit terms this year.

Suppose inventory went up, say, 30 percent, but sales revenue increased only 10 percent. The business obviously bought or manufactured more products than it sold — quite a bit more. At the next annual stockholders meeting, I would definitely ask the CEO about this. And I would ask what the company plans to do next year to bring inventory back into line with sales.

Unusually large increases in assets that are greatly out of line with the company's sales revenue growth put pressure on cash flow and could cast serious doubts on the company's solvency — which I explain in the next section.

# Are There Any Signs of Financial Distress? Will the Business Be Able to Pay Its Liabilities?

A business can build up a good sales volume and have very good profit margins, but if the company can't pay its bills on time, its profit opportunities could go down the drain. *Solvency* refers to the prospects of a business being able to meet its debt and other liability payment obligations on time. Solvency analysis asks whether a business will be able to pay its liabilities, looking for signs of financial distress that could cause serious disruptions in the business's profit-making operations. In short, even if a business has a couple billion bucks in the bank, you should ask: How does its solvency look?

To be solvent does not mean that a business must have cash in the bank equal to its total liabilities. Suppose, for example, that a business has $2 million in non-interest-bearing operating liabilities (mainly accounts payable and accrued expenses payable), $1.5 million in short-term notes payable (due in less than one year), and $3.5 million in long-term debt (due over the next five years). Thus its total liabilities are $7 million. To be solvent, the business does not need $7 million in its checking account. In fact, this would be foolish.

There's no point in having liabilities if all the money were kept in the bank. The purpose of having liabilities is to put the money to good use in assets other than cash. A business uses the money from its liabilities to invest in *noncash* assets that it needs to carry on its profit-making operations. For example, a business buys products on credit and holds these goods in inventory until it sells them. It borrows money to invest in its fixed assets.

Solvency analysis asks whether assets can be converted quickly back into cash so that liabilities can be paid on time. Will the assets generate enough cash flow to meet the business's liability payment obligations as they come due?

*Short-term* solvency analysis looks a few months into the future of the business. It focuses on the *current* assets of the business in relation to its *current* liabilities; these two amounts are reported in the balance sheet. A rough measure of a company's short-term liability payment ability is its *current ratio* — current assets (cash, accounts receivable, inventory, and prepaid expenses) are divided by current liabilities (accounts payable and accrued expenses payable, plus interest-bearing debt coming due in the short term). A 2-to-1 current ratio usually is a reasonable benchmark for a business — but don't swallow this ratio hook, line, and sinker.

The current ratio does not have to be 2-to-1 for many businesses. Much depends on the products a business sells and the established financing practices in the industry. For example, auto dealers rely on very heavy short-term borrowing to carry their huge inventories of cars and light trucks. They survive and remain solvent on very low current ratios. Lenders know the financing needs of the businesses they deal with, and they judge current ratios accordingly. A 2-to-1 current ratio is fairly conservative. Many businesses can get by on a lower current ratio without alarming their sources of short-term credit.

Business investors and creditors also look at a second solvency ratio called the *quick ratio.* This ratio includes only a company's *quick assets* — cash, accounts receivable, and short-term marketable investments (if the company has any). Quick assets are divided by current liabilities to determine the quick ratio. It's also called the *acid-test ratio* because it's a very demanding test to put on a business. More informally, it's called the *pounce ratio,* as if all the short-term creditors pounced on the business and demanded payment in short order.

Many people consider a safe acid-test ratio to be 1-to-1 — $1 of quick assets for every $1 of current liabilities. However, be careful with this benchmark. It may not be appropriate for businesses that rely on heavy short-term debt to finance their inventories. For these companies, it's better to compare their quick assets with their quick liabilities and exclude their short-term notes payable that don't have to be paid until inventory is sold.

The current and acid-test ratios are relevant. But the solvency of a business depends mainly on the ability of its managers to convince creditors to continue extending credit to the business and renewing its loans. The credibility of management is the main factor, not ratios. Creditors understand that a business can get into a temporary bind and fall behind on paying its liabilities. As a general rule, creditors are slow to pull the plug on a business. Shutting off new credit may be the worst thing lenders and other creditors could do. This may put the business in a tailspin, and its creditors may end up collecting very little. Usually, it's not in their interest to force a business into bankruptcy, except as a last resort.

# Are There Any Unusual Assets and Liabilities?

One thing I do in reading a balance sheet is to look for out-of-the-ordinary assets and liabilities. These may be legitimate, but I want to know what they are and whether they affect the profit of the business. The usual assets (to name the major ones) include accounts receivable, inventory, and fixed assets. The usual liabilities include accounts payable, accrued expenses payable, short-term and long-term debt accounts, and, of course, the owners' equity accounts for capital invested by the owners and for retained earnings. Once you get off this beaten path, you never know what you'll discover.

Most businesses report a miscellaneous, catch-all account called *other assets.* Who knows what might be included in here? If the balance in this account is not very large, trust that the CPA auditor did not let the business bury anything important in this account.

*Marketable securities* is the asset account used for investments in stocks and bonds (as well as other kinds of investments). Companies that have more cash than they need for their immediate operating purposes put the excess funds to work earning investment income rather than let the money lie dormant in a bank checking account. The accounting rules for marketable securities are fairly tight; you needn't be concerned about this asset.

If you encounter an asset or liability you're not familiar with, look in the footnotes to the financial statements, which present a brief explanation of what the accounts are and whether they affect profit accounting. (I know, you don't like reading footnotes; neither do I.) For example, many businesses have large liabilities for unfunded pension plan obligations for work done in the past by their employees. The liability reveals that the business has recorded this component of labor expense in determining its profit over the years. The liability could be a heavy demand on the future cash flow of the business.

# How Well Are Assets Being Utilized?

Every business needs assets to make profit, and every business has to raise capital from debt and equity sources. Both sources of capital have a cost — business managers should never lose sight of the *time cost of money*. Interest must be paid on debt, and net income must be earned on equity capital. A business has to make enough *earnings before interest and tax* (EBIT) to pay interest, pay income tax (unless it is a pass-through entity), and provide a residual net income that is sufficient for the amount of equity capital being used. Leaving land to lie fallow for a season or two may be smart farming, but business assets have to be put to good use all the time.

The overall test of how well assets are being used is the *asset turnover ratio,* which equals annual sales revenue divided by total assets. (You have to calculate this ratio; most businesses do not report this ratio in their financial statements, although a minority do.) This ratio tests the efficiency of using assets to make sales. Some businesses have low asset turnover ratios, less than 2-to-1. Some have very high ratios, such as 5-to-1. Each industry and retail sector in the economy has a standard asset turnover ratio, but these differ quite a bit from industry to industry and from sector to sector. There is no standard asset turnover ratio for all businesses. A supermarket chain couldn't make it if its annual sales revenues were only twice its assets. Capital-intensive heavy manufacturers, on the other hand, would be delighted with a 2-to-1 asset turnover ratio.

Financial report readers are wise to track a company's asset turnover ratio from year to year. If this ratio slips, the company is getting less sales revenue bang for each buck of assets. If the company's profit ratio remains the same, it gets less profit out of each dollar of assets, which is not good news for equity investors in the business.

# What Is the Return on Capital Investment?

I need a practical example to illustrate the *return on capital investment* questions you should ask. Suppose a business has $12 million total assets, and its accounts payable and accrued liabilities for unpaid expenses are $2 million. Thus its *net operating assets* — total assets less its non-interest-bearing operating liabilities — are $10 million.

I won't tell you the company's sales revenue for the year just ended. But I will tell you that its earnings before interest and tax (EBIT) were $1.32 million for the year. The basic question you should ask is this: How is the business doing in relation to the total capital used to make this profit?

EBIT is divided by assets (net operating assets, in my way of thinking) to get the *return on assets* (ROA) ratio. In this case, the company earned 13.2 percent ROA for the year just ended:

```
$1,320,000 EBIT ÷ $10,000,000 net operating assets =
              13.2% ROA
```

Was this rate high enough to cover the interest rate on its debt? Sure; it's doubtful that the business had to pay a 13.2 percent interest rate. Now for the bottom-line question: How did the business do for its *owners*, who have a lot of capital invested in the business?

The business uses $4 million total debt, on which it pays 8 percent annual interest. Thus its total owners' equity is $6 million. The business is organized as a regular corporation that pays a combined 40 percent federal and state income tax on its taxable income.

Given the company's capitalization structure, its EBIT (or profit from operations) for the year just ended was divided three ways:

- ✔ **$320,000 interest on debt:** $4,000,000 debt × 8% interest rate = $320,000

- ✔ **$400,000 income tax:** $1,320,000 EBIT – $320,000 interest = $1,000,000 taxable income × 40% tax rate = $400,000 income tax

- ✔ **$600,000 net income:** $1,320,000 operating earnings – $320,000 interest – $400,000 income tax = $600,000 net income

Net income is divided by owners' equity to calculate the *return on equity* (ROE) ratio, which in this example is

```
$600,000 net income ÷ $6,000,000 owners' equity = 10% ROE
```

Some businesses report their ROE ratios, but many don't — generally accepted accounting principles do not require the disclosure of ROE. In any case, as an investor in the business, would you be satisfied with a 10 percent return on your money?

You made only 2 percent more than the debt holders, which is not much of a premium for the additional risks you take on as an equity investor in the business. But you may predict that the business has a bright future and over time your investment will increase two or three times in value. In any case, ROE is a good point of reference — although this one ratio does not give you a final answer regarding what to do with your capital. Reading Eric Tyson's *Investing For Dummies* (published by IDG Books) can help you make a wise decision.

# What Does the CPA Auditor Say?

A final question: What does the CPA auditor say? Publicly owned businesses are required to have their annual financial reports audited by an independent CPA firm who is elected by their stockholders (well, I should say selected by the board of directors subject to approval by a vote of the stockholders). Many privately held businesses have their annual reports audited, even though an audit is not legally required. Small businesses may not have an audit, but instead have a CPA review or compile their financial statements — in these cases, the CPA does not express an opinion on the financial statements. A business pays a lot of money for its audit, and you should read what the auditor has to say.

The auditor's report is attached to the financial statements, sometimes right before the statements or, alternately, following the footnotes. (Chapter 15 explains the auditor's report.) I'll be frank: The wording of the auditor's report is tough going. Talk about jargon! In any case, focus on the sentence that states the auditor's *opinion* on the financial statements. In rough terms, the CPA gives the financial statements a green light, a yellow light, or a red light — green meaning that everything's okay, yellow meaning that you should be aware of something that prevents the CPA from giving a green light, and red meaning that the financial statements are seriously deficient.

Look for the key words *fairly present.* These code words mean that the CPA firm has no serious disagreement with how the business prepared its financial statements. This unqualified opinion is called a *clean opinion.* Only in the most desperate situations does the auditor give an adverse opinion, which in essence says that the financial statements are misleading. You either see a clean opinion, or the audit opinion will be modified. For example, the CPA may disagree with an accounting method used by the business, or the CPA may judge that the financial report needs more disclosure of certain items. But overall, the CPA is satisfied that the financial statements are not misleading.

If the audit firm can't give a clean opinion on the financial statements or thinks that something about the financial statements should be emphasized, a fourth paragraph is added to the standard three-paragraph format of the audit report (or additional language is added to the one-paragraph audit report used by the Big 5 CPA firm PricewaterhouseCoopers). The additional language is the tip-off; look for a fourth paragraph (or additional language), and be sure to read it. The auditor may express doubt about the business being able to continue as a going concern. The solvency ratios discussed earlier should have already tipped you off. When the auditor mentions it, things are pretty serious.

# Appendix A

# Glossary: Slashing through the Accounting Jargon Jungle

• • • • • • • • • • • • • • • • • • • • • • • • • • • • • • • • • • • • • • • • • • • • • • • •

**ABC (activity based costing):** A relatively new scheme for allocating indirect *overhead costs*. Overhead costs provide various support functions in a business. The ABC approach classifies overhead costs into separate categories of support activities that are needed in manufacturing operations and in other areas of the business organization (such as a sales territory). Cost drivers are developed for each support activity to measure the extent of usage of that support. The annual cost of each support activity is allocated to manufacturing and other areas according to how many cost driver units are used.

**accelerated depreciation:** One of two basic methods for allocating the cost of a fixed asset over its useful life and for estimating its useful life. Accelerated depreciation allocates greater amounts of depreciation in early years and lower amounts in later years, and also uses short life estimates. For comparison, see also *straight-line depreciation*.

**accounting:** The methods and procedures for analyzing, recording, accumulating, and storing financial information about the activities of an entity, and preparing summary reports of these activities internally for managers and externally for those entitled to receive financial reports about the entity. The managers of a business and the investors in the business, as well as lenders to the business, depend on accounting reports called *financial statements* to make informed decisions. Accounting also encompasses preparing tax returns that must be filed with government tax authorities by the entity.

**accounting equation:** Assets = Liabilities + Owners' Equity. This basic equation is the foundation for *double-entry accounting* and reflects the balance between a business's assets and the sources of capital that is invested in its assets, which fall into two basic groups — liabilities and owners' capital.

**accounts payable:** One main type of the short-term liabilities of a business, representing the amounts owed to vendors or suppliers for the purchase of products, various supplies, parts, and services that were bought on credit; these do not bear interest (unless the business takes too long to pay).

**accounts receivable:** The short-term asset representing the amounts owed to the business from sales of products and services on credit to its customers. Customers are not normally charged interest, unless they do not pay their bills when due.

**acid-test ratio:** See *quick ratio.*

**accrued expenses payable:** One main type of short-term liabilities of a business that arise from the gradual buildup of unpaid expenses, such as vacation pay earned by employees or profit-based bonus plans that aren't paid until the following period. **Caution:** The specific titles of this liability vary from business to business; you may see accrued liabilities, accrued expenses, or some other similar account name.

**accumulated depreciation:** The total cumulative amount of depreciation expense that has been recorded since the fixed assets being depreciated were acquired. In the *balance sheet* the amount in this account is deducted from the cost of fixed assets. (Thus it is sometimes referred to as a contra account.) The purpose is to report how much of the total cost has been depreciated over the years. The balance of cost less accumulated depreciation is included in the total assets of a business — which is known as the *book value* of the assets.

**accrual-basis accounting:** Unfortunately, "accrual" is not a familiar term to most people. A better term would be "full-basis," or "complete-basis" accounting. From the profit accounting point of view this refers to recording revenue at the time sales are made (rather than when cash is actually received from customers), and recording expenses to match with sales revenue or in the period benefited (rather than when the costs are paid). From the financial condition point of view this refers to recording several assets, such as receivables from customers, cost of inventory (products not yet sold), and cost of long-term assets (fixed assets) — and, recording several liabilities in addition to debt (borrowed money), such as payables to vendors and payables for unpaid expenses.

**annualized rate of interest and rate of return:** The result of taking a rate of interest or a rate of return on investment for a period shorter than one year and converting it into an equivalent rate for the entire year. Suppose you earn 2.00 percent interest rate every quarter (three months). Your annualized rate of interest (as if you received interest once a year at the end of the year) equals 8.24 percent rounded — which is not simply 4 times the 2.00 percent quarterly rate. (The annualized rate equals [1+.02] raised to the fourth power minus one.) This is also called the effective annual rate, although it would make as much sense to call it the equivalent annual rate. See also *compound interest.*

**asset turnover ratio:** A measure of how effectively assets were used during a period, usually one year. To find the asset turnover ratio, divide annual sales revenue either by total assets or by *net operating assets*, which equals total assets less short-term, non-interest-bearing liabilities.

**audit report:** A one page statement issued by a CPA, after having examined a company's accounting system, records, and supporting evidence, that gives an opinion whether the company's financial statements and footnotes are presented fairly in conformity with *generally accepted accounting principles*. Annual audits are required of publicly-owned corporations; many privately held businesses also have audits. The CPA auditor must be independent of the business. Instead of a clean opinion, which means that the auditor has no material objections to the financial statements prepared by the business, the auditor may render a qualified opinion in which the CPA takes exception to one or more aspects of the company's financial statements and footnotes. A CPA auditor expresses doubts about the financial viability of a business if it is in dire financial straits.

**bad debts:** The particular expense that arises from a customer's failure to pay the amount owed to the business from a prior credit sale. When the credit sale was recorded the accounts receivable asset account was increased. When it becomes clear that this debt owed to the business will not be collected the asset account is written-off and the amount is charged to bad debts expense.

**balance sheet:** The *financial statement* that summarizes the assets, liabilities, and owners' equity of a business at an instant moment in time. Prepared at the end of every profit period, and whenever needed, the balance sheet shows a company's overall financial situation and condition.

**basic earnings per share (EPS):** Equals *net income* for the year (the most recent twelve months reported, called the trailing twelve months) divided by the number of capital stock shares of a business corporation that have been issued and are owned by stockholders (called the number of shares outstanding). See also *diluted earnings per share*. Basic EPS and its close sibling diluted EPS are the most important factors that drive the market value of stock shares issued by publicly owned corporations.

**book value of assets:** Refers to the recorded amounts of assets which are reported in a *balance sheet* – usually the term is used to emphasize that the amounts recorded in the accounts of the business may be less than the current replacement costs of some assets, such as fixed assets bought many years ago that have been depreciated.

**book value of owners' equity, in total or per share:** Refers to the *balance sheet* value of owners' equity, either in total or on a per-share basis for corporations. Book value of owners' equity is not necessarily the price someone would pay for the business as a whole or per share, but it is a useful reference, or starting point for setting market price.

**breakeven point (sales volume):** The annual sales volume (total number of units sold) at which total *contribution margin* equals total annual *fixed expenses* — that is, the exact sales volume at which the business covers its fixed expenses and makes a zero profit, or a zero loss depending on your point of view. Sales in excess of the breakeven point contribute to profit, instead of having to go towards covering fixed expenses. The breakeven sales volume is a useful point of reference for analyzing profit performance and the effects of *operating leverage*.

**budgeting:** The process of developing and adopting a profit and financial plan with definite goals for the coming period — including forecasting expenses and revenues, assets, liabilities, and cash flows based on the plan. Actual performance during the coming period is compared against budgeted goals to determine progress or lack of progress; or, the budget may be used for general planning purposes only, especially for determining additional capital that will be needed for growth.

**burden rate:** An amount per unit that is added to the direct costs of manufacturing a product according to some method for the allocation of the total indirect fixed manufacturing costs for the period, which can be a certain percent of direct costs or a fixed dollar amount per unit of the common denominator on which the indirect costs are allocated across different products. Thus, the indirect costs are a "burden" on the direct costs. For a very simple example, manufacturing fixed costs may be charged at the rate of 25 percent of raw material costs on every product made during the year. (Supporters of *ABC* will be horrified by this example.)

**capital expenditures:** Outlays for *fixed assets* — to overhaul or replace old fixed assets, or to expand and modernize the long-lived operating resources of a business. Fixed assets have useful lives from 3 to 39 (or more) years, depending on the nature of the asset and how it's used in the operations of the business. The term "capital" here implies that substantial amounts of money are being invested that are major commitments for many years.

**capital stock:** The certificates of ownership issued by a corporation for capital invested in the business by owners; total capital is divided into units, called shares of capital stock. Holders of capital stock shares participate in cash dividends paid from profit, vote in board member elections, and receive asset liquidation proceeds; and, they have several other rights as well. A business corporation must issue at least one class of capital stock called *common stock*. It may also issue other classes of stock, such as *preferred stock*. Both common and preferred capital stock shares of thousands of large corporations are traded on the New York Stock Exchange and over NASDAQ.

**cash flow(s):** In the most general and broadest sense this term refers to any kind of cash inflows and outflows during a period — monies coming in, and monies paid out. Frequently the term is used as shorthand for *cash flow from profit*. The *cash flow statement* classifies cash flows into three different categories: *operating activities, investing activities,* and *financing activities.*

**cash flow from profit:** In the *cash flow statement* this is called *cash flow from operating activities*. Equals net income for the period, adjusted for changes in certain assets and liabilities, and for depreciation expense. Some people call this *free cash flow* to emphasize that this source of cash is free from the need to borrow money, issue capital stock shares, or sell assets. **Be careful:** The term free cash flow is also used to denote cash flow from profit minus capital expenditures. (Some writers deduct cash dividends also; usage has not completely settled down.)

**cash flow from operating activities:** see, *cash flow from profit.*

**cash flow statement:** This financial statement of a business summarizes its cash inflows and outflows during a period according to a threefold classification: *cash flow from profit* (or, *operating activities*), *investing activities*, and *financing activities*. **Editorial comment:** In far too many cases, based on my experience, the cash flow statement is too detailed, too technical, and too difficult to decipher; furthermore, several items reported in this financial statement do not reconcile with changes in assets and liabilities reported in the company's comparative balance sheet.

**certified public accountant (CPA):** The CPA designation is a widely recognized and respected badge of a professional accountant. A person must meet educational and experience requirements and pass a national uniform exam to qualify for a state license to practice as a CPA. Many CPAs are not in public practice; they work for business organizations, government agencies, and nonprofit organizations, or teach accounting (a plug for educators here if you don't mind). CPAs in public practice do audits of financial statements, and also provide tax and management consulting services in an ever-expanding range of areas (such as personal financial planning, for example).

**chart of accounts:** The official, designated set of accounts used by a business that constitute its *general ledger,* in which the transactions of the business are recorded. These accounts must be used, unless the chief accounting officer of the organization (the *Controller*) authorizes new accounts to be added to the list.

**common stock:** The one class of capital stock that must be issued by business corporations. It has the most junior, or "last in line" claim on the business's assets in the event of liquidation, after all liabilities and any senior capital stock (such as *preferred stock*) are paid. Common stock has voting rights in the election of the board of directors, although a business may issue both voting and nonvoting classes of common stock. Common stock receives dividends from profit only after preferred stockholders (if any) are first paid.

**compound interest:** "Compound" is a code word for reinvested. Interest income *compounds* when you don't remove it from your investment, but instead leave it in and add it to your investment or savings account. Thus you have a bigger balance on which to earn interest the following period. You earn interest on interest by compounding. More correctly, you earn interest on reinvested income. See also *annualized rate of interest and rate of return.*

**comprehensive income:** Includes net income which is reported in the *income statement* plus certain technical gains and losses in assets and liabilities that are recorded but don't necessarily have to be included in the income statement. Most companies report their comprehensive gains and losses (if they have any) in their *statement of changes in owners' equity.*

**contribution margin:** Equals sales revenue minus cost of goods sold expense and minus all *variable expenses* (in other words, contribution margin is profit before *fixed expenses* are deducted). On a per unit basis, contribution margin equals sales price less *product cost* per unit and less variable expenses per unit. Contribution margin is an exceedingly important measure for analyzing profit behavior and for making sales price decisions.

**controller:** The chief accounting officer of an organization. The controller may also serve as the chief financial officer in business and other organizations, although in large organizations the two jobs are usually split.

**cooking the books:** Refers to any one of several fraudulent (deliberately deceitful with intent to mislead) accounting schemes used to overstate profit and to make financial condition look better than it really is. Cooking the books is different from *profit smoothing* and *window dressing,* which are tolerated — though not encouraged — in financial statement accounting. Cooking the books for income tax is just the reverse: It means overstating, or exaggerating, deductible expenses or understating revenue to minimize taxable income. **Warning:** A conviction for income tax evasion is a felony.

**cost of capital:** For a business this refers to joint total of the interest paid on debt capital and the minimum net income it should earn to justify the owner's equity capital that it uses. Interest is a contractually set amount of interest; no legally set amount of net income is promised to owners. A business's *return on assets (ROA)* rate should ideally be higher than its weighted-average cost of capital rate (based on the mix of its debt and equity capital sources).

**creative accounting:** Does not refer to the artistic side of accountants, but rather the use of dubious accounting techniques and deceptions designed to make profit performance or financial condition appear better that things really are. See *profit smoothing* and *cooking the books.*

**current assets:** Includes cash plus *accounts receivable, inventory,* and *prepaid expenses* (and marketable securities if the business owns any). These assets are cash or assets that will be converted into cash during one *operating cycle.* Total current assets are divided by total current liabilities to calculate the *current ratio,* which is a test of short-term solvency.

**current liabilities:** Short-term liabilities, principally *accounts payable, accrued expenses payable, income tax payable,* short-term notes payable, and the portion of long-term debt that falls due within the coming year. This group includes both non-interest bearing and interest-bearing liabilities that must be paid in the short-term, usually defined to be one year. Total current liabilities are divided into total *current assets* to calculate the *current ratio.*

**current ratio:** A test of a business's short-term solvency (debt-paying capability). Find the current ratio by dividing total its *current assets* by its total *current liabilities.*

**debits and credits:** These two terms are accounting jargon for decreases and increases that are recorded in assets, liabilities, owners' equity, revenue, and expenses. When recording a transaction, the total of the debits must equal the total of the credits. The rules for what's a debit and what's a credit stem from the *accounting equation.* "The books are in balance" means that the sum of debit balance accounts equals the sum of credit balance accounts. Even so, accounting errors happen when transactions are not recorded or are recorded with wrong amounts or in wrong accounts.

**depreciation expense:** Allocating (or spreading out) a fixed asset's cost over the estimated useful life of the resource. Each year of the asset's life is charged with part of its total cost as the asset gradually wears out and loses its economic value to the business. Either *accelerated depreciation* or *straight-line depreciation* is used; both are acceptable under *generally accepted accounting principles (GAAP).* A choice must be made. (Only the straight-line method is allowed for long-life buildings.)

**diluted earnings per share (EPS):** First, please refer to *basic earnings per share (EPS),* which equals annual net income divided by the actual number of stock shares outstanding. In contrast, diluted earnings per share equals net income divided by the sum of the actual number of shares outstanding plus any additional shares that will be issued under terms of stock options awarded to managers and for the conversion of senior securities into common stock (if the company has issued convertible debt or *preferred stock* securities). Other factors may also cause the number of stock shares to be increased. In short, this measure of profit per share is based on a larger number of shares than basic EPS. The larger number causes a diminution, or dilution in the amount of net income per share. Although hard to prove for certain, market prices of stock shares are driven by diluted EPS more than basic EPS. (For many businesses the two EPS measures are very close.)

**dividend yield:** Measures the cash income component of return on investment in stock shares of a corporation. The dividend yield equals the most recent 12 months of cash dividends paid on a stock, divided by the stock's current market price. If a stock is selling for $100.00 and over the last 12 months has paid $3.00 cash dividends, its dividend yield equals 3.0 percent.

**double-entry accounting:** Symbolized in the *accounting equation,* which means both the assets of a business as well as the sources of money for the assets (which are also claims on the assets). *Accrual-basis accounting* uses the discipline of *debits and credits* for recording individual transactions to keep the accounts in balance; this means the total accounts with debit balances equals the total accounts with credit balances.

**earnings before interest and income tax (EBIT):** Sales revenue less cost of goods sold and all operating expenses — but before deducting interest on debt and income tax expenses. This measure of profit also is called *operating earnings, operating profit,* or something similar; terminology is not uniform.

**earnings management:** See *profit smoothing.*

**earnings per share: See** *basic earnings per share* **and** *diluted earnings per share.*

**EDGAR:** The acronym for the web-based database of financial reports and other required filings under federal securities laws with the Securities & Exchange Commission (SEC). Go to: www.sec.gov/edgarhp.htm.

**effective interest rate:** The rate actually applied to your loan or savings account balance to determine the amount of interest for that period. A period can be one month, or one quarter of a year or some other time unit. The effective interest rate is determined by dividing the nominal (in name only) annual percentage rate by the number of periods for which interest is computed during the year. For example, if the annual rate is quoted at 12.0 percent and interest is figured quarterly, the effective quarterly interest rate is 3.0 percent. See also *annualized rate of interest and rate of return.*

**equity capital:** See *owners' equity.*

**external financial statements:** The financial statements included in financial reports that are distributed outside a business to its stockholders and debtholders (who are entitled to a periodic accounting on the financial performance and condition of the business). Internal financial statements to managers, although based on the same accounting methods, are prepared differently and contain more detail, which managers need for decision-making and control.

**extraordinary gains and losses:** Just what the term implies. These are unusual, non-recurring gains and losses that happen infrequently and that are aside from the normal, ordinary sales and expenses of a business. These gains and losses, in theory, are one-time events that come out of the blue. But, in actual practice many businesses record these gains and losses too frequently to be called nonrecurring. These gains and losses (net of income tax effects) are reported separately in the income statement; the implication is that they won't happen again in the near future. In this way attention is directed to net income from the normal, ordinary operations of the business — as if the special gains and losses should be put out of mind. These items pose a serious dilemma in investment analysis.

**Financial Accounting Standards Board (FASB):** The highest authoritative, private-sector, standard-setting body of the accounting profession in the United States. The FASB issues pronouncements that establish *generally accepted accounting principles (GAAP)* and that supersede previous standards. These statements on accounting standards and accounting methods are very technical, written by CPAs for CPAs. Plain-English, digest versions of FASB pronouncements are reported in the financial press and can be found at other sources geared to non-accountants.

**financial leverage:** The term is used generally to mean using debt capital on top of equity capital in any type of investment. For a business it means using debt in addition to equity capital to provide the total capital needed to invest in its *net operating assets.* The strategy is to earn a rate of *return on assets (ROA)* higher than the interest rate on borrowed money. A favorable spread between the two rates generates financial leverage gain to the benefit of *owners' equity.*

**financial reports:** The periodic financially-oriented communications from a business (and other types of organizations) to those entitled to know about the financial performance and position of the entity. Financial reports of businesses include three primary financial statements (*balance sheet, income statement,* and *statement of cash flows),* as well as footnotes and other information relevant to the owners of the business. The content, structure, and conventions of financial reports are highly developed in the United States — governed by private-sector originated standards but subject to federal government oversight, mainly by the Securities & Exchange Commission (SEC).

**financial statement:** The generic term for *balance sheet, cash flow statement, and income statement,* all three of which present summary financial information about a business. Sometimes financial statements are called simply "financials."

**financing activities:** One of three types of *cash flows* reported in the *cash flow statement*. These are the dealings between a business and its sources of debt and equity capital — such as borrowings and repayments of debt, issuing new stock shares and buying some of its own stock shares, and paying dividends.

**first-in, first-out (FIFO):** One of two widely used accounting methods by which costs of products when they are sold are charged to cost of goods sold expense in chronological order, so the most recent acquisition costs remain in inventory at the end of the period. However, the reverse order also is acceptable, which is called the *last-in, first-out (LIFO)* method.

**fixed assets:** The shorthand term for the long-life (generally three years or longer) resources used by a business, which includes land, buildings, machinery, equipment, tools, and vehicles. The most common account title for these assets you see in a balance sheet is "property, plant, and equipment."

**fixed expenses (costs):** Those expenses or costs that remain unchanged over the short run and do not vary with changes in sales volume or sales revenue — common examples are building rent under lease contracts, salaries of many employees, property taxes, and monthly telephone bills for local calls. Fixed expenses provide capacity for carrying out operations and for making sales. Fixed manufacturing costs provide production capacity.

**footnotes:** Think of footnotes in a book. Footnotes are attached to the three primary financial statements, to present detailed information that cannot be put directly in the body of the financial statements. Footnotes have the reputation of being difficult to read, poorly written, overly detailed, and too technical. Unfortunately, these criticisms have a lot of truth behind them.

**free cash flow:** Many people use this term to mean the amount of *cash flow from profit* — although some writers deduct capital expenditures from this number, and others deduct cash dividends as well. This term is relatively new, and not everyone uses it in exactly the same way. Make sure you know what the person means when using the term.

**general ledger:** The complete collection of all the accounts used by a business (or other entity) to record the financial effects of its activities. More or less synonymous with *chart of accounts*.

**generally accepted accounting principles (GAAP):** The authoritative standards and approved accounting methods that should be used by businesses and private nonprofit organizations to measure and report their revenue and expenses, and to present their assets, liabilities, and owners' equity, and to report their cash flows in their financial statements. Many elements of GAAP haven't changed for many years, but other elements are subject to change and updating.

**going-concern assumption:** The accounting premise that a business will continue to operate and will not be forced to liquidate its assets. A reasonable assumption to make in the great majority of situations, but the accountant is on the lookout for any evidence to the contrary, in which case different accounting methods may be appropriate.

**goodwill:** Goodwill has two different meanings, so be careful. The term can refer to the product or brand name recognition and the excellent reputation of a business that provide a strong competitive advantage. Goodwill in this sense means the business has an important but invisible "asset" that is not reported in its balance sheet. Second, a business may purchase and pay cash for the goodwill that has been built up over the years by another business. Only purchased goodwill is reported as an asset in the balance sheet.

**gross margin (profit):** Equals sales revenue less cost of goods sold for the period. On a per unit basis, gross margin equals sales price less product cost per unit. Making an adequate gross margin is the starting point for making bottom-line *net income*.

**imputed cost:** A hypothetical cost used as a benchmark for comparison. One example is the imputed cost of equity capital. No expense is recorded for using owners' equity capital during the year. However, in judging net income performance, the company's rate of *return on equity (ROE)* is compared with the rate of earnings that could be earned on the capital if it were invested elsewhere. This alternative rate of return is an imputed cost. Close in meaning to the economic concept of *opportunity cost*.

**income smoothing:** See *profit smoothing*.

**income statement:** The *financial statement* that summarizes sales revenue and expenses for a period and reports one or more *profit* lines. Also, *extraordinary gains and losses* are reported in this financial statement. The income statement is one of the three primary financial statements of a business.

**income tax payable:** That part of income tax expense for the year that hasn't yet been remitted to the government at the end of the year, but will be soon. The federal income tax law requires that most (preferably all) of the annual income tax be paid before the close of the year, but in many cases part of the total tax bill is still owed to the government at the end of the year.

**internal (accounting) controls:** Accounting forms, procedures, and precautions that are established primarily to prevent and minimize errors and fraud (beyond what would be required for record keeping). Common internal control procedures include requiring the signature of two managers to approve transactions over a certain amount, restricting entry and exit routes of employees, using surveillance cameras, enforcing employees to take their vacations away from the business, and conducting surprise inventory counts and inspections.

**investing activities:** One of three classes of *cash flows* reported in the *cash flow statement*. In large part these are the *capital expenditures* by a business during the year, which are major investments in long-term assets. A business may dispose of some of its fixed assets during the year, and proceeds from these disposals (if any) are reported in this section of the cash flow statement.

**last-in, first-out (LIFO):** One of two widely used accounting methods by which costs of products when they are sold are charged to cost of goods sold expense in reverse chronological order, one result being that the ending inventory cost value consists of the costs of the earliest goods purchased or manufactured. The opposite order is also acceptable, which is called the *first-in, first-out (FIFO)* method. The actual physical flow of products seldom follows a LIFO sequence. The method is justified on the grounds that the cost of goods sold expense should be the cost of replacing the products sold, and the best approximation is the most recent acquisition costs of the products.

**leverage:** see *financial leverage* and *operating leverage*.

**LIFO liquidation gain:** A unique result of the *last-in, first-out (LIFO)* method, which happens when fewer units are replaced than sold during the period. The decrease in inventory requires that the accountant go back into the old cost layers of inventory for part of the cost of goods sold expense. Thus, there is a one-time windfall gain in *gross margin,* roughly equal to the difference between the historical cost and the current cost of the inventory decrease. A large LIFO liquidation gain should be disclosed in a footnote to the financial statements.

**limited liability company (LLC):** A relatively new type of legal form of business organization that is a hybrid between a partnership and a corporation. A LLC can elect to be a *pass-through tax entity* for federal income tax purposes. This legal form of business organization has more flexibility regarding the apportionment of profit and management authority among the owners as compared with a corporation.

**lower of cost or market (LCM):** A special accounting test applied to inventory, that can result in a write-down and charge to expense for the loss in value of products held for sale. The recorded costs of products in inventory are compared with their current replacement costs (market price) and with net realizable value if normal sales prices have been reduced. If either value is lower, then recorded cost is written down to this lower value. **Note:** Inventory is not written up when replacement costs rise after the inventory was acquired.

**management accounting:** The branch of accounting that prepares internal financial statements and various other reports and analyses to assist managers do their jobs. These internal accounting reports help managers carry out their planning, decision-making and control functions. The detailed information provided in these reports is confidential and is not circulated outside the business. Internal management income statements focus on *profit margin* and sales volume, and should separate *variable expenses* from *fixed expenses*. Management accounting includes *budgeting*, developing and using standard costs, and working closely with managers regarding how costs are allocated.

**margin of safety:** Equals the excess of actual sales volume over the company's *breakeven point*; often expressed as a percent. This information is used internally by managers and is not disclosed in external financial reports.

**market cap:** The total value of a business calculated by multiplying the current market price of its capital stock times the total number of capital stock shares issued by the business. This calculated amount is not money that has been invested in the business, and the amount is subject to the whims of the stock market (which has become more volatile in recent years).

**net income:** Equals sales revenue less all expenses for the period; also any *extraordinary gains and losses* for the period are counted in the calculation to get bottom-line net income. "Bottom line" means everything has been deducted from sales revenue (and other income the business may have) so that the last profit line in the income statement is the final amount of profit for the period. (But, see *comprehensive income*.) Instead of "net income" you may see terms such as "net earnings," or "earnings from operations," or just "earnings." However, you do not see the term "profit" very often.

**net operating assets:** The total amount of assets used in operating a business, less its short-term non-interest bearing liabilities. A business must raise an equal amount of capital. Suppose a business's total net operating assets add-up to $25 million. Thus, the company must have raised $25 million from interest-bearing debt and equity sources of capital — remembering that undistributed profit (called *retained earnings*) is counted as part of owners' equity.

**operating activities:** The profit-making activities of a business — that is, the sales and expense transactions of a business. See also *cash flow from operating activities*.

**operating assets:** The several different assets, or economic resources used in the profit-making operations of a business. Includes cash, accounts receivable from making sales on credit, inventory of products awaiting sale, prepaid expenses, and various fixed, or long-life assets. The company's short-term, non-interest-bearing liabilities are deducted from its total operating assets to get *net operating assets*. A business may have other assets not essential to its mainstream sales and expense operations. For example, a business may invest excess cash in marketable securities, or in real estate that is held for long-term opportunities.

**operating cycle:** The repetitive sequence over a period of time of producing or acquiring inventory, holding it, selling it on credit, and finally collecting the account receivable from the sale. It is a "cash-to-cash" circle — investing cash in inventory, then selling the products on credit, and then collecting the receivable. The length of the operating cycle be a relatively short time (a few weeks) or a relatively long time (several months) — which varies from industry to industry.

**operating earnings (profit):** See *earnings before interest and income tax (EBIT)*.

**operating leverage:** Once a business has reached its *breakeven point* a relatively small percent increase in sales volume generates a much larger percent increase in profit; this wider swing in profit is the idea of operating leverage. Making sales in excess of its breakeven point does not increase total fixed expenses, so all the additional *contribution margin* from the sales goes to profit.

**operating liabilities:** Short-term liabilities generated spontaneously in the profit-making operations of a business. The most common ones are *accounts payable, accrued expenses payable,* and *income tax payable* — none of which are interest bearing unless a late payment penalty is paid, which is in the nature of interest.

**opportunity cost:** An economic definition of cost referring to income or gain that could have been earned form the best alternative use of money, time, or talent foregone by taking a particular course of action. Suppose you earn $100,000 on your money, time, and effort. Suppose you could have earned, say, $85,000 if you had followed the next best alternative. The opportunity cost is the $85,000 that you gave up by following the course of action you did. Your economic profit is the marginal $15,000 you're ahead by choosing the better alternative.

**overhead costs:** Sales and administrative expenses, and manufacturing costs that are indirect, which means they cannot be naturally matched or linked with a particular product, revenue source, or organizational unit — one example is the annual property tax on the building in which all the company's activities are carried out. Many overhead costs are fixed and cannot be decreased over the short run — such as payment for the general liability insurance carried by a business. Manufacturing overhead costs are allocated among the different products made during the period through the use of a *burden rate* — in order to account for the full cost of each product. In this way the manufacturing overhead costs are absorbed in product cost.

**owners' equity:** The ownership capital base of a business. Owners' equity derives from two sources: investment of capital in the business by the owners (for which *capital stock* shares are issued by a corporation), and profit that has been earned by the business but has not been distributed to its owners (called *retained earnings* for a corporation). The current market value of owners' equity is usually different than the recorded amount (*book value*) reported in the balance sheet.

**pass-through tax entity:** A type of legal organization by which the business entity itself does not pay income tax but instead serves as a conduit of its annual taxable income — the business *passes through* its annual taxable income to its owners, who include their respective shares of the amount on their individual income tax returns. Partnerships are pass-through tax entities by their very nature. Limited liability companies (LLCs) and corporations with 75 or fewer stockholders (called S corporations) can elect to be treated as a pass-through tax entity.

**preferred stock:** A second class, or type of capital stock that can be issued by a business corporation in addition to its *common stock*. Preferred stock derives its name from the fact that it has certain preferences over the common stock — it is paid cash dividends before any can be distributed to common stockholders, and in the event of liquidating the business, preferred stock shares must be redeemed before any money is returned to the common stockholders. Preferred stock usually does not have voting rights and may be callable by the corporation, which means that the business can redeem the shares for a certain price per share.

**prepaid expenses:** Expenses that are paid in advance, or up-front for future benefits. The amount of cash outlay is entered in the prepaid expenses asset account. For example, a business writes a $60,000 check today for fire insurance coverage over the following six months. The total cost is first entered in the asset account; then, each month, $10,000 is taken out of the asset and charged to expense. Though not insignificant, prepaid expenses are usually much smaller than a business's inventory and accounts receivable assets.

**price/earnings (P/E) ratio:** The current market price of a capital stock divided by its most recent, or "trailing" twelve months *diluted earnings per share (EPS),* or *basic earnings per share* if the business does not report diluted EPS. A low P/E may signal an undervalued stock or a pessimistic forecast by investors. A high P/E may reveal an overvalued stock or may be based on an optimistic forecast by investors.

**product cost:** Equals the purchase cost of goods that are bought and then resold by retailers and wholesalers (distributors). In contrast, a manufacturer combines four different types of production costs to determine product cost: direct materials, direct labor, and variable and fixed manufacturing *overhead costs.* Overhead costs are allocated to different products in order to account for the full cost of making products, which is called absorption costing.

**profit:** A very general term that can have different meanings. It may mean gains less losses, or inflows less outflows, or other kinds of increases minus decreases. In business, the term means sales revenue (and other sources of income) minus expenses for a period of time, such as one year. In an *income statement,* the final or bottom-line profit is called *net income*, which equals sales revenue less all expenses (plus any extraordinary gains and less any extraordinary losses). For public corporations net income is also put on a per share basis, called *earnings per share.*

**profit and loss (P&L) statement:** An alternative title for the *income statement,* which may be used informally by a business but hardly ever is seen in external financial reports to investors. The title was used in external financial reports years ago, but not today. Also, the term "P&L" is tossed around loosely to refer to the profit or loss prospects of a venture, or when referring to the profit performance of a product line or a specific investment. It has a certain ring to it that sounds good — even though if you look at it closely, how can a business have profit and loss at the same time?

**profit ratio:** Equals *net income* divided by sales revenue. Measures net income as a percentage of sales revenue. A closely watched ratio by both business managers and investors.

**profit smoothing:** Manipulating the timing of when sales revenue and/or expenses are recorded in order to produce a smoother profit trend year to year. Investors prefer steady trend lines instead of widely fluctuating ones. This needs the implicit or explicit approval of top management, because these techniques require the override of normal accounting procedures and methods for recording sales revenue and expenses. Instead of letting the chips fall where they may, top management intercedes and gives approval to methods that delay or accelerate the recording of some expenses (and perhaps of some sales) in order to produce a "better" profit number for the year. CPA auditors generally go along with a reasonable amount of profit smoothing — which is also called *income smoothing,* or *earnings management.*

**proxy statement:** The annual solicitation from a corporation's top executives and board of directors to its stockholders that requests that they vote a certain way on matters that have to be put to a vote at the annual meeting of stockholders. In larger public corporations most stockholders cannot attend the meeting in person, so they delegate a proxy (stand-in person) to vote their shares yes or no on each proposal on the agenda. So, these solicitations are called proxy statements. The company's executives and its board of directors use proxy statements to persuade the stockholders to vote one way or the other on agenda items; they are not neutral on these issues.

**quick ratio:** The number calculated by dividing the total of cash, *accounts receivable,* and marketable securities (if any), by total *current liabilities.* This ratio measures the capability of a business to pay off its current short-term liabilities with its cash and near-cash assets. Note that inventory and prepaid expenses, the other two current assets, are excluded from assets in this ratio. (Also called the acid-test ratio.)

**retained earnings:** One of two basic sources of owners' equity of a business (the other being capital invested by the owners). Annual profit (*net income*) increases this account, and distributions from profit to owners decrease the account. Retained earnings does not refer to cash or any particular asset. In fact, a business could have a small cash balance but a very large retained earnings balance – you often see this in balance sheets.

**return on assets (ROA):** Equals *earnings before interest and income tax (EBIT)* divided by the *net operating assets* (or by total assets, for convenience), and is expressed as a percent. The ROA rate is the basic test of how well a business is using its assets so that it can pay the interest rate on its debt and can earn a satisfactory rate of *return on equity (ROE)* for its owners.

**return on equity (ROE):** Equals *net income* divided by the total *book value of owners' equity*, and is expressed as a percent. ROE is the basic measure of how well a business is doing in providing "compensation" on the owners' capital investment in the business.

**return on investment (ROI):** A very broad and general term that refers to the income, profit, gain, or earnings on capital investments, expressed as a percentage of the amount invested. The most relevant ROI ratios for a business are *return on assets (ROA)* and *return on equity (ROE).*

**sales revenue–driven expenses:** Expenses that vary in proportion to, or as a fixed percent of changes in total sales revenue (total dollars). Examples are sales commissions, credit card discount expenses, and rent expense and franchise fees based on total sales revenue. (Compare with *sales volume–driven expenses.*)

**sales volume–driven expenses:** Expenses that vary in proportion to, or as a fixed amount with changes in sales volume (quantity of products sold). Examples include delivery costs, packaging costs, and other costs that depend mainly on the number of products sold or the number of customers served. (Compare with *sales revenue–driven expenses.*)

**Securities & Exchange Commission (SEC):** The federal agency established by the federal Securities Exchange Act of 1934, which has broad jurisdiction and powers over the public issuance and trading of securities (stocks and bonds) by business corporations. In certain circumstances the SEC can suspend trading in a security, begin an investigation, and start legal actions against a business.

**statement of cash flows:** See *cash flow statement.*

**statement of changes in owners' (stockholders') equity:** More in the nature of a supplementary schedule than a full-fledged financial statement — but, anyway, its purpose is to summarize the changes in the owners' equity accounts during the year. These changes include distributing cash dividends, issuing additional stock shares, buying some of its own capital stock shares, *comprehensive income* gains and losses, and who knows what else.

**straight-line depreciation:** Spreading the cost of a fixed asset in equal amounts of depreciation expense to each year of its useful life. Depreciation is the same amount every year by this method. Although this method has much intuitive appeal and must be used to depreciate the cost of buildings, for other fixed assets many businesses select an *accelerated depreciation* method.

**variable expenses (costs):** Any expense or cost that is sensitive to changes in sales volume or sales revenue. (See *sales revenue–driven expenses* and *sales volume–driven expenses.*) In contrast, *fixed expenses* (costs) do not change over the short run in response to changes in sales activity.

**window dressing:** Accounting devices that make the short-term liquidity and solvency of a business look better than it really is. One common technique is to hold the books open a few business days after the close of the accounting year in order to record additional cash receipts (as if the cash collections had occurred on the last day of the year). A type of "fibbing" in the *balance sheet.* This term does not refer to manipulating recorded profit (see *profit smoothing* for comparison).

# Appendix B

# Accounting Software

• • • • • • • • • • • • • • • • • • • • • • • • • • • • • • • • • • • • • • • • • •

*L*arge business organizations write their own computer accounting programs, which contain thousands and thousands of lines of instructions and computer code. Fortunately, those of you who don't have computer programmers on your staff (or the money to pay for outside professional programmers) can buy a simple, ready-to-use accounting program right off the shelf. You can find accounting software at your local computer store or in your favorite mail-order computer catalog. That's the good news.

The bad news is that you have to decide *which* accounting software package is best for your particular business. Because quite a few good programs are on the market, you should consider your business needs in order to narrow down your choices.

The following list gives you some general pointers for narrowing down your choices and deciding which accounting software package is right for your business:

✔ **Get your bookkeepers and accountants involved in the selection process early on.** They know which features are most critical for your business, even though they may not know all the technical points about computers and software. They're the ones who will have to use the software and make it work for your business.

✔ **Make a list of the features that you need.** Some accounting programs intended for small businesses are designed around a "typical" business and may not support the accounting needs of your particular business. For example, if you collect sales taxes, you need to make sure that the software program supports sales tax collection and remittance to the tax agencies. Or if you're a contractor who bases each job on a custom order, you need an accounting program that includes *job order* accounting.

✔ **Get a software recommendation from your business friends and associates who are already using an accounting program (or have your accountant talk with their accountants).** This step is possibly the most important. Try to get a feel for how much work *they* went through in picking out, setting up, and actually using the software. Zero in on the particular strengths and weaknesses that they've discovered in the accounting program that they're using.

✔ **Pay attention to the features and flexibility of the accounting program.** For example, how much customization of source documents and financial statements does the program allow? You want a certain amount of flexibility to tailor forms and formats to your needs. On the other hand, you may be intimidated by the idea of customizing accounting forms, so a program with plenty of ready-made forms may be right for you. Also, the program's capability to leave good *audit trails* (documentation that you'd need if audited) is important.

✔ **Check whether the software comes with a good user's manual and other documentation.** The trend these days is to put most or all of the help information in the software itself, meaning that the program needs to be up and running and you access the help information on the fly. Alternatively, the owner's manual can be printed out so that you have a hard copy available for reference.

✔ **Think about how simple or difficult the program is to set up.** Although the initial cost of the software may not be a factor for you (all the accounting programs that I list here sell for a couple hundred bucks or less), be sure to consider the cost and time required to get the software up and running.

One option is to use a computer consultant (such as a CPA with the appropriate experience) to help you choose the right software package and to help you with the initial setup of the software. This option is certainly less expensive than hiring professional programmers to write a program based on your business's needs, but you may want to try a do-it-yourself approach first, before paying for outside help. You can find computer consultants in the Yellow Pages.

Here's a list of several popular small business accounting programs (for Windows 98 operating systems) to get you started on your search for the best program for you. I include the names of the software companies, followed by their toll-free telephone numbers and their web site addresses. (Some of these accounting programs are available in Macintosh versions, but you have to check.) The street prices of these software packages are generally under $200.

✔ The Sage Group offers three accounting programs geared to small businesses: phone 800-854-3415; www.sage.com

- **DacEasy**; www.daceasy.com

- **Peachtree**; www.peachtree.com

- **BusinessWorks**; www.us.sage.com/businessworks

✔ **MYOB Accounting Plus**: MYOB US Inc.; phone 800-322-MYOB; www.myob.com

✔ **One-Write Plus**: NEBS Inc.; phone 800-225-6308; www.nebs.com

✔ **Great Plains Accounting**: Great Plains Software Inc.; phone 800-477-7736; www.gps.com

✔ **QuickBooks**: Intuit Inc.; phone 800-433-8810; www.intuit.com

✔ **Simply Accounting**: ACCPAC International; phone 800-773-5445; www.accpac.com

# Index